While he was undoubtedly the most popular author of his day and well loved by readers in succeeding generations, Charles Dickens has not always been a favorite with critics. For half a century after his death, the writer celebrated for his novels advocating social reform was often ridiculed by those academics who condescended to write about him. Only the faithful band of devotees who called themselves Dickensians kept alive an interest in his work. Then, during the Second World War, Dickens underwent a kind of resurrection by critics, and within two decades he was once again being hailed as the foremost writer of his age, a literary genius whose work can stand beside that of Shakespeare and Milton. In the last thirty years Dickens has once again been taken to task, this time by a new breed of literary theorists who find fault with his chauvinism and imperialist attitudes. Whether he has been adored or despised, however, one thing is certain: no other Victorian novelist has generated more critical commentary.

Laurence Mazzeno's book traces the history of Dickens's reputation from the earliest reviews by his contemporaries through the work of early twenty-first-century commentators. Chapters concentrate on the way judgments of Dickens changed as new standards for evaluating fiction came to dominate academic discussion. Special attention is paid to important late nineteenth- and twentieth-century studies by George Gissing, G. K. Chesterton, F. R. Leavis, George Orwell, Edmund Wilson, Humphry House, Edgar Johnson, J. Hillis Miller, Philip Collins, Michael Slater, and Harry Stone. Mazzeno also places emphasis on the past three decades, showing how literary theory has opened up new ways of reading Dickens. What becomes clear is that, in attempting to provide fresh insight into Dickens's writings, critics often reveal as much about the predilections of their own age as they do about the novelist.

Laurence W. Mazzeno is President Emeritus of Alvernia University, Reading, Pennsylvania. He is the author of *Jane Austen: Two Centuries of Criticism* (Camden House, 2011), *Tennyson: The Critical Legacy* (Camden House, 2004), *Matthew Arnold: The Critical Legacy* (Camden House, 1999), *Herman Wouk* (1994), and annotated bibliographies of eighteenth-century fiction, nineteenth-century poetry, and nineteenth-century fiction. He is a former editor of *Nineteenth-Century Prose*.

*Studies in European and American Literature and Culture:
Literary Criticism in Perspective*

About *Literary Criticism in Perspective*

Books in the series *Literary Criticism in Perspective* trace literary scholarship and criticism on major and neglected writers alike, or on a single major work, a group of writers, a literary school or movement. In so doing the authors—authorities on the topic in question who are also well-versed in the principles and history of literary criticism — address a readership consisting of scholars, students of literature at the graduate and undergraduate level, and the general reader. One of the primary purposes of the series is to illuminate the nature of literary criticism itself, to gauge the influence of social and historic currents on aesthetic judgments once thought objective and normative.

The Dickens Industry

Critical Perspectives 1836–2005

Laurence W. Mazzeno

CAMDEN HOUSE
Rochester, New York

Copyright © 2008 Laurence W. Mazzeno

All Rights Reserved. Except as permitted under current legislation, no part of this work may be photocopied, stored in a retrieval system, published, performed in public, adapted, broadcast, transmitted, recorded, or reproduced in any form or by any means, without the prior permission of the copyright owner.

First published 2008 by Camden House
Transferred to digital printing 2010
Reprinted in paperback 2011

Camden House is an imprint of Boydell & Brewer Inc.
668 Mt. Hope Avenue, Rochester, NY 14620, USA
www.camden-house.com
and of Boydell & Brewer Limited
PO Box 9, Woodbridge, Suffolk IP12 3DF, UK
www.boydellandbrewer.com

Paperback ISBN-13: 978-1-57113-515-5
Paperback ISBN-10: 1-57113-515-4
Hardback ISBN-13: 978-1-57113-317-5
Hardback ISBN-10: 1-57113-317-8

Library of Congress Cataloging-in-Publication Data

Mazzeno, Laurence W.
    The Dickens Industry: critical perspectives 1836–2005 / Laurence W. Mazzeno.
       p. cm. — (Studies in European and American literature and culture) (Literary criticism in perspective)
    Includes bibliographical references and index.
    ISBN-13: 978-1-57113-317-5 (acid-free paper)
    ISBN-10: 1-57113-317-8 (acid-free paper)
    1. Dickens, Charles, 1812–1870 — Criticism and interpretation — History. I. Title. II. Series.

PR4587.3.M39 2008
823'.8—dc22

2008008292

This publication is printed on acid-free paper.

Cover photograph: Re-touched version of Charles Dickens by (George) Herbert Watkins, albumen print, arched top, 1858. © National Portrait Gallery, London.

Contents

Acknowledgments		vii
Introduction		1
1:	The Dickens Phenomenon (1836–1870)	12
2:	The Birth of the Dickens Industry and the Reaction against Victorianism (1870–1914)	31
3:	Dickens among the Moderns (1915–1940)	62
4:	The Tide Turns (1940–1959)	91
5:	Dickens and Mainstream Academic Criticism (1960–1969)	119
6:	The Dickens Centenary and After (1970–1979)	141
7:	Dickens in an Age of Theory I: New Theories, New Readings (1980–2000)	170
8:	Dickens in an Age of Theory II: The Persistence of Traditional Criticism (1980–2000)	212
9:	The Future of Dickens Studies: Trends in the Twenty-First Century	239
Major Works by Charles Dickens		261
Chronological List of Works Cited		263
Index		305

Acknowledgments

I WANT TO PAY TRIBUTE to several people who are part of the "industry" that has allowed me to bring this project to fruition. First are a group of librarians at the University of Richmond and Virginia Commonwealth University, where I prowled the rows of shelves for months. Thanks also to the people at the College of William & Mary, where everyone — from the staff in the Swem Library to the ladies in the Security Office who processed my frequent requests for parking passes — made me realize that stories of Virginians' hospitality are all true. Though I suspect no one there knows me, their kindness in answering questions and providing help when I needed assistance with the new, self-serve checkout machine was a real blessing.

I continue to be grateful to the staff of the Franco Library at Alvernia College, where I worked for eight years and where I am still considered a member of the academic community. Their continuing support in helping with research, tracking down leads, and obtaining materials has been invaluable. First among equals there is Roberta Rohrbach, whose cheerful assistance (and exceptional persistence) has made my research nearly effortless.

I have been fortunate to have had two distinguished young Dickensians read my manuscript and offer cogent suggestions for improvement: Professor John Drew of the University of Buckingham and Professor Grace Moore of the University of Melbourne. I believe this book is better for their efforts, although for whatever errors may remain I am, of course, fully responsible.

I also want to thank Jim Walker and Katie Hurley at Camden House for their invaluable guidance and assistance in getting this book into print. And finally, I must acknowledge the support of my family, who indulge me by giving me the time to pursue my hobby, away from home among the library stacks where I can "converse" with the critics whose work on Dickens and others continues to reveal to me stories worth telling.

Introduction

"THE LITERARY SENSIBILITY of Charles Dickens is possibly the most amply documented literary sensibility in history." So writes Jane Smiley, herself a popular novelist, on the first page of her critical biography *Charles Dickens* (2002). A cursory glance at any research library's catalog would suggest Smiley is probably right. Books, articles, and reviews about Dickens and his work number in the thousands. For nearly two centuries he has been idolized and demonized. He has been cherished and dismissed. He has been taken to task for poor plotting and outrageous characterization, and held in awe for his ability to unite the disparate elements of the complex society about which he wrote. He has been celebrated as the upholder of Victorian values — and for being his age's most severe critic. He has been classified as an unexplainable genius, and intensely psychoanalyzed to discover the hidden sources of his creative powers. He has been deconstructed, reevaluated from the perspectives of gender studies and New Historicism, and adapted for the movies and television. What he *hasn't* been is ignored. No other English writer save Shakespeare has received so much attention. As a result, Lyn Pykett's pithy admonition in her 2002 critical survey of Dickens sums up the present state of Dickens criticism: "The twenty-first century critic writing about the nineteenth-century novelist Charles Dickens," she says, "must inevitably engage with that complex historical phenomenon, the Dickens industry" (2).

I have borrowed my title from Pykett and others who have used it before her because in *The Dickens Industry* I want to call attention to the significant critical business that has grown up around Dickens and his work. In this commentary on Dickens's critical reputation during the past 170 years I am concerned with several large questions: How was Dickens perceived? How did perceptions change over time? What works were valued by the Victorians, by their children and grandchildren, and by the academic community and the general public throughout the twentieth century? What critical issues occupied the attention of those writing about Dickens during the past 170 years? And finally, what does criticism of Dickens tell us about his critics? The last question is the most intriguing, of course, for as Angus Wilson observed more than fifty years ago, "To analyze the changing reputation of an author who has commanded the respect of such an enormous variety of readers and the high regard of such a miscellaneous collection of serious critics must surely, I have always thought, throw great light not only upon his own work but upon the nature of English literary taste in the last hundred years" (75). My hope is that by foregrounding the assumptions of critics who have written on Dickens and focusing on their methodologies I can provide insight in two directions simultaneously, both on Dickens as a writer *and* on the critics and their times.

The work of the Dickens critics has been made possible by the efforts of many scholars who have labored to provide reliable texts from which others can form critical judgments. I feel some obligation to mention a few of the more significant or representative efforts in this line, since I say little about them in my survey of criticism. First, there has never been a time when critics had difficulty finding a copy of a Dickens novel. Editions of his fiction began to appear long before Dickens died. Dickens personally supervised the production of some of these; his eldest son brought out a complete edition of the novels some years later. Between 1870 and 1950 dozens of "collected editions" were issued, often under the guidance of highly regarded writers such as Andrew Lang, George Gissing (although the edition he worked on was suspended before all the novels appeared), and G. K. Chesterton. As early as the late nineteenth century, trade publishers began turning out editions of individual novels for use in colleges and high schools. In the 1960s a group of British scholars secured an agreement with Oxford University Press to issue annotated editions of each of the novels. "The Clarendon Dickens" was intended by its editors "to present the text as Dickens meant his readers to see it, free from the corruptions that have taken place during a century and more" (*Bookseller* 1966). For the past half-century a team of respected Dickensians has been at work to fulfill the promises made in the original editors' prospectus.

Dickens's minor writings and his nonfiction have received similar treatment, and by 2004 usable, accurate editions of virtually everything Dickens wrote had become available to scholars and students. Notable among these projects are Kenneth Fielding's edition of Dickens's speeches (1960), Philip Collins's edition of the public readings (1975), Harry Stone's two-volume edition of Dickens's writings from *Household Words* (1969), and Michael Slater's four-volume *Dent Uniform Edition of Dickens's Journalism* (1996–2000). More specialized studies worth noting are Merle Bevington's *The Saturday Review 1855–1868* (1941), which includes a discussion of the treatment Dickens received from the magazine's reviewers (and some intriguing comments on the backlash from the magazine's readers to hostile commentaries), and Anne Lohrli's *Household Words: A Weekly Journal 1850–1859* (1973), an examination of the periodical Dickens edited for nearly a decade, which includes a compilation of the Table of Contents, indexes of article titles, and an essay on the journal's history.

Editions of Dickens's letters have been available since the 1890s. Among those published during the first half of the twentieth century, the most notable is Walter Dexter's *Letters of Charles Dickens* (1938), identified in Dickens circles as the Nonesuch Edition. In 1912 R. C. Lehmann collected letters between Dickens and Henry Willis, his sub-editor at *Household Words* and *All the Year Round*, in *Charles Dickens as Editor*. In 1933 Flora Livingston edited Dickens's letters to Charles Lever, a writer and frequent contributor to *All the Year Round*. The novelist's letters to Angela Burdett-Coutts were published by Charles Osborne, Burdett-Coutts's private secretary, in 1932; a more scholarly volume was brought out by Edgar Johnson in 1953. In the 1950s a group of Dickens scholars led by Humphry House and Kathleen Tillotson developed an ambitious plan for a scholarly edition that would collect and annotate all known correspondence. The first volume of The Pilgrim Edition of Dickens's letters appeared in 1965, the twelfth and final one in 2002. House died in 1955 before serious work could begin on the project, but Tillotson was joined over the years by a distinguished group of colleagues including Graham Storey, Madeline House, K. J. Fielding, Angus Easson, Nina Burgess, and dozens of assistants. Even before the Pilgrim Edition had been completed, David Paroissien brought out *Selected Letters of Charles Dickens* in 1985, choosing letters that illustrate Dickens's personal life, social and political concerns, and work as a writer and editor.

Scholars have also been busy creating dictionaries, encyclopedias, and similar collections intended as guides to his work. These have been surprising popular: Gilbert Pierce's 1872 *Dickens Dictionary* was reissued several times well into the twentieth century, Thomas Fyfe's *Who's Who in Dickens* (1913) was popular enough to merit a second edition, and Alexander Philip and W. L. Gadd's *A Dickens Dictionary* (1909) not only went into a second edition in 1928, but was reprinted in 2002. Most provide brief plot summaries and lists of characters, while others like Mary Williams's *The Dickens Concordance* (1907) are limited to listing first appearances of characters and cataloging the works. When it comes to Dickens at least, such books were not simply historical anomalies fueled by the Victorians' mania for cataloging and classifying everything in their world. Publications such as Norman Page's *A Dickens Companion* (1984) and *A Dickens Chronology* (1988), Fred Levit's *A Dickens Glossary* (1990), Donald Hawes's *Who's Who in Dickens* (1997), and George Bynum and Wolfgang Mieder's *The Proverbial Dickens: An Introduction to Proverbs in the Works of Charles Dickens* (1997) attest to the continuing popularity (and marketability) of such books when Dickens is the subject. There are dozens of others, among them some quite useful guides such as *Dickens Dramatized* (1987), in which H. Philip Bolton provides a listing of dramatic performances (stage, radio, and television) based on Dickens's fiction. George Newlin's rather imposing handbooks, *Every Thing in Dickens* (1996) and three volumes of *Everyone in Dickens* (1995), are among the first to be produced with the aid of a computer. Dickens biographer Fred Kaplan describes them in the foreword as supplanting all previous work of this kind.

Of greater academic value, perhaps, but certainly less compendious is the *Dickens Index* (1988), prepared by noted scholars Michael Slater, Nicholas Bentley, and Nina Burgis. This volume contains a listing of Dickens's works annotated with descriptions of themes, citations of literary allusions, a detailed chronology, and a bibliography of Dickens's writings. Other publications offering sophisticated commentary for students of Dickens are Paul Schlicke's *The Oxford Reader's Companion to Dickens* (1999) and its "competitor," John Jordan's *The Cambridge Companion to Charles Dickens* (2001), both of which include the same kinds of summary work but also provide exceptionally good commentary on the critical tradition.

Anyone trying to gain some comprehensive understanding of critical perspectives on Dickens soon recognizes his or her debt to dozens of scholars who have taken on the painstaking and often thankless task of identifying and indexing the massive body of secondary source materials. Beginning in 1886 with the appearance of Frederic G. Kitton's *Dickensiana: A Bibliography of the Literature Relating to Charles Dickens and His Writings,* attempts have been made to catalog not only Dickens's corpus but also the thousands of reviews, notices, commentaries, articles, and books about him and his work. The Modern Language Association's annual *International Bibliography* has long been a convenient source for identifying criticism about Dickens; since the mid-1980s brief summaries are provided for entries. For more than thirty years the editors of *Dickens Studies Annual* have published an annual essay in which a noted Dickens scholar summarizes the most important work done in the previous year.

However, the sheer volume of critical materials makes the bibliographer's task a daunting one. J. Don Vann's "A Checklist of Dickens Criticism, 1963–1967" (1969) covers only five years and yet runs twenty-three pages of small type. Joseph Gold's *The Stature of Dickens: A Centenary Bibliography* (1971), admittedly not comprehensive, lists more than three thousand entries — and this was assembled before Dickens studies exploded during the last three decades of the century. In 1982, Alan M. Cohn and K. K. Collins published a continuation of Gold's work, *The Cumulated Dickens Checklist 1970–1979* containing more than three thousand entries for that ten-year period. Their work followed closely on the heels of John Fenstermaker's *Charles Dickens, 1940–1975* (1979), a guide to criticism of the novels and Christmas stories published during thirty-five years subsequent to the appearance of Edmund Wilson's "Dickens: The Two Scrooges," the work Fenstermaker considers the watershed separating old ideas about Dickens from modern judgments. While more selective than Fenstermaker's work, R. C. Churchill's *A Bibliography of Dickensian Criticism 1836–1975* (1975) covers a longer time span and is lightly annotated, largely with Churchill's evaluation of individual entries. Duane DeVries's *General Studies of Charles Dickens and His Writings and Collected Editions of his Works: An Annotated Bibliography* (2004) provides brief summaries of approximately sixteen hundred works.

The magnitude of the task awaiting anyone wishing to read everything written about Dickens is suggested by Terri Hasseler's "Recent Dickens Studies: 2004" in the 2006 *Dickens Studies Annual*. This evaluative summary of a single year's work runs for nearly eighty pages — the size of a small monograph. Through the years, however, several scholars have written about the history of Dickens criticism — with varying degrees of success. Prominent among these studies are the entries in the Modern Language Association's two editions of *Victorian Fiction: A Guide to Research*, Ada Nisbet's in the 1964 volume and Philip Collins's in the 1978 revision. By far, however, the most influential study of Dickens's reception and reputation is George Ford's *Dickens and His Readers* (1955), a careful analysis of Dickens's reception among his contemporaries. Ford extends his study well into the twentieth century, providing some idea of the causes and impact on Dickens's reputation of what came to be known as The Reaction against the Victorians. Although Ford is most frequently cited as the authority on Dickens's reputation from 1836 until 1940, he was not the first to write an extended study on this issue. While not as comprehensive nor as scrupulously researched, Amy Cruse's *The Victorians and Their Reading* (1935) examines readers' reaction to novels published during the six decades of Victoria's reign. Irma Rantavaara's *Dickens in the Light of English Criticism* (1944) focuses on revisions in Dickens's reputation since the publication of John Forster's biography in the 1870s.

A number of highly credible studies have done much to extend Ford's work. Fred Boege's "Recent Criticism of Dickens" (1953) summarizes critical studies done in the 1930s and 1940s. In 1955 Edgar Johnson, whose *Charles Dickens: His Tragedy and Triumph* (1952) had been hailed by many as the definitive biography of the novelist, contributed a brief essay to the *Victorian Newsletter* containing a broad assessment that describes the landscape of Dickens studies quite succinctly. "The seventy years of Dickens scholarship following his death were predominantly devoted to exploring the biographical data and filling in the outlines where Forster's great biography were scanty," he says, while "the amount of significant esthetic criticism and of attempted psychological or sociological interpretations" was "relatively small." By contrast, since 1940 "these endeavors have been of increasing importance" (4).

In 1962 four of the "big names" in Dickens studies — George Ford, Edgar Johnson, J. Hillis Miller, and Sylvère Monod — met at a symposium in Boston where they sketched out what they called the "four staves" of Dickens criticism as it then existed: *biographical* criticism, which conference moderator Noel Peyrouton called "the farthest advanced" at the time; *historical*, which aimed to "recreate or reconstruct" Dickens's works in relation to the times in which they appeared and identify topical allusions or sources for his fiction; *psychological*, which Peyrouton describes as a technique used to examine Dickens's characters, myths and symbols "outside of any particular historical context"; and *analytical*, "a neutral ground approach" that focuses on a study of the texts themselves in an attempt to establish definitive readings. Just a decade later, of course, a whole new wave of theoretical study would expand this list considerably.

During the 1960s and 1970s representative commentary from nineteenth- and early twentieth-century critics was made available to wider audiences of scholars and students in a number of anthologies. Some are discussed later in this book because they indicate the kinds of critical inquiry being valued at the time these anthologies were published. In 1970, Stephen Wall reprinted prefaces from various editions of the novels that appeared during Dickens's lifetime in *Charles Dickens: A Critical Anthology*, supplementing Dickens's own assessment of his work with commentary by Victorian and post-Victorian critics. While the selections from other critics are limited in Wall's work, since 1971 those interested in learning first-hand what Dickens's earliest critics thought of his work have been fortunate to have a generous representative sampling available in Philip Collins's *Dickens: The Critical Heritage*. These excerpts are supplemented by Collins's extensive and insightful critiques. Collins reprised this kind of work in *Dickens: Interviews and Recollections* (1981), two volumes of comments from men and women who knew Dickens. Kathryn Chittick's *The Critical Reception of Charles Dickens 1833–1841* (1989) and *Dickens and the 1830s* (1990) supplement the work of Ford and Collins in examining that first decade during which Dickens established his reputation among his contemporaries.

An even larger selection of critical commentary is now available in *Charles Dickens: Critical Assessments* (1995), four volumes assembled and edited by Michael Hollington. Like Collins, Hollington provides an informative introduction; additionally, he collects criticism from sources outside England and America, and includes considerable material from the twentieth century. More limited in scope, Corinna Russell's *Lives of Victorian Literary Figures I: Eliot, Dickens, and Tennyson by Their Contemporaries* (2003) contains excerpts of accounts of Dickens's life and work by his contemporaries. Early in the twenty-first century essays by two authorities on Dickens and the Victorians provide further insights into the history and status of Dickens's reputation: Frederick Karl's "Recent Dickens Studies" (2003), a review of late-twentieth and early twenty-first century commentaries, and Sylvère Monod's "Dickens Biography: Past, Present, and Future: An Outline of History" (2004), a retrospective on attempts to examine Dickens's life and career.

In *The Victorians: An Age in Retrospect* (2002), John Gardiner says "our sense of the range and depth of Dickens's vision has coalesced in the years since his death" (162). Gardiner traces briefly the trajectory of Dickens criticism through the twentieth century, pointing out how Dickens was first seen as an advocate for family and national values, then later as a subversive force undermining those same values. While the moderns rejected him because his novels did not fit their definition of what constituted good fiction, the general reading public continued to read and enjoy his works. After the Second World War Dickens was used to rally support for rebuilding London and England, literally as well as metaphorically. But by the 1970s, Gardiner says, he was once again celebrated for his radicalism. The "recognizably 'modern' Dickens" — the novelist celebrated throughout the latter half of the twentieth century — "took shape around the 1940s, the years in which a distinctive breakthrough was made in appreciating the artistry that underpinned his creative vision" (172). This he attributes to four factors: the development of psychological criticism, the professionalization of literary criticism as a discipline, the appearance of fresh insights into the novelist's life, and the "visualization" of Dickens's work in movies and on television.

In *The Dickens Industry* I expand on Gardiner's brief outline. Although my major focus is on the critical texts themselves, I have tried to follow Frederic Jameson's mandate to "always historicize," offering where appropriate some commentary on the historical, literary, or political context that shaped individual works. In keeping with the guidelines of the Literary Criticism in Perspective series, I have organized the work along chronological lines, although I have made no attempt to adhere to a strict time line, especially in the two chapters covering the last decades of the twentieth century. My desire is to indicate something of the "conversation" that has taken place among critics as one responds to the work of another. Of course, I make no pretense of providing a comprehensive bibliographic essay; a book of that sort would run considerably longer than this one. As a consequence, however, I have found little room to include discussions of technical issues or explications of individual passages, or entire novels. Even the casual reader of this volume will notice that books are privileged, while the large body of Dickens criticism existing in dozens of fine journals is given relatively little notice. Also, I have refrained from making any significant comment on the various adaptations of Dickens's work for the movies and television. I realize these are themselves interpretations and by extension criticisms of his work, but others have handled this task recently, and I see no need to repeat their work. Finally, if this book seems to be weighted toward more recent critical examination, I can say only that I do not wish to repeat the work of others who have covered the same ground in previous decades. What I hope to accomplish is to give *my* readers a sense of how Dickens has mattered to students and scholars of literature, and perhaps to the larger audience who still buy and read his books.

Works Cited

Bentley, Nicholas, Michael Slater, and Nina Burgis. *The Dickens Index*. Oxford: Oxford UP, 1988.

Bevington, Merle Mowbray. *The Saturday Review 1855–1868: Representative Educated Opinion in Victorian England*. New York: Columbia UP, 1941. Reprint, New York: AMS Press, 1966.

Boege, Fred W. "Recent Criticism of Dickens." *Nineteenth Century Fiction* 8 (December 1953): 171–87.

Bolton, H. Philip. *Dickens Dramatized*. New York: G. K. Hall, 1987.

Bynum, George B., and Wolfgang Mieder. *The Proverbial Charles Dickens: An Index to Proverbs in the Works of Charles Dickens*. New York: Peter Lang, 1997.

Churchill, R. C. *A Bibliography of Dickensian Criticism 1836–1975*. New York: Garland, 1975.

"The Clarendon Dickens: Aim to Present Text Readers Were Meant to See." *Bookseller* (8 October 1966): 1928–34.

Chittick, Kathryn. *The Critical Reception of Charles Dickens 1833–1841*. New York: Garland, 1989.

———. *Dickens and the 1830s*. Cambridge: Cambridge UP, 1990.

Cohn, Alan M. and K. K. Collins. *The Cumulated Dickens Checklist 1970–1979*. Troy, NY: Whitson, 1982.

Collins, Philip A. W. "Charles Dickens." In *Victorian Fiction: A Second Guide to Research*, rev. ed. edited by George Ford, 34–113. New York: Modern Language Association, 1978.

———, ed. *Charles Dickens: The Public Readings*. Oxford: Clarendon, 1975.

———, ed. *Dickens: Interviews and Recollections*. 2 vols. Totowa, NJ: Barnes & Noble, 1981.

———. *Dickens: The Critical Heritage*. London: Routledge & Kegan Paul, 1971.

Cruse, Amy. "Dickens." *The Victorians and Their Reading*, 151–73. Boston: Houghton Mifflin, 1935. Issued as *Victorians and Their Books*. London: G. Allen and Unwin, 1935.

DeVries, Duane. *General Studies of Charles Dickens and His Writings and Collected Editions of his Works: An Annotated Bibliography.* New York: AMS Press, 2004.

Dexter, Walter, ed. *The Letters of Charles Dickens.* 3 vols. London: Nonesuch Press, 1938.

Fenstermaker, John. *Charles Dickens 1940–1975: An Analytical Subject Index to Periodical Criticism of the Novels and Christmas Books.* Boston: G. K. Hall, 1979.

Fielding, K. J., ed. *The Speeches of Charles Dickens.* Oxford: Clarendon P, 1960.

Ford, George H. *Dickens and His Readers: Aspects of Novel Criticism Since 1836.* Princeton, NJ: Princeton UP, 1955: New York: Norton, 1965.

Ford, George H. et al. *Dickens Criticism: Past Present, and Future Directions.* Cambridge, MA: Charles Dickens Reference Center, 1962.

Forster, John. *The Life of Charles Dickens.* London: Chapman & Hall, 1872–74. Boston: Osgood, 1875. Reprint, London: Palmer, 1928.

Fyfe, Thomas A. *Who's Who in Dickens.* London: Hodder & Stoughton, 1913.

Gardiner, John. *The Victorians: An Age in Retrospect*, 161–79. London: Hambledon & London, 2002.

Gold, Joseph, comp. *The Stature of Dickens: A Centenary Bibliography.* Toronto: U of Toronto P, 1971.

Hasseler, Terri. "Recent Dickens Studies: 2004." *Dickens Studies Annual* 37 (2006): 137–215.

Hawes, Donald. *Who's Who in Dickens.* New York and London: Routledge, 1997.

Hollington, Michael, ed. *Charles Dickens: Critical Assessments.* 4 vols. Sussex, England: Helm, 1995.

House, Madeline, and Graham Storey, eds. *The Letters of Charles Dickens.* 12 vols. Pilgrim Edition. Oxford: Clarendon Press, 1965–2002.

Johnson, Edgar. *Charles Dickens: His Tragedy and Triumph.* 2 vols. New York: Simon and Schuster; Toronto: Musson, 1952. London: Gollancz, 1953.

———, ed. *Letters of Charles Dickens to Angela Burdett-Coutts 1841–1865.* London: Cape, 1953.

———. "The Present State of Dickensian Studies." *Victorian Newsletter* 7 (April 1955): 4–9.

Jordan, John O., ed. *The Cambridge Companion to Charles Dickens.* Cambridge: Cambridge UP, 2001.

Karl, Frederick R. "Recent Dickens Studies." *Victorian Literature and Culture* 31.2 (2003): 593–611.

Kitton, Frederic G. *Dickensiana; A Bibliography of the Literature Relating to Charles Dickens and his Writings.* London: Redway, 1886.

Lehmann, R. C. *Charles Dickens as Editor.* London: Smith, Elder, 1912.

Levit, Fred. *A Dickens Glossary.* New York: Garland, 1990.

Livingston, Flora, ed. *Charles Dickens's Letters to Charles Lever.* Cambridge, MA: Harvard UP, 1933.

Lohrli, Anne. *Household Words: A Weekly Journal 1850–1859.* Toronto: U of Toronto P, 1973.

Monod, Sylvère. "Dickens Biography: Past, Present, and Future: An Outline of History." *Biography and Source Studies* 8 (2004): 139–61.

Newlin, George, ed. *Every Thing in Dickens.* Westport, CT: Greenwood Press, 1996.

———, ed. *Everyone in Dickens.* 3 vols. Westport, CT: Greenwood, 1995.

Nisbet, Ada. "Charles Dickens." In *Victorian Fiction: A Guide to Research*, edited by Lionel Stevenson, 43–55. New York: Modern Language Association, 1964.

Osborne, Charles. *Letters of Charles Dickens to the Baroness Burdett-Coutts.* New York: E. P. Dutton, 1932.

Page, Norman. *A Dickens Chronology.* Boston: G. K. Hall, 1988.

———. *A Dickens Companion.* New York: Schocken, 1984.

Paroissien, David, ed. *Selected Letters of Charles Dickens.* Boston: Twayne, 1985.

Philip, Alexander J. and W. L. Gadd. *A Dickens Dictionary.* New York: Dutton, 1909. 2nd ed., revised and enlarged. London: Simpkin, Marshall, 1928.

Pierce, Gilbert. *A Dickens Dictionary.* Boston: Osgood, 1872.

Pykett, Lyn. *Charles Dickens.* Critical Issues series. London: Palgrave, 2002.

Rantavaara, Irma. *Dickens in the Light of English Criticism.* Helsinki, Finland. 1944.

Russell, Corinna. *Lives of Victorian Literary Figures I: Eliot, Dickens, and Tennyson by Their Contemporaries.* London: Pickering & Chatto, 2003.

Schlicke, Paul, ed. *Oxford Reader's Companion to Dickens.* Oxford: Oxford UP, 1999.

Slater, Michael, ed. *'The Amusements of the People' and Other Papers: Reports, Essays and Reviews 1834–1851.* Dent Uniform Edition of Dickens's Journalism. Vol. 2. London: J. M. Dent, 1996.

———. *'Gone Astray' and Other Papers from Household Words 1851–1859*. Dent Uniform Edition of Dickens's Journalism. Vol. 3. London: J. M. Dent, 1998.

———. *Sketches by Boz and Other Early Papers 1833–1839*. Dent Uniform Edition of Dickens's Journalism. Vol. 1. London: J. M. Dent, 1994.

Slater, Michael, and John Drew, eds. *'The Uncommercial Traveller' and Other Papers 1859–1870*. Dent Uniform Edition of Dickens's Journalism. Vol. 4. London: J. M. Dent, 2000.

Smiley, Jane. *Charles Dickens*. New York: Viking, 2002.

Stone, Harry, ed. *Uncollected Writings of Charles Dickens: Household Words 1850–1859*. 2 vols. Bloomington: Indiana UP, 1968; London: Allen Lane, Penguin, 1969.

Vann, J. Don. "A Checklist of Dickens Criticism, 1963–1967." *Studies in the Novel* 1 (Summer 1969): 255–78.

Wall, Stephen, ed. *Charles Dickens*. Penguin Critical Anthologies. Harmondsworth, England: Penguin, 1970.

Williams, Mary. *The Dickens Concordance*. London: Francis Griffiths, 1907.

Wilson, Angus. "Novels and Highbrows." *Encounter* 31 (April 1956): 75–77.

Wilson, Edmund. "Dickens: The Two Scrooges." *New Republic* 102 (March 1940): 297–300, 339–42. Reprinted, revised, and enlarged, in *The Wound and the Bow: Seven Studies in Literature*. Boston: Houghton, Mifflin, 1941. Reprint in *Eight Essays*. New York: Doubleday, 1954.

1: The Dickens Phenomenon (1836–1870)

THE RECEPTION OF DICKENS'S WORK by his contemporaries has been the subject of several studies, the most significant among them George Ford's *Dickens and His Readers* (1955). Ford's influential and oft-quoted book has been supplemented by Philip Collins in his introduction to *Dickens: The Critical Heritage* (1971) and Kathryn Chittick in *The Critical Reception of Charles Dickens 1833–1841* (1989). As a consequence, the present brief summary is not intended to replace earlier scholarship, but instead to review trends in criticism that provide necessary background for understanding what happened later in Dickens studies.

As Chittick observes in her analysis of Dickens's earliest works, as soon as his first sketches started appearing, newspapers began to run brief notices and commentaries on their quality (47). Predictably, periodicals began carrying longer reviews of Dickens's work almost as soon as *Sketches by Boz* was in print. Dickens's initial reviewers were especially interested in characterization and verisimilitude, and not all of them were positive. The reviewer for the *Examiner* (1836) complained that Dickens relied too heavily on caricatures of Cockney figures, meliorating that criticism by remarking "this broad, common-place sort of thing is unworthy of the author" whose talents suggested he was capable of greater accomplishments (Chittick 61).[1] George Hogarth, Dickens's future father-in-law, went even farther in putting forward the notion that Dickens was destined to be more than a jocular entertainer. Writing in the *Morning Chronicle* (1836), Hogarth cited "A Visit to Newgate" as an example of Dickens's powers as a social commentator (Chittick 61). In a similar vein, an early reviewer wrote in the *Metropolitan Magazine* (1836) that Dickens provided "a perfect picture of the morals, manners, [and] habits of the greater portion of English society," and while the "succession of portraits does not reach higher than those of the best of the middle classes," Dickens does manage to portray "with a startling fidelity" the "lowest of the low" (Collins 30). A reviewer for the same journal writing about *Pickwick Papers* in 1837 claims "the renowned Mr. Pickwick" is "the legitimate successor to Don Quixote" (Collins 31). As the monthly numbers of Dickens's first remarkable comic novel emerged, the British reading public embraced the young novelist as *the* new voice in fiction.

During the first five years of his career Dickens was treated much like a rock star would be more than a hundred years later. Lionized by the public, he became almost overnight one of the most talked-about figures in England. Reviewers were comparing him with Shakespeare, Fielding, Smollett, and Sterne, and speaking of him as the successor to Scott and Byron, writers who enjoyed immense popularity among the previous generation. In 1837, Charles Buller was already attempting to explain to readers of the *London and Westminster Review* the reasons for "a popularity extraordinary on account of its sudden growth, its vast extent, and the recognition which it has received from persons of the most refined taste, as well as from the great mass of the reading public" (Collins 52). Buller seems amazed to discover that Dickens's "excellence appears indeed to lie in describing just what everybody sees every day" (Collins 53). But he offers some unsolicited advice to the young tyro, suggesting that he will not "leave some lasting monuments in our literature" without study, labor, or care (Collins 54).

Many were worried that Dickens would burn out too quickly. After all, at one time he was working on three novels simultaneously while trying to establish himself as a journal editor. In reviewing *Pickwick* and *Sketches by Boz* for the *Quarterly Review* (1837), Abraham Hayward wonders if Dickens can sustain his popularity. "The fact is, Mr. Dickens writes too often and too fast," Hayward says. "If he persists much longer in this course, it requires no gift of prophecy to foretell his fate — he has risen like a rocket, and he will come down like the stick; but let him give his capacity fair play, and it is rich, vigorous, and versatile enough to insure him a high and enduring reputation" (Collins 62).

Surveying Dickens's early work through *Nicholas Nickleby* for the *Edinburgh Review* (1838), Thomas Henry Lister calls Dickens "a very original writer" not likely to lose his popularity, because he has already become "the truest and most spirited delineator of English life, amongst the middle and lower classes, since the days of Smollett and Fielding" (Hollington 251). Curiously Lister finds Dickens's forte is "less in drawing characters than in describing incidents" (Collins 75), but like so many of his Victorian contemporaries Lister believes a Dickens novel owes its success "not to its merits as a whole, but to the attractiveness of detached passages" (Collins 76). The idea that the parts are somehow greater than the whole would be championed by Dickens lovers for more than a century, until formalist critics found ways to describe the underlying principles unifying the novels. Lister, too, admonishes Dickens to go slower, avoid imitation, "keep nature steadily before his eyes," and "check all disposition to exaggerate" (Collins 77).

Detractors appeared almost immediately, of course. Richard Ford rather snidely suggests in the *Quarterly Review* (1839) that Dickens writes best about the lower classes because he does not know the upper classes firsthand. He is also critical of Dickens's ability to construct a plot. A year later, the anonymous writer of "Charles Dickens and His Work" in *Fraser's Magazine* (1840) claims his characters are not drawn from life. This writer identifies another of the issues that would become a bugbear for critics antithetical to Dickens's work: serial publication. "The necessity of filling a certain quantity of pages per month imposed upon the writer a great temptation to amplify trifling ingredients, and well sentence after sentence with any sort of words that would occupy space." While this writer likes much in Dickens, he confesses somewhat sadly, "we do not like this novel-writing by scraps against time" (Collins 90).

By 1840, however, some reviewers thought early predictions of Dickens's great success were already being fulfilled. A notice in *Fraser's Magazine* (1840) expresses amazement that Dickens has achieved such "extensive popularity" without resorting to "mean" or "unjustifiable panderings to public favour," or to "the use of low arts of tricking, puffery, or pretence" (Collins 86). A reviewer in *Metropolitan Magazine* (1840) indicates another Victorian bias when he praises Dickens for "now performing most efficaciously the office of a moral teacher" (Collins 93). Although Thomas Hood faults Dickens for poor construction, he observes in his *Athenaeum* review of *Master Humphrey's Clock* and *The Old Curiosity Shop* that, "We invariably rise from the perusal of his volumes in better humour with the world; for he gives us a cheerful view of human nature and paints good people with a relish that proves he has himself a belief in, and sympathy with, their goodness" (Hollington 287).

The British were not the only ones to love Dickens's early works; Americans were equally effusive in their praise. The writer of "The Reception of Mr. Dickens" in *United States Magazine and Democratic Review* (1842) celebrates him as a social reformer. "We see that his mind is strongly possessed," the writer says, "with a true sense of the unjust suffering, moral and physical, by which the mass of mankind are everywhere pressed down to the dust." He goes on to "warn Wellington and Peel" and "Toryism in general, against this young writer" whose work is "calculated to hasten on the great crisis of the English Revolution (speed the hour!) far more effectively than any of the open assaults of Radicalism or Chartism" (Collins 117). The parenthetical ejaculation may suggest as much about the essayist as it does about Dickens, but the idea that the novelist wanted to change the world through his writings was fast catching on among contemporaries.

While Dickens was immensely popular among the masses, some among the more discerning, conservative elite expressed serious reservations about both his methods and his themes. The author of "Modern Novels" in the *Christian Remembrancer* (1842) thought Dickens was entering treacherous waters in his more recent novels. In these works aimed ostensibly at social reform, the writer asserts, Dickens is pandering to "the popular will" by railing against "the privileged classes, recognized officials, ancient institutions, the laws and their administration" — a "proceeding the unfairness of which is fully equaled by its danger" (Collins 159). Similarly, John Wilson Croker, who had previously savaged both Keats and Tennyson, has some deprecatory comments to make about Dickens in his 1843 *Quarterly Review* article. "Dickens is, as everybody knows, the author of some popular stories published originally in periodical parts — remarkable as clever exhibitions of very low life." But Croker expresses serious doubt "whether the power — or perhaps we should say the habits of his mind — are equal to any sustained exertion." Additionally, the "continuous repetition of scenes of low life — though, as we have said, seldom *vulgarly* treated — becomes at last exceedingly tedious" (Collins 136). It should be remembered, however, that the latest Dickens book people were reading was *American Notes for General Circulation*, a polemic against America that brought howls of protest from critics on both sides of the Atlantic.

Criticism such as Croker's did not seem to dampen the public's zeal for Dickens's work. A sense of early Victorians' appreciation of him is apparent in R. H. Horne's *A New Spirit of the Age* (1844), a three-volume collection of essays prepared by Horne (with the assistance of Elizabeth Barrett) to provide Victorian readers an introduction to the new voices in poetry and prose. The essay on Dickens occupies the first seventy-six pages of the first volume. A brief glance at Horne's analysis reveals much about the aesthetic and moral expectations of the Victorians. Horne praises Dickens for his characterization, claiming he does not engage in caricature but instead offers an "inexhaustible variety and truth of character" (6). He applauds the young novelist for being able to deal with sordid subjects without becoming sordid, and for achieving verisimilitude without giving offense to even the most delicate reader. Recognizing that Dickens was somehow violating early Victorian conventions of fiction by writing about the lower classes, Horne explains the novelist's high-minded motives in trying to bring attention to those in need. Aesthetically, Horne places Dickens in the class of writers to which Shakespeare had been assigned, calling him "instinctive" (57) — as opposed to refined, one would assume. Finally, Horne makes sure to praise Dickens for his strong spirit of Christian charity. Although at the time of this assessment Dickens had published only five novels, Horne was already predicting he would be the representative novelist of his age.

At the time Horne was writing, Dickens was actually scrambling to regain the high regard he had reached among readers with his early novels — and to make enough money to support his family and meet his professional obligations. The publication of *A Christmas Carol* in 1843 marked a new phase of Dickens's relationship with his readers, and issued in a form of fiction for which he would become equally famous, the Christmas story. Ironically, the story of Ebenezer Scrooge was not an immediate commercial success, but the tale soon took on a kind of mythic status, as the young W. M. Thackeray observed in an 1844 review for *Fraser's Magazine:* "Who can listen to objections regarding such a book as this?" (Collins 149). E. L. Blanchard echoed these sentiments in *Ainsworth Magazine,* asserting *A Christmas Carol* is "not to be talked about or written of according to ordinary rules" (Collins 143). Subsequent stories sold better but tended to be less well received. In writing about *The Cricket on the Hearth* the reviewer for *Chambers's Edinburgh Journal* (1846) suggests this "picture of humble life, contemplated in its poetic aspects and at its more romantic crises" shows Dickens is "in one sense, ambitious of becoming the Wordsworth of prose fiction" — though not quite there yet, as he remains "deficient in the profundity and stern power of that great master" (Hollington 320).

Despite some of the usual objections, the good reviews were probably welcome news to Dickens, as *Martin Chuzzlewit* was not universally loved by its first critics. The long assessment published in *North British Review,* probably by Thomas Cleghorn, finds Dickens declining in power: "no one can read even a single chapter of *Martin Chuzzlewit* without perceiving a very striking declension from the purity and unassuming excellence which marked his earlier compositions" (Collins 187). Of course, time would prove Dickens right; the novel eventually earned praise from numerous critics, and among its characters Sarah Gamp became one of Dickens's most memorable.

Although sales of Dickens's next novel, *Dombey and Son,* were quite good, the reviews were mixed. High praise such as that from the writer for the *Westminster Review* (1847), who proclaims "No other writer can approach Dickens in a perfect analysis of the mind of children" (Collins 225), were balanced by negative estimates such as those of *Blackwood's Magazine* reviewer John Eagles (1848), who dismisses the novel as Dickens's "greatest failure, as a whole" (Collins 231). Eagles even accuses Dickens of writing with the express, mischievous purpose to "decry, and bring into contempt as unfeeling, the higher classes" (Collins 230). A reviewer for *Macphail's Edinburgh Ecclesiastical Journal* (1849) takes a swipe at both Dickens and his readers, claiming the public "admire Mr. Dickens's humourous and pathetic pictures of life, however extravagantly drawn; and, though it be evident that now — exhausted and emptied — he is but reproducing, with some slight modifications, old sketches, he is still as popular as ever." Unfortunately, the reviewer goes on to say, "his immense popularity has inspired him with a confidence which is rather presumptuous; and for some time back, he has sought to be the solemn teacher, as well as the lighthearted jester, of the age" (Collins 179–80).

Despite the carping about hasty writing and frustration at the lack of tightly structured plots, by mid-century some critics began admitting that Dickens had staying power. The American scholar Edwin P. Whipple, who wrote frequently about him, remarks in "Novels and Novelists: Charles Dickens" (1849) that "Dickens has an open sense for all the liberal influences of his time, and commonly surveys human nature from the position of charity and love" (Collins 239). Whipple also thinks Dickens represents the attitudes of his age: "The humanity, the wide-ranging and healthy sympathies, and especially, the recognition of the virtues which obtain among the poor and humble, so observable in the works of Dickens, are in a great degree characteristic of the age, and without them popularity can hardly be won in imaginative literature" (Collins 239). Writing about *David Copperfield,* the reviewer for *Fraser's Magazine* (1850) remarks that "there is no single individual who, during the past fourteen years, has occupied so large a space in the thoughts of English folk as Charles Dickens," adding that "innumerable reputations have flared up and gone out; but the name and fame of Charles Dickens have been exempt from all vicissitude" (Hollington 331). Of course not everyone saw either the novel or its author in such lofty terms. As Philip Collins wryly notes in his editorial commentary, "Few reviewers have prognosticated with such decisive erroneousness as the *Spectator*'s on *David Copperfield* — 'likely to be less popular than many of the previous tales of Mr. Dickens, as well as rather more open to unfavourable criticism'" (Collins 242). To be fair, the remark may simply reflect the journal's bias against Dickens rather than a considered judgment of the novel, and it was a decidedly minority opinion at the time. Collins says there was widespread agreement among the Victorians that *David Copperfield* was his masterpiece.

Inevitably, the appearance of *Vanity Fair* in 1847 sparked immediate comparisons between Thackeray and Dickens. In a lengthy essay in the *North British Review* (1851), later expanded in *British Novelists and Their Styles* (1859), David Masson claims both have given English prose "a fresh impulse" and "a new set of characteristics" (239). But Masson is quick to point out that, because both are yet living, the critical attention they are receiving at mid-century may not last; "a time will come," he cautions, "when they shall have their settled places" (239). He seems to prefer Dickens over Thackeray not only because the former has greater range in his subject matter, but also — and perhaps more importantly — because he has a "genial, kindly, cheerful, and sentimental" outlook on life (249). This kind of comparison, made frequently during the remainder of the century, was eventually reduced to a kind of critical commonplace, aptly summarized by the nineteenth-century historian Justin McCarthy in *A History of Our Own Time* (1894): "Dickens set out on the literary theory that in life everything is better than it looks; Thackeray with the impression that it is worse" (I.638). Viewing Masson's assessment historically, it is clear the Victorians valued novels for their ability to teach life lessons and make people feel good.

The novels written after *David Copperfield* were not as well received as Dickens's earlier work. While there was always an occasional good review, the general belief among critics was that Dickens had run out of steam, and his creative juices had dried up. Of course, as Philip Collins remarks in the introduction to *Dickens: The Critical Heritage*, "Throughout his career, the fatal decline of Dickens's talent was confidently proclaimed," though like those about Mark Twain, "reports of his literary demise were later discovered to have been greatly exaggerated" (10). But in 1853, when *Bleak House* was published, many critics were ready to pounce on Dickens for abandoning the humor of his early days for this grim portrait of English society. Some like George Brimley, who reviewed the novel for the *Spectator* (1853), found it simply bad: "*Bleak House* would be a heavy book to read through at once, as a properly constructed novel ought to be read. But we must plead guilty to having found it dull and wearisome as a serial" (Hollington 351). Others had mixed feelings. "In some respects," the reviewer for *Bentley's Miscellany* (1853) writes, it is "the worst of Mr. Dickens's fictions, but, in many more, it is the best" (Collins 287). "There are *parts*," he writes emphatically, "which, without hesitation, may be pronounced more powerful and more tender than anything that Dickens ever wrote — but the whole is disappointing" (Collins 288). Dickens's friend and confidante John Forster, who frequently wrote glowing reviews of the novelist's work, observes in the *Examiner* that, "The judgments on *Bleak House* are, in short, as various as judgments are apt to be upon a man whose failings it is thought a subtle test of criticism to discover, for the very reason that all the world admires and likes him, and his books are bought and read by everybody" (Collins 290). As for growing complaints that Dickens did not provide sufficient character development, Forster counters by saying, "They know little how much there is in any one man's head or heart who expect to have every character in a tale laid bare before them as on a psychological dissecting table and demonstrated minutely" (Collins 292).

Shortly after *Bleak House* was published, James Augustine Stothert offered a rather caustic summary of the reasons for Dickens's popularity — and his problems with critics — in an 1854 *Rambler* article. "Charles Dickens is, in fact, pre-eminently a man of the middle of the nineteenth century. He is at once the creation and the prophet of an age which loves benevolence without religion, the domestic virtues more than the heroic, the farcical more than the comic, and the extravagant more than the tragic." He is, Stothert concludes, "the product of a restlessly observant but shallow era" (Hollington 357). Whether one liked him or not, however, it was hard to deny his influence. "It is scarcely conceivable," writes Harriet Martineau, "that any one should, in our age of the world, exert a stronger social influence than Mr. Dickens has in his power" (Collins 235).

Dickens followed *Bleak House* with his shortest novel, *Hard Times,* and the critics chose to give it short shrift. Predictably, John Forster felt "its many beauties blind us, as they will blind other generations, to its few defects" (Collins 303), and John Ruskin recommended the novel be studied "with close and earnest care by persons interested in social questions" (Collins 314). However, a majority of critics were closer in their judgments to Richard Simpson of *The Rambler* (1854), who declared that "on the whole, the story is stale, flat, and unprofitable; a mere dull melodrama, in which character is caricature, sentiment tinsel, and moral (if any) unsound" (Collins 303). Even Edwin Whipple had some harsh things to say about Dickens's sense of political economy displayed in the novel: "The fact that men like Carlyle, Ruskin, and Dickens can write economic nonsense without losing intellectual caste shows that the science of political economy, before its beneficent truths come to be generally admitted, must go through a long struggle with benevolent sophisms and benevolent passions" (Hollington 380).

Despite the growing trend in negative criticism, by the 1850s Dickens's novels were being translated into a number of languages and he had a following on the Continent. Unfortunately, one of the leading European critics, Hippolyte Taine, thought him shallow. In a review essay in *Revue des Deux Mondes* (1856) Taine observes that "The imagination of Dickens is like that of monomaniacs." Dickens "does not perceive great things," Taine says; "he has vigour" but "does not attain beauty." Further, his "inspiration is a feverish rapture, which does not select its objects." On the other hand, Taine admits "there is no writer who knows better how to touch and melt; he makes us weep, absolutely shed tears." But the novelist's philosophical outlook is decidedly limited and simplistic. "The novels of Dickens," Taine says, "can be reduced to one phrase, to wit: Be good, and love; there is genuine joy only in the emotions of the heart; sensibility is the whole man" (Collins 337–42). The French novelist Gustave Flaubert dismissed Dickens even more vigorously, calling him an "ignoramus! A giant of good fellows," perhaps, but "second-rate." The basis for this dismissal reveals something about Flaubert's critical prejudices: "How little [Dickens] cares for art! Not once does he mention it" (Maurois 120).

Flaubert's criterion for judging excellence was coming to be shared by a later generation of artists who placed new demands on the novel. Writing in 1856, George Eliot lamented that the English have at present "one great novelist who is gifted with the utmost power of rendering the external traits of our town population; and if he could give us their psychological character — their conceptions of life, and their emotions —

with the same truth as their idiom and manners, his books would be the greatest contribution" (Collins 343). The theologian Peter Bayne's critique of Dickens in *Essays in Biography and Criticism* (1857) is similar in its indictment of Dickens's tendencies to stray too far from the tenets of realism in his fiction. Bayne admits Dickens has "a sympathy of extraordinary range" (385) for the poorer classes whose lot he wished to improve. While conceding Dickens's ability to evoke emotional responses in his readers, however, Bayne suggests his aesthetic and moral principles are flawed. In Bayne's view, Dickens has been willing to "dishonor" (353) his genius by resorting to caricature to please readers who were not interested in complex characterization. Tricks and mannerisms, Bayne laments, substitute for real character analysis.

Indeed, Eliot and Bayne were part of a growing movement that would find Dickens deficient in ways the early Victorians did not. As George Ford observes in *Dickens and His Readers,* beginning at mid-century "the seeds of revolution were being sown by gifted and perceptive readers of fiction" (155) who would apply new standards to their assessment of the novel — ones by which Dickens's work would be judged and found wanting. An important voice among these revolutionaries was James Fitzjames Stephen, who at age twenty-six published his "theory of the novel" in an essay titled "The Relation of Novels to Life" (1855). That Stephen was brash and overly self-confident in his judgments of literature seems obvious in hindsight. (A lawyer by training, he gave up writing about literature later in his career.) Philip Collins calls Stephen's tone "a blend of undergraduate iconoclasm, patrician contempt for the masses, and mandarin defence of cultural tradition against the inroads of commercial barbarians" (13). Small wonder that Stephen did not appreciate Dickens. He attacked Dickens's methods and his choice of subjects in "License of Modern Novelists" (1857). But his harshest criticisms appeared in four essays written for the *Saturday Review,* a relatively new journal that devoted considerable space to literary matters. Ford describes Stephen's series of hostile *Saturday Review* articles as "a head-on attack with a cudgel" (151). Stephen takes Dickens to task in "Mr. Dickens as a Politician" (1857) for his naïve approach to social reform, and ridicules him for his poor skills at construction — and his attack on the legal profession — in a review of *Little Dorrit* (1857). A year later, Stephen blasts away at Dickens again for his sentimentality, heavy-handed characterization, and general muddle-headedness in "Mr. Dickens" (1858) — a critique so savage that nearly seventy years later Albert Mordell would think it worthy of inclusion in his collection *Notorious Literary Attacks* (1926).

The vitriolic tone of Stephen's criticism is nowhere better exemplified than in his review of *A Tale of Two Cities* (1859). Comparing this novel to an ill-prepared meal, Stephen says that in the *Tale* the discerning reader "will have an opportunity of studying in its elements a system of cookery which procured for its ingenious inventor unparalleled popularity, and enabled him to infect the literature of his country with a disease" that corrupts long-accepted standards of literature. If one accepts the principles Dickens follows in writing novels, one can only conclude that "the principal results of a persistent devotion to literature are an incurable vulgarity of mind and of taste, and intolerable arrogance of temper" (Ford and Lane 39). Dickens cannot create a plausible plot or believable, complex characters. Instead, Stephen says, he achieves his popularity by "working upon the feelings by the coarsest stimulants" and "setting common occurrences in a grotesque and unexpected light" (41). As he does in earlier essays on Dickens, Stephen once again lambastes the novelist for his inaccurate portrayal of the workings of the law. In that observation, George Ford suggests, lies the real reason for Stephen's visceral dislike of Dickens. Stephen thought the character of Tite Barnacle, head of the family that profits from the nefarious and Byzantine workings of the Circumlocution Office in *Little Dorrit*, was modeled on his father, Judge James Stephen. For that unforgivable sin, Dickens deserved to be punished. One might wonder, too, if that motivated other members of the distinguished Stephen family. Fitzjames's younger brother Leslie wrote much about the novel as a genre but almost nothing about Dickens, and his 1885 *Dictionary of National Biography* article on Dickens offers only begrudging admiration for some of the novelist's accomplishments while relishing his many limitations. The muted appreciation of Dickens offered by Leslie Stephen's daughter Virginia Woolf in her 1925 essay on *David Copperfield* is only slightly more positive in its assessment of Dickens's abilities.

All through the 1850s and 1860s the critics began to pile on, heaping scorn upon *Little Dorrit, A Tale of Two Cities,* and *Our Mutual Friend;* only *Great Expectations* seemed to escape universal execration. William Forsyth complained in *Fraser's Magazine* (1857) that Dickens continues to write "too much and too fast" and "seems to have no conception of a well-constructed plot." Additionally, "his characters are all exaggerations. We doubt if there is one which, as he has drawn it, occurs in real life." Worst of all is Dickens's "habit of pushing an idea to the extreme." In Forsyth's opinion, "No man ever rode a metaphor harder than Mr. Dickens" (Collins 350–52). E. B. Hamley remonstrates with Dickens in *Blackwood's Magazine* (1857), urging him to abandon his crusade for social reform. "As a humourist," Hamley says, "we prefer Dickens to all living men — as artist, moralist, politician, philosopher, and ultra-philanthropist, we prefer many living men, women and children to Dickens" (Collins 358). Writing shortly thereafter, Walt Whitman applauded Hamley's article for exposing "the degeneracy so evident" in Dickens's later work (Collins 358). A *Saturday Review* critic finds his "bizarre and grotesque literary taste, and the curious light under which he sees almost all the common things and the common events of life, drag him down, in his intervals of weakness, into the mire," and his "attempts to portray or to caricature or to satirize the upper classes of society have always been ludicrous failures" (Collins 417).

Walter Bagehot's assessment in the *National Review*, published in 1858 when Dickens was being pilloried for abandoning humor in favor of social criticism, is a bit more balanced. Conceding there is "no contemporary English writer" who can give pleasure simultaneously "to the servants as well as to the mistress, to the children as well as to the master" (Collins 390), Bagehot begins by laying out Dickens's faults, which are many. His genius is "essentially irregular and unsymmetrical," emerging from a "copious mind" that is not "harmonious" (Collins 391). He cannot reason, he cannot develop a good plot, he cannot write a love story. He can use sentiment to his own purposes, but tends to overuse it. What he excels in, Bagehot says, is his ability to portray city life and draw memorable characters. But Bagehot finds himself forced to admit Dickens's most recent works represent a distinct falling off, a result of what Bagehot sees as the inherent "deficiency" in Dickens of the "masculine faculties" of "reasoning, understanding and firm far-seeing sagacity" (Collins 401).

Surprisingly, even the *Saturday Review* (161) allowed its anonymous critic to praise *Great Expectations*. "Mr. Dickens may be reasonably proud of these volumes," the reviewer observes. "After a long series of his varied works — after passing under the cloud of *Little Dorrit* and *Bleak House* — he has written a story that is new, original, powerful, and very entertaining," worthy of standing "beside *Martin Chuzzlewit* and *David Copperfield*" (Collins 427). Edwin Whipple comments in the *Atlantic Monthly* (1861) that in *Great Expectations* Dickens is able to gain control over his tendency toward the pathetic and the ideal to produce an "artistic creation" that demonstrates he "is now in the prime, and not in the decline of his great powers" (Collins 428–29). However, E. S. Dallas, an important Victorian critic, was less enthusiastic in his *Times* review. "*Great Expectations* is not, indeed, his best work," he suggests, "but it is to be ranked among his happiest" (Collins 431).

Dallas also liked *Our Mutual Friend*, claiming in his *Times* review (1865) that the novel is "really one of his finest works, and one in which on occasion he even surpasses himself" (Collins 464). In the same review Dallas takes issue with those who praise *Pickwick Papers* as Dickens's best work. Even though it remains funny on numerous readings, he says, "we refuse to measure a work of art by the amount of visible effect which it produces; and we are not going to quarrel with tragedy because it is less mirthful than comedy." By contrast with this earlier work, Dallas says, one of the "remarkable" aspects of *Our Mutual Friend* is "the immense amount of thought which it contains" (Collins 466).

Dallas was in a distinct minority in writing about Dickens's last completed novel. The *Saturday Review* returned to its usual stand against Dickens, claiming *Our Mutual Friend* demonstrates once again that Dickens "has always been, and always will be, essentially a caricaturist" (Collins 461). To make matters worse, the reviewer goes on, in this novel the caricatures "are without either of Mr. Dickens's characteristic excellences. They are not very witty or humorous." Further, "the execution is coarse and clumsy, and the whole picture is redolent of ill-temper and fractiousness" (Collins 462). This reviewer admires Dickens for his "sincere hatred of that form of cant which implies that all English habits and institutions are the highest product of which civilization is capable," and applauds his justifiable "abhorrence of much in the administration of the Poor Law." But he feels Dickens exaggerates his case and thereby diminishes the effectiveness of his argument. "On the whole, this makes a very tedious performance, and the general verdict will probably be that *Our Mutual Friend* is very hard reading" (Collins 463). The reviewer for the *Westminster Review* (1866) suggested "the closer we look at Mr. Dickens's characters, the more we detect the trickery of an artificer." The novelist's "whole art" is "founded upon false principles" (Collins 474). In this reviewer's opinion, "true art has nothing to do with such ephemeral and local affairs as Poor Laws and Poor Law Boards; and whenever [Dickens] tries to serve such a double purpose, it is like an egg with two yolks, neither is ever hatched." Certainly, he goes on, if Dickens "knows anything of human nature, he must know that the practical English mind is, as a rule, repelled by any advocacy in the shape of fiction" (Collins 476).

Certainly, however, the review most influential in shaping future opinion of Dickens's artistry was that written by the young American expatriate Henry James, who was already making a name for himself in London literary circles. The publication of his assessment of *Our Mutual Friend* in the *Nation* (1865), written when he was just twenty-two years old, hints at a new standard for judging novels — what George Ford in *Dickens and His Readers* calls "the high aesthetic line" (199). Calling the novel the poorest of Dickens's works and faulting it as lacking in inspiration, James criticizes Dickens for the rather cavalier organization of all of his novels and consistently failing to explore beneath the surface of reality. For the young aspiring critic and novelist, the first principle of great fiction is its ability to mirror society not by creating exaggerated caricatures but by carefully delineating the inner lives of people who appear, at least, to be real human beings with complex feelings and delicate sensibilities. Dickens is prone to focus on oddities of human nature, James says, rather than examine real people in everyday situations. The "truly great novelist" sees no "alternatives," no "oddities"; for such a writer, James says, "there is nothing outside of humanity. He cannot shirk it; it imposes itself upon him" (Ford and Lane 53). By contrast, Dickens is unable to write about humankind with any degree of insight because he lacks "the intellectual superiority" over his characters to "prosecute those generalities in which alone consists the real greatness of a work of art" (53). James calls Dickens "the greatest of superficial novelists," stating that it would be "an offense against humanity to place Mr. Dickens among the greatest novelists" (52). In "The Art of Fiction," written two decades later, James would articulate a theory of fiction that makes Dickens's novels marginal: "the only reason for the existence of a novel," he proclaims, "is that it does attempt to represent life" in all its complexities (Allen and Clark 543). Nevertheless, it is good to be reminded that James's approach, while it might be appealing to certain readers, can also be a kind of straitjacket. No less an artist than James's admirer and contemporary Edith Wharton observed that his "literary judgments had long been hampered by his increasing preoccupation with the structure of the novel, and his unwillingness to concede that the vital center (when there was any) could lie elsewhere." It was impossible to convince him, she said, that "there might be merit in the work of writers apparently insensible to these sterner demands of the art" (323). Nonetheless, James and his disciples — among them Percy Lubbock, E. M. Forster, F. R. Leavis, and his wife Q. D. Leavis — would all find Dickens sorely deficient by the standards James had established for judging a novel's value, and their opinion would hold sway in academic circles for more than half a century.[2]

Interestingly, James's strictures were anticipated by the author of the *London Review* (1865) assessment of *Our Mutual Friend,* who claims to be "almost oppressed by the fullness of life which pervades the pages of this novel" (Hollington 422). The writer goes on in what can only be a direct rebuttal to James and others of the new generation of novel writers and readers: "We are prepared to hear from a certain class of critics who can tolerate nothing beyond the civilities of everyday life, and who seem to think that great passions are among those vulgar mistakes of nature to which novelists should be superior" (Collins 457).

Retrospectives written in the late 1860s suggest how critics on both sides of the Atlantic felt about the novelist who for thirty years had strode the literary landscape like a colossus. Writing in the *Atlantic Monthly* in 1867, Edwin Whipple reflects on Dickens's accomplishments while recognizing some of his pervasive limitations. "In the foundation of his character, Dickens agrees with the majority of well-meaning mankind. He has no paradoxes in morality to push, no scientific view of human nature to sustain, no philosophy of society to illustrate, no mission to accomplish." On the other hand, "Nobody ever thinks of going to his writings for light on such moral problems as are opened in Hamlet and Faust. Intellectually, he seems incapable of generalization" (Collins 479). Whipple praises Dickens for his ability to create characters, even though he sometimes exaggerates: "This exaggeration, however, is not caricature, for caricature never gives the impression of reality"; besides, he says, "Dickens caricatures only when his special object is to satirize" (Collins 480–81). Whipple admits the "plots of his romances, though frequently improbable in themselves, always seem probable in relation to the characters they are devised to bring vividly out." More importantly, the "impression left by all his books is not only humane but humanizing" (Collins 482). "Why, then," Whipple asks, "is Dickens not to be ranked with the greatest masters of characterization?" Because great characterization consists in creating "great natures," and while "the natures which Dickens creates may be original, strange, wild, criminal, humorous, lovable, pathetic, or good," they "are never great" (Collins 486).

Like Whipple, British critics of the 1860s were trying to get their arms around the phenomenon known as Charles Dickens. That he had been immensely popular early in his career was a given; that he had suffered a downturn in more recent decades when he abandoned humor in favor of social protest was also evident. What did all this mean for posterity? In a retrospective written for the *Contemporary Review* (1869), George Stott says that while the possibility of Dickens's being "popular a century hence is a question quite impossible to decide, and therefore very unprofitable to discuss," coming generations will be forced to acknowledge Dickens as "one of the great literary facts of the age. As such he is worthy of careful investigation" (Collins 492). Like a good Victorian, Stott insists there is "a preliminary question that may be asked of Mr. Dickens, as of all artists whatever their degree. Is he artist only, or moralist as well?" Stott maintains that "in all his novels Mr. Dickens has a distinct and conscious moral aim which inspires and dominates over the narrative," making him "an Idealist, not a Realist" (Collins 493). Stott finds Dickens at his best as a caricaturist, but when "he abandons the field of farce for loftier aims, where its methods are inapplicable, he at once makes us sensible of his deficiencies." Although he is adept at "idealizing the grotesque, [Dickens] fails in higher efforts, through the limitation both of his knowledge of, and imaginative sympathy with, human nature, and the insufficiency and unsuitableness of his methods in an unfamiliar field" (Collins 495). Not only is Dickens "insensible to beauty," Stott asserts; "he is no less so to intellectual excellence, and the aims and pursuits of intellectual men. We can hardly fail to be struck by the marked absence in him of anything like loftiness of thought" (Collins 498). This deficiency, coupled with "narrowness of mind," make Dickens unqualified for "that *rôle* of social reformer which he is so ambitious of filling" (Collins 499). If there is a philosophy underlying Dickens's work, Stott believes it is best defined as "an expansion of the idea of Christmas," a "gospel of geniality that Mr. Dickens sets himself to preach; the feelings and sympathies supposed to be evoked by the annual holiday are to be the ruling principles of life" (Collins 500). Stott finds this simplistic approach distasteful. "Mr. Dickens has very possibly not fully grasped the bearing of the doctrines he has laid down in one part of his works and another; but if he had the power to reform the world according to his own principles, the result would be to turn it into the vulgar Arcadia we have been depicting — fit habitation only for those benevolent but eccentric elderly gentlemen, virtuous artisans, and gushing young ladies on whom his warmest admirations are lavished" (Collins 500). Unfortunately, Stott concludes, "All that gives interest to life, and makes it worth the living, would be gone" (Collins 501).

Later in the same year R. H. Hutton, one of the most widely read critics of the Victorian era, contributed a brief article to the *Spectator* titled "Mr. Dickens's Moral Services to Literature" (1869) in which he declares, "That Dickens's moral influence has been, on the whole, healthy and good we heartily believe. It has been certainly profoundly humane" (Collins 489). "Still" — and this is a very strong caveat — "the last moral service we should think of ascribing to Dickens's literary influence would be the diffusion of a genuine reverence for absolute sincerity and realism." Too often he "falls into the most mawkish and unreal sentimentalism" (Collins 490). Hutton believes Dickens's "greatest service to English literature will, after all, be not his high morality, which is altogether wanting in delicacy of insight, but in the complete harmlessness and purity of the immeasurable humour into which he moulds his enormous stores of acute observation." Dickens is worth reading, Hutton concludes, because "he provides almost unlimited food for a great people without infusing any really dangerous poison into it" (Collins 491). Humorous, humane, harmless — admirable attributes to be sure, but in an age that valued moral earnestness, Hutton's summation suggests the critical tide had definitely turned against Dickens as the great moralist and social reformer that many had thought him just a generation earlier.

Notes

[1] I have provided in the "Works Cited" listings the full citation for each of the reviews from which I quote. However, because few scholars and students have access to the nineteenth-century periodicals in which these reviews appear, I have cited pages from Kathryn Chittick's *The Critical Reception of Charles Dickens 1833–1841*, volume 1 of Michael Hollington's *Charles Dickens: Critical Assessments* (1995), Philip Collins's *Dickens: The Critical Heritage* (1971) or George Ford and Lauriat Lane's *The Dickens Critics* (1961) to facilitate identification of these passages.

[2] The relationship between Dickens and James, and the former's influence on the American novelist and critic, has been the subject of several studies, including H. Blair Rouse, "Charles Dickens and Henry James: Two Approaches to the Art of Fiction" (*Nineteenth Century Fiction* 1950), and Q. D. Leavis, "A Note on Literary Indebtedness: Dickens, George Eliot, Henry James" (*Hudson Review* 1955).

Works Cited

Allen, Gay Wilson, and Harry Hayden Clark, eds. *Literary Criticism*. 2 vols. Detroit, MI: Wayne State UP, 1962.

Anon. Review of *Bleak House*. *Bentley's Miscellany* 34 (October 1853): 372–74.

Anon. Review of *The Cricket on the Hearth*. *Chambers's Edinburgh Journal* n.s. 5 (17 Jan 1846): 44–48.

Anon. Review of *Dr. Marigold's Prescriptions*. *Saturday Review* 20 (16 December 1865): 763–64.

Anon. Review of *Dombey and Son*. *Westminster Review* 47 (April 1847): 5–11.

Anon. Review of *Great Expectations*. *Saturday Review* 12 (20 July 1861): 69.

Anon. Review of *The Haunted Man*. *Macphail's Edinburgh Ecclesiastical Journal* 6 (Jan 1849): 423–31.

Anon. Review of *Master Humphrey's Clock*. *Metropolitan Magazine* 30 (December 1840): 111.

Anon. Review of *Our Mutual Friend*. *London Review* (28 October 1865): 467–68.

Anon. Review of *Our Mutual Friend*. *Saturday Review* 20 (11 November 1865): 612–13.

Anon. Review of *Our Mutual Friend*. *Westminster Review* n.s. 29 (April 1866): 582–85.

Anon. Review of *Pickwick Papers*. *Metropolitan Magazine* 18 (January 1837): 6.

Anon. Review of *Sketches by Boz*. *Metropolitan Magazine* 15 (March 1836): 77.

Bagehot, Walter. "Charles Dickens." *National Review* 7 (October 1858): 458–86.

Bayne, Peter. *Essays in Biography and Criticism*, 363–92. First series. Boston: Gould and Lincoln, 1857.

Blanchard, E. L. Review of *A Christmas Carol*. *Ainsworth's Magazine* 5 (January 1844): 86.

Brimley, George. Review of *Bleak House*. *Spectator* 26 (24 September 1853): 923–25.

Buller, Charles. "The Works of Dickens." *London and Westminster Review* 29 (July 1837): 194–215.

"Charles Dickens and David Copperfield." *Fraser's Magazine* 42 (December 1850): 698–700.

"Charles Dickens and His Works." *Fraser's Magazine* 21 (April 1840): 381–400.

Chittick, Kathryn. *The Critical Reception of Charles Dickens 1833–1841*. New York: Garland, 1989.

Cleghorn, Thomas. "Writings of Charles Dickens." *North British Review* 3 (May 1845): 65–87.

Collins, Philip A. W., ed. *Dickens: The Critical Heritage*. London: Routledge & Kegan Paul, 1971.

Croker, John Wilson. Review of *American Notes. Quarterly Review* 71 (March 1843): 502–28.

Dallas, E. S. Review of *Great Expectations. The Times* (17 October 1861): 6.

———. Review of *Our Mutual Friend. The Times* (29 November 1865): 6.

Eagles, John. "A Few Words about Novels — a Dialogue." *Blackwood's Magazine* 64 (October 1848): 468–69.

Eliot, George [Marian Evans]. "The Natural History of German Life." *Westminster Review* 66 (July 1856): 55.

Ford, George H. *Dickens and His Readers: Aspects of Novel Criticism Since 1836*. Princeton, NJ: Princeton UP, 1955: New York: Norton, 1965.

Ford, George H., and Lauriat Lane, Jr., eds. *The Dickens Critics*. Ithaca, NY: Cornell UP, 1961.

Ford, Richard. Review. *Quarterly Review* 64 (June 1839): 83–102.

Forster, John. Review of *Bleak House, Examiner* 8 (October 1853): 643–45.

———. Review of *Hard Times. Examiner* 9 (September 1854): 568–69.

Forsyth, William. "Literary Style." *Fraser's Magazine* 55 (March 1857): 260–63.

Hamley, E. B. "Remonstrance with Dickens." *Blackwood's Magazine* 81 (April 1857): 490–503.

Hayward, Abraham. Review of *Pickwick Papers* and *Sketches by Boz. Quarterly Review* 62 (October 1837): 484–518.

Hogarth, George. Review of *Sketches by Boz. Morning Chronicle* 20 (11 February 1836).

Hollington, Michael, ed. *Charles Dickens: Critical Assessments*. 4 vols. London: Helm, 1995.

Horne, R. H. *A New Spirit of the Age*. 3 vols. London: Smith, Elder, 1844. Reprint, New York: Garland, 1986.

Hood, Thomas. Review of *Master Humphrey's Clock* and *The Old Curiosity Shop*. *Athenaeum* 7 (November 1940): 887–88.

Hutton, R. H. "Mr. Dickens's Moral Services to Literature." *Spectator* 42 (17 April 1869): 474–75.

James, Henry. "*Our Mutual Friend*." *Nation* 1 (December 1865): 786–87. Reprinted as "The Limitations of Dickens." *Views and Reviews*. Boston: Ball, 1908.

Leavis, Q. D. "A Note on Literary Indebtedness: Dickens, George Eliot, Henry James." *Hudson Review* 8 (Autumn 1955): 423–28.

Lister, Thomas Henry. Review of *Sketches by Boz, Pickwick Papers, Oliver Twist*, and *Nicholas Nickleby*. *Edinburgh Review* 68 (Oct 1838): 75–97.

"Literary Examiner." *Examiner* 1456 (28 February 1836): 132–33.

Martineau, Harriet. *A History of England During the Thirty Years' Peace 1816–1846*. 4 vols. London: C. Knight, 1849. London: G. Bell, 1877–78.

Masson, David. *British Novelists and Their Styles: Being a Critical Sketch of the History of British Prose Fiction*. London: Macmillan; Boston: Gould and Lincoln, 1859. Reprint, Boston: W. Small, 1928.

———. "*Pendennis* and *Copperfield:* Thackeray and Dickens." *North British Review* 15 (May 1851): 57–89.

Maurois, André. *Dickens, His Life and Work*. Translated by Hamish Miles. London: J. Lane, 1934.

McCarthy, Justin. "Dickens and Thackeray." *A History of Our Times*, 255–59. Rev. ed. Vol. 2. New York: Lovell, Coryell & Co., 1894.

"Modern Novels." *Christian Remembrancer* 4 (December 1842): 585–96.

Mordell, Albert, ed. *Notorious Literary Attacks*. New York: Boni & Liveright, 1926.

Oliphant, Margaret. "Sensation Novels." *Blackwood's Edinburgh Magazine* 91 (May 1862): 564–84.

"The Reception of Mr. Dickens." *United States Magazine and Democratic Review* (April 1842): 315, 320.

Rouse, H. Blair. "Charles Dickens and Henry James: Two Approaches to the Art of Fiction." *Nineteenth Century Fiction* 5 (September 1950): 151–57.

Ruskin, John. *Unto this Last*. *Cornhill Magazine* 2 (August 1860): 159.

Simpson, Richard. Review of *Hard Times*. *The Rambler* n.s. 2 (October 1854): 361–62.

Stephen, James Fitzjames. "License of Modern Novelists." *Edinburgh Review* 106 (July 1857): 124–56.

———. "*Little Dorrit*." *Saturday Review* 4 (July 1857): 15–16.

———. "Mr. Dickens." *Saturday Review* 5 (May 1858): 474–75. Reprinted in Albert Mordell, ed., *Notorious Literary Attacks*. New York: Boni & Liveright, 1926.

———. "Mr. Dickens as a Politician." *Saturday Review* 3 (January 1857): 8–9.

———. "The Relation of Novels to Life." *Cambridge Essays*, 148–92. London: J. N. Parker, 1855.

———. "*A Tale of Two Cities.*" *Saturday Review* 8 (17 December 1859): 741–43.

Stephen, Leslie. "Dickens, Charles." *Dictionary of National Biography*. Vol. 5, 925–37. 1885. Reprint, London: Smith, Elder, 1908.

Stothert, James Augustine. "Living Novelists." *The Rambler* n.s. 1 (January 1854): 41–51.

Stott, George. "Charles Dickens." *Contemporary Review* 10 (January 1869): 203–25.

Taine, Hippolyte. "Charles Dickens: son talent et ses oeuvres." *Revue des Deux Mondes* n.s. 1 (1 February 1856): 618–47.

Thackeray, W. M. "A Box of Novels." *Fraser's Magazine* 29 (Feb 1844): 166–69.

Wharton, Edith. *A Backward Glance*. London: Appleton-Century, 1934.

Whipple, Edwin. "The Genius of Dickens." *Atlantic Monthly* 19 (May 1867): 546–54.

———. "*Great Expectations.*" *Atlantic Monthly* 8 (September 1861): 380–82.

———. "Novels and Novelists: Charles Dickens." *North American Review* 69 (October 1849): 383–407.

———. Review of *Hard Times*. *Atlantic Monthly* 39 (March 1877): 353–58.

Whitman, Walt. "Charles Dickens." *Brooklyn Daily Times*, 6 May 1857.

Woolf, Virginia. "*David Copperfield.*" *Nation and Athenaeum* 37 (August 1925): 620–21. Reprinted in *The Moment and Other Essays*. London: Hogarth, 1947. Reprinted in *Collected Essays*. Vol. 1. London: Hogarth, 1966.

2: The Birth of the Dickens Industry and the Reaction against Victorianism (1870–1914)

WHEN DICKENS DIED in 1870, there was a rush to publish memorial tributes. Among the first to appear was one by George Augustus Sala, who had worked with Dickens on *Household Words* and *All The Year Round* and been considered one of his protégés. Sala originally published a testimonial to his mentor in the *Daily Telegraph*, then expanded his narrative fourfold for publication under the title *Charles Dickens* later in 1870. Writing more a celebratory funeral oration than critical analysis, Sala claims Dickens was "as original as he who imagined Achilles' wrath, as he who conjured up Falstaff's salt humors, and who painted Satan in awful blackness" (7). Such favorable comparisons to Homer, Shakespeare, and Milton might have been expected from someone who owed his career to Dickens's sponsorship, but they are also typical of the ways Victorian critics tended to judge a writer's merits. Sala praises Dickens for discovering what the people of his age wanted, and then giving it to them — humor without grossness — and for being a model citizen. Typical of Victorian biographers, Sala focuses on the novelist's public accomplishments while saying of his private life, "it behooves me not at this time to speak" (94). Certainly Sala knew something of Dickens's mid-life crises, but as a good Victorian, he preferred not to expose the clay feet of his idol.

A much longer biography appeared in the same year. Robert Shelton MacKenzie's *Life of Charles Dickens* (1870) is more comprehensive than Sala's and contains considerably more commentary on the novels. An American, MacKenzie makes a concerted effort to give Americans great credit for Dickens's popularity, claiming that in the United States he had fifty readers for every one in England. MacKenzie celebrates Dickens as the "champion of the oppressed" and the "censor of the selfish rich" (29). His judgments of individual novels parallel conventional opinion among nineteenth-century readers: the earlier novels receive the highest praise, while later works are given considerably less critical attention. What is most interesting about MacKenzie's study, though, is his consistent attempt to turn Dickens into a kind of Horatio Alger figure, the boy from a very humble background who became incredibly successful but never let success go to his head. MacKenzie's method of scouring the fiction for clues to real-life sources is characteristic of a practice that would occupy hundreds of Dickens lovers for nearly half a century — and earn them the scorn of critics who were already applying formalist and aesthetic principles to literary analysis.

Shortly after Dickens died, one of the first of what might be called "specialty studies" appeared, Charles Kent's *Charles Dickens as a Reader* (1872). Kent's aim was modest: to document Dickens's career as a public performer. A member of the group that would eventually create The Dickens Fellowship in 1903, Kent intended his study as a reminder to future generations that Dickens achieved his popularity not only by writing his novels but by bringing them to life in dramatic readings that captivated large audiences in England and America. While not exceptionally scholarly, the book helped solidify what might be called the "Dickens Myth," reinforcing the notion that the novelist was a larger-than-life figure who, like Shakespeare before him, had special insights into human character and a unique way of presenting them to both the reading and theater-going publics.

It is important to point out, however, that the seeds of discontent planted as early as the 1850s began to blossom almost immediately after Dickens died. The trend should not be surprising; as Edgar Johnson observed eighty years later, "when the literary king is dead there is a strong temptation to disparage his triumphs, and even before that there are always youthful rivals seeking to topple him from his throne" ("Turning Tides" 644). Such was the fate Dickens suffered at the hands of many who managed to outlive him.

Nothing could be farther from Kent's salutary assessment than George Henry Lewes's essay on Dickens published in the *Fortnightly Review*. "Dickens in Relation to Criticism" (1872) set the trend for critics who had a low regard for Dickens's accomplishments in fiction. Although Lewes and Dickens had been friends for some time, Lewes was no doubt irked that Dickens was held in higher esteem by the public than George Eliot — that is, Marian Evans, with whom Lewes had lived for years. Lewes had already shown his displeasure with Dickens's cavalier treatment of science, complaining in 1853 about the novelist's suggestion in *Bleak House* that one of his characters had died from spontaneous combustion. A proponent of realism and complex characterization, Lewes was hardly a fan of Dickens's techniques of exaggeration and rhetorical embellishment. To be fair, however, it must be pointed out that "Dickens in Relation to Criticism" is aimed not simply at Dickens himself but even more so at uncritical admirers, specifically John Forster, who had only recently released the first volume of his *Life of Charles Dickens*. Opening his essay with an admission that Dickens has achieved "a popularity almost unexampled," Lewes asks, "Surely it is a task for criticism to exhibit the sources of that power?" (143). In what would seem to be a tribute to Dickens, Lewes locates the principal source of Dickens's genius in his imagination, a faculty Lewes calls "imperial" (144). Yet he qualifies this by observing somewhat snidely that, while he has never found traces of insanity in Dickens, "there is considerable light shed upon his works by the action of the imagination in hallucination" (145). His characters, Lewes goes on to say, are "universally intelligible, no matter how fantastic and unreal," but "their falsity" is obscured for some readers by "the blaze of their illumination" (146). These "unreal figures," Lewes says, "affected the uncritical reader with the force of reality" (146). And he goes on: "Think how little the mass of men are given to reflect on their impressions, and how their minds are for the most part occupied with sensations rather than ideas, and you will see why Dickens held an undisputed sway" (146). Apparently thousands of shallow readers were taken in by this clever author for whom "the world of thought and passion lay beyond his horizon" (147).

Against these unthinking, gullible readers Lewes sets himself up as the discerning critic whose knowledge of literature makes him capable of rendering more objective judgments on Dickens's accomplishments. A genuine critic "is distressed to observe" in Dickens's novels "the substitution of mechanisms for minds, puppets for characters" (148). Of course, Lewes admits, some critics dwell too much on an artist's technical merits — or deficiencies — and underrate the artist's ability to please an audience. Though he insists Dickens displayed immense talent in being able to touch the heartstrings of his readers, most of those who devoured his novels had no sense of the "refinements of Art and Literature" (151). It is hard to imagine Lewes being anything but cynical when he says that "thought is strangely absent" from Dickens's works, or that since "his was merely an *animal* intelligence" [Lewes's emphasis] Dickens's "early education was more fruitful and less injurious than it would have been to a nature constructed on a more reflective and intellectual type" (151). Since most readers of Lewes's essay would have just read Forster's account of Dickens's chaotic childhood and known he had little formal education, the remark is particularly barbed. Lewes closes by returning to his observation that Dickens's prodigal imagination goes a long way toward overcoming his faults, but for those skilled in critical reading, he is little more than a cheap trickster.

Many who enjoyed Dickens may have been annoyed at Lewes's critique, but Dickens's closest friend and literary executor John Forster was outraged, especially since the first volume of his biography of Dickens had been the impetus for Lewes's stinging commentary. Forster was not going to let that judgment go unchallenged. The final two volumes of *The Life of Charles Dickens* (1872–74) were recrafted to meet Lewes's charges head-on. Forster inserted materials to give the lie to assertions about Dickens's lack of technical merit and his understanding of human nature. Among readers already predisposed to admire Dickens, Forster's rebuttal was sufficient to reassure them that Lewes was simply being mean-spirited; as a consequence, in the history of Dickens criticism, Lewes has long been considered one of the fathers of the anti-Dickens movement.

Meanwhile, Forster's *Life of Charles Dickens* instantly became not only the standard for evaluating the novelist's work, but also for judging his character. Forster met Dickens while the novelist was still establishing his reputation and quickly became Dickens's closest confidante, his trusted unofficial editor and business advisor, and his literary executor. A man of letters who edited several periodicals and newspapers and wrote biographies of British statesmen and writers such as Oliver Goldsmith and Walter Savage Landor, Forster intended his *Life of Charles Dickens* to be the work that would establish his own place in English literary history. There is little doubt Forster saw himself performing the same work that James Boswell had done so admirably in documenting the life of Samuel Johnson. Dickens actually cooperated in the venture first by telling Forster as early as 1848 that he would like to have his life story told. He had been composing an autobiography at the time, but broke off work on it to write *David Copperfield*, a fictional account based loosely on his own life. Before he died he gave Forster the autobiographical fragment; Forster used this document, along with correspondence he had exchanged with Dickens over more than thirty years, to construct a story that would appeal to Victorian readers. In Forster's hands, Dickens becomes a kind of "Hero as Novelist," to adapt Carlyle's terminology from *Heroes and Hero-Worship*. Revealing for the first time Dickens's deprived childhood, including his humiliating service in a factory where he was put on display in the shop window sealing bottles of shoe-blacking, Forster creates the image of a young man emerging from a psychologically devastating home life to become the darling of the English reading public.

Although he acknowledges at times that his hero was not faultless, Forster glosses over deficiencies in Dickens's character in favor of descriptions of his great insights into human nature, his ability to describe minutely the people and places he met and saw, his intense concern for the poor and disenfranchised, his deep-seated faith in the essential goodness of humanity, and his indefatigable capacity for work. A century before the New Historicists began examining novelists and novel-making as economic enterprises, Forster wrote about the way "Dickens" became a commodity, and how the man Charles Dickens traded on his name to amass both wealth and social status — a fortune he put to good use and a fame he did not really relish, if one is to believe Forster.

While he was quick to bring out the obstacles Dickens had to overcome as a young man, Forster was much more reticent in dealing with the mess Dickens made of his personal life in the 1850s. The novelist's separation from his wife in 1858 had been a public affair — in large part because Dickens himself had made it so by publishing a letter in *Household Words* explaining why he had left her — but Forster opts to gloss over details. Of course, Forster knew Dickens had kept up some kind of relationship with the young actress Ellen Ternan from 1856 until his death in 1870. But he chose not to even mention Ternan in the biography, simply attributing the separation to the "unsettled feeling" Dickens experienced at this point in his life, "the satisfactions which home should have supplied" but did not (2.193). The point is important for understanding something about Forster's approach to his subject, and about the Victorians' expectations regarding literary biographies. Forster wanted to make Dickens a hero, and the reading public was glad to have a portrait of their favorite novelist that presented him as a generous, hardworking, public-spirited man who had risen from poverty to become both rich and well-regarded. Forster's one-sided portrait, written in the face of evidence to the contrary, would supply grist for future biographers' mills for the next century.

As a literary critic, Forster was a man of his time, but some of his observations about Dickens's works displayed more perspicacity than many of his contemporaries demonstrated. He appreciates *Pickwick Papers* but judges it unpolished, especially when compared to later novels. He praises *Oliver Twist* and *The Old Curiosity Shop,* but strains to find something good to say about *Barnaby Rudge.* He thinks *Martin Chuzzlewit* deserves a better reputation than it had earned with its first critics, and considers *Dombey and Son* well constructed — not a common opinion among Victorian readers. Naturally he adores *David Copperfield,* but what is more noteworthy is his praise for *Bleak House,* a novel panned by contemporaries: "in the very important particular of construction," he observes, it is "perhaps the best thing done by Dickens" (2.114). However, he agrees with Victorian critics who found *Little Dorrit* and *Our Mutual Friend* disappointing. Forster attributes the deficiencies of these later works to Dickens's exhaustion and the trials of his separation from Catherine Dickens.

The biography actually received mixed reviews among Forster's first readers. Some found it too detailed (a curious charge in an age when biographies typically filled several volumes). Others objected, perhaps rightly, that Forster's over-reliance on his own correspondence with Dickens and his failure to collect many documents and reminiscences from others who knew the novelist made it appear Forster was principally responsible for Dickens's great success. Writing four decades later about a new edition of Forster's biography, critic Stewart Ellis would acknowledge the adverse reception by some earlier critics, pointing out some of the book's "faults both of omission and commission." Despite his judgment that Forster is "egotistical and at times prejudicial," Ellis claims it is "a great biography, the greatest, it is safe to say, of its great subject, and one that will never be superseded" (85–86). Certainly it is true that, for seventy-five years after it first appeared, Forster's *Life of Charles Dickens* remained the most read and most cited biography. It was reprinted several times in its entirety, abridged by George Gissing in 1903, edited by B. W. Matz in 1912, by J. W. T. Ley in 1928, and again by A. J. Hoppé in 1965. At the beginning of the twenty-first century it continues to appear in abbreviated lists of "must read" works for Dickens scholars.

The extent to which Forster influenced subsequent biographies can be seen in Adolphus Ward's *Charles Dickens* (1882), prepared for the English Men of Letters series. In keeping with the guidelines for books in this series, Ward concentrates on the personal traits that make his subject a great man. Consequently, he stresses the importance of Dickens's experiences as a child, especially his humiliations at the blacking factory, and his work as a reporter, about which Ward says, "Already we notice in him what were to remain, through life, two of his most marked characteristics — strength of will and a determination, if he did a thing at all, to do it thoroughly" (9–10). Like Forster, he is hesitant to delve too deeply into Dickens's personal life, especially the troubled years of the 1850s and 1860s. He begs off discussing the novelist's separation from his wife, saying that if Forster could not judge Dickens's actions, neither will he. Nevertheless, he does attempt, especially in his final chapter, to account for Dickens's genius, which he believes derives from the writer's ability to be in touch with his readers and from his penchant for the dramatic.

In critiquing individual novels, Ward shows his preference for Dickens's humor over his social criticism. His comments on *David Copperfield*, "the most perfect" of all his novels "as a work of art" (103), perpetuate the Victorians' belief that this was Dickens's masterpiece. Like many of his contemporaries, he has only faint praise for novels written after this one — except for *Great Expectations,* which he says ranks among Dickens's best. Ward's last chapter, "The Future of Dickens's Fame," is a surprisingly evenhanded assessment of the novelist's place in English literature. Presciently, Ward suggests future generations might not rank Dickens as highly as his Victorian contemporaries did. He was already being proven right.

Like Ward, Frank Marzials looks to Forster's biography as well as the newly published volumes of the *Letters of Charles Dickens* edited by his daughter Mary and sister-in-law Georgina Hogarth, and to F. G. Kitton's bibliography, *Dickensiana* (1886), for his *Life of Charles Dickens* (1887) prepared for the Great Writers series. Valuing the earlier comic work over the social commentaries of Dickens's later years, Marzials judges *David Copperfield* "the culminating point in Dickens's career as a writer" (111).

He refutes critics who had faulted Dickens for his implausible plots by asserting that plausibility was unnecessary in a writer who reaches "a higher unity than that of mere plot" (85). In providing critical analysis that is both conventional and somewhat opinionated, Marzials aligns himself with a growing number of Dickens lovers who refuse to recognize any fault in their idol. This carries over into his commentary of Dickens's life and character, which perpetuates and expands on the myth of Dickens as the hale-fellow-well-met Victorian gentleman, always pure in his thoughts and always acting from the highest motives. "Petty jealousies found no place in the nature of this great writer," he asserts flatly (53). He blasts those who blamed Dickens for separating from Catherine, bemoaning the slanders these people have hurled at a man whose character simply could not be impugned. Only near the end of his study does Marzials acknowledge that, nearly two decades after Dickens's death, changing fashions might affect his reputation. "Some loss of immediate, vital interest is inevitable," he admits. "Nevertheless, in Dickens's case, all will not die" (162).

In contrast to these loving tributes, Leslie Stephen's article on Dickens in the *Dictionary of National Biography* (1885) suggests the backlash against Dickens was being carried forward by the group that had always considered him the poster child for sentimental fiction. In sketching the story of his life, Stephen praises Dickens's work as an editor, glosses over the separation from his wife, and expresses admiration for Dickens's abilities as a businessman and provider for his family and others. When writing about the novels, however, Stephen is skilful in his ability to damn with faint praise. Though not as vitriolic as his brother FitzJames had been in attacking Dickens three decades earlier, Stephen is careful to balance any compliments with sly comments that undermine the novelist's claim to greatness. To that end, Stephen stresses two qualities: Dickens's "exuberant animal spirit" and his "amazing fertility in creating comic types" (927). The earlier novels rank higher in his opinion because in them the "humourist is not yet lost in the satirist" (927). In his concluding remarks, Stephen begins by praising Dickens's personal character, but then undercuts his high assessment by noting that the novelist's "weaknesses are sufficiently obvious, and are reflected in his writings." Of course, Stephen observes, "If literary fame could be safely measured by popularity with the half-educated, Dickens must claim the highest position of English novelists." But more sophisticated critics can see at a glance that "his merits are such as suit the half-educated": his "pathos" has "little real depth of feeling," and his political and social views favor "spontaneous instinct" over "genuine reasoned conviction." In sum, "His books are inimitable [no doubt the word choice is intentional] caricatures of contemporary 'humours' rather than the masterpieces of a great observer of human nature" (935).

Less caustic, perhaps, but no less deprecatory, were the comments of Margaret Oliphant, the novelist and critic whose 1892 survey *The Victorian Age of English Literature* offered an assessment of the development of the novel during the nineteenth century. Oliphant's judgment of Dickens had not changed much in thirty years; her 1862 *Blackwood*'s essay "Sensation Novels" had compared *Great Expectations* unfavorably to Wilkie Collins's *The Woman in White*. Oliphant had accused Dickens of letting his considerable artistic powers go to waste, calling him "the careless, clever boy who could do it twice as well, but won't take pains" (Collins 442). In her 1892 reevaluation, Oliphant continues to insist that the best of Dickens is the early Dickens. Though he "never achieved any particular eminence as a story-teller" (252), he was able to create memorable characters. Oliphant has little use, however, for Dickens's "sentimental or pathetic passages" (256), and his Christmas books are particularly offensive examples of his tendency to rely on sentimentality rather than to draw believable characters reacting realistically in everyday situations.

These rather dismissive appraisals represented one trend in Dickens studies, but by no means did the novelist fall out of favor completely. A generation that had grown up in the latter half of the century reading about Pickwick, Oliver Twist, Nicolas Nickleby, David Copperfield, and Pip carried their admiration into adulthood. The most fanatic among them could not get enough of their hero. They collected editions of Dickens's work and personal memorabilia. They searched diligently for the real-life models of people and places depicted in the fiction. Gradually, they came to be referred to as "Dickensians" — a title they bore with pride, but which often met with ridicule from those who considered themselves more sophisticated and modern than their Victorian fathers and grandfathers.

Typical of these fanatic Dickens lovers was Frederic G. Kitton. Born in 1856 in Norwich, he read Dickens as a boy and was immediately captivated. Kitton went to London in 1873 to apprentice as an artist, working for some time as an etcher. But he found his true calling as a writer, publishing memoirs of two men who had illustrated Dickens's books, Hablot Browne ("Phiz") and John Leech. Beginning in 1886, Kitton began producing books about Dickens: *Dickensiana*, a bibliography of the author's works; *Charles Dickens By Pen and Pencil* (1890), a collection of reminiscences and anecdotes about the novelist; a bibliography of the novels (1897) and a separate one on the minor writings (1900); a study of Dickens and his illustrators (1899); a biography, largely redacted from other sources (1902); an edition of Dickens's verse (1903); and a monograph prepared in collaboration with G. K. Chesterton (1903). By the time he died — prematurely in 1904 — Kitton had become the foremost

Dickens scholar in the world. His *Dickens Country* (1911), a posthumously published account of the real-world places Dickens used as models for his fiction, was welcomed by those who cherished the memory of the novelist as the man who created Christmas and represented all that was good and wholesome in the English character.

Kitton rarely wrote criticism, however; that was left to others, and the field soon became crowded, with one writer after another attempting to provide some insight into Dickens's artistry or his philosophy on issues such as social reform, religion, or morality. In the late nineteenth century, it was common practice for critics to combine a series of essays on various literary figures into a single volume; sometimes there was an overriding theme that connected individual pieces, sometimes not. In both types of works, the focus tended to be on the character of the writer rather than the content of his or her work. Furthermore, identifying general trends was more important than providing detailed analysis of individual novels. Dickens figures prominently in many of these collections, a few of which may serve as examples of this form of critical treatment.

The first, Samuel Davey's *Darwin, Carlyle, and Dickens* (1876), treats Dickens independently, not attempting to judge him in comparison with other figures about whom Davey writes. Nevertheless, like most critics writing in the decade after Dickens's death, Davey devotes considerable attention to "placing" Dickens not only among his contemporaries but also among writers in the English tradition. Focusing on characterization, Davey applauds Dickens for being able to depict "the darker passions" (149) and infuse "a moral purpose" (150) even in his descriptions of the "vilest conceptions of human nature" (150). Nevertheless, Davey is equivocal about Dickens's permanence — and his greatness. Though he calls him the most beloved novelist of his time, he may not be the greatest, Davey says, answering the charge of critics like Henry James by admitting that, "if he could not sound the depths or tumult of the soul, he could touch those lighter feelings which play upon the surface of our nature" (122–23).

A second example of mainstream Victorian commentary is James Crabbe Watt's *Great Novelists: Scott, Thackeray, Dickens, Lytton* (1880). Even more than Davey, Watt is interested in the character of the man rather than the quality of the works. The Dickens he presents to readers bears similarities to people celebrated by Carlyle in works like *Heroes and Hero-Worship* or Samuel Smiles in his series of biographies: men shaped by early experiences into becoming self-reliant, self-made geniuses. Watt is much more interested in chronicling Dickens's triumph over adversity than in critiquing individual novels; in fact, the ten novels written after *The Old Curiosity Shop* are dismissed in a mere two pages. Perhaps Watt knew his audience was more interested in learning to apply the "lesson" of Dickens's life to their own.

In an essay originally published in the *Athenaeum* and included in *Views and Reviews: Essays in Appreciation* (1890) W. E. Henley praises Dickens as "an artist in the best sense of the term" (4). He traces with admiration Dickens's growth from a simple humorist to a serious novelist, defining the starting point for the change as the publication of *Nicholas Nickleby*. Though Dickens may have had faults, Henley says, they are ones shared with Sir Walter Scott or Shakespeare — writers whose stock was high in the nineteenth century. Henley's commentary is representative of Dickens lovers who would persevere in their unstinting praise during the next half-century, in spite of the prevailing trend in academic circles to disparage Dickens as a mere entertainer. "I love to think," Henley writes at the conclusion of his brief essay, "that while English literature endures he will be remembered as one that loved his fellow-men and did more to make them happy and amiable than any other writer of his time" (8).

Similar sentiments were echoed by Frederic Harrison, whose essay on Dickens in the *Forum* (1895) opens with a caution that assessing Dickens is risky at a time when he is still beloved by many readers. Harrison prefers the early novels, where Dickens excels in his ability to write humorous fiction; in those works, Harrison observes, the novelist's inability to create a good plot is not so noticeable. Like other writers of his own time, however, Harrison finds the "restless gaiety" of the novels "too often growing fatiguing" (138) — a sentiment that certainly sat well with a generation of late-century readers constantly being told that great novels should paint more realistic, and somber, portraits of life and society.

By the 1890s the earnest moralists who had been giants among the Victorians were being summarily discredited and dismissed by the modernists who found their values questionable and their hypocrisy repulsive. Walter Crotch reports in a retrospective published in 1919 that at the end of the nineteenth century, "It was customary among the Smart Set — the smart literary set" — to "denounce [Dickens] as crude, catholic, and an apostle of the obvious" (121). Half a century earlier readers had wept openly when they read Dickens's highly charged account of the death of Little Nell in *The Old Curiosity Shop*. By contrast, the *fin-de-siècle* attitude is best captured in the famous witticism of Oscar Wilde: "One must have a heart of stone to read the death of Little Nell without laughing" (Beckson 163).

The status of Dickens criticism at the end of Victoria's reign is evident in the work of the most influential critic of the age, George Saintsbury. The leading light in both French and English criticism for nearly forty years, Saintsbury had spent time as a journalist and was for twenty years a professor at the University of Edinburgh. Prolific and wide-ranging in his interests, Saintsbury's judgments were much respected both by readers of popular, upscale periodicals such as the *Saturday Review* and by university teachers. In *Corrected Impressions* (1895) Saintsbury observes that it is hard to write about Dickens because "current public opinion about him seems to have got in a kind of tangle" (117). Actually, Saintsbury had done much to contribute to the diminishment of Dickens's reputation in academic circles by writing consistently about the novelist's faults. While Dickens was a great humorist, Saintsbury says, he is simply not a great novelist. His forte is fantasy, and his propensity for mannerism and exaggeration limits his artistry. Further, he could not plot, he did not understand the nobility, and he was "destitute of the faculty of self-criticism" (130). Saintsbury had expressed similar opinions in his 1892 collection *Miscellaneous Essays* and would do so again in his 1896 study *Essays on English Literature*.

Saintsbury would repeat his charges in *A Short History of English Literature* (1898) wherein, after calling Dickens one of the two greatest prose writers in English, he recites a litany of faults that diminish his artistic achievements. The greatest deficiency Dickens suffers, however, is "a lack of anything like real acquaintance or sympathy with great and high regions of thought, and an unfortunate proneness to talk about what he did not understand" (743). Although he always had good words for the early novels, Saintsbury never forgave Dickens for what he thought was ill-informed social commentary, delivered in an overly theatrical style. He had not changed his opinions by the time he came to write *The English Novel* in 1913, in which he lumps Dickens in with other mid-century novelists as successors to Austen and Scott. Nor did his entry on Dickens for the *Cambridge History of English Literature* in 1916 reflect a change of heart. Like G. H. Lewes, Saintsbury valued novels of ideas and complex characterization, and since his books became staples of college study for several decades, especially in England, his comments on Dickens helped to shape the opinion a generation of university students.

At the end of the century Americans were still reading Dickens, even if the new wave of critics found him deficient in the many aspects of social realism that were coming to define the best fiction. One of his most important champions was Henry James's good friend William Dean Howells. The editor and novelist had loved Dickens from the time he was a boy, as he explains in his autobiographical memoir *My Literary Passions* (1895). Dickens had captivated him, he says, because "when I read him, I was in a world where the right came out best, and where merit was crowned with — success" (75). Howells published a series of three articles on Dickens's women in *Harper's Bazaar* in 1900, which he reprinted in *Heroines of Fiction* (1901), and also wrote a fond account of his favorite Dickens novel, *David Copperfield*, for *Munsey's Magazine* in 1897. But his appreciation was muted when he was forced to consider Dickens's work in light of the new critical principles being developed for evaluating the novel.

Writing in *Criticism and Fiction* (1891), Howells has only modest praise for his favorite novelist. Although he cautions against establishing hard-and-fast rules for judging fiction that may be too restrictive, he is nevertheless unable to find Dickens's work sufficiently realistic to pass the litmus test then being applied to the genre. Dickens's "pathos appears false and strained," Howells admits, "the humor largely horse-play," "the character theatrical," and "the psychology commonplace" (175–76). Measured against the grim but accurate realism of novels by Gissing, James, and of course Howells himself, Dickens comes up short.

While many American readers were still sympathetic toward Dickens, a growing chorus of criticism was beginning to be heard in the United States. Charles Dudley Warner, American novelist, editor, and critic observes in the preface to volume 8 of *Library of the World's Best Literature* (1897) that, although he still appreciates Dickens's ability to captivate readers, his status among most serious critics had definitely fallen. The essay on Dickens written by Laurence Hutton for this volume does little more than sketch Dickens's life and offer perfunctory praise for his ability to create memorable characters. In *Victorian Literature: Sixty Years of Books and Bookmen* (1897) the American critic Clement Shorter observes that while Dickens remains "the most popular writer our literature has ever seen," the spate of negative commentary makes it hard at this time to "gauge his precise position" (42–43) among English novelists. Finally, in his sweeping survey *The Development of the English Novel* (1899), Yale professor Wilbur Cross places Dickens on the side of the idealists in what Cross sees as a continual struggle in fiction between realistic and idealistic tendencies. While he celebrates Dickens as the foremost exemplar of the humanitarian novel, he admits Dickens sometimes strays into exaggeration. Nevertheless, Cross has harsh words for Dickens's detractors: "against the current offhand condemnation of Dickens' sentimentalism history, however, will surely protest" (186). Whether Cross thought that sentimentalism would return to vogue, or that critics would eventually see something more than overt sentimentalizing in the novels, is not made clear. Perhaps that is why he is so exuberant to report in his 1912 essay "The Return to Dickens" that Dickens appeared to be weathering the storms of criticism that were still swelling around his work.

The first of the truly important and influential critics to write admiringly of Dickens was a young novelist, George Gissing. At the request of the editors of the Victorian Era Studies series, Gissing turned his hand from fiction to write *Charles Dickens: A Critical Study* (1898). The work would turn out to be the starting point for modern assessments of Dickens as a literary artist. Gissing had admired Dickens's novels from an early age, but as he developed his own ideas about the nature of fiction — ideas that privileged realism — he began to see the places at which Dickens succeeded and those where he missed the mark. Gissing was familiar with what had been written about Dickens. He knew the trajectory in Dickens studies was downward; for every one person who celebrated Dickens (usually for his humor or "fellow feelings" about humanity) there were a dozen who were quick to point out the novelist's limitations. Gissing was not very pleased with Adolphus Ward's volume in the English Men of Letters series, and he was determined not to devote much attention to biographical matters. Instead, in *Charles Dickens: A Critical Study* Gissing attempts to apply the practices being popularized by critics such as Henry James to the Dickens canon. His study examines the novels as works of art, judging them not by ranking them against each other (Gissing dismissed attempts to determine which was the greatest of Dickens's novels as "uncritical" [159]), or against the work of other novelists, or by their ability to present some larger "approved" social message. Instead he examines the ways Dickens creates plots, draws his characters, structures his work to achieve effect, and develops his themes. He traces the development of Dickens's artistic ability chronologically, noting places at which he seems to advance in his craft, and points where he falls back on conventions either to please his audience or to meet the deadlines of serial publication. In fact, Gissing argues these were the two most important reasons Dickens did not fully realize his talents as an artist. He seldom had time to work out inconsistencies in plotting or characterization, and too frequently he felt constrained by "the characteristics, moral and intellectual, of Victorian England" (176) to deal candidly with some topics.

Gissing's Dickens is a great but flawed artist. He "had not the tragic gift" (149), but he was a great humorist and possessed great insight into society. In his early work he was willing to subordinate theme to characterization (especially when the characters were inherently interesting, such as those in *Martin Chuzzlewit*). In novels such as *Dombey and Son* his "famous shortcomings are abundantly exemplified" (148), among them poor and improbable plotting, and caricature substituted for genuine characterization. Nevertheless, Gissing has much good to say about Dickens's novels, and his insistence that they be read in historical context helped future critics take a more reasoned look at what Dickens was able to do with his material and still retain his popularity. Gissing went on to write several introductions to the Rochester edition of Dickens's novels, and when that series failed before completion, he continued writing about each of the works. These essays were eventually published posthumously in *Critical Studies of the Works of Charles Dickens* (1924) and *The Immortal Dickens* (1925).

Gissing's contributions to Dickens studies go beyond comments on individual novels, however; his approach to novel-reading marked a new turn in critical analysis of the novelist. As Michael Cronin observes in his

2001 essay "Gissing's Criticism of Dickens," the most important contribution the younger novelist made in advancing Dickens studies was to present Dickens as "a middle-class radical and moralist who is politically conservative and thoroughly representative" of his age (26). Additionally, Cronin notes, in writing about Dickens's artistry Gissing "made the reading of novels into an intellectual activity in a manner which Dickens's original readers could not have dreamed of" (30). Hence the ground for literary analysis was shifting, from judging the novel as a kind of public performance (like the theater, which figured prominently in Dickens's own life and in many of his novels) to a private experience.

The initial reception of Gissing's study was positive, although the reviewer in the *Saturday Review* (the same periodical that published FitzJames Stephen's hostile comments on Dickens four decades earlier) thought Gissing's assessment too generous. Dickensians celebrated the work, of course, and soon Gissing was ranked with Frederick G. Kitton as the two most prominent and influential Dickens scholars. Gissing's prominence among Dickens critics was proclaimed by Clement Shorter in 1903, and seconded by G. K. Chesterton, who would in a short time supplant Gissing as the foremost critic of Dickens. As late as 1940 Gissing's work was still held in high regard. Edmund Wilson, whose 1940 essay "Dickens: The Two Scrooges" helped usher in a revolution in Dickens studies, observed in *The Wound and The Bow* (1941) that Gissing was "an admirable critic" whose book on Dickens is not only "the best thing on Dickens in English but stands out as one of the few really first-rate pieces of literary criticism produced by an Englishman of the end of the century" (2).

At the turn of the twentieth century there was a glimmer of hope for Dickens lovers that his critical reputation might be once again on the upswing. The controversial but influential poet A. C. Swinburne had helped to spur the upward swing a bit with his essay on Dickens in the *Quarterly Review* (1902), in which he justifies Dickens's place as England's greatest novelist and blasts critics who cannot see his merits. After noting that Dickens possessed "the quality of a great tragic and comic poet or dramatist in prose fiction" and those of "a great humorist and born master of the arts of narrative and dialogue" (224), Swinburne says that only the "blatant boobies" among critics would "deny truthfulness and realism to the imagination of Charles Dickens" (237). As early as 1903, the poet Alice Meynell was writing appreciatively of Dickens. In "Charles Dickens as a Man of Letters," an essay that appeared in *Atlantic Monthly* and in other places, including her collection *Hearts of Controversy* (1917), she defends Dickens against those who found him vulgar. Though her own opinion may have been colored by the fact that Dickens had been a friend of her father's, Meynell appreciates Dickens's humor, admires his ability to create what she calls "dramatic tragedy" and to use "inanimate things and landscape" in his fiction (291). She is particularly impressed with his ability to write narration, a trait she says is most unusual in novelists. Similar sentiments were expressed by Arthur Compton-Rickett in "The Genius of Dickens" (1906). Compton-Rickett thought the harsh critical commentary of the previous two decades was sparked by a reaction against early reviewers who had made too much of the "messages" of great writers (viii).

The most significant event in the history of Dickens criticism occurred in 1902, when a score of Dickens admirers joined together to form The Dickens Fellowship. Its members intended to promote the novelist's memory and celebrate his writings. The headquarters of the Fellowship was in London, naturally. One of the initial goals of the founders was to establish some form of publication to facilitate an exchange of ideas and information about Dickens and his circle. Knowing such ventures could easily fail if not sufficiently supported financially, leaders of the Fellowship decided to delay starting this publication to see how popular their society would become. They hadn't long to wait; within two years the Fellowship grew to include 6,500 members enrolled in thirty branches worldwide. Confident that a new journal would find wide readership (and subscribership), on January 1, 1905, the leadership of the society launched *The Dickensian,* "A Magazine for Dickens Lovers and a Monthly Record of the Dickens Fellowship."

With the enthusiasm typical of people dedicated to a cause, the Dickens Fellowship set out to produce monthly issues of their new periodical. Bertram Waldrom Matz, a lifelong devotee of Dickens and author of a 1902 biography, was selected as the first editor. It is possible that he was the second choice, as the most prominent Dickens scholar of the late nineteenth century, F. G. Kitton, died only months before the magazine was launched. The initial plan was that the *Dickensian* would be thirty-two pages long and include original articles, illustrations, photographs, reviews, and reprints (some dating back to the early nineteenth century), as well as news of clubs and branches. Most contributions were brief, but the slim green-covered volumes — reminiscent of the monthly numbers of Dickens novels that had appeared in serial form years earlier — became the principal source for information about Dickens and the scholars who had committed themselves to his memory. The tenacity and devotion of Dickens lovers for their special periodical can be seen in the frequency with which a number of them sent in articles and information; the same names reappear among the contributors for decades. During the first sixty-five years of its publication — a notably long stretch for any journal — only three men served as editors. Matz headed the journal until his death in 1925. He was replaced by Walter Dexter, another fanatical Dickens lover, ardent bibliophile, and eventually editor of Dickens's letters. Dexter served in the position from 1925 to 1945. Upon his death Leslie Staples, a frequent contributor to the journal and an authority on Dickens's times, took over the editorship, holding the post from 1945 until 1968.[1]

From its first issue, however, the *Dickensian* was met with skepticism and even disdain by many in academic circles and those who had rejected Dickens and all he stood for. There were several reasons for this reaction. First, neither Matz nor his two successors was affiliated with a university, a credential becoming increasingly important as literary criticism became a more established profession requiring formal study. Second, the tendency to include ephemera and to continue publishing arcane and sometime trivial information alongside more traditional scholarship and criticism made the journal appear less scholarly than other new publications springing up in the universities and professional associations. It was not uncommon to see notes about the discovery of the real-life model for a fictional character or location described in one of Dickens's novels running in the same issue as articles discussing his social criticism or artistic ability.

Furthermore, some of the contributors wrote of Dickens as if he were beyond criticism. The generation of academics brought up in the early decades of the twentieth century wanted nothing to do with Victorian enthusiasm and hero-worship. Unfortunately, for many academics the journal became synonymous with this attitude — an unfair charge, as a 1930 article in the *Dickensian* itself makes clear. In "'Biting' Critics," J. Cuming Walters, a noted scholar who had published books on Dickens, Shakespeare, and Tennyson, claims blind adulation does a great disservice to Dickens. "The best form of tribute" to the novelist, he says, "is to read and consider him impartially and discerningly." By contrast, the devotee who "shouts 'Wonderful!' 'Excellent!' 'Perfect!' is offering no tribute at all; he is only making a noise." What's wanted by all true Dickens lovers, Walters asserts is "not the fulsome eulogist, not the man who is forever pasting the same old ornamental label upon everything that Dickens wrote, not the man who lumps together as of equal merit *David Copperfield* and *Oliver Twist* — no, what we want is the judicious and reasonable student. And Dickens is far too great to suffer by that process" (285). Appearing when it did, however, this judgment was probably noted by few in the academic world and in any case unheeded by old-fashioned Dickensians who may have stumbled upon it. More than half a century later, however, Peter Ackroyd would offer a strong endorsement of the *Dickensian:* "There is more information and pertinent material within these green-covered magazines," he observes in his biography of Dickens, "than in a host of more apparently imposing volumes" (*Dickens* 1085).

Those who loved Dickens unconditionally were delighted to have a forum for sharing ideas and learning more about him. Among the more active members of the new Fellowship was Percy Fitzgerald. In his youth Fitzgerald was one of the aspiring writers whom Dickens befriended in the years before his death. Claiming in later life to have also been a special protégé of John Forster, Fitzgerald had earlier founded a society he called "The Boz Club" that concentrated on Dickens's life rather than his works. Perhaps hoping to appeal to the new generation of Dickens lovers inspired by the foundation of the Dickens Fellowship, Fitzgerald brought out two books that highlighted his own relationship with the novelist. *The Life of Charles Dickens, as Revealed in his Writings* (1905) is intended to supplement Forster's *Life;* according to Fitzgerald, Forster had been "somewhat scared by criticism, and suppressed himself a good deal" (x). But Fitzgerald adds little to the Dickens story in his disjointed and derivative biography. His *Memories of Charles Dickens* (1913), a collection of his reminiscences of Dickens and those of several others who knew the novelist, is typical of late-Victorian and Edwardian publications providing tame gossip and anecdotes that satisfy the curious but do little to advance the critical reputation of the writer. Nevertheless, it is a sure bet that these books, and others like them, filled the shelves of Dickensians everywhere, while the novelist's reputation in academic circles continued to languish.

Other members of the Dickens Fellowship were busy collecting materials about Dickens's life and writings, publishing their findings in the *Dickensian* or in scholarly monographs. Unquestionably, some of their efforts can be classified as simply antiquarian. Others, however, have proven of greater value to scholars. One example of more lasting contributions produced by a Dickens Fellow is William Glyde Wilkins's *Charles Dickens in America* (1911). This collection of published newspaper accounts, letters, and other documents relating to the novelist's visits to the United States and his dealing with American authors, publishers, and readers contains little analysis, but is nevertheless an excellent compendium of material that might otherwise be hard to ferret out of newspaper morgues or private collections.

In 1906 G. K. Chesterton published *Charles Dickens,* a book that immediately established Chesterton as a major voice in Dickens studies. Chesterton was already well known in literary circles for his poetry and his works on Robert Louis Stevenson and Tolstoy. Three years earlier, he had collaborated with the Dickensian F. G. Kitton to produce a brief tribute to the novelist. The 1906 study, a loosely organized biography that disguised a strident proclamation of the novelist's "genius," defends Dickens from his detractors and proclaims his importance in English letters and English life.

From the outset, Chesterton saw himself engaged in a war with the proponents of realism, naturalism and modernism who would deny Dickens's greatness. "Even the fastidious and unhappy who cannot read his books without a continuous critical exasperation" will concede he is a "great writer even if he is not a good writer" (2), he insists. Acknowledging his debt to Gissing, whom he considers "the soundest of the Dickens critics" (3), Chesterton sets out to correct his predecessor's view of the grim Victorian world depicted in Dickens's novels by pointing out what he sees as their undercurrent of "hope and humanity" (4). The figure that emerges from Chesterton's 1906 study is an eternal optimist whose special strength lies in his ability to depict character and express faith in the innate goodness of people to overcome the evils of society. Against charges that Dickens fails both in plotting and in achieving a sense of verisimilitude, Chesterton simply asserts "Dickens's work is not to be reckoned in novels at all" (35). Instead, he claims "Dickens was a mythologist rather than a novelist" (38). At times Chesterton resorts to *ad hominem* argument to blast critics who dare to attack his hero. He defends Dickens's sentimentality as a form of optimism, excusing his excesses of characterization by saying that he did not "point out things, he made them" (105). Page after page of his study sings the praises of the man whose ability to create figures such as Pickwick, Micawber, Fagin, Dick Swiveller, Miss Havisham and Sarah Gamp exempts him, Chesterton insists, from the kinds of criticism appropriate for mere mortals among the novel-writing crowd.

Lest it appear Chesterton is without discrimination in his critique, it should be noted that he did find a gradual diminishment in Dickens's creative powers as the novelist aged. The reasons he gives for the decline, however, are a further slap at those who seek realism in the novel. Has Dickens "lost or gained," Chesterton asks in concluding his assessment of the later work, "by the growth of technique and probability in his later work?" Certainly his later characters "were more like men; but were not his earlier characters more like immortals?" (104). For Chesterton, the greatest of Dickens's work was his first, *Pickwick Papers*. The rest are very good, even great, but nothing quite measures up to that original *tour de force* that set the reading public abuzz and introduced a new form of writing into English — and world — literature. The optimism and idealism of Pickwick's world is that which is unique in Dickens, and these qualities earn him his deserved place at the head of English novelists past, present, and presumably future as well.

Because his opinion was not widely held by critics outside of the circle of Dickensians, defending Dickens became for Chesterton something of a cottage industry. He spent the next three decades stubbornly making the case for Dickens in a series of books and articles. His 1906 monograph was reissued as *Charles Dickens: A Critical Study* in 1913 and again as *Charles Dickens: The Last of the Great Men* in 1942, six years after Chesterton himself had died. He redacted his case in his study *The Victorian Age in Literature* (1913), comparing Dickens most favorably with his contemporaries. From 1906 until 1921 he contributed introductions for a new edition of the novels. He included essays on Dickens in many of his own collections such as *Tremendous Trifles* (1909), *Generally Speaking* (1929), *Come to Think of It* (1931), *Sidelights on New London and Newer York* (1932), and *The Common Man* (published posthumously in 1950). His tribute to Dickens, "The Great Gusto," appeared in *The Great Victorians* (1932), a collection of essays by noted critics.

The argument in these later pieces follows the line of reasoning worked out in the 1906 study. Writing in 1931, Chesterton excuses the novelist's prolixity by saying he "suffered from a sort of premature Big Business" mentality that forced him to keep himself in front of his audience (*Come to Think of It* 254). A year later he claims Dickens remains popular with the public, if not with academics, because he was an iconoclast in his day. "He did not really belong to that world of seriousness which some called Victorian" (*Sidelights* 247); he was "singularly free of the illusions of his time" (250). In "The Great Gusto" he celebrates Dickens's liberalism, a trait Chesterton finds running through all of his fiction. Chesterton insists Dickens was "pre-Victorian" rather than a mainstream Victorian novelist; his aim was always to carry on the traditions of the comic novel initiated by Fielding and Smollett. The "pressures of Victorianism" forced him to refine his techniques so that his later work "is still comic but no longer coarse" (163). In Chesterton's view, virtually unchanged over three decades, Dickens remained throughout his career a great comic novelist whose work is only occasionally marred by sentimentality and melodrama.

On occasion Chesterton acknowledges some fault with his hero. Dickens is prone to exaggeration, he admits. But he defends him as an important and ultimately successful self-made man, against whom criticism seems mean-spirited. Never one to let his hero suffer vilification for his work or his life, Chesterton takes to task those who would speculate too much about the novelist's separation from his wife, claiming "very little good is done by making guesses about a story of which the spiritual balance and proportion were probably never known to more than three or four people" (*Last of the Great Men* 219). In the same essay, he states flatly that when critics called Dickens "vulgar" it meant "nothing except that the critics themselves were snobbish" (221).

For nearly half a century, Dickens lovers worldwide looked to Chesterton as their champion against those who would belittle the novelist's accomplishments. However, the extent to which this consistently positive view of Dickens gets in the way of objective criticism was ruefully acknowledged by one of Chesterton's editors, Alexander Woolcott, who admits in the Reader's Club edition of *Charles Dickens* (1942) that this book — and by extension, the body of Chesterton's criticism — is far less a critical study than a "hymn of praise" (ix). What Chesterton did for Dickens studies is admirable in that he kept alive the debate over the novelist's value as an artist and social commentator. The extent of his influence and the critical principles that inform his work are the subjects of David Derus's "Gissing and Chesterton as Critics of Dickens" (1985) and of four other articles in a special number of the *Chesterton Review* (1985), in which the authors all point out that the Dickens who emerges from the pages of Chesterton's criticism is as much a creation of the critic as he is the historical figure who produced fifteen novels between 1836 and 1870.

Actually, one might wonder why Chesterton felt compelled to launch such a systematic and strident campaign to defend Dickens, since Dickens continued to enjoy immense popularity among the general population. As James Milne points out in "How Dickens Sells" (1906), while "Shakespeare is our best-selling author," there "can be little doubt" that Dickens stands next in line (773). The American scholar Paul Elmer More openly questioned the need for such excessive praise as Chesterton's. In volume 5 of his *Shelburne Essays* (1908), More claims Dickens's popularity had not waned at all, but instead that Chesterton and other Dickensians seemed to find it necessary to "erect some bogus enemy, whom they thereupon proceed to knock over." "Is it possible," More asks, "they are protesting against a reservation in their own minds?" (22). An intellectual disciple of Matthew Arnold, More sought the presence of "high seriousness" in a literary work as the litmus test for its greatness. Not discovering that quality in Dickens, he could find little to admire. More looked askance at what he considered the excesses — and especially the exaggerated humor — that characterizes Dickens's work. In his view Dickens never acquired "discipline" or the ability to suppress flamboyant eccentricities for the sake of his art (29). More faults him as a stylist and takes him to task for his inability to create characters, especially tragic ones, which he says "will not bear analysis" (42). "In place of tragic art," More concludes, "he has given us tears" (34).

Some critics, however, were not as "disinterested" as the neo-Arnoldian More claims to be. The novelist and critic Edwin Pugh appropriated Dickens for his own purposes, producing a polemic appropriately titled *Charles Dickens: The Apostle of the People* (1908). Originally published in installments in *New Age* magazine, a socialist tract, Pugh's study is among the first in a long line of modern works to remake Dickens in the image of the critic writing about him. It is probably not surprising that Pugh was drawn to Dickens because, as a novelist himself, Pugh was considered a sentimental moralist by critics of his fiction. What he makes of Dickens, however, goes beyond a simple apology for the Victorian novelist's literary characteristics. In a manner reminiscent of Blake writing about Milton, Pugh claims Dickens "was a Socialist without knowing it" (315).

Observing that Dickens had a lifelong interest in politics, Pugh develops a consistent reading of the novels that highlights his liberal — at times radical — ideology. He aims to demonstrate that the kind of social justice Dickens advocates in his novels is compatible with the ideals of proponents of the French Revolution and their descendants, Socialists such as Robert Owen — and Pugh himself. That some considered Dickens vain and arrogant seems not to bother Pugh at all; these people were simply envious of the Victorian novelist's successes. Even Pugh has to acknowledge, however, that his thesis can be stretched too far. After all, he says, "Of all Dickens's books, *Great Expectations* is the present writer's favorite — as it seems, in his opinion, to be also the best of them all. The best in every way, except — alas! — in the Socialist way." There is little in this novel, he admits, "that directly serves my present purpose" (250). Notwithstanding this disclaimer, Pugh continues to make his case for Dickens as a champion of "the respectable, self-respecting poor" (281) whose prescription for progress points the way to a better society.

Pugh was certainly not alone in celebrating the uses to which Dickens's work had been put. In the November 1910 issue of the *Bookman* the editor asserts "the good influence of Dickens's novels cannot be overestimated," and anyone seeking to maintain and increase that influence should be considered a "public benefactor" (70). In an article in the same number, B. W. Matz outlines the ways Dickens "strove in all his books to set right what was wrong with the world as well as to amuse and entertain those who lived in it" (79). Clearly the notion of Dickens as the "apostle of the people" was alive and well in some circles.

The early years of the twentieth century saw the publication of a number of handbooks and surveys of English literature, and discussions of Dickens figure prominently in many of them. But as one might expect from the tenor of criticism at the time, assessments of his value as a novelist and social critic vary widely. William Dawson's *Makers of English Fiction* (1905) offers a positive portrait of Dickens and his work. Dawson considers Dickens a natural genius, unspoiled by education, whose powers of observation and strong imagination combined to produce some of the best novels in the language. Though he admits that at times Dickens had a "tendency to fancifulness, to romance, to the grotesque" (109), Dawson believes Dickens's occasional lapses must be overlooked in favor of his stunning achievement. "Tastes may change," he asserts, "new reputations rise and wane, but the time will never come when the great creative artist is dethroned and finally forgotten" — and in Dawson's view Dickens is just such a creative genius (122). The American critic Holbrook Jackson devotes a chapter to Dickens in his *Great English Novelists* (1908), praising him for breathing new life into a genre that was dying in the 1830s. Though Jackson is willing to admit some faults — Dickens cannot construct plots, and is too given to emotional excess, as in the death scene of Little Nell, where "the pathos is laid on with a trowel" (252) — he still finds Dickens "as quick today as ever he was," a master of "laughter and tears" and "the genius of a lamp that shines for all" (243). The critic Richard Burton is somewhat less enthusiastic, noting in *Masters of the English Novel* (1909) that while Dickens exhibited creativity and energy throughout his career, his early works can scarcely be called novels at all.

Several authors of critical surveys chose to lump Dickens and Thackeray together for discussion. Sometimes Dickens appears superior to his contemporary, at other times he falls short by the comparison. For example, in his chapter "Dickens and Thackeray" in *The Literature of the Victorian Era*" (1910), Hugh Walker concludes Dickens is decidedly inferior to Thackeray as a social satirist. Like Chesterton, he calls *Pickwick Papers* "the greatest" of Dickens's books (665) and thinks it was a mistake for Dickens to turn his novels into tracts for social reform. "At an early date in his career," Walker notes, "Dickens began to take himself seriously and, to his own detriment, as many believe, to exhibit a purpose in his work" (684). "Not one" of the novels written after *Little Dorrit* — including *Great Expectations* — is "of the first class" (677). Echoing both Gissing and the proponents of Arnoldian high seriousness, Walker admits "there is a good deal in Dickens that offends a cultured taste" (679), a fault not shared by Thackeray. Walker predicts Dickens will never recover from the decline his reputation suffered in the forty years since his death.

Albert Canning does not share Walker's pessimistic view, however. In *Dickens and Thackeray Studied in Three Novels* (1911), Canning expresses a rather benign view of Dickens as a social critic, claiming his object was "never to induce the most wronged and suffering to desire revolution," but instead to "induce the common intelligence of the country, in all its different classes, to redress real grievances and alleviate undesirable sufferings" (21). Unfortunately, most of Canning's book consists of plot summary and commentary on the novelist's ability to create memorable characters. The fact that he examines two early works is also suggestive of the relative disrepute in which Dickens's later work was held at the beginning of the twentieth century.

Writing three years later, the American critic William Phelps includes a previously published essay on Dickens in his *Essays on Books* (1914) that reinforces this view of the novelist as a benevolent optimist. "The great work in which Dickens was engaged" throughout his career, Phelps says, was "the work of cheering us all up" (179). In Phelps's view, Dickens excels in dramatizing his faith in God and humanity; charges that he was simply a caricaturist or was careless in his art are nonsense. Phelps is so convinced of Dickens's greatness, however, that he finds it unnecessary to provide any evidence for the author's technical ability, resorting instead to amassing quotations from the novels without commentary, as if to say to other critics, "See!" Phelps's conclusion dispels any lingering question about his high regard for Dickens: "He is so great that we can only measure ourselves by him" (191). Phelps makes his case again in *Advance of the English Novel* (1916), reprinting materials from an earlier *Bookman* article and arguing that the period between 1850 and 1860 was "the greatest decade in the history of the English novel" (104).

One of the most important, extensive defenses of Dickens as a benevolent reformer and consummate artist came from yet another ardent Dickensian. J. Cuming Walters had been a member of the Dickens Fellowship since its inception, and served as its president in 1910–11. In 1911, he collected his addresses to the Fellowship into *Phases of Dickens: The Man, His Message, and His Mission*. Walters operates from the premise that Dickens was not only a first-rate novelist, but also a great "teacher with a moral gospel" (ix). In a fashion typical of British writers before the First World War, Walters adopts a rather chauvinistic view, calling Dickens "a crusader" who was "engaged in as holy a war as the Knight Templar" (xv). This kind of hyperbole characterizes much of Walters's commentary, in which he celebrates Dickens's fight to promote healthy ideals of manhood, womanhood, justice, and patriotism, struggling always against the great evil of hypocrisy. He praises Dickens for his conscious attempt to "knit in bonds of sympathy the classes which had stood apart" (266), although he recognizes the novelist is "rather the exposer of evils than the mender" (271). Despite adopting a methodology and a viewpoint that links him more with his nineteenth-century forebears than with contemporaries or future Dickens scholars, Walters at times seems to be moving toward a critical position that would become popular among scholars of the coming decades. Rather than claiming that Dickens was the spokesperson for the Victorians, Walters says he was "in conflict with his age. Rightly or wrongly, he believed it was an age of severities and shams" (xix). Unfortunately, insightful observations like these are overshadowed in Walters's study by claims such as, "Of what there is to say of Dickens little has by now been left unsaid" (ix).

To celebrate the centenary of Dickens's birth in 1912, Dickens lovers paid homage to him in several publications. Among the more prominent was B. W. Matz's edition of Forster's biography. The *Bookman* published a special issue devoted to the novelist in February, the month of his birth. Included was a brief note by Matz, who has nothing but praise for Dickens's artistry and nothing but disdain for those who question it. Reminiscences from twenty-six noted writers, including Chesterton, Thomas Hardy, Alfred Wallace, Andrew Lang, and George Bernard Shaw are compiled from questionnaires sent to them by the magazine's editor. These range from the effusive to the desultory, such as Thomas Hardy's observation regarding the influence Dickens had on him: "I do not know that my literary efforts owed much to his influence. No doubt they owed something unconsciously, since everybody's did in those days" (247). By contrast Shaw, in his usual acerbic manner, attests that "my works are all over Dickens; and nothing but the stupendous illiteracy of modern criticism could have missed this glaring feature of my methods" (247).

Tributes appeared in many reputable publications: A. C. Benson's in the *North American Review* in March, Alice Meynell's in the *Dublin Review* in April, H. C. Biron's in the *National Review* in May, Henry Van Dyke's in *Scribner's Magazine* in June. In October, the *Yale Review* carried a lengthy commentary by Wilbur Cross titled "The Return to Dickens," which explains why the novelist had remained popular and why critics were slowly coming to ignore the negative comments of the late nineteenth century and recognize Dickens as a great artist. A similar appreciative review of Dickens's career was published by Darrell Figgis in various forums, first in the *Nineteenth Century* in February, then reprinted in *Living Age* in March 1912, and again as a chapter in his *Studies and Appreciations* later in the year. Dedicated to Chesterton and written specifically as a centenary notice to "reach the central note that should elucidate the perplexing" aspects of Dickens's fiction (13), the essay is as much an answer to negative critics as it is a positive commentary on what makes Dickens great. Figgis ends up repeating what earlier defenders had said: Dickens cannot be judged by the strict definitions of the novel created by critics of the late nineteenth century, but instead must be compared with his real peers — Cervantes, Rabelais, and Bunyan.

While many of the moderns saw fit to ignore Dickens when they were not disparaging his accomplishments, one became his champion. George Bernard Shaw was a lifelong fan of the Victorian novelist. His contributions to the special number of the *Bookman* cited above are indicative of the debt he felt to Dickens. He insists further that "Dickens was one of the greatest writers that ever lived; an astounding man, considering the barbarous ignorance of his period" (*Bookman* 1912, 247). Shaw began writing about Dickens as early as 1887, and speaking about him in lectures even before that date. While he acknowledged the popularity of the early work — his first published piece was a review of a new edition of *Pickwick Papers* — he was consistent in arguing the later novels were Dickens's greatest achievements. Shaw may be accused of special pleading on occasion, since the novels he finds most praiseworthy are ones that expose the kinds of evils Shaw himself, a Fabian and closet Marxist, found so abominable. In his review of the 1892 edition of *Pickwick*, Shaw suggests the book has remained Dickens's most popular because "it is the only one which can be read without an occasional uncomfortable suspicion that the author was in downright earnest after all" (23).[2] The good-natured laughter one expends on this early novel is very different, Shaw says, from the kind of self-conscious, slightly uncomfortable risibility aroused by the comic characters in the later, darker novels.

In 1913 Shaw wrote an Introduction for the Waverly Edition of *Hard Times,* a novel in which he detects a major shift in Dickens's vision of society, indeed his conversion experience. In this novel "we see Dickens" for the first time "with his eyes newly open and his conscience newly stricken by the discovery of the real state of England" (27). In this novel Dickens aligns himself with the truly perceptive critics of British society: "This is Karl Marx, Carlyle, Ruskin, Morris, Carpenter, rising up against civilization itself as against a disease, and declaring that it is not our disorder but our order that is horrible." Dickens is finally ready to admit that "until Society is reformed, no man can reform himself except in the most insignificantly small ways" (29). No longer is Dickens the light-hearted humorist who occasionally becomes annoyed with the ills he sees around him; now "the occasional indignation has spread and deepened into a passionate revolt against the whole industrial order of the modern world" (29). Shaw acknowledges that in these later novels Dickens drops all pretense of verisimilitude in favor of biting social commentary designed to make readers uncomfortable. The only weakness in *Hard Times* is Dickens's portrait of the factory workers; Shaw believes Dickens's negative attitude toward the workers' efforts to organize themselves is simply wrongheaded. In taking this stance, Dickens "turns his back frankly on Democracy, and adopts the idealized Toryism of Carlyle and Ruskin," a position he sticks to for the remainder of his life (34). One can sense the disappointment Shaw feels for a hero not ready to make the ultimate leap into the abyss.

Shaw would go on to write a preface for *Great Expectations* in 1937, a novel he calls "the most perfect of Dickens's works" (57). In his essays, however, he speaks less about the novel than about Dickens's revolutionary tendencies. Shaw has concluded by this time that if readers had heeded Dickens's message they may not have had to learn the hard lessons of Fascism and Communism. He considers Dickens a prophet, not a mere popularizer who pandered to his public. While Marx may have known he was a revolutionary while Dickens did not, the novelist's best work can stand with that of the father of Communism, Shaw concludes, stating flatly that "*Little Dorrit* is a more seditious book than *Das Kapital*" (51). Shaw had said as much in 1908: "One of the greatest books in the English language is *Little Dorrit*," he told an audience in Liverpool, "and when the English nation realizes it is a great book and a true book there will be a revolution in this country" (111). Of course, it would not be long before the English would be fighting, but not in a revolution. Rather, young men would be dying on battlefields in France to defend

British interests against the Germans and their allies, and Dickens would be enlisted to serve his country once again.

Notes

[1] The history of the early years of the *Dickensian* is described in detail in J. W. T. Ley's "History of the *Dickensian*" (*Dickensian* 1926).

[2] Shaw's commentary on Dickens is scattered throughout his writings, much of it in unpublished letters or in the texts of speeches he delivered at various public functions. For this reason he may not have had the influence on Dickens criticism that Chesterton and Gissing had. Fortunately, in 1985 Dan H. Laurence and Martin Quinn collected all of Shaw's commentary in a single volume, *Shaw on Dickens*, adding a perceptive introduction that makes no bones about Shaw's perversion of Dickens for his own socialist purposes. All page references in my text are to reprints of Shaw's essays in that volume. The relationship between the two writers has been examined extensively in other places as well, including Edgar Johnson, "Dickens and Shaw: Critics of Society" (1958) and Jean-Claude Amalric, "Shaw as a Critic of Dickens" (1982).

Works Cited

Ackroyd, Peter. *Dickens*. London: Minerva, 1990.

Amalric, Jean-Claude. "Shaw as a Critic of Dickens." *The Independent Shavian* 19.3 (1982): 63–68.

Beckson, Karl. *I Can Resist Everything Except Temptation, and Other Quotations from Oscar Wilde*. New York: Columbia UP, 1996.

Benson, Arthur C. "Charles Dickens." *North American Review* 195 (March 1912): 381–91.

Biron, H. C. "The Plots of Dickens." *National Review* 59 (May 1912): 514–23.

Bookman. Extra Number. *Charles Dickens*. London: Hodder & Stoughton, 1910.

Bookman. Extra Number: *Charles Dickens*. London: Hodder & Stoughton, 1912. Reprint, 1914.

Burton, Richard. "Dickens." *Masters of the English Novel: A Study of Principles and Personalities*, 175–94. New York: Henry Holt, 1909.

Canning, Albert S. *Dickens and Thackeray Studied in Three Novels*. London: T. F. Unwin, 1911. Reprint, New York: Kennikat, 1971.

Chesterton, G. K. *Charles Dickens*. London: Methuen, 1906. Reprinted as *Charles Dickens: A Critical Study*. London: Dodd, Mead, 1913. Reprinted as *Charles Dickens: The Last of the Great Men*. Edited by Alexander Woolcott. New York: The Press of the Readers Club, 1942.

———. "Dickensian." *Tremendous Trifles*, 96–103. London: Methuen, 1909.

———. "The Great Gusto." In *The Great Victorians*, edited by H. J. and Hugh Massingham, 163–71. London: Nicholson and Watson; New York: Doubleday, Doran, 1932. Reprinted in *A Handful of Authors*, edited by Dorothy Collins. London: Sheed and Ward, 1953.

———. "On Dickens and After." *Come to Think of It*, 250–60. New York: Dodd, Mead, 1931.

———. "On *Edwin Drood*." *Generally Speaking*, 261–67. New York: Dodd, Mead, 1929.

———. "The Popularity of Dickens." *Spectator* 141 (November 1928): 43–44. Reprinted in *Sidelights on New London and Newer York, and Other Essays*. New York: Dodd, 1932.

———. "A Tale of Two Cities." *The Common Man*. New York: Sheed & Ward, 1950.

———. *The Victorian Age in Literature*. London: Williams and Norgate, 1913. Reprint, London: Oxford UP, 1966.

Chesterton, G. K., and Frederic G. Kitton. *Charles Dickens*. London: Hodder & Stoughton, 1903.

Chesterton Review: The Journal of the G. K. Chesterton Institute 11.4 (November 1985). Special issue on Dickens and Chesterton.

Compton-Rickett, Arthur. *Personal Forces in Modern Literature*, 143–85. London: Dent, 1906. Reprint, New York: AMS Press, 1970.

Cronin, Michael. "Gissing's Criticism of Dickens." In *A Garland for Gissing*, edited by Bouwe Postmus, 23–31. Amsterdam, Netherlands: Rodopi, 2001.

Cross, Wilbur L. "The Realistic Reaction (Dickens)." *The Development of the English Novel*, 168–96. New York: Macmillan, 1899.

———. "The Return to Dickens." *Yale Review* 2 (October 1912): 142–62.

Crotch, W. Walter. "The Decline — and After!" *Dickensian* 15 (July 1919): 121–27.

Davey, Samuel J. "Charles Dickens." *Darwin, Carlyle and Dickens, With Other Essays*, 121–56. London: James Clark, 1876. Reprint, New York: Haskell House, 1971.

Dawson, William J. *The Makers of English Fiction*. London: Hodder & Stoughton; Toronto: F. H. Revell, 1905.

Derus, David L. "Gissing and Chesterton as Critics of Dickens." *The Chesterton Review: The Journal of the G. K. Chesterton Institute* 12.1 (February 1986): 71–81.

Dickens, Charles. *The Letters of Charles Dickens*. Edited by Mary Dickens and Georgina Hogarth. 2 vols. London: Chapman & Hall, 1879.

Ellis, Stewart M. "Dickens and Forster." *Chambers Journal* (20 January 1912). Reprinted in *Mainly Victorian*, 80–88. London: Hutchinson, 1925.

Figgis, Darrell. "Praise of Dickens." *Nineteenth Century* 71 (February 1912): 274–84. Reprinted in *Living Age* 272 (March 1912): 524–32. Reprinted in *Studies and Appreciations*. London: Dent, 1912.

Fitzgerald, Percy. *The Life of Charles Dickens, as Revealed in his Writings*. 2 vols. London: Chatto & Windus, 1905.

———. *Memories of Charles Dickens*. London: Simpkin, Marshall, Hamilton, Kent & Co., 1913.

Forster, John. *The Life of Charles Dickens*. London: Chapman & Hall, 1872–74. Boston: Osgood, 1875. Reprint, London: Palmer, 1928.

Gissing, George. *Charles Dickens: A Critical Study*. London: Blackie, 1898. Reprinted in *Collected Works of George Gissing on Charles Dickens*, edited by Pierre Coustillas. Vol. I. Surrey, England: Grayswood, 2004.

———. *Critical Studies of the Works of Charles Dickens*. New York: Greenberg, 1924.

———. *The Immortal Dickens*. Edited by B. W. Matz. London: Palmer, 1925. Reprint, New York: Haskell House, 1965.

Harrison, Frederic. "Charles Dickens." *Forum* 18 (January 1895): 545–53. Reprinted as "Dickens's Place in Literature." *Studies in Early Victorian Literature*, 128–44. London: E. Arnold, 1895.

Henley, William E. "Dickens." *Views and Reviews: Essays in Appreciation*, 1–8. London: David Nutt, 1890. London: David Nutt; New York: Scribner's Sons, 1906.

Howells, William Dean. *Criticism and Fiction*. New York: Harper; London: Osgood, 1891. Reprinted in *Criticism and Fiction and Other Essays by W. D. Howells*, edited by Clara M. and Rudolph Kirk. New York: New York UP, 1959.

———. "Dickens." *My Literary Passions*, 88–103. New York: Harper, 1895.

———. "The Earlier Heroines of Charles Dickens." *Harper's Bazaar* 33 (September 1900): 1192–97. Reprinted in *Heroines of Fiction*. Vol. 1. New York: Harper, 1901.

———. "Heroines of Dickens's Middle Period." *Harper's Bazaar* 33 (September 1900): 1287–92. Reprinted as "Heroines of Charles Dickens's Middle Period." *Heroines of Fiction*. Vol. 1. New York: Harper, 1901.

———. "Later Heroines of Dickens." *Harper's Bazaar* 33 (October 1900): 1415–21. Reprinted as "Dickens's Later Heroines." *Heroines of Fiction*. Vol. 1. New York: Harper, 1901.

———. "My Favorite Novelist and His Best Book." *Munsey's Magazine* (April 1897). Reprinted in *Criticism and Fiction and Other Essays by W. D. Howells*, edited by Clara M. and Rudolph Kirk, 97–100. New York: New York UP, 1959.

Hutton, Laurence. "Charles Dickens, 1812–1870." In *Library of the World's Best Literature, Ancient and Modern*. Vol. 8, edited by Charles Dudley Warner, 4625–88. New York: R. S. Peale and J. A. Hill, 1896–99.

Jackson, Holbrook. "Charles Dickens." *Great English Novelists*, 215–54. London: Grant Richards, 1908.

Johnson, Edgar. "Dickens and Shaw: Critics of Society." *Virginia Quarterly Review* 33 (Winter 1957): 66–79.

———. "Turning Tides." *Virginia Quarterly Review* 31 (Autumn 1955): 644–48.

Kent, Charles. *Charles Dickens as a Reader*. London: Chapman & Hall, 1872. Reprint, New York: Haskell House, 1973.

Kitton, Frederic G. *Charles Dickens, By Pen and Pencil*. London: F. T. Sabin, 1890.

———. *Charles Dickens, His Life, Writings and Personality*. London: T. C. and E. C. Jack, 1902.

———. *Dickens and his Illustrators*. London: Redway, 1899.

———. *The Dickens Country*. London: A. and C. Black, 1911.

———. *Dickensiana: A Bibliography of the Literature Relating to Charles Dickens and His Writings*. London: Redway, 1886.

———. *The Minor Writings of Charles Dickens: A Bibliography and Sketch*. London: E. Stock. 1900.

———. *The Novels of Charles Dickens: A Bibliography and Sketch*. London: E. Stock, 1897.

———, ed. *The Poems and Verses of Charles Dickens*. London: Harper, 1903.

Laurence, Dan H., and Martin Quinn, eds. *Shaw on Dickens*. New York: Frederick Ungar, 1985.

Lewes, George Henry. "Dickens in Relation to Criticism." *Fortnightly Review* 17 (February 1872): 141–54.

Ley, J. W. T. "History of the *Dickensian*." *Dickensian* 22 (January 1926): 11–22, 121–29.

MacKenzie, Robert Shelton. *Life of Charles Dickens*. Philadelphia: T. B. Peterson, 1870.

Marzials, Frank T. *Life of Charles Dickens*. London: W. Scott, 1887.

Matz, Bertram W. "Charles Dickens and Reform." *Bookman* 39 (November 1910): 79–86. Reprinted in *Bookman Extra Number* (1914): 186–93.

———. *Charles Dickens: The Story of His Life and Writings.* London: Dickens Fellowship, 1902.

Meynell, Alice. "Charles Dickens as a Man of Letters." *Atlantic Monthly* 91 (January 1903): 52–59. Reprinted in *Hearts of Controversy.* London: Burns and Oates, 1917.

———. "Notes of a Reader of Dickens." *Dublin Review* 150 (April 1912): 370–84. Reprinted in *Living Age* 69 (May 1912): 461–69. Reprinted as "Dickens as Man of Letters." *Hearts of Controversy.* London: Burns and Oates, 1917.

Milne, James. "How Dickens Sells: He Comes Next to the Bible and Shakespeare." *Book Monthly* 3 (August 1906): 773–76.

More, Paul Elmer. "The Praise of Dickens." *Shelburne Essays.* 5th series, 22–44. New York: Putnam, 1908.

Oliphant, Margaret. "Sensation Novels." *Blackwood's Edinburgh Magazine* 91 (May 1862): 564–84.

———. *The Victorian Age of English Literature.* London: Tait, 1892.

Phelps, William L. *The Advance of the English Novel.* New York: Dodd, Mead, 1916.

———. "Dickens." *Essays on Books,* 178–91. New York: Macmillan, 1914.

Pugh, Edwin. *Charles Dickens: The Apostle of the People.* London: New Age Press, 1908. Reprint, New York: Haskell House Publishers, 1971.

Saintsbury, George. "Charles Dickens." *Corrected Impressions: Essays on Victorian Writers,* 117–37. London: Heinemann, 1895.

———. "Dickens." *A History of Nineteenth Century Literature 1780–1895,* 145–50. New York: Macmillan, 1896.

———. "Dickens." In *Cambridge History of English Literature.* Vol. 13, edited by A. W. Ward and A. R. Waller, 303–39. Cambridge: Cambridge UP, 1907–16.

———. *The English Novel.* London: Dent, 1913.

———. *Essays on English Literature.* London: Rivington, Percival, 1896.

———. *Miscellaneous Essays.* London: Percival, 1892.

———. *A Short History of English Literature.* London: Macmillan, 1898.

Sala, George Augustus. *Charles Dickens.* London: Routledge, 1870.

Shaw, George Bernard. "Introduction." *Hard Times.* Waverley edition. London: Waverley Book Co., 1913. Reprinted in *Shaw on Dickens,* edited by Dan H. Laurence and Martin Quinn. New York: Frederick Ungar, 1985.

———. "On Dickens." *Dickensian* 10 (June 1914): 150–51. Reprinted in *The Bookman* Extra Number (1914). 103–4.

Shorter, Clement. *Victorian Literature: Sixty Years of Books and Bookmen.* New York: Dodd, Mead, 1897. Reprint, New York: Bart Franklin, 1970.

Stephen, Leslie. "Dickens, Charles." *Dictionary of National Biography.* 1885 edn. Vol. 5, 925–37. London: Smith, Elder, 1908.

Swinburne, Algernon C. "Charles Dickens." *Quarterly Review* 196 (July 1902): 20–39. Reprint with additions as *Charles Dickens,* edited by T. Watts-Dunton. London: Chatto & Windus, 1913. Reprinted in *Swinburne as Critic,* edited by Clyde K. Hyder, 223–42. London: Routledge & Kegan Paul, 1972.

Van Dyke, Henry. "The Good Enchantment of Charles Dickens." *Scribner's Magazine* 51 (June 1912): 656–65. Reprinted in *Companionable Books and Their Authors.* London: Hodder & Stoughton, 1912.

Walker, Hugh. "Dickens and Thackeray." *The Literature of the Victorian Era,* 660–706. Cambridge: Cambridge UP, 1913.

Walters, J. Cuming. "'Biting' Critics." *Dickensian* 26 (Autumn 1930): 282–85.

———. *Phases of Dickens: The Man, His Message, and His Mission.* London: Chapman & Hall, 1911. Reprint, New York: Haskell House Publishers, 1971.

Ward, Adolphus W. *Charles Dickens.* English Men of Letters Series. London: Macmillan, 1882.

Watt, James C. "Dickens." *Great Novelists: Scott, Thackeray, Dickens, Lytton,* 163–218. Edinburgh: Macniver and Wallace, 1880.

Wilkins, W. Glyde. *Charles Dickens in America.* London: Chapman & Hall, 1911.

Wilson, Edmund. "Dickens: The Two Scrooges." *New Republic* 102 (March 1940): 297–300, 339–42. Reprinted, revised and enlarged, in *The Wound and the Bow: Seven Studies in Literature.* Boston: Houghton, Mifflin, 1941. Reprinted in *Eight Essays.* New York: Doubleday, 1954.

3: Dickens among the Moderns (1915–1940)

WHEN THE CONFLICT THAT WOULD COME to be known for a time as The Great War broke out, Britain mobilized all its resources to defeat the Germans and their allies. Dickens became a tool to boost morale among those who stayed behind while young men went off to the trenches in France and Belgium. While it may seem strange to students of literature in the twenty-first century to see fiction employed for such overtly jingoist purposes, the idea did not seem at all unusual in 1914. Some sense of how Dickens was used as propaganda can be gleaned from J. W. T. Ley's 1915 *Dickensian* article, "Dickens and Our Allies." Ley's tone is more akin to patriotic rhetoric than literary criticism: "The Editor has asked me to write something about Dickens and his association with or references to the peoples who are fighting with us in this great war of Freedom" (286). His was no small task, given that among Britain's allies were the Russians, against whom Britain had fought in the Crimean War, and the French and Italians, peoples long distrusted by Englishmen. Ley begins by pointing out that Dickens was "impatient" with England's "insularity," and recognized his country's faults and failings (285), the worst of which was an unmerited chauvinism. Ley waxes passionately about Dickens's great humanitarianism, assuring readers he was "a man of too broad sympathies not to know that the foreigner is a human being like the Englishman" (286). Ley focuses principally on Dickens's attitudes toward France and Italy, but the underlying tone of his article is clear: If Dickens could find goodness in these nations, certainly those who love Dickens should embrace them in this time of crisis.

Although not intended directly as propaganda, the novelist John C. Powys's praise for Dickens in his collection *Visions and Revisions* (1915) highlights Dickens's special ability to "endow the little everyday objects that surround us" with "the fetish-magic of natural 'animism'" (96). Powys defends Dickens from the attacks of those who insist that only realists can be great novelists. In fact, Powys applauds Dickens for being a "shameless sentimentalist" and a "monstrous melodramatist" because these qualities make life interesting. Powys would temper his praise in an essay published two decades later in *Enjoyment of Literature* (1938), remarking there on Dickens's "unfortunate sentimentality" (327). On the other hand, Powys thinks Dickens's ability to bring to life the ugly as well as the beautiful has in some ways limited his readership. "One still encounters nervous and fastidious persons," he says, "devotees of Walter Pater or of Henry James, who 'can't read Dickens'" (331). However, if one can believe John Middleton Murry, certainly no ardent fan of Dickens or the Victorians, "a marked revival of interest and admiration for Dickens among the younger generation" began concurrently with the start of the First World War (331).

Among Dickensians, interest in the man continued to be as high as interest in the novels. In 1919 Ley attempted to set the record straight on a number of Dickens's attachments in *The Dickens Circle: A Narrative of the Novelist's Friendships* (1919). This volume is intended to supplement Forster's biography, which Ley found "disappointing" because it was too narrowly focused on the Dickens-Forster connection (vii). Although he admits the bond between Dickens and his biographer was "the greatest of them all" (336), Ley wants Dickens lovers to know there were others with whom the novelist shared time and interests, among them Francis Jeffrey, Samuel Rogers, Leigh Hunt, Thomas Carlyle, and a host of people less famous but nonetheless important to Dickens during his career.

Sidney Dark shares Ley's interest, as his *Charles Dickens* (1919) makes abundantly clear. Deriving most of his ideas from Chesterton, Dark provides a sympathetic reading of Dickens's life, especially the turbulent 1850s when he was "working to save his soul, trying to put out of mind the family unhappiness which was beginning to be insupportable" (22). Dark defends Dickens's decision to leave his wife, and even calls him "an affectionate father" (26) — perhaps because he did not know what some of the Dickens children had said about the way their father behaved toward them. He exalts the novelist as a great teacher whose "gospel" cannot be disregarded (26), especially at the time Dark is writing: "Few things," he says, are "of more vital importance to the Englishman of today than that he understand Dickens completely and rightly" (28). While no one who had emerged from the war could still believe in the idea of equality, Dark says, "men have always yearned for liberty, and the spirit of liberty breathes in the pages of the Dickens novels." Dickens is "the most English of all the great writers" Dark claims, even "more English than Shakespeare" (37). Of course, what drives Dark to that conclusion is his heartfelt conviction that Dickens's message was one his country needed at the moment. In Dark's estimation, Dickens believed that "life was thrilling and splendid and funny, that freedom was the one essential to happiness, that all cruelty was merely silly, that the simple and the poor were more lovable than the learned and the rich, that kindness was the greatest of all virtues, and humbug the worst of all sins" (45). The stridency of Dark's encomium suggests how much he wants to believe in the "Christmas story" Dickens, and no doubt there were thousands in England who shared his view.

For largely the same reasons, William Walter Crotch is even more insistent in championing the novelist in *The Secret of Dickens* (1919). An ardent Dickensian, Crotch was never shy in declaring his belief that Dickens was not only a great artist but a great patriot. Crotch focuses on ways Dickens touched English society, positioning his own work as a call for his countrymen to rediscover their roots. "In summoning the public interest once more to the greatest novelist of modern times, I feel I am doing the specific work of our Western civilization against the hated reactionaries of Germany," he proclaims. "Any study of Dickens means a spiritual arming of the people for democracy" (xiv–xv).

Crotch's blatant xenophobia and anti-Teutonic feelings lead him to link the evils of the Kaiser's regime with the equally damaging effects of an even greater enemy — greater, because more insidious — the rise of modernism and the modern novel. "We have only to glance at the morbidities of modern German literature to realize how fatal to the Soul of the people they have proved" (5). He expresses deep concern that English literature is following that same path. Writers like Compton MacKenzie and D. H. Lawrence are, he says, causing English literature to lose its way. By contrast Dickens is essentially wholesome and decidedly English while being universal in his outlook on humankind. The glimmer of renewed interest in Dickens heartens Crotch, because "this new study of the novelist may safeguard us" not only from "the perils of literary vacuity" (7) but more importantly from the possibility that English literature might lose "its essentially English characteristics," becoming "cosmopolitan, and, therefore, anemic and soulless" (8).

On the other side of the Atlantic, Richard Burton was writing with an eye toward critics who had for several decades disparaged Dickens's work. He observes in the opening pages of *Charles Dickens: How to Know Him* (1919), that it was now beginning "to look very much as if the works of Charles Dickens were more than those of a representative author" of his day; rather, they are being seen as "a permanent contribution to the literature of the English-speaking peoples" (2). Burton laments the fact that, after his death, Dickens was frequently compared unfavorably to Thackeray, denied any artistic merit, and called a careless workman whose didacticism "injured his craftsmanship" (4). The critics who said this, Burton claims, simply have not come to understand that "life is larger than what is called art." Fortunately, the general public never lost their love for Dickens, and Burton is heartened to note that even some critics — perhaps inspired by the events of the war, which put art and life into sharper perspective — are coming to adopt a "broader and saner view" (5). Throughout his survey of the novelist's career, he points out how sound and wholesome Dickens is, implying of course that those who criticize him are simply wrongheaded in their assessment of his value. Burton sees hope for the "rising generation" (293) to appreciate Dickens once again, and he points to sales figures to support his belief that Dickens would survive his current round of detractors.

The New Critics

By the time the war ended, a new generation of critics, safely housed, for the most part, in British and American universities, was beginning to reshape attitudes about literature according to principles espoused by Henry James and the members of the aesthetic movement. In the opening chapter of *The Craft of Fiction* (1921) Percy Lubbock outlines the changes that would divide the Victorian and Edwardian critics from the new breed that emerged after the War. Following the lead of James and anticipating I. A. Richards and the Cambridge critics who would advocate a more scientific approach to literary criticism, Lubbock proposes a more objective way of viewing a work of fiction. To date, he says, the role of the critic had been rather straightforward: "We discuss the writer, we discuss the people in his book, we discuss the kind of life he renders and his success in the rendering" (5). The new critic, by contrast, should be concerned with "form, design, composition" (10). "The beginning of criticism," he declares, "is to read aright" (13). Lubbock turns to Dickens to illustrate his new way of reading, examining form as a controlling principle in *David Copperfield*. His analysis suggests that point-of-view is the device through which Dickens controls his narrative. In hindsight this may seem almost a truism, but to students of literature in the 1920s, the shift of critical focus from the writer and his world to the writer as craftsman and artist was revolutionary. Lubbock finds many qualities to praise in Dickens's work, particularly his ability to use what Lubbock calls the "pictorial" method, painting a social panorama filled with interesting people (215). He praises *Bleak House* as a particularly good example of that technique. There is, of course, a certain irony in Lubbock's giving high marks to that novel. Like Henry James, whose work he admired, Lubbock is prone to value novels with a consistent point of view. But *Bleak House* alternates between a first-person narrative and an omniscient narrator in whom Dickens vests powers of observation, insight, and moral discourse that would certainly have made James uncomfortable.

Despite the growing shift toward analysis of technical merit, many Dickens lovers remained busy extolling his personal virtues. His abilities as a storyteller figure prominently in W. C. Phillips's *Dickens, Reade and Collins: Sensation Novelists* (1919), which traces changes in English society — both sociological and technological — that led readers to alter their expectations of novelists. Oliver Elton's *Survey of English Literature* (1920) places great stress on Dickens's moral outlook in the novels, but

Elton suggests that to really appreciate Dickens's attempts at social reform one must read his journalism. Although raised in the generation that grew up adoring *Pickwick Papers,* Elton insists those who believe Dickens went into decline after writing *David Copperfield* are wrong. The idea that the later novels deserve equal scrutiny was slowly starting to catch on in critical circles. The philosopher George Santayana admired Dickens greatly, but was less enthusiastic about his abilities as a thinker than Elton, observing in the *Dial* (1921) that "it is remarkable, in spite of his simplicity and openness of heart, how insensible Dickens was to the greater themes of the human imagination — religion, science, politics, art" (59). He also expresses his belief that Dickens was forced frequently to "cheapen in execution what his inspiration had so vividly conceived" (62) in order to meet the demands of his audience and his publication schedule. Nevertheless, Santayana insists that this "perfect comedian" (65) is able to celebrate Christian virtues without the trappings of organized religion, and through his constant exaggeration get to the core of the human spirit. Not everyone appreciates him, Santayana admits, but frequently, he says, "what displeases us in Dickens is that he does not spare us" (67). He makes people face up to traits about human nature and society they would rather avoid.

Dickens's reputation among university students at this time can be inferred from the work of two professors from prestigious institutions. In *Charles Dickens and Other Victorians* (1925), Cambridge professor Arthur Quiller-Couch is not shy about assigning Dickens to the highest rank: "I do not see what English writer we can choose to put second to Shakespeare," he asserts, "save Dickens" (21). What cannot be predicted, Quiller-Couch says, is whether Dickens will pass the true test of greatness, that is, whether his work will go on "meaning more, under quite different conditions, to succeeding ages" (23). At the same time in America, University of Pennsylvania Professor Cornelius Weygandt writes in *A Century of the English Novel* (1925) that he finds "something of the simplicity of a folk imagination in the story-telling of Dickens" (64), a combination of vivid characterization and a fairy-tale quality phantasmagoria that continues to fascinate readers and make him a beloved figure among the general populace. Technically, Weygandt considers Dickens a satirist whose real predecessor is Hogarth rather than Richardson. In fact, he goes so far as to say that Dickens stands outside the main tradition of English writers, relying on neither the Bible nor the classics as sources for inspiration. Weygandt also judges the later novels as Dickens's best work, an opinion slowly growing in popularity among American critics. Presumably, what Weygandt wrote is what he was telling his students, so his ideas may be considered seminal in forming attitudes toward future Dickens studies in America.

The ground there was fertile, as Clarence Cason notes in "Charles Dickens in America To-day" (1926). According to Cason, a newspaper a decade earlier had posed the question, "Who was called the 'Jesus Christ of literature'?" and the answer was "Charles Dickens." Cason's article reports results of a survey of American professors of literature, almost all of whom have good things to say about Dickens. But not everyone in America thought highly of him at this time. In "Is Dickens Still a Hero?" (1927) H. H. Kidd seems to take great pleasure in denouncing him as a "journalistic," "mechanical" writer (280) who had "a penchant for plagiarizing the works of his best friends" (285) and borrowing without acknowledgment from a host of other sources.

Nor did Dickens fare well with the Bloomsbury Group and other modern writers in his own country. Perhaps no one in that circle expressed their enigmatic feelings for Dickens any more forcefully than John Galsworthy, who declares in a 1927 essay ("Six Novelists in Profile") that while Dickens was "a born teller of tales, with an amazing knowledge of human nature and human beings" he was also "an extraordinary artless writer" (*Candelabra* 133). Certainly, Galsworthy says, "no one would dream of going to Dickens to learn consciously the art of novel-writing" (135). Despite this glaring flaw, Galsworthy considers him "the greatest English novelist, and the greatest example in the annals of all novel-writing of the triumph of sheer exuberant genius" (135).

The same kind of love-hate relationship characterizes the commentary of Virginia Woolf, who begins her 1925 essay on *David Copperfield* by asserting that Dickens's "sentiment is disgusting and his style commonplace"; to read him "every refinement must be hidden and every sensibility kept under glass" (*The Moment and Other Essays* 76). Further, she asserts, he did not understand the upper classes and was unable to treat "mature emotions" adequately (77). Yet despite these faults, Woolf finds his work mesmerizing. Often Dickens is able to win over readers because of his ability at creating memorable characters, she says, but *David Copperfield,* "the most perfect of all the Dickens novels," has much more to recommend itself as a work of art (80). Perhaps the same motivation prompted Lillian Rainey's comment in the *Century* magazine a year later: "I like Dickens," she writes, "though I am aware that is a thing one does not air promiscuously" (304).

But not everyone was down on Dickens. Orlo Williams initiates his discussion of Dickens in *Some Great English Novelists: Studies in the Art of Fiction* (1926) by admitting that "one sits down to write about Dickens with an acute sense of discouragement." Williams is concerned that there is not much left to be said. "From Taine to Chesterton," Dickens "has been exhaustively criticized, descried and appreciated" (26). Williams's language recalls that of the generation of critics who wrote before literary criticism was overtaken by the dispassionate language of scientific investigation. Using *Martin Chuzzlewit* as his example, he concludes that Dickens is guided by three emotions, "love, humor, and moral indignation" (37), the last quality emerging from "a very generous heart which had known much misery" (46). Like a wine connoisseur, Williams proclaims that "a draught of Dickens is reviving and full of potent flavors" (28).

After James and Lubbock, the most influential theorist to write about Dickens was E. M. Forster. His *Aspects of the Novel* (1927) could in fact be considered the bible of modernist approaches to fiction, incorporating Jamesian principles and defining the terms for discussing fiction that would survive for half a century. Like Woolf, Forster admits he appreciates Dickens but ultimately determines he was not a great novelist. Linking him with H. G. Wells, Forster says Dickens was "generous-minded" and a hater of "shams," qualities that made him a "valuable social reformer." Unfortunately, "the world of beauty was largely closed to Dickens" (33). Technically the problem with his novels is even greater; he is not capable of creating "round" characters, ones who grow in the course of a work of fiction and therefore provide the greatest interest to sensitive readers. "Dickens's people are nearly all flat," Forster asserts. "Nearly every one can be summed up in a sentence." Or so it would seem; but even Forster has to acknowledge that when reading Dickens one experiences a distinct "feeling of human depth" that defies simple characterizations (108-9). Dickens is able to "use types and caricatures" to achieve "effects that are not mechanical and a vision of humanity that is not shallow." While those who dislike him can certainly make a case for their position, Forster believes Dickens's "immense success with types suggests that there may be more in flatness than the severer critics admit" (109).

Writing in the same year as Forster, T. S. Eliot offers only tepid praise for Dickens in "Wilkie Collins and Dickens" (1927). Yet Eliot, too, finds more substance to Dickens than his detractors would like to admit. Noting he worked in what Eliot calls "the golden age of melodrama," when distinctions between highbrow and popular fiction were less rigid, Dickens was a master of the craft as it was practiced in his own time (409). Eliot claims *Bleak House* is Dickens's best novel — a judgment somewhat unusual at the time, but one that critics of succeeding generations would embrace heartily. Like Forster, Eliot finds "Dickens excelled" in "the creation of characters of greater intensity than human beings" (410). Perhaps what Eliot was suggesting is what George Orwell would express openly a decade later: Dickens is great even if he does not follow rules critics have laid out for judging what is best in literature.

Others were quick to accept Forster's and Eliot's assessments. The novelist, poet and critic Edwin Muir makes only passing references to Dickens's novels in *The Structure of the Novel* (1928), a work heavily influenced by James, E. M. Forster, and Lubbock. Muir says Dickens was exceptionally skilled at creating memorable characters but unable to construct a decent plot. It would be nearly forty years before Muir would alter his assessment, finally suggesting in "The Dark Felicities of Charles Dickens" (1965) that, in the later novels, the "careless improvisation of the earlier stories" (206) gives way to carefully crafted plots usually focused on "imprisonment in its various forms" (208). Muir's insight at this date is noteworthy in that it presages the work of D. A. Miller, Jeremy Tambling, and a host of others who would discover in the writings of the French philosopher Michel Foucault a means of explaining Dickens's fascination with this phenomenon.

Ford Madox Ford also had little to say about Dickens, but what he does say in *The English Novel: From the Earliest Days to the Death of Joseph Conrad* (1930) is mostly derogatory. He seems more interested in the controversies Dickens stirred up than in the quality of his work, and one telling remark encapsulates his attitude quite succinctly: "My father thought Dickens was vulgar" (108). Aldous Huxley was even more caustic. In "The Vulgarity of Little Nell" (in *Vulgarity in Literature* [1930]) he finds Dickens seriously wanting in taste. Defining "vulgarity" as a "lowness that proclaims itself" (248), Huxley asserts it is "vulgar, in literature, to make a display of emotions which you do not naturally have" (278). Influenced by the new science of psychology and by anti-Victorian attitudes prevalent at the time, Huxley observes sardonically that Dickens had "an overflowing heart; but the trouble was that it overflowed with such curious and even rather repellent secretions" (298). When he becomes emotional, Huxley argues, he "ceases instantly to lose his intelligence," and "ceases even to wish to see reality" (299). Unfortunately, Huxley concludes, "the quality of Dickens's sentimentality" is "truly pathological" (303).

But there were new champions emerging as well. In 1929 a fresh voice — powerful, opinionated, and destined to be prolific — made itself heard. Edward Wagenknecht was a young scholar who published *The Man Charles Dickens* (1929) several years before he submitted it as his dissertation at the University of Washington. Wagenknecht calls his book a psychobiography modeled on techniques made popular by Gamaliel Bradford decades earlier. Wagenknecht is less concerned with chronicling the details of Dickens's life than in discovering the sources of his genius. He also scoffs at the personal and professional charges currently being made against Dickens, countering with the claim that "Dickens is justly celebrated for the purity of his imagination and his humor" (182). As one might expect from a disciple of Bradford, Wagenknecht's portrait of Dickens is drawn not only from previously published books and unpublished sources but also from the fiction, which Wagenknecht insists is a window into the novelist's personality. The book contains long accounts of the way Dickens measures up to what Wagenknecht calls the five tests of character: generosity, attitudes toward children, relations with servants, behavior toward animals, and especially behavior toward friends and acquaintances. What is particularly striking are claims Wagenknecht makes for his own role in the Dickens Industry. In the preface to his 1966 revision of *The Man Charles Dickens,* Wagenknecht looks back at the history of critical commentary since his book's first appearance in 1929 and concludes that he almost single-handedly initiated modern Dickens studies — by which he seems to mean the kind of study that became common practice in the 1940s. A number of his essays published subsequent to the 1929 edition defend Dickens against charges that he had had an affair with Ellen Ternan. Wagenknecht repeats his assertions regarding Dickens's character and talent in a review of recent scholarship on Dickens in the *Virginia Quarterly Review* (1934) and again in the chapter on Dickens in his widely circulated *Cavalcade of the English Novel* (1943).

Despite Wagenknecht's claims about his unique place in Dickens studies, by the 1930s Dickensians were beginning to find more allies among mainstream academic critics — although these were not always fulsome in their praise. For example, in *The Facts of Fiction* (1932) Norman Collins calls Dickens "the first journeyman of genius in modern times" (155) but claims Dickens would have been delighted by the reproaches of modern critics that he wrote for the public. Collins thinks it unfortunate that "Dickens has won a false reputation as a social reformer" (161) since what he really wanted to do was entertain. Collins finds it sad that Dickens took this role beyond the bounds of reason, as his reading tours were significantly detrimental to his career: they demeaned his character and crushed his creativity. "There is something rather chilling to the spirit," he observes, "in the notion of an aging author abandoning the quietude of the study to become a sort of giant performing flea" (164). Like Collins, Joseph Warren Beach argues in *The Twentieth-Century Novel: Studies in Technique* (1932) that despite current assertions to the contrary, Dickens was "most interested in technique," although he suffers from a "want of realism" (4). That is not intended as a criticism, however, as Beach explains later in his commentary. He believes Dickens is concerned "chiefly to provide as much entertainment as possible," and judged by this standard, "the greatest of all masters in this art" (124). Beach explains how Dickens uses sentimentalism, melodrama, chiaroscuro, and intricate plotting to provide his readers great enjoyment. Dickens is "the classic example of the novelist pure and simple, and unaffected by the preoccupation of realism" (128). He succeeds, Beach suggests, precisely because he is not bound by the demands placed on the realistic novelist who must portray "the typical reactions of human nature in typical circumstances" (128).

Bucking the trend of the New Critics, Robert Lovett and Helen S. Hughes argue in *The History of the Novel in England* (1932) that to appreciate a novel fully, readers must understand the "literary circumstances" in which an author worked, including prevailing ideas about beauty, character, and morality, and have some knowledge of the author's life and experiences (2). In their analysis of Dickens they find the sources for his success in "the hardship of his early life" (228), his training as a journalist, and his "dramatic experience" (230). While they fault Dickens for weak plotting and an inability to draw characters "in the round" (234), they note that "technical qualities have far less weight in determining the success of novels in England than in France" (235) — so Dickens escapes critical damnation and emerges as "the universal entertainer of the English reading public," a role that gave him his "chief social importance" (236).

By the 1930s even some members of the Bloomsbury group had begun to express admiration for Dickens publicly. Osbert Sitwell's brief monograph, *Dickens* (1932), opens with a plea for "a revaluation" (5) that would restore balance to Dickens's reputation. After all, Sitwell observes, even after more than five decades of disparagement, Dickens is still being read, because readers admire his energy and imagination and discover in his novels an inherent design — something missed by many critics of Sitwell's generation. Sitwell argues Dickens's "sense of social justice" is "too strong" to permit him "to attain any ultimate perfection of art" (46). Apparently for Sitwell, meaning well trumps writing well. Sitwell would write about Dickens again five years later, turning his 1937 Northcliff Lecture into "Dickens and the Modern Novel" for inclusion in *Trio* (1938), a collection of his essays. Still an admirer, Sitwell admits that while Dickens is much loved by readers, his influence on modern novelists is "not a very considerable one" (4).

More typical of critical analysis during the 1930s, however, is Pelham Edgar's *The Art of the Novel from 1700 to the Present Time* (1933). Modeled on Lubbock's *The Craft of Fiction,* the book traces the "structural evolution of the English novel" (3). Edgar's interest is in form, not content, and predictably his criticisms of Dickens are harsh. "In a constructional sense Dickens was his own worst enemy," he asserts (117). He would have been a better novelist if only he had "been a shade more self-critical and intelligent" (117). Edgar believes Dickens pandered too much to his audience, which demanded complex and sensational stories and did not care about careful construction. Ironically, Edgar seems to *like* Dickens's novels, but he cannot reconcile Dickens's apparent lack of concern for form with twentieth-century critics' demand that great art be well constructed. The same seems to be true for Hillaire Belloc, who complains in "Dickens Revisited" (1927) that "the first thing a modern like myself would say about him is that he is damnably crude" — but, Belloc admits, so were Molière and Shakespeare. Belloc is struck by "the amazing power of his good rhetoric in the midst of whole washtubs of bad rhetoric" (444). Yet despite his faults, "he gets exactly" the "motives of hypocrisy and vanity in our average selves." This, Belloc concludes "is an amazing achievement for a man whose sentimentalism ran so false" and who, being uneducated and unaware of literary tradition, "had no guide to keep him in touch with reality" (445).

Dickens is dealt with even more unkindly by David Cecil in *Early Victorian Novelists* (1934), an assessment of nineteenth-century writers by one well schooled in post-Victorian ideology. Cecil is bothered by the inability of Victorian writers to deal honestly with "the animal side of human nature" (8) and by their unwillingness to tackle "the broader, more impersonal objects that occupy mankind; his relation to thought, to art, to public affairs" (9). None of this group, Cecil says, is able to "stir those profounder feelings to which the very greatest art appeals" (9). They do tell stories well, he acknowledges, and they are all good at creating interesting characters, even if they do not delve deeply into the human psyche. Probably for those reasons, Cecil surmises, Dickens's popularity "has suffered no sensible decline"; still, he argues, Dickens's work contains "a great deal that is bad" (27). His novels lack strong construction and artistic unity. He relies too heavily on conventions established by earlier generations of novelists. He frequently overstates his case. He has "no sense of form" and an "uncertain grasp of character" (49). Dickens may be "the greatest humourist that England had ever produced," Cecil concludes (46), but he really is limited by his education and experience so much that he needs to create a fantasy world as a substitute for the real world he simply does not understand. He was, at best, "an average nineteenth-century Cockney," Cecil concludes; "only he had genius" (49).

While Cecil is not willing to tackle the issue of Dickens's moral vision, he does suggest that what he considers the rather simplistic worldview expressed in the novels, with their affirmation of goodness and the value of human affections, continues to appeal to the general public. There is another point worth observing about Cecil's assessment, however, even though he does not make much of it in his discussion. In commenting on Dickens's style, Cecil claims Dickens's novels are reminiscent of Elizabethan dramatic poetry. That suggestion would be taken up by the irascible F. R. Leavis within a decade and used as one reason to exclude Dickens from the ranks of England's greatest novelists.

Before that would happen, however, Leavis's wife, Q. D. Leavis, herself a distinguished Cambridge professor, would publish the initial salvo leveled by the couple at the Victorian novelist. In her wide-ranging study *Fiction and the Reading Public* (1932) Leavis hints at the problems she and her husband have with Dickens's work. Unlike so many of her contemporaries using tools of psychology to find clues about the author's personality and psychoses in his fiction, Leavis concentrates on the social context of the novels and on their internal workings. Her principal interest in this book is the impact of changes in readership on the production of novels. She is quick to attribute Dickens's popularity to a shift in the kind of people who began reading novels in the 1830s. His novels were produced for "a naïve public, not that of the old circulating libraries or that could afford to buy Scott, but for the shopkeeper and the working man" (156). Dickens resorted to crude sentimentality and overstatement because these qualities pleased such an audience. "Anyone who runs a critical eye over a novel or two" by Dickens can quickly discern, Leavis states categorically, "that his originality is confined to recapturing a child's outlook on the grown-up world." He is not only "uneducated, but also immature" (157). Dickens was satisfied to achieve cheap effects in each serial number, since by employing this method he was sure to keep his readers waiting for the next installment. Nevertheless, Leavis says in a backhanded compliment, "Dickens himself has a personal outlook and idiom which, though elsewhere present only in patches, succeed in getting the upper hand in *David Copperfield* and *Great Expectations* sufficient for these novels to be called literature" (158). It would be thirty-eight years before the Leavises decided there was substantially more to Dickens than they initially conceded.

Biography between the Wars

While critics such as Cecil and Leavis were establishing Dickens's reputation as a writer during the postwar years, others were revisiting the novelist's life to discover hitherto unknown information that would paint a decidedly different portrait than the one created by John Forster, Chesterton, and their fellow Dickensians. Although Dickens lovers had done much to supplement Forster's three-volume life study of Dickens by publishing articles and notes in the *Dickensian,* it was not until 1935 that anyone made any significant addition to biographical studies. In fact, the only notable new full-length biography to be published in the 1920s was Ralph Straus's *Charles Dickens: A Biography from New Sources* (1928), printed in England as *Charles Dickens: A Portrait in Pencil.* Straus is almost apologetic in explaining that his book concentrates on the life rather than the novels. "I have little enough to say of his books," Straus says, because "Gissing and Chesterton, it seems to me, have said all that it is necessary to say on the matter" (xiv). He argues correctly, though, that a new biography is needed because so much new material has come to light since Forster's work appeared in the 1870s. Straus has good things to say about Forster, although he believes Forster's close friendship with Dickens made him reluctant to write about sensitive personal issues. He is much harder on F. G. Kitton, whose *Charles Dickens, His Life, Writings and Personality* (1902) he considers a pastiche assembled by "sift[ing] Forster and 'The Letters of Charles Dickens,' coolly reprinting whole sentences from these works as his own" (xii). Among the new materials Straus had at his disposal was an extensive collection of Dickensiana including family correspondence assembled by the collector Charles J. Sawyer. Straus uses these documents to weave a new tale of the novelist's life, frequently embellished to liven up the narrative. Even with considerable new information, however, Straus holds back in his portrait, claiming "there are incidents in Dickens's life which even now need not be told, and I dare say that I, too, have been rather more discreet than I need have been" (xiii). Unfortunately, it is sometimes hard to know what is original to Straus and what is borrowed, since he does not provide footnotes or a bibliography. Straus would make another stab at chronicling the novelist's career in *Dickens: The Man and the Book* (1936), which is actually a collection of selected quotations from the novels, strung together along a biographical thread, intended to make the case that Dickens is Shakespeare's equal.

Five years after Straus's biography appeared, Bernard Darwin, grandson of the famous naturalist, took time away from writing about golf to write *Dickens* (1933) for Duckworth's Great Lives series. Drawing principally from Forster and other published sources for details of Dickens's life, and on Chesterton and other Dickensians who favored the early work, Darwin writes a summary that offers little new information for those who had been keeping up with Dickens studies. What makes Darwin's book of interest — largely because of what would follow within a year of its publication — is his commentary on the novelist's separation from his wife. Acknowledging that the separation "came as a bombshell to the bulk of [Dickens's] admirers," Darwin says, "the first thing that strikes us is that it ought to have happened long before. The notion that a man and woman living together in a state of obvious unhappiness and continuing to produce children is repugnant" (110). Of course, Darwin seems to be taking Dickens's side in the matter. That same line of reasoning is applied to his assessment of Dickens's relationship with Ellen Ternan. In citing Dickens's letter in which the novelist alludes to her as "innocent and pure," Darwin says "there's no scrap of evidence to show that Dickens's words about her were not absolutely true" (114). Certainly Darwin's grandfather and his contemporaries would have come to the same conclusion, but contemporaries of Bernard Darwin, grown suspicious of the Victorians' claims of earnestness and purity, had begun to view such protestations in a different light.

One of those who had a different view was Thomas Wright, a literary biographer of sorts, who had previously published lives of William Cowper,

William Blake, Edward FitzGerald, and Daniel Defoe. The kind of work in which he specialized can be seen in the subtitle of the last volume mentioned, which contains the promise of "entirely new information respecting Defoe." Wright first published his discoveries about Dickens's private life in "Charles Dickens Begins His Honeymoon" in the April 3, 1934 issue of the *Daily Express.* A year later he would detail his findings more fully in his *Life of Charles Dickens* (1935). Wright's revelations about the real nature of the novelist's relationship with Ellen Ternan initiated a small revolution in Dickens studies. He was the first to assert unequivocally — and in print — that Dickens had kept Ternan as his mistress during the last decade of his life, and that he separated from his wife so he could spend his time with Ternan. Release of this startling and somewhat titillating news could not have been better timed. Attacks on Victorian hypocrisy were at their height. Biographical readings of fictional works were in vogue, aided by the application of the tools of psychoanalysis to critical study, which frequently suggested meanings and interpretations hidden not only from the general public but even from the writers themselves.

Wright's portrait of Dickens as callous and self-centered was not original, of course, but he had a heavy task on his hand, considering he was refuting two influential eyewitnesses to the novelist's behavior. Mary Dickens's *Charles Dickens, by His Eldest Daughter* (1885) and reprinted in 1897 under the title *My Father as I Knew Him,* describes a home life that is not exactly rosy, but Mary manages to present her father in a favorable light as one who cherished his family above everything else. Henry Dickens, the novelist's eighth child, wrote frequently about his father, contributing articles to periodicals such as the *Dickensian, Harper's Weekly, Lloyd's Weekly,* the *New York Times Magazine,* and the London *Times.* Henry Dickens expanded the last two pieces into a short book, *Memories of My Father* (1928), a cheery account with only a passing acknowledgment of the "heavy moods of deep depression" that plagued the novelist, a condition his son attributes to his "sensitive and emotional nature" (14).

There is no sense of late-Victorian reticence in Wright's work, although he claims to have begun his biography in 1893 and completed it in 1904. He says the account of Dickens's affair with Ternan was relayed to him by Canon William Benham, who ostensibly heard the story firsthand from Ternan. Unfortunately, Benham died in 1910, Ternan in 1914, so by 1935 neither was around to dispute Wright's account, and Wright himself died the year after he published his startling news of Dickens's affair. Actually, however, much of the information about Dickens's relationship with Ellen Ternan had been available for some time to those willing to ferret out the story. The first bequest in Dickens's will is to Ternan, and Wright is certain the family and many of Dickens's close friends knew about the liaison. Apparently, though, no one seemed willing to despoil the memory of the great champion of Victorian family life, so the "secret" stayed buried until Wright incorporated the story into his work.

Wright's is an interesting combination of biography and criticism. For many of the details of Dickens's early life he relies on Forster and on *David Copperfield*, although he believes Dickens's friend and first biographer was in part responsible for driving Dickens away from his wife and into Ternan's arms. Wright's interpretations of novels written before 1856 are not particularly enlightening, but as he asserts in his introductory remarks, his revelation of Dickens's affair with Ternan proves that "most of the theories respecting Dickens's later years" put forth by Forster and other Dickensians "were supremely ridiculous" (7). Ellen Ternan, Wright says, was the inspiration for many of Dickens's later heroines — Estella in *Great Expectations,* Helena Landless in *Edwin Drood,* and especially Bella Wilfer in *Our Mutual Friend.* "It will be noticed," he says, "that there is no real heat in the love scenes in Dickens's stories until we get to those in which Miss Ternan covertly figures" (255). Wright's rather flamboyant and at times voyeuristic account startled some Dickens lovers, infuriated others, and added further ammunition to the arsenal of critics bent on debunking the Victorians' collective high-minded sense of moral superiority. But seventeen years later, when a more dispassionate — and definitive — account of the relationship was published by Ada Nisbet, Wright's essential claims were upheld. Additionally, since 1935 no critic has been able to read any of Dickens's later work without taking into account the affair that inspired the novelist in the final decade of his life.

Wright's initial revelations in his 1934 article had an immediate impact. Even before his longer biography was published, the prolific Victorian debunker Hugh Kingsmill Lunn, writing under his pseudonym Hugh Kingsmill, used information from Wright's *Daily Express* piece to rush into print a scathing attack on Dickens. *The Sentimental Journey: A Life of Charles Dickens* (1934) represents the nadir of critical estimation of Dickens's character and fiction. Informed by the tools of psychological analysis and shaped by Kingsmill's disdain for the Victorians, the book attacks Dickens as vain, self-centered, and immature in his personal life, and decidedly inferior in his artistic endeavors.

Kingsmill sets himself up as a kind of champion for modernism in dealing with a Victorian icon by noting that Dickens's enduring popularity among the general public has created a problem for someone such as himself, since "millions of dumb admirers" have made it hard to present a detached view of the man and his work (3). Kingsmill is willing to grant that Dickens had a marvelous flair for depicting the grotesque and ludicrous. He even admits, somewhat begrudgingly, that the early novels have some merit, principally for their comedy — a quality lamentably absent from the later, darker novels. "Had he been able to harmonize his comic genius and his emotions he would have been a writer of the first order," Kingsmill speculates — perhaps with a degree of sarcasm. "But the opposition between them was innate and irreconcilable" (7).

Kingsmill finds every way he can to highlight this opposition and stress the egotism that dominated Dickens's life and destroyed the people around him. He finds Dickens responsible for the suicide of his first illustrator, Robert Seymour, claiming Dickens's shameful treatment of him provided the "last straw" that drove Seymour to take his own life. By contrast, Kingsmill says, that "last straw" would "not have been placed on [Seymour's] back by Shakespeare, or Cervantes, or Fielding, or any other writer whose comic genius was fully nourished by his human feelings" (53). But Dickens had no such feelings, Kingsmill says, as seen again in his ill-treatment of Maria Beadnell when he renews his acquaintance with her years after she had rejected him. The cruel portrait of her as Flora Finching in *Little Dorrit* demonstrates that "while rigidly faithful to his own emotions" Dickens "could not preserve any sympathy or affection for someone who no longer fitted into his emotional panorama" (172). And of course the best example of the novelist's harsh dismissal of someone he no longer needed is exhibited, for Kingsmill, in the horrific treatment of his wife. Far from being a great lover of humanity, Dickens was simply a lover of himself, ready to trample on the feelings of others to get what he wanted. Kingsmill is not content to attack Dickens for these qualities; he even goes after Ellen Ternan. "Miss Ternan was an actress," he observes wryly, "and knew how to make her resentment against poverty appealing to Dickens." However, she was equally adept at making "her resentment against Dickens harrowing to Canon Benham," the man to whom, as Wright had pointed out, she confided her feelings about the time she had spent under the novelist's protection (220).

Whenever he can, Kingsmill makes clear his disdain for the criticism of Dickens lovers such as G. K. Chesterton. His readings of the novels are highly autobiographical, usually aimed at explaining how the self-absorbed novelist put himself and those he loved or hated into his fiction. Certainly those who admired Lytton Strachey's character assassinations in *Eminent Victorians* would have relished every page of Kingsmill's diatribe.

Dickens seemed to fare much better among North American critics. In 1933, the Canadian writer Stephen Leacock published what might be considered the last biography of Dickens prepared without widespread knowledge of the novelist's true relationship with Ellen Ternan. It is certainly the last in the tradition of Forster, Chesterton, and the Dickensians for whom *any* negative criticism was too much. Leacock opens *Charles Dickens: His Life and Work* (1933) with an acknowledgement that Dickens is not as widely read as he once was, but the fault for this lies not with the novelist but with modern readers. "We live in a badly damaged world,"

Leacock laments, while "Dickens lived in a world that is visibly passing, the age of individual eminence that is giving place to the world of universal competence" (2). This nostalgic outlook colors Leacock's reading of the fiction, and leads him to ascribe greater value to the earlier work. Even though ardent Dickens lovers "are unwilling to accept any idea of a decline or waning of his powers in later life, of an inferiority of his later books" (237), Leacock insists that after publishing *David Copperfield*, "the highest reach of his achievement" (121), Dickens suffered a notable downturn in creative genius. *Hard Times* is a failure. *Little Dorrit* is so complicated and confusing that "few readers follow it and none remember it" (190). *Our Mutual Friend* "never is, and never was, very readable" (239).

Leacock had published an essay on Dickens's novels nearly twenty years earlier in his collection *Essays and Literary Studies* (1916) in which he had taken on critics who were asserting Dickens did not write well or create realistic characters. That same approach reappears in Leacock's biography, and while his literary criticism is hardly groundbreaking, his assessment of Dickens's career and character makes his work particularly intriguing to historians of Dickens's reputation. In writing about Dickens's perspectives of other countries, Leacock seems to have gotten it right: Dickens misunderstood Americans, and he "never really saw the Continent. He carried to it the limitations of his nation" (132). By contrast, Leacock is sympathetic to Dickens's sentimentalism, finding it a means of the novelist's coping with death, especially the death of children, in an age that may have been the first to feel real compassion for the suffering of the lower and middle classes.

What Leacock misses — or chooses to ignore — is the role Ellen Ternan might have played in Dickens's life. He attributes Dickens's darkening mood in the 1850s and 1860s to his separation from Catherine, and even faults Forster for not being more forthcoming in discussing the strained relationship. Somewhat prophetically, Leacock notes that after Dickens published his infamous letter outlining his reasons for leaving his wife, "a sort of decent conspiracy of silence" had fallen over this phase of the novelist's life. More than sixty years later it still "lies under a veil" (211–12). Yet, ironically, he discusses at some length the bequests Dickens makes in his will but ignores the first one, which was to Ternan for £1,000. Apparently Leacock did not have time to investigate this curious gift, or like so many Dickens lovers before him, opted not to delve too deeply into a subject that might paint the novelist in a bad light.

Continental Criticism: A Snapshot

Critics in England and America were not the only ones writing about Dickens during the first four decades of the twentieth century, of course, and on occasion a particularly influential study was translated for the benefit of English-speaking students and scholars. Andre Maurois's *Dickens,* a book that combines biography with critical analysis, offers some insight into ways the Victorian novelist was being revalued on the Continent in the years between the world wars. Although his book was published in French in 1927, English-speaking readers were able to get some idea of Maurois's estimate from his 1929 *Forum* article "The Philosophy of Dickens." Unfortunately, an English translation of Maurois's book did not appear until 1934, after Wright published his "new" information about Dickens and Ellen Ternan. In the preface composed for the American edition published in 1935, Maurois acknowledges that, during the eight years since his work was first published, the appearance of "certain new documents" made him "re-read and simplify the French text" because, from "letters which hitherto had remained unpublished, critics and biographers had contrived to depict the character of Dickens in a rather unpleasing light. They have shown him as vain, unjust," even "hypocritical" (vii). Maurois wishes to counter these charges, demonstrating how Dickens's personal life had only minimal effect on his status as an artist. He is quick to defend Dickens against those who find fault with his artistic ability. Unlike Chesterton, whose method of dealing with detractors "consists of depicting the pettiness of the critic in contrast to the greatness of the work criticized" (141), Maurois is willing to concede that the critics are right on some counts, but certainly not on all of them. Dickens's memorable characters are like those of the great dramatists, Maurois says, and while he was perhaps not always realistic, one needs to remember that "the epoch which was foremost in rejecting Dickens was that of naturalism" (157). "What we require of the artist," Maurois counters, "is not fidelity to reality, but fidelity to *his* reality" (161). Maurois can be critical at times, for example in faulting Dickens for railing against social ills without suggesting specific reforms, and for failing to deal with religious issues in any meaningful way. On the other hand, he says, an artist should not be blamed too much for failing to deal with abstractions. In the end, Maurois finds Dickens essentially English in his outlook. His work leaves "two or three essential impressions" that constitute his "message" (175). Dickens has a "boundless optimism" (176) in approaching a world he saw as "a battlefield" where good constantly struggles against evil (178). He believes in progress, Maurois says, the kind which will eventually lead to a world in which "men will attain a kind of everlasting Christmas" (179).

A complementary view is offered by the Austrian writer Stefan Zweig. One of Europe's leading novelists and biographers during the first decades of the century, Zweig published a lengthy essay on Dickens in 1919. His work influenced German readers and critics but was not available in English until four years later, and then only in limited circulation, appearing in a 1923 issue of the *Dial*. More widely available in *Three Masters* (1930), a volume including essays on Balzac and Dostoevsky, Zweig's account values Dickens for his ability to "construct a canvas, peopling it with types of his own working, giving it laws of gravitation that apply to it alone." Like Balzac and Dostoevsky, Dickens is able to build up "a law of life and a concept of life by means of the characters" in his novels, "so that we are given a vision of a new kind of world" (ix–x). This provocative notion may not have attracted much attention among British and American critics, but nearly four decades later it would reappear as the central thesis of one of the most influential studies of Dickens, J. Hillis Miller's *Charles Dickens: The World of His Novels* (1958).

Zweig says, however, that because Dickens embodies English tradition, he was not a real revolutionary: "The artist in him never played traitor to the Englishman" (57). Applying the criteria of a revolutionary socialist theory — a form of Marxism, to be sure — to Dickens's novels, Zweig concludes the novelist's "wonderful imagination" was fettered to "the rock of success" and his "artistic aspirations were burdened by a deep feeling of contentment" (63). Despite a genuine desire to bring about social reform, Dickens was shackled to his middle-class contemporaries too tightly to break free from their values; as a result, "the whole entourage of Dickens's novels is one of bourgeois smugness" (66). Throughout his career, Zweig notes a bit sadly, Dickens "claps a censorship on [his] emotions, instead of allowing them free vent" (83). Throughout Zweig's commentary, one senses more than a hint of disappointment that Dickens did not have the courage to break with the hypocritical society in which he lived — and which supported his lifestyle by buying his books.

Early Signs of Changes in Critical Esteem

While Zweig may have mourned over Dickens's inability to become a true revolutionary, others were celebrating his success at having been one. In *Charles Dickens: The Progress of a Radical* (1937), T. A. Jackson, a Marxist critic, offers the first extended reading of the Dickens canon that links the Victorian novelist to the radical political tradition that was reaching the height of its popularity in Western Europe when this book appeared. Dickens had long been considered a favorite novelist among socialists, as Pugh's 1908 book on Dickens as the "apostle of the people" and Shaw's 1913 comment about the revolutionary character of *Little

Dorrit make clear. The Socialist Harold Laski had even praised Dickens in a 1932 article in the *Daily Herald,* calling him "a great social reformer," although Laski believes he was deeply rooted in English traditions. Jackson notes in his foreword that *Humanité,* the French Communist daily, ran *David Copperfield* as a serial during 1936, and that a Belgian Communist journal printed extracts from *A Tale of Two Cities* during the previous summer. For his own part, Jackson is not a simplistic propagandist, and although he approaches Dickens through the lens of Marxist ideology, he is neither blind to other readings nor unaware that the novelist was not a Socialist agitator. Acknowledging that Dickens has been embraced by people of all political persuasions, Jackson is intent on showing how the tendency of critics of the 1920s and 1930s to equate Dickens's popularity among the general readership with artistic inferiority is a telltale sign that beneath the surface optimism of the novels lies a strain of radicalism that makes Dickens a kind of *communist manqué.*

Jackson's approach is to read each novel in its historical context, noting the important social and political movements that form the background to each work. He believes Dickens developed contempt for government during his days as a parliamentary reporter and found nothing but similar corruption in all forms of society. He sees Dickens's career following a natural progression from optimistic reformer to hardened critic of a corrupt society. All Dickens lacked was a nudge that would have pushed him into the Socialist camp. The "radicalism" that emerged at the end of his career, Jackson says, "stiffened, hardened, and deepened into something that with a little outside aid might easily have emerged as positive Socialism or Communism" (11).

As one might expect, Jackson considers the lynchpin work in the Dickens canon to be *Hard Times,* an attack on capitalism that contains passages "in which Dickens takes a ground indistinguishable from that taken by Marx and Engels" (39). Jackson also devotes considerable attention to *American Notes* — quite unusual for a critic of his day — in an attempt to explain Dickens's revulsion for America. "At the time," Jackson says, Dickens "did not realize that the things which horrified him most were only the normal consequences of that political emancipation of the bourgeoisie for which as a Radical he was enthusiastic" (50). In his detailed analysis of Dickens's major works, Jackson reveals his own Marxist bent, concentrating not only on the "literary-technical" merits, but also on "the relative preponderance of optimism or its converse in the general world outlook" and "the class-sympathy implicit in the working-out of each novel" (101). He admits, finally, that Dickens was not a philosopher like Marx, but instead was a great reporter with a gift for caricature, a quality Jackson considers a virtue, "because men in his society *were* caricatures — and couldn't help being so, given social conditions" (253).

Jackson is also pleased that Dickens showed no theological bias. In fact, he finds Dickens to be a closet atheist who may have harbored some belief in God but certainly had no use for organized religion. Through a bit of ideological legerdemain, Jackson is able to offer readings of the Christmas stories that strip them of their religious overtones.

Taken as a whole, Jackson says, the Dickens canon represents an "assault upon the bourgeois order" (283). To those who really understood him, Dickens was something of a threat. Jackson is especially hard on John Forster, who apparently discerned Dickens's tendencies toward radicalism but chose to suppress or ignore the implications of his insights. "Forster's philistine imperviousness" is regrettable, he suggests (249). But he admits "Dickens never fully realized the cumulative force of his own indictment of bourgeois society" (295). Jackson attributes the failure to Dickens's decision to remain aloof from the political process, and to his innate fear of the power of imagination — two traits better realized, Jackson implies without stating, in the work of the century's greatest radical, Karl Marx, of whom Dickens is but a pale shadow.[1]

To get some sense of the extremes of Dickens criticism in the 1930s, one might place beside Jackson's strident polemic O. F. Christie's *Dickens and his Age: An Essay* (1939). Like Jackson, Christie is interested chiefly in ways Dickens reflects and shapes his times. Christie comments on various social, technical, and political issues with which Dickens engages, weaving comments about the novels into an overview of the nineteenth-century scene. Born when Dickens was still alive and a household name, Christie writes in the style of his Victorian forebears, and his study is reminiscent of the "Dickens Country" genre of F. G. Kitton and the early Dickensians. His Dickens is cheerful and hopeful, annoyed with social ills but hardly ready to toss out the social superstructure that has been built over the centuries in his beloved homeland.

If there is such a thing as a mainstream view of Dickens in the 1930s, it can be found in Ernest Baker's ten-volume *History of the English Novel*. Its enduring popularity as a source for undergraduate research and general information on the development of the genre make it a useful gauge of critical opinion on Dickens in the period between the world wars. Volume 7, *The Age of Dickens and Thackeray* (1936), contains two long chapters on Dickens in which Baker repeats information about the novelist's professional life gleaned from other sources, particularly Forster's life, which he calls "one of the great biographies" in English (237). Despite five decades of negative criticism, Dickens remains in Baker's view the preeminent novelist of his age. Yet Baker's judgments seem in most instances as derivative as his information about Dickens's career. He asserts that "Dickens knew the worst of humanity, yet he believed in the best"; that his "genius was for the extensive, not the intensive vision" (248), which is a coded criticism of the novelist's inability to delve deeply into the inner lives of his characters. Later in the essay, Baker makes the point more explicitly, claiming Dickens lacked the ability "to see far below the outward and visible idiosyncrasies of mankind" (321). While Baker finds his "monstrous concoctions of sheer nonentities" that populate his early works to be achievements (259), he complains that during his formative years Dickens displayed a "besetting clumsiness and carelessness in spinning his plots" (279). With *Dombey and Son,* Baker argues, Dickens turned a corner in his development as a novelist, mastering in a fashion the ability to plot carefully. The novel that followed, *David Copperfield,* is a perennial favorite with critics and general readers, though Baker says that, despite its realism (a positive quality) it is "not entirely free from the ensnaring device of poetic justice" (283).

Clearly influenced by the critical tenets of realism and psychological character development, Baker finds Dickens's later works rise and fall on the novelist's ability to approximate the world around him and present believable characters and situations. For this reason, he equivocates about *Bleak House,* a "novel of purpose" (294) in which Dickens displays "his power of evoking an emotional and moral atmosphere out of physical objects" (296) — but a work in which he attempts too much for a single book. He is clearly vexed with *Little Dorrit,* finding it tortuous. He dismisses both *Hard Times* and *A Tale of Two Cities* as uncharacteristic of Dickens. He pays great attention to *Great Expectations,* which he considers a masterpiece of verbal artistry, but is considerably less taken with *Our Mutual Friend,* calling it "a coat of various colours" — with the coat being "shabby and second-hand" (313–14).

Since the purpose of his study is to explain the development of the novel and help place practitioners in some kind of "order of merit," Baker finds himself offering an assessment of Dickens that gives him great credit for his strengths but does not ignore weaknesses — at least, weaknesses according to the criteria made fashionable by the formalists. Of all the novelists who have written in English, Baker says, Dickens "is the one with the largest natural endowment, the one with most prolific imagination, and the richest humour" (325). But his lack of education limited him in many ways, especially in "the finer requirements of craftsmanship, in a sense of the duties and prerogatives of an artist, in the niceties of good taste" (325). This Jamesian view leads Baker to lament the fact that Dickens "was given to vulgar sentimentality and emotionalism — as was his age — qualities that jar on a later age" (326). But his concluding observation contains in it more than Baker himself might have imagined. Dickens is not a realist, he asserts. Even though a number of his characters and scenes evoke an aura of the real world because of his ability to provide minute descriptions, the people and places Dickens depict exist in "a world of his own imagination" (330). A later generation of critics, armed with new tools and new ways of viewing literary productions, would confirm Baker's claim and in the process elevate Dickens to undisputed pre-eminence among Victorian novelists.

As the foregoing discussion demonstrates, there was never really any hiatus in critical commentary on Dickens. But there was a sense in the academic community, especially during the first four decades of the twentieth century, that Dickens was a writer too often overrated by fans who ignored significant faults of style and intellectual prowess. Certainly not everyone felt this way, and some of Dickens's defenders were men and women of critical sensitivity and extensive learning. Guy Boas wrote enthusiastically of his abilities in 1939, calling him together with Shakespeare "the greatest of such miracles in our literature" (314). But Boas admits he is not writing criticism, but rather an appreciation of Dickens's accomplishments and a lament that the world Dickens described has long since passed. The idea that the novelist merited only qualified appreciation remained the dominant view until the outbreak of the Second World War. A notable change in attitudes began to occur at that time, brought about by two essayists who were not themselves part of academe, but whose influence over the study of literature can hardly be overestimated: the Englishman George Orwell and the American Edmund Wilson.

Orwell's essay on Dickens first appeared in his collection *Inside the Whale* in 1940, and was reprinted in the widely circulated *Dickens, Dali and Others* (1946). Orwell seeks to answer two important questions. The first is one of critical evaluation: "Where exactly does [Dickens] stand, socially, morally, and politically?" (3). The second, however, is both more personal and in some ways more profound: "Why does anyone care about Dickens? Why do *I* care?" (57). In answering the first, Orwell offers an observation that elevates the Victorian novelist above the ranks of the mere entertainers: "Dickens's criticism of society" in his novels "is almost exclusively moral" (5). While he seldom offers specific suggestions for improving the world around him, Orwell notes, Dickens is intent on exposing corruption, hoping that a "change of spirit" (22) might lead to reformation. He was a proponent of progress, as others have suggested; but, Orwell says, "when he speaks of progress, it is usually in terms of *moral* progress," not advances in technology. He was not, Orwell insists, a revolutionary; in fact, Dickens "is very sure revolution is a monster" (14). As he grew older, though, he became increasingly despondent because he felt society was beyond reformation, and his novels became darker as his hopes for change faded.

Much of Orwell's essay is given over to examining Dickens's limitations and faults. Orwell believes Dickens was a product of his middle-class upbringing, and hence did not understand the aristocracy or the very poor. Despite Dickens's frequent depictions of criminals, Orwell finds he does not really appreciate these social outcasts. While he admired the working poor, he did not really understand their lives. "A thing that strikes one when one looks beneath the surface of Dickens's books is that, as nineteenth-century novelists go, he is rather ignorant" about the details of the world of work; as a consequence, "work" always happens "off-stage" (45). Orwell faults Dickens for his poorly constructed plots, but he is less bothered by the lack of structure than critics such as E. M. Forster and Henry James.

Still, Orwell has a sense that his criticisms will not be appreciated by Dickens devotees. At a point two-thirds of the way through his essay, he observes that "By this time, anyone who is a lover of Dickens" will "probably be angry with me" (58). But Orwell insists Dickens deserves to be read, not for his message, which may be remote to modern audiences, but for his methods. Dickens is a master at creating memorable characters and circumstances. He is at his best, Orwell says, in his digressions. "The outstanding, unmistakable mark of Dickens's writing is the *unnecessary detail*" (59). He is a writer "whose parts are greater than his wholes. He is all fragments, all details" (65). Orwell says Dickens may break all so-called rules of plotting, characterization, or realism, and still deserve readers' attention. In the final analysis, Orwell says, "There are no rules in novel-writing, and for any work of art there is only one test worth bothering about — survival" (68). That Dickens has survived for seventy years after his death is sufficient testament to his greatness. Orwell offers a final thought on the reasons for Dickens's continuing relevance. While "no grown-up person can read Dickens without feeling his limitations," the novelist's "native generosity, which acts as a kind of anchor" seems to keep him "where he belongs" (73). Dickens continues to matter to modern readers because, despite any faults, he remains the great celebrator of "the native decency of the common man" (74). With Orwell's blessing, it was now acceptable for the educated classes to read Dickens without apology.

What Orwell did for Dickens's reputation in England, Edmund Wilson did in America. Though not affiliated with any university, Wilson was widely respected as a literary critic, so it was no surprise that he created a revolution in Dickens studies in 1940 with three brief articles in the *New Republic*. The following year he combined and expanded them into the opening chapter of *The Wound and the Bow* (1941). Choosing the evocative title "Dickens: The Two Scrooges," Wilson argues persuasively that Dickens has been unjustly maligned by lovers of modern novelists and generally misunderstood even by his most ardent admirers. The key to appreciating his novels, Wilson says, is in understanding the novelist's life — a life characterized by rejection, disappointment, and restlessness that find expression in the fiction that made him famous.

Most of Wilson's commentary is a survey of the novels in which he stresses the relationship between Dickens's life and his art. The writer emerges from Wilson's study as a tormented soul at odds with his society and himself. Claiming Dickens "was probably the most antagonistic" among his contemporaries "to the Victorian Age itself" (29), Wilson sees in his career a growing sense of frustration with the hypocrisy and materialism he witnessed around him. But Wilson manages to celebrate Dickens as a social critic without turning him into a Communist, refusing to brand him as T. A. Jackson did as a radical completely beyond the mainstream. Instead, Wilson explains how the fiction becomes a release for torments Dickens was forced to undergo. He also believes Dickens is a master of psychological portraiture, improving as his career advanced. By Wilson's lights, the later, darker novels are superior to earlier efforts, largely because they reflect the multiple levels on which Dickens found himself estranged.

While Wilson may not have been the first to celebrate the dark, alienated Dickens, his essay seemed to establish that view — at least in America — as the dominant one. For the next four decades, virtually every critic wishing to explain something of Dickens's genius as a writer found it necessary to acknowledge a debt to Wilson. It would not be an overstatement to say that Wilson ushered in a new era in Dickens criticism, one that in a sense gave permission to critics armed with the tools of formalism and psychology to explore the novelist's work. "Dickens: The Two Scrooges" showed it was possible to find modern relevance in the work of the most celebrated Victorian novelist — if one simply took time to look for it.

Notes

[1] In contrast to Jackson, with his lengthy treatise on Dickens's latent communist tendencies, the man often considered the father of modern Marxist literary criticism, Georg Lukács, had little to say about Dickens. But in *The Historical Novel*, a work that appeared in German in 1955 but not in English until 1962, the Hungarian philosopher laments that "even with a writer of Dickens's rank the weaknesses of his petty bourgeois humanism and idealism are more obvious and obtrusive in his historical novel of the French Revolution [*A Tale of Two Cities*] than in his social novels." Dickens's weakness, Lukács says, is in his insistence on separating the human and moral aspects of life from the social forces that drive individual actions. What makes these comments noteworthy, despite their brevity, is the fact that they contradict the claims of earlier Marxists such as Jackson, who see Dickens as a revolutionary, not a member of the bourgeoisie.

Works Cited

Baker, Ernest A. *The Age of Dickens and Thackeray.* Vol. 7 of *The History of the English Novel.* London: H. F. and G. Witherby, 1936.

Beach, Joseph W. *The Twentieth Century Novel: Studies in Technique.* New York: Century, 1932.

Belloc, Hillaire. "Dickens Revisited." *New Statesman* 28 (January 1927): 444–45.

Boas, Guy. "Charles Dickens To-day." *Blackwood's Magazine* 245 (March 1939): 314–26.

Burton, Richard. *Charles Dickens: How to Know Him.* Indianapolis: Bobbs-Merrill, 1919.

Cason, Clarence E. "Charles Dickens in America To-day." *Literary Digest International Book Review* 4 (September 1926): 603–7.

Cecil, Lord David. "Charles Dickens." *Early Victorian Novelists,* 27–63. London: Constable, 1934; Indianapolis: Bobbs-Merrill, 1935. Reprinted in *Victorian Novelists: Essays in Revaluation.* Chicago: Chicago UP, 1958.

Christie, O. F. *Dickens and His Age.* London: H. Cranton, 1939. Reprint, New York: Phaeton Press, 1974.

Collins, Norman. "Charles Dickens." *The Facts of Fiction,* 155–65. New York: Dutton, 1933.

Crotch, W. Walter. *The Secret of Dickens.* London: Chapman & Hall, 1919. Reprint, New York: Haskell House, 1972.

Dark, Sidney. *Charles Dickens.* London: T. Nelson, 1919. Reprint, New York: Haskell House, 1975.

Darwin, Bernard. *Dickens.* London: Duckworth; New York: Macmillan, 1933. Reprint, New York: Haskell House, 1973.

Dickens, Sir Henry F. *Memories of My Father.* London: Gollancz, 1928; New York: Duffield, 1929.

Dickens, Mary. *Charles Dickens by His Eldest Daughter.* London: Cassell, 1885. Reprinted as *My Father as I Knew Him.* London: Roxburghe Press, 1897. Reprint, New York: Harmon & Irwin, 1928.

Edgar, Pelham. *The Art of the Novel from 1700 to the Present Time.* New York: Macmillan, 1933. Reprint, New York: Russell & Russell, 1965.

Eliot, T. S. "Wilkie Collins and Dickens." *Times Literary Supplement* (4 August 1927): 525–26. Reprinted in *Selected Essays, 1917–1932.* New York: Harcourt, Brace, 1932, new ed. 1950.

Elton, Oliver. "Charles Dickens." *Survey of English Literature: 1830–1880,* 194–221. Vol. 2. London: E. Arnold, 1920. Rev. and reprinted in *Dickens and Thackeray.* London: E. Arnold, 1924.

Ford, Ford Madox. *The English Novel: From the Earliest Days to the Death of Joseph Conrad.* London: Lippincott, 1930.

Forster, E. M. *Aspects of the Novel.* London: E. Arnold, 1927.

Forster, John. *The Life of Charles Dickens.* London: Chapman & Hall, 1872–74. Boston: Osgood, 1875. Reprint, London: Palmer, 1928.

Galsworthy, John. "Six Novelists in Profile." *Castles in Spain and Other Screeds,* 201–35. New York: Scribner, 1927. Reprinted in *Candelabra.* New York: Scribner, 1933.

Huxley, Aldous. "The Vulgarity of Little Nell." *Vulgarity in Literature,* 54–59. London: Chatto & Windus, 1930. Reprinted in *Music at Night and Other Essays.* London: Chatto & Windus, 1931.

Jackson, Thomas A. *Charles Dickens: The Progress of a Radical.* London: Lawrence and Wishart, 1937; New York: International, 1938. Reprint, New York: Haskell House, 1971.

Kidd, H. H. "Is Dickens Still A Hero?" *South Atlantic Quarterly* 26 (July 1927): 280–89.

Kingsmill, Hugh [Hugh Kingsmill Lunn]. *The Sentimental Journey: A Life of Charles Dickens.* London: Wishart, 1934; New York: William Morrow, 1935.

Kitton, Frederic G. *Charles Dickens, His Life, Writings and Personality.* London: T. C. and E. C. Jack, 1902.

Laski, Harold. "In Praise of Dickens." *Daily Herald* (24 December 1932).

Leacock, Stephen. *Charles Dickens: His Life and Work.* London: Davies, 1933; New York: Doubleday, Doran, 1934.

———. "Fiction and Reality: A Study of the Art of Charles Dickens." *Essays and Literary Studies,* 159–88. London: John Lane, 1916.

Leavis, F. R. *The Great Tradition.* London: Chatto & Windus, 1948.

Leavis, Q. D. *Fiction and the Reading Public.* London: Chatto & Windus, 1932.

Ley, J. W. T. "Dickens and Our Allies." *Dickensian* 11 (November 1915): 285–90.

———. *The Dickens Circle: A Narrative of the Novelist's Friendships.* London: Chapman & Hall; New York: Dutton, 1919.

———. "History of the *Dickensian.*" *Dickensian* 22 (January 1926): 11–22, 121–29.

Lovett, R. M. and H. S. Hughes. *The History of the Novel in England.* Boston: Houghton Mifflin, 1932.

Lubbock, Percy. *The Craft of Fiction*. London: J. Cape, 1921.

Lukács, Georg. *The Historical Novel*. Translated by Hannah and Stanley Mitchell. London: Merlin Press, 1962.

Maurois, André. *Dickens, His Life and Work*. Translated by Hamish Miles. London: J. Lane, 1934.

———. "The Philosophy of Dickens." *Forum* 81 (January 1929): 54–59.

Miller, J. Hillis. *Charles Dickens: The World of His Novels*. Cambridge, MA: Harvard UP, 1958. Reprint, Bloomington: Indiana UP, 1969; Cambridge, MA: Harvard UP, 1974.

Muir, Edwin. "The Dark Felicities of Charles Dickens." *Essays on Literature and Society*, 206–14. Cambridge, MA: Harvard UP, 1965.

———. *The Structure of the Novel*. London: L. and V. Woolf, 1928; New York: Harcourt, Brace, 1929.

Murry, John Middleton. "The Dickens Revival." *Times* 19 (May 1922): 16.

Orwell, George. "Charles Dickens." *Inside the Whale*, 9–85. London: Gollancz, 1940. Reprinted in *Critical Essays*. London: Secker & Warburg, 1946; *Dickens, Dali and Others*. New York: Reynal and Hitchcock, 1946; *A Collection of Essays*. New York: Doubleday, 1954; *Collected Essays*. London: Secker & Warburg, 1961.

Phillips, Walter C. *Dickens, Reade and Collins: Sensation Novelists*. New York: Columbia UP, 1919. Reprint, New York: Russell and Russell, 1962.

Powys, John C. "Dickens." *Visions and Revisions*, 119–31. New York: Shaw, 1915. Reprint, London: Macdonald, 1955.

———. *Enjoyment of Literature*, 321–41. New York: Simon and Schuster, 1938. Reprinted in *Pleasures of Literature*, 321–41. London: Cassell, 1938.

Quiller-Couch, Sir Arthur T. *Charles Dickens and Other Victorians*. Cambridge: Cambridge UP, 1925.

Rainey, Lillian F. "Dickens Up To Date." *Century* 3 (February 1926): 504–6.

Santayana, George. "Dickens." *Dial* 71 (November 1921): 537–49. Reprinted in *Soliloquies in England and Later Soliloquies*. New York: Scribner, 1922. Reprint, Ann Arbor: U of Michigan P, 1967.

Sitwell, Sir Osbert. *Dickens*. London: Chatto & Windus, 1932. Reprint, New York: Haskell House, 1973.

———. "Dickens and the Modern Novel." *Trio: Dissertations on Some Aspects of National Genius*, 1–45. London: Macmillan, 1938.

Strachey, Lytton. *Eminent Victorians*. New York and London: G. P. Putnam's Sons, 1918.

Straus, Ralph. *Charles Dickens: A Portrait in Pencil.* London: Gollancz, 1928. Issued as *Charles Dickens: A Biography from New Sources.* New York: Cosmopolitan Books, 1928.

———. *Dickens: The Man and the Book.* London: Nelson, 1936.

Wagenknecht, Edward. *Cavalcade of the English Novel*, 173–268. New York: Holt, Rinehart and Winston, 1943.

———. *The Man Charles Dickens: A Victorian Portrait.* Boston: Houghton Mifflin, 1929. Rev. ed. Norman: U of Oklahoma P, 1966.

———. "Review of Recent Dickens Literature." *Virginia Quarterly Review* 10 (July 1934): 455–59.

Weygandt, Cornelius. *A Century of the English Novel.* New York: The Century Co., 1925.

Williams, Orlo. *Some Great English Novels: Studies in the Art of Fiction.* London: Macmillan, 1926.

Wilson, Edmund. "Dickens: The Two Scrooges." *New Republic* 102 (March 1940): 297–300, 339–42. Reprinted, revised and enlarged, in *The Wound and the Bow: Seven Studies in Literature.* Boston: Houghton, Mifflin, 1941. Reprinted in *Eight Essays.* New York: Doubleday, 1954.

Woolf, Virginia. "*David Copperfield.*" *Nation and Athenaeum* 37 (August 1925): 620–21. Reprinted in *The Moment and Other Essays.* London: Hogarth, 1947. Reprinted in *Collected Essays*, vol. 1. London: Hogarth, 1966.

Wright, Thomas. *The Life of Charles Dickens.* London: H. Jenkins, 1935.

Zweig, Stefan. "Charles Dickens." Translated by Kenneth Burke. *Dial* 74 (January 1923): 1–24. Reprinted in *Three Masters.* Translated by Eden and Cesar Paul. New York: Viking, 1930.

4: The Tide Turns (1940–1959)

IN REVIEWING GEORGE FORD'S *Dickens and His Readers* in 1955, Edgar Johnson observed that, "Few things are more dangerous to an author's later fame" than for him "to have won great acclaim and, worse yet, popularity in his lifetime." That nearly guarantees a negative reaction from the next generation, often for no better reason than to express its independence from their elders. But often, Johnson says, "some decades later still, the critical tide turns again, and something like the old reputation may be restored, even enhanced by subtler shades of appreciation than it had formerly enjoyed" ("Turning Tides" 644). The seminal revaluations of Orwell and Wilson in 1940 ushered in just such a reversal in Dickens's fortunes among the critics — a reversal that began during the tumultuous years when Europe was ablaze with war, and that has lasted, with few exceptions, into the twenty-first century.

As had occurred during the First World War, after hostilities began again in 1939, the British public was encouraged to seek solace in the pages of a Dickens novel in times of great stress. In "Return to Dickens," an article that appeared in a 1940 issue of the *St. Martin's Review,* the publication of St. Martin's Church, official church of the Admiralty, Bernard Darwin recommends Dickens as an escape from the harsh realities of war. Darwin calls the novelist "an old and familiar friend" (30). He encourages people to read Dickens's novels because they have "no plot, or none that any reasonable being can remember for five minutes at a time," and because he is "long," which is advantageous for those who have "more and longer evenings in which to read" (30). Darwin considers Dickens an escapist novelist, never writing about soldiers or wars. Best of all, Darwin says, he is "the apostle of snugness," one whose work can be appreciated by curling up in front of a roaring fire (31). The literary purist may cringe at these suggestions, but one need only to look "fore and aft," to borrow a naval term, to see what Darwin was up to. The article preceding "Return to Dickens" in the *Review* is R. H. Mottram's "A Tonic for the Times," in which the author encourages reading great English authors as a means of coping with the madness of the war. In the one that follows Darwin's essay, "Munitions of the Spirit," Albert Mansbridge argues for the need to practice religion during the war. Like a good Englishman, Dickens is being pressed into service once again to fight those who would destroy the British way of life.

The Dickens Fellowship continued to be active in promoting study of the novelist, and lifelong devotees like the poet Alfred Noyes did what they could to advance his stature. His 1940 volume *Pageant of Letters* contains an essay on Dickens originally delivered as an address to the Dickens Fellowship. Prepared as the war raged in England, the lecture-turned-essay stresses Dickens's modernity. Reprising the language of many publications of the First World War era, Noyes says that "the world has never been in such tragic need for [Dickens's] just and gentle heart, his broad and deep humanity, his tenderness for the weak" (162). At a time when Europe is in danger of being dehumanized, "Dickens comes like a wealth of redeeming sanity through the raucous yelling of a madhouse" (184). Dickens is relevant, Noyes says, because he speaks to his readers about values they cherish. Noyes does devote some attention to matters of literary criticism as well, noting "the art of Dickens deserves a far closer study on its technical side than it has yet received" (170).

Noyes's call for serious study was already being heeded in America. Participants at a 1939 meeting of the Victorian Group of the Modern Language Association decided the time was right to provide a "reinterpretation of a literature of great significance to us today," because, as editor Joseph Baker says in his preface to the resulting book, *The Reinterpretation of Victorian Literature,* "the writers of Victorian England first tried to salvage humane culture for a new world of science, democracy, and industrialism" (4). Though the book did not appear until 1950, it reflects trends in Dickens scholarship during the decade between the conference and its publication. However unprompt, the scholars who collaborated with Baker brought to their task both skills and attitudes that set them apart from the generation of critics who rose to prominence during and after the First World War. Ostensibly freed from the prejudices that had caused people of an earlier generation to view all things Victorian with disdain, the new breed sought to discover whether previous generations had been wrong about writers like Dickens. Bradford Booth's essay in the collection, "Forms and Techniques in the Novel," celebrates the vision and technical accomplishments of Victorian novelists in general, claiming the so-called "advance" of the novel in the twentieth century has been seriously overrated. While "some subtilization of technique and form" has occurred, there has been in his view "no marked intensification of overall merit" (67). Booth defends Dickens from detractors — some of whom he calls "critical vultures" (75) — claiming Dickens was a conscious craftsman whose faults can all be ascribed to the demands placed on him by "the vicious influence of serial publication" (76). Booth is willing to admit the novelist was sometimes too quick to give in to public demand for happy stories, but he insists Dickens is a master of characterization.

Before the war it was unusual to find an Oxford don displaying any scholarly interest in Dickens; Humphry House was the exception. Working in an atmosphere where Dickens may have been read for entertainment but was certainly not thought worthy of scholarly study, House painstakingly began research on the novelist and his age. His initial work culminated in the publication of *The Dickens World* in 1941, a book that was to become one of the classics in Dickens studies. Noting that "in recent years nearly all of the most valuable work" on Dickens "has been biographical" (11), House focuses his attention in another direction. His principal aim, he says, is "to show in a broad and simple way the connexion between what Dickens wrote and the times in which he wrote it, between his reformism and some of the things he wanted reformed, between the attitude to life shown in his books and the society in which he lived" (14). House challenges the prevailing notion that Dickens was not a mature thinker or social reformer, describing ways he used his own experiences, especially those from his childhood, to craft novels that exposed social ills. House points out how Dickens was influenced by the ideas of Jeremy Bentham, although not by the work of many of Bentham's disciples. Contradicting Orwell's assertion that Dickens knew little about the workplace, House also reveals how much Dickens was fascinated by the world of work, suggesting that in the novels "work plays an essential part in the characters' approach to life" (55). Though this assertion would be challenged by future critics, House was the first to observe that "the minute attention to the business of life gives Dickens's novels their immense solidity" (58). He is also among the first to pay attention to Dickens's use of religion, which he says was "one of the chief causes of his success as a popular moralist and reformer." Dickens managed to strike "a good religious note," House says, "without committing himself beyond the common stock of Christian phrases" (110).

House takes specific exception to the portraits of the novelist created by Jackson and Chesterton. "A great deal has been written and said about Dickens as a writer for 'the people,'" House notes. "Yet his chief public was among the middle classes, rather than among the proletariat." House thinks Dickens was not "the leader of a kind of 'peasants' revolt in Bloomsbury," nor was he — as Jackson claimed — "devoted to the uniting of the workers of the world" (152). He believes Dickens was perfectly comfortable with the class system in England, although he railed against abuses within that system. Dickens attacked many political schemes he thought wrongheaded and criticized people engaged in politics; but all the while, House asserts, he supported the general premises on which the English system of government was based. He promoted reform, not revolution.

House's concentration on the content of the novels and on the relationship of fictional events to real-world people, events, and ideas has the danger of making Dickens's work something more akin to journalism than fiction. House anticipates this objection and provides a clever response. Dickens was a journalist all his life, House says, if one means by that a chronicler of the people and events of the age; in that sense, Dickens "was in fact a journalist of the finest kind" (215). Frequently quoted by other scholars, challenged by no less a Dickens critic than J. Hillis Miller, *The Dickens World* instantly became the standard for sociological criticism against which subsequent works would be measured. House's work had a further distinction. It was the first scholarly book exclusively devoted to Dickens published by Oxford University Press.

Of course, most students of the 1940s learned of Dickens not from books like House's or scholarly journals but from surveys and histories of literature. What they were learning can be seen in publications such as Ifor Evans's *A Short History of English Literature* (1940). Evans tells readers Dickens is certainly "the greatest novelist that England has yet produced," but — and this is a very significant "but" — he was "hampered by his age, which demanded sentiment and reticence." Evans suggests that had he not been so constrained but instead received "the encouragement of a less squeamish age," Dickens "might have been Shakespearean" (170). Dickens knew much more than he was able to reveal in his fiction. He wrote about the virtues of cheerfulness and love because that would please his readers. But Evans insists he was temperamentally alienated from the society that lionized him. This notion would gain traction among critics as the decade progressed.

Another sweeping survey of fiction, Gordon Gerould's *The Patterns of English and American Fiction* (1942) attempts to apply formalist theory to fiction without becoming bogged down in terminology. Hoping to help more readers understand the development of fiction, Gerould attempts to avoid "various critical terms in common use, such as 'realistic' and 'psychological'" and to use "plain language" (vi) in reviewing the careers of individual writers to discern the patterns and themes that emerge and recur over the centuries. He argues the popularity Dickens achieved as a humorist masks his real artistic talent. Like many other critics, Gerould laments Dickens's occasional descent to cheap tricks for evoking pity or sympathy, and his tendency to cater too much to popular demands. Gerould's Dickens is the unlettered tyro made popular by Chesterton, a writer bent on social reform but with "no ordered philosophy of life," who "steered his course by intuition and knowledge won through keen observation" (267). Though his style is "ragged and uneven," it is frequently "touched by genius" (267). Gerould's judgments may not seem original, but his work is important for those interested in the history of Dickens criticism because Gerould was a professor at Princeton, and his published views indicate what undergraduates were learning about Dickens at the time his survey appeared.

Students were no doubt also influenced by Edward Wagenknecht's strident defense of Dickens in *Cavalcade of the English Novel* (1943), in which Wagenknecht claims to be interested in literature rather than "the factors by which it is conditioned" (vii). Wagenknecht cleverly describes Dickens's "place among novelists" as akin to "that of the woman in the Gospels who was a sinner. Much is forgiven him because he loved much. He has enough faults to sink a whole flotilla of lesser writers" (213).

Wagenknecht's own judgments regarding Dickens's fiction had not changed much since the publication of his first major commentary on the novelist, *The Man Charles Dickens* (1929). What had changed was the state of Dickens criticism. Despite his protestations that "insofar as there has ever been any critical reaction against him, it has now spent its force utterly" (213), Wagenknecht finds it necessary to address some of the critical studies that appeared between 1929 and 1943 — and he seems to have little use for much of what he has read. Reaching back even farther into the history of Dickens criticism, he takes issue with George Bernard Shaw's assessment that *Little Dorrit* is the best Dickens has to offer to help more readers understand the development of fiction. Those "interested in literature primarily for its propaganda values" would naturally reach that conclusion, but "a more disinterested judgment" would see the novel as "the titanic effort of a very tired man" (218). As for Edmund Wilson's 1940 essay ("Dickens: The Two Scrooges"), it is "a completely irresponsible piece of criticism" (218). Although Wagenknecht catalogs a number of Dickens's shortcomings, he has little use for virtually anyone else who finds fault with the novelist: "Most of the unfortunate people who are unable to like Dickens would grant much of what I have so far written. But, they would add, all this shows he was second-rate" (224). For Wagenknecht, it is not Dickens but these critics who are decidedly second-rate.

The idea of Dickens as alienated from Victorian society began to catch on quickly with a group of critics who saw this as a way of rescuing the novelist from charges that he was too much the spokesperson for Victorian values. One of the first to follow Wilson along that line of reasoning was Lionel Stevenson. His essay "Dickens's Dark Novels" (1943) examines three of the later novels to explain how external political forces combined with the trauma of personal crises to influence Dickens in writing what Stevenson considers some of his most powerful fiction. Another is V. S. Pritchett, author of two articles on Dickens in the *New Statesman* (1944, 1946), who says in *The Living Novel* (1946) that "the whole of Dickens's emotional radicalism, his hatred of the utilitarians and philanthropists and all his attacks on institutions, are based on his strongest and fiercest sense:

isolation" (88). Rex Warner follows the same line of reasoning in *The Cult of Power* (1946). Claiming Dickens is being left unread by his fellow Englishmen, Warner challenges both the formalists and the psychological critics who dismiss Dickens or misinterpret him to reevaluate his work. He has little use for the categories established by E. M. Forster for judging a novel's value; in his view, Dickens is great in the same way Fielding and Smollett are, even if he does not provide the kind of complex characterization as, say, Samuel Richardson. Further, Warner says, while he may have written for a Victorian audience, "to imagine Dickens as tainted" with the prevailing vices of the period "is really nonsensical" (35). Dickens was adept at pointing out the hypocrisies of his age. His optimism is not a fault, but rather his way of acknowledging his faith in human nature while still recognizing human fallibility. While Warner calls his own work a minority report, by the late 1940s his view was hardly that of the minority in academic circles.

However, amidst all the newly discovered strengths of the novelist, what seemed like a truly minority opinion on Dickens was issued by the influential and highly opinionated Cambridge scholar F. R. Leavis. The author of several books of literary and cultural criticism, Leavis had founded the journal *Scrutiny* in 1932. By the late 1940s he was the recognized leader of a conservative group of literary critics who combined techniques of close reading with a belief in the critical tradition championed by Matthew Arnold nearly a century earlier. In 1947 Leavis authored an essay on *Hard Times* for *Scrutiny* to inaugurate a series he titled "The Novel as Dramatic Poem." A year later he published his influential work *The Great Tradition* (1948), in which he states unequivocally that "the great English novelists are Jane Austen, George Eliot, Henry James, and Joseph Conrad" (1). Dickens is dismissed almost without comment until the last pages of the study, where Leavis appends the essay on *Hard Times*.

Why exclude Dickens? The answer lies in Leavis's approach to the novel, one that follows principles espoused by Arnold and Henry James and subscribed to by, among others, E. M. Forster, Percy Lubbock, and New Humanists such as Paul Elmer More. Leavis knows he will be charged with being too narrow in his definition of greatness, but he argues that distinctions are needed at this point in the development of critical studies because "the present vogue" (1) in evaluating works of the Victorian age is leading to what he considers wrongheaded judgments. Like Arnold and T. S. Eliot, Leavis is exceptionally discriminating, and he is hard on critics who do not agree with his demanding criteria for assessing literary merit. However, Leavis is not quite as harsh as his own critics have suggested; he does have good things to say about other novelists, including Dickens, but he guards jealously the territory he has staked out as the arena where greatness dwells.

It may be easier to see why Dickens does not make Leavis's list of great novelists by examining the criteria Leavis established for judging a novelist's achievements. The writers he places in the first rank "not only change the possibilities of art for practitioners and readers," they are also "significant in terms of the human awareness they promote: awareness of the possibilities of life" (2). "The great novelists," he says, are "all very much concerned with 'form'; they are all very original technically" (7). Dickens is, by implication, not in that group. Leavis admits Conrad was influenced by Dickens, but in distinguishing the pupil from his teacher Leavis explains why Conrad is more worthy to be called a great novelist. Conrad, he says, handles his materials in such a way that "the end is a total significance of a profoundly serious kind." Dickens simply never reaches this level of sophistication. "That Dickens was a great genius and is permanently among the classics is certain," Leavis admits. "But the genius was that of a great entertainer, and he had for the most part no profounder responsibility as a creative artist than this description suggests." As a result, "the adult mind" does not find in Dickens "an unusual and sustained seriousness" (19). Curiously, the one place Leavis finds Dickens approaching this level of seriousness is in *Hard Times*. Leavis claims "the prose" in this novel is "that of one of the great masters of English, and the dialogue — very much a testing for such an undertaking — is consummate; beautifully natural in its stylization." Unfortunately, Leavis concludes, "there is only one *Hard Times* in the Dickensian *oeuvre*" (20). With this judgment he relegates Dickens to the ranks of those unsophisticated geniuses who manage to entertain but not really enlighten readers.

It is hardly surprising to discover opinions of Dickens found in *Scrutiny* support Leavis's judgment. For example, in an earlier *Scrutiny* article R. C. Churchill says it is difficult to write about Dickens because so many critics have "attributed to their author their own opinion" of his character and merit, finding him at one time or another "a typical Victorian, a typical anti-Victorian, a Marxist, a Royalist" (*Importance* 182). Churchill believes, as Leavis does, that Dickens is a writer of uneven quality, identifying the source of that unevenness in Dickens's constant need to pander to his reading public.

Dickens continued to have his detractors outside academe as well. Somerset Maugham's 1948 *Atlantic Monthly* article on Dickens, reprinted in *Ten Novels and Their Authors* (1954), reinforces the notion that Dickens lacks "high seriousness." "I find myself still immensely amused by his humor," Maugham says of Dickens, "but his pathos leaves me cold" (144). Dickens does not do a good job portraying reality, Maugham concludes, but his work is nevertheless entertaining — hardly a ringing endorsement of Dickens's artistic ability.

The fluctuating nature of Dickens's reputation is reflected in an interesting postwar account of Dickens by the poet, critic, and historian Richard Aldington. In "The Underworld of Young Dickens," in his *Four English Portraits* (1948), Aldington chooses Dickens as a representative of the emerging middle class, familiar with the lower classes but ultimately unable to appreciate the upper classes. Aldington's account of Dickens's life is hardly groundbreaking, and he seems to subscribe to late nineteenth-century attitudes about biography and art. He considers the early novels Dickens's best work, claiming that "as a serious novelist Dickens is inadequate, timid and prudish when compared with Balzac and Flaubert" (177), in general placing Dickens somewhere between faultless and worthless — admitting, however, that Dickens and other writers would be best served if critics would realize that "no generation — still less an individual critic — is competent to act as a final court of appeal" when "passing judgment on the faults of a writer" (148).

At mid-century, a new round of "history of the English novel" surveys appeared, some written by scholars whose insights were formed by the older, humanistic traditions of Arnoldian scholarship, others by proponents of newer formalist methodologies. Whatever their critical predispositions, many were also influenced by the revisionist thinking that had characterized study of the Victorians for at least the past two decades. A brief comparison of surveys published at the mid-point of the twentieth century with those published a half-century earlier reveals how high Dickens's star had risen. Whereas George Saintsbury had only begrudgingly admitted Dickens into the company of important fiction writers, Walter Allen has great praise for him in *The English Novel: A Short Critical History* (1954) and *Six English Novelists* (1955), in which Allen praises Dickens for his "exuberant energy of creation" (95). His assessment in *The English Novel* attempts to answer specifically the criticisms leveled against Dickens by George Santayana and F. R. Leavis. Comparing him to Shakespeare — unthinkable to Saintsbury — Allen says it is "absurd to explain genius" (98). Allen does not consider Dickens's characters to be caricatures, but rather claims his portraits emerge from a childlike vision of the world.

Arnold Kettle writes in his historical survey *An Introduction to the English Novel* (1951) that previous critics of the novel "appear to have shirked, with a few notable exceptions, the business of analysis and of disciplined critical evaluation" (7). What he means by this is that others have not been sufficiently explicit in explaining the kinds of novels that have been produced. Curiously, he selects *Oliver Twist* to illustrate Dickens's methodology. Given that choice, it is not surprising that he finds Dickens no realist, at least, not in the sense that Jane Austen is. Instead Kettle sees him as a symbolist rather than a social historian. The poor plotting he discovers in *Oliver Twist* does not seem to detract from its impact, however, as "the truth and depth of the central vision are such that a vitality is generated which struggles against and survives the plot" (138).

Richard Church's *The Growth of the English Novel* (1951) is organized around the controlling idea expressed in its title. Church makes this clear even in his chapter headings, calling individual sections by names such as "The Seed Bed" and "Four Mighty Limbs." Dickens is placed among the "Kings of the Forest," and Church's effusive, non-scholarly discussion continues the clichés of earlier, favorable critics: "No novelist has had more direct influence as a reformer," he repeats, and "in all his instincts [Dickens] was democratic," working "through instinct rather than through reason" (122). Apparently unaware of the generally favorable treatment emerging in scholarly journals, Church feels compelled to tell readers that "Dickens stands at the head of all our novelists, in spite of what the higher critics might say, and in spite too of our own personal reservations" (123).

In her survey *The English Novel: Form and Function* (1953) Dorothy Van Ghent includes a critique of *Great Expectations* in which she focuses on Dickens's use of language. As she had done in her oft-reprinted *Sewanee Review* article "The Dickens World: A View From Todgers'" (1950), Van Ghent concentrates on the way Dickens tends to isolate characters within their own language, a technique reflecting his view that "human separatedness" is the ordinary condition of life (127). She is convinced that Dickens employs the pathetic fallacy and the principle of reification to highlight the inhuman traits of many of his characters. Her examination of these and other stylistic qualities leads her to a conclusion that directly contradicts the one reached by Walter Allen. Van Ghent insists Dickens had a dark vision of a world turned upside down, a vision best realized in his later novels.

Finally, *The Mirror in the Roadway: A Study in the Modern Novel* (1956) is instructive not simply because it was written by the popular Irish writer Frank O'Connor (the pseudonym for Michael O'Donovan), but because it is based on a series of lectures given at Harvard during the 1953–1954 academic year, and hence reflects what students and the public were then being told about Victorian literature and about Dickens. O'Connor challenges the views held by early modernists regarding the aims of the novel, arguing instead that the genre emerged across Europe as a middle-class vehicle of art with realism as its hallmark — but realism broadly defined. "I suspect," he says, "that one real difficulty in dealing critically with Dickens and his contemporaries is that none of our critical approaches apply" because Victorian novelists frequently blended elements of realism and romance (72). However, O'Connor thinks Dickens responded too quickly to the demands of his public, thereby compromising his art. He was good at "handling the problems raised by the conversion of an extremely private art into a more public one," playing to his audience like a good actor (77). The "typical Dickens novel" is, in O'Connor's judgment, "a romance, usually with a romantic subplot, the whole thing padded out with scores of supernumeraries. The thinness of the romance is usually concealed by the richness of the different character parts" (79–80). Yet for all Dickens's faults, O'Connor admires him because he works with a great love of his craft and carries readers along by injecting the fairy-tale element into his novels.

New Biographies

Among the most significant developments in Dickens studies during the decade immediately following the Second World War was in the area of biography. For seventy years John Forster's *Life of Charles Dickens* stood as the standard account of the novelist's life. Virtually every subsequent biography was somehow derivative of Forster's exhaustive narrative, notwithstanding Wright's additions regarding Dickens's relationship with Ellen Ternan. In 1945, however, Una Pope-Hennessy published *Charles Dickens*, the first biography based on the recently published three-volume Nonesuch Edition of Dickens's letters. Pope-Hennessy is quick to give credit to Forster, whose work she calls "the first and greatest book on Dickens" (x), but she extends his commentary significantly by using letters which Forster did not have or chose not to use in constructing his account of Dickens's life. Like Forster, Pope-Hennessy is captivated by her subject, calling Dickens "a great seer as well as a very great novelist" (xii). In fact, if there is a notable fault in this otherwise carefully documented piece of modern scholarship, it is Pope-Hennessy's insistence that Dickens was not only a genius but a martyr who rose from the humiliations of the blacking factory to achieve a social standing few writers could rival. Refuting the contentions of earlier biographers, Pope-Hennessy believes Dickens's work as a parliamentary reporter made him quite familiar with the upper classes — and at the same time instilled in him a zeal for reform.

Early in her book, Pope-Hennessy sets up Catherine Hogarth as the person responsible for the failure of her marriage to Dickens. Dickens's growing social success indeed took a toll on his marriage, but Pope-Hennessy lays fault for the strain with his wife. Likewise, Pope-Hennessy excuses his behavior in his dealings with his various publishers, ascribing difficulties to Dickens's misplaced loyalties or to "one of those nervous and temperamental breakdowns which overtook him whenever things became vexacious or disappointing" (237). She is willing to admit he had a mercurial temper that made personal relationships difficult at times, but in her view "his temperament cannot be accounted for; it is only possible to state how it operated" (86). Later biographers would spend considerable effort to provide just such an accounting.

"Even now, it is not generally recognized," Pope-Hennessy says, "the high price [Dickens] had to pay for his triumphs and successes" (248). A Romantic by nature, he was unusually affected by events such as the humiliation of working in the blacking factory, the rejection by Maria Beadnell, and the death of Mary Hogarth. "Dickens had in an extreme degree a faculty that we only have in a lesser degree. Because of it he never, in spite of all his warm friendships, his high spirits, his acting, his huge successes, was a truly happy man" (276). This spirit of restlessness, touched on only obliquely by Forster and others, becomes a major theme in Pope-Hennessy's narrative.

Nowhere is Pope-Hennessy more disingenuous than in her discussion of Dickens's relationship with Ellen Ternan. She could not ignore it; Thomas Wright's biography had been out for more than a decade, and critics had already begun to speculate on the significance of that liaison on Dickens's fiction. "As far as Forster was concerned," Pope-Hennessy says, "Ellen Ternan did not exist and therefore could have had nothing to do with the separation" from his wife. Wright, who "made a specialty of discoveries in the private lives of the eminent" (401), had made it impossible for her to follow Forster's course. She seems hesitant to take on this task, however, portraying Dickens as a reluctant participant in the affair and labeling his sister-in-law Georgina a co-conspirator in the breakup of Dickens's marriage, managing to get Catherine ejected from the family circle while maintaining her own position in the household.

Pope-Hennessy's portrait of Dickens as a kind of Byronic hero whose life matched his fiction in its intensity and *angst* found a welcome audience among Dickens critics. Her characterization certainly rescued Dickens from the welter of anti-Victorian sentiment that marked the work of Hugh Kingsmill and Wright. Perhaps, however, she went too far in trying to justify all of the novelist's character flaws. Modern trends in biographical study were already moving toward a more balanced view of a subject. Even Hesketh Pearson's highly derivative biography, *Dickens: His Character, Comedy, and Career* (1949), presents a more even-handed if somewhat jaunty portrait of the novelist. Additionally, because Edgar Johnson's monumental biography appeared only seven years later, Pope-Hennessy's book was quickly relegated to a position of secondary importance among studies of the novelist's life.

Given the growth in psychological criticism in the twentieth century, it was only a matter of time before a full-scale psychological biography of Dickens would be published. Jack Lindsay calls *Charles Dickens: A Biographical and Critical Study* (1950) the first "serious attempt to grapple with his creative process" (5). Signaling to his readers the importance of his own work beyond the boundaries of literary criticism, Lindsay claims that Dickens, along with William Blake, "holds the key to the nature of our cultural crisis today" (5); to understand him is to gain some measure of control over the postwar troubles facing Western societies. Like most psychological critics, Lindsay looks for clues in Dickens's childhood that influenced his creative powers later in life. This is an especially fruitful exercise, Lindsay says, because "no important writer has drawn so continuously and directly on his personal experiences as Dickens. There is scarcely any gap between the experience and the creative image" (24). Like a good Freudian, Lindsay finds the key to understanding Dickens in his relationship with his mother, and to a lesser extent his father; his readings of the novels emphasize how the novelist transforms real-life disappointments and traumas into art. Lindsay asserts that Dickens, resentful of being excluded from his mother by her subsequent pregnancies but satisfied by his experiences in Chatham as a youngster, exhibits a psychological "death wish," a desire to "arrest life at the point of maximum harmony, maximum levity" (63) — accounting for his continuing fascination with children and his desire to create fairy-tale endings for even the most complex adult problems.

The story Lindsay tells does little to advance the accounts given by early biographers. For him, correct interpretation of biographical details is more important. For example, Lindsay argues that Dickens's compulsion to marry, a result of his unconscious need to recreate the fantasy he had built up about his early childhood years, drove him into a bad union with Catherine Hogarth. Throughout his adult life, Lindsay argues, Dickens was obsessed with economic pressures that he feared would sap his creativity, and these fears emerge in his novels. His mind, given to dreams and nightmares, became a storehouse of images that achieved symbolic dimensions in the fiction. Lindsay finds deep psychological significance in dreams, in images of clocks and trains, which represented for Dickens "avenging forces, a nemesis, a monster" (387), and in his obsession with murder.

Dickens was, in Lindsay's view, the "first writer in England after Shakespeare (except Blake) who is centrally and continuously aware of the problems of dissociation" (412), the struggle of the individual against an increasingly insensitive society. Lindsay's Dickens is a street fighter, a hero battling the impersonal forces of modernity. His true ancestors are not the eighteenth-century novelists but the great Romantic poets — and his descendants are the symbolists, both groups sharing with him the sense that "a new organic integration of art and life" was needed if society were to survive and thrive (417). The novelist's great achievement lies in his ability to turn personal trauma into art, to shape a vision for society from his individual anxieties and losses.

Close on the heels of Lindsay's book, the crime writer Julian Symons also published a psychological study, *Charles Dickens* (1951). In the first third of the book, a summary of the novelist's life, Symons says that some of Dickens's activities were "pathological" (24) and that he was, at his core, a manic depressive. As a result, much of what Dickens wrote was "emotional expression produced by relentless psychological necessity." Fortunately, Symons says, it is possible for the critic to separate the conscious from the unconscious elements of the fiction, revealing Dickens as an artist "struggling to make a rational world from his own passionate and apparently ceaseless exaltation and depression" (29). Symons's critical analysis follows the same line, mining the novels for evidence of Dickens's mania or depression. Symons sees Dickens as a man with a grudge against the world, a radical who felt constantly at odds with mainstream Victorian society. Especially in the later novels, Dickens "impales on the skewer of his own bitterness the bureaucracy that had rebuffed his work as a reformer, the aristocracy that had rejected him as a social equal, the friends and lovers who had failed to live in the fantasy world of his imagination" (43). In Symons's view, Dickens could never have succeeded as an artist because he was forced to conform to "the deadly conventions in literature demanded by his class" (82). Only the Victorians would have accepted the "pathetic creations" (82) Dickens provided; "certainly," Symons assures his readers, "they could not have been accepted, or expressed, in any other age" (83). Far from seeing Dickens as a great radical, Symons says that "consciously, Dickens desired nothing more than to be the spokesman for the rising Victorian bourgeoisie" (93). Only in his unconscious could he be the rebel that modernists really wanted — or hoped — to discover in his writings.

The reception of Lindsay's and Symons's books among Dickens scholars was predictably mixed. Not everyone was ready to accept the idea that any novelist, not even one as overtly disgruntled and restless as Dickens was known to have been, can best be explained as a jumble of neuroses that somehow combine to spur the creative imagination and are the real sources of genius. For two years, Lindsay's book, in particular, did command some attention, but when Edgar Johnson's biography appeared in 1952, Lindsay's became relegated to that group of books which receive an occasional obligatory citation but fail to maintain continuing notice among scholars.

By contrast, Johnson's *Charles Dickens: His Tragedy and Triumph* (1952) is not only a classic in Dickens studies, but a superb example of mid-century biography. The product of years of painstaking research that uncovered hundreds of documents tucked away in libraries and private collections, Johnson's two volumes run to nearly twelve hundred pages. Though clearly influenced by Forster's work, Johnson balances that narrative (which had privileged Forster's relationship with Dickens) with information from other sources, including the work of Pope-Hennessy. The metaphor of contrast suggested by Johnson's title is carried through in the narrative, and in the structure of the book itself, as Johnson interleaves chapters providing critical commentary on the novels and stories with those focused on the central narrative of Dickens's life. Throughout, Johnson strives for objectivity, trying to balance Dickens's successes with his faults — both literary and personal. Without straying too far from his sources, he attempts to enliven his narrative by dramatic scene-painting, constructed from letters, newspaper accounts and diaries that hint at the atmosphere surrounding key episodes in the novelist's life. The narrative is peppered with comments such as the one describing Dickens's feeling on the success of his reporting on Parliament: "How far behind now was the ten-years-past misery of the warehouse and the prison!" (66).

Like most critics of his day writing about fiction and poetry, Johnson seeks the underlying principles that unite the seemingly disparate events of Dickens's domestic and professional careers. He finds the "unifying thread of Dickens's entire career" in his "critical analysis of modern society and its problems," an analysis "hardly surpassed in grasp or scope either by his contemporaries or by any more recent novelists" (viii). There is more than an occasional hint of the influence of psychological criticism in Johnson's assessments, such as this description of Dickens's reaction to his breakup with Maria Beadnell: "The wounds of his defeat left him to heal as best he could," eventually discovering "two ways of sublimating his self-pity until they formed a characteristic psychological pattern. A grief or an annoyance, he found, could be exorcised by being magnified to such grotesque proportions that it exploded into the comic and was lost in laughter"; or, Johnson continues "the private emotion could be transcended by being used as a means of understanding and sympathizing with other living creatures" (81). This kind of analysis suggests the approach Johnson takes between Dickens's life and his fiction. While he does not read all the novels and stories as fictionalized autobiography, Johnson acknowledges what he considers Edmund Wilson's keen insight into Dickens's character and method of composition. Hence, throughout Johnson's work there is the strong suggestion that life and art were inexorably intertwined. Additionally, given his overarching thesis regarding Dickens as a social critic, Johnson finds evidence of this more serious strain even in the earliest comic work, going so far as to claim that in *Pickwick Papers, Oliver Twist,* and *Nicholas Nickleby* "there already runs the vein of social criticism that was to become dominant in Dickens's entire career" (273). Johnson is at his best as a critic when discussing later novels, where in chapters such as "The Anatomy of Society" he reveals how Dickens creates in *Bleak House* "the novel of the social group, used as an instrument of social criticism" (764).

Johnson does his best to describe Dickens the man with the same kind of analytical dispassion he applies to his critiques of the novels. The early chapters read like a Horatio Alger novel, as the boy suffering from poverty and humiliation rises to be the toast of England. But he is also careful to explore the restlessness that permeated Dickens's character, a quality Johnson suggests drove him to be ruthless in his business dealings, cruel toward his wife, and ever intent on recapturing the innocence of youth — as he imagined it should be, not necessarily as he lived it. On occasion, however, Johnson reveals himself to be an apologist for Dickens, as in his comments regarding adverse critical reaction to *A Christmas Carol*. "There have been readers who objected to Scrooge's conversion as too sudden and radical to be psychologically convincing. But this," Johnson insists, "is to mistake a semi-serious fantasy for a piece of prosaic realism." Yet it is not really a generic misunderstanding that lies at the heart of such criticisms. "It may be that what really gives the skeptics pause is that Scrooge is converted to a gospel of good cheer. They could probably believe easily enough if he espoused some gloomy doctrine of intolerance" (488). What Johnson believes about Dickens is best summed up in his concluding paragraph: "More than eighty years have passed since Charles Dickens died. His passionate heart has long crumbled to dust. But the world he created shines with undying life, and the hearts of men still vibrate to his indignant anger, his love, his tears, his glorious laughter, and his triumphant faith in the dignity of man" (1158). The words could have been written by Dickens himself.

After *Charles Dickens: His Tragedy and Triumph* appeared, Johnson was much in demand for his insights into Dickens's work, and his reviews and brief commentaries are scattered throughout scholarly journals. Some even appear in publications with wider circulation among the general public, such as his *Saturday* Review article "The Scope of Dickens." In 1967 he contributed an essay titled "Dickens and the Spirit of the Age" to *Victorian Essays: A Symposium* in which he argues Dickens's work "is a mirror reflecting almost all the emergent forces and all the major problems of the Victorian age" (288), at the same time taking to task those critics who would divorce literature from its social surroundings. He did not write extensively about Dickens after 1952, however, choosing to let his own reputation stand on the work that instantly attracted notice from fellow scholars worldwide while he turned his attention to other novelists. He did bring out an edition of Dickens's letters to Angela Burdett-Coutts in 1953, and coedited the *Dickens Theatrical Reader* in 1964.

Johnson's biography was reviewed not only in scholarly journals but in newspapers and periodicals as well. While a few like John Butt cautioned against calling it the definitive biography since "it has been written while our knowledge of Dickens is still growing" (151), most applauded its appearance. The literary luminary Lionel Trilling published a review that he reprinted in *A Gathering of Fugitives* (1956), where in addition to commenting on Johnson's work he includes some important comments relative to Dickens's reputation in the years before the Second World War. Trilling says he always considered Dickens "one of the two greatest novelists in England, Jane Austen being the other" (45). Yet, he says, when he was an undergraduate at Columbia University in New York he was scoffed at for suggesting Dickens had any literary merit. "Our contemporary literature [by which Trilling means Proust, Joyce, Faulkner] has had the effect of bringing to light" the "importance and the profundity and accuracy of Dickens" in his view of modern society (48). The following year, in an introduction to *Little Dorrit*, reprinted in *The Opposing Self: Nine Essays in Criticism* (1955), Trilling observes how cannily Dickens manages to employ the prison as a metaphor for the individual in society. In general, Trilling strongly advocates a symbolist view of Dickens's fiction, comparing *Little Dorrit* in this respect to classics such as *Piers Plowman, Pilgrim's Progress,* and even *The Divine Comedy* as a portrait of society and the individual's place in it.

In 1952, the same year Johnson's biography appeared, Ada Nisbet published *Dickens and Ellen Ternan*, a carefully researched exploration intended to determine the validity of the claim that Dickens had conducted a lengthy affair with the actress. Why such a study is important is made clear by Edmund Wilson in the book's preface: "There is something more to our interest in the private lives of great men than the mere desire to pry into other people's affairs" (vii). This is especially true in the case of Dickens, he argues, because "the personality of Ellen Ternan evidently plays an important role in Dickens's later works" (x). Of course, when Thomas Wright published the first detailed account of the scandal, he was attacked vigorously by old-school Dickensians who refused to let go of the notion that their hero was as wholesome as the heroes and heroines who populate his novels. Such a response should have been anticipated, says Nisbet. By 1935, "The Dickensian cult" had grown "to such proportions that to find fault with Dickens is, as one once remarked about Longfellow, like carrying a rifle into a national park" (2). For her part, Nisbet is one of the new generation of critics who does not believe that learning the truth about a novelist's life in any way diminishes the writer's literary accomplishments. Her study establishes the fact that Dickens had a relationship with Ternan, although the exact nature of their liaison is not clear. Nevertheless, Nisbet says, understanding something of Ternan can help critics make sense of much that Dickens includes in his later novels, especially his portraits of young women. The reaction to Nisbet's book stirred a different kind of controversy than Wright's did. In a review for *Nineteenth Century Fiction,* Edgar Johnson gently chided her for "recapitulating the material" already available — and covering the same ground as he does in his recent biography (297). Gerald Grubb complains Nisbet is "neither objective nor definitive" and simply fails to prove her thesis (129). On the other hand Kenneth Fielding, then establishing his reputation as a Dickens scholar, writes favorably of the book, claiming Nisbet has managed to "turn aside from the controversy" surrounding the alleged affair to discover "new information about what actually happened" (323). Even if she does repeat much of what is already known, Fielding says, "it is hardly less valuable to have a general review of the whole affair outlined with such accuracy and care" (324).

Critical Trends at Mid-Century

In America, criticism in the 1950s was dominated by proponents of formalism, so that studies like Fred W. Boege's *PMLA* article "Point of View in Dickens" (1950) appeared with great regularity. Even historical studies of literature tended to focus on questions of technique, as Robert Gorham Davis's "The Sense of the Real in English Fiction" (1951) in *Comparative Literature* attests. British critics, as a rule more interested in the social and historical dimensions of fiction, were finally able to get beyond their prejudices about the Victorians, as Angus Wilson noted in "Dickens and the Divided Conscience" (1950), re-examining Dickens's life and works to discover how these may "tell us something of the fundamental anxieties of the externally optimistic Victorian world" (350).

Since the publication of *The Dickens World* in 1941, Humphry House had remained a busy and prolific scholar, writing and speaking about Dickens in academic forums and public gatherings. In 1955, he collected a number of his essays and talks from BBC radio programs into a critical anthology, *All in Due Time.* This eclectic volume suggests the range of House's interests in Dickens, and offers some insight into ways British scholars approached the novelist in the 1940s and 1950s. House's talk on "The Macabre Dickens" explains how Dickens uses the macabre for effect, and how the technique allows the novelist to exploit his keen psychological insight. House also includes an extended commentary on George Bernard Shaw's essay on *Great Expectations,* which he finds full of insight but decidedly too political. "Far too much that has been written and said about Dickens's politics," House argues, has been done "with the misguided expectation of finding something definite and almost sympathetic" (217). Included in this category, no doubt, would be T. A. Jackson's Marxist critique, and probably the work of the Freudians as well. House prefers the gentler, humanist approach. One of the great ironies about this volume, however, emerges from the text of a BBC program in which House outlines plans for a new edition of Dickens's letters, a project to which he had devoted considerable time. His enthusiasm for what would certainly be the definitive work on the novelist's correspondence is apparent throughout. Tragically, House did not live to see the publication of the first volume; he died in 1955, and others, notably Graham Storey, Kathleen Tillotson, and Madeline House, had to take up the task.

Tillotson was an appropriate successor to House as editor of Dickens's letters. In the year before House died she published one of the most influential twentieth-century studies of Victorian fiction, *Novels of the Eighteen-Forties* (1954), which contains a lengthy discussion of *Dombey and Son*. Perhaps the most important aspect of Tillotson's work is the premise from which she conducts her examination. She asserts at the outset that the historical context is critical to understanding any novel; her purpose, then, is "to learn more about particular novels and their time, and about the novel as a 'kind'" (2). Her focus, however, is on "English novels — not English novelists" (2). About half her book is given over to examining the production of fiction during the decade she is studying. She has great praise for *Dombey and Son*, claiming "the social criticism" cannot be "abstracted from the novel"; it is so well integrated that "abstraction distorts" (201). Her close textual analysis, coupled with a deep understanding of the historical period in which Dickens worked, is characteristic of the best British scholarship that would emerge over the next four decades.

One of the last consistently negative assessments of Dickens appears in Mario Praz's *The Hero in Eclipse in Victorian Fiction* (1956). Dickens is the subject of the first chapter in the book's second section, which Praz titles "The Decline of the Hero." Countering the arguments made by T. A. Jackson for Dickens's radical status, and the more recent heroic portraits by Humphry House and Una Pope-Hennessy, Praz considers Dickens essentially bourgeois, conventional in his approach to moral issues, and typically evasive in dealing with sexual matters. Interestingly, Praz thinks Dickens shied away from writing about sexual matters not only to accommodate conventions of his day, but because he was hesitant to say anything that might hint at the true nature of his relationship with Ellen Ternan. Praz tries to expose what "was not going well behind the comfortable façade of Dickens's novels" (137). He finds many contradictions and inconsistencies, and even accuses Dickens of relishing sadism and being driven almost exclusively by concerns for money. There "may seem to be realism" in Dickens, Praz argues, but this is "merely delight in the picturesque." The novelist "is debarred from true realism partly by his tendency toward theatricalism, partly by his Victorian repugnance for everything that is crude and offensive to delicacy" (149).

Praz has little good to say about Dickens's craftsmanship, either. He finds his techniques common to his time, especially his reliance on the conventions of sensationalism. "Although of the moral fibre of the reformer of manner," he says, Dickens "was, fundamentally, a slave to the mechanical conventions of the novel, and was incapable of adapting his means of expression to his nature" (163). He believes the Edwardians were right to criticize Dickens for his reliance on sensationalism and excessive pathos. "The Dickens who appeals to the Moderns, on the other hand, the Dickens I have hinted at more than once," he says, "is the original, the more genuine Dickens, the one who would always have been a writer of the first rank — not a Dickens of minor importance — if the fashion for the serial novel and the course of English social evolution had not directed his activity into paths other than the essay and the genre picture" (169). This truly remarkable Dickens emerges at times, Praz says, when he distorts reality to present a world of genuine horror. But these scenes are few among works that are, in Praz's assessment, bourgeois pap for bourgeois readers. The times indeed made the writer, and made him badly.

But Praz, like Jack Lindsay, was destined to become little more than a footnote in the history of Dickens criticism. By the late 1950s the Dickens Industry had set up shop in colleges and universities in England and America. Scholars at Oxford and Cambridge, Harvard and Yale, and hundreds of other institutions of higher learning were beginning to treat Dickens with the respect accorded to Shakespeare, Milton, Chaucer, Richardson, Fielding, and Austen. For example, the notion of Dickens as a conscious craftsman and consummate artist was advanced greatly by Kathleen Tillotson and John Butt in an influential 1957 study, *Dickens at Work*. Concentrating on the novelist's methods of composition, Tillotson and Butt operate from "the conviction of Dickens's greatness as a creative artist" (9). The two make clear how conditions of publication affected Dickens's work, especially serialization. They explain how the author used part of each weekly or monthly number to prepare readers for what was to come. They recount in detail how Dickens wrote and how a novel went from manuscript to finished publication and describe how and when Dickens revised his work through various editions. They are also concerned with ways Dickens used external research in his historical works. This work of exceptional scholarship was to influence a generation of scholars interested in Dickens's artistry.

Also interested in Dickens's craftsmanship, Morton Dauwen Zabel included three essays on the novelist in *Craft and Character: Texts, Methods, and Vocation in Modern Fiction* (1957). All were versions of previously published work, some dating back as far as 1942. The first is of particular interest in a study of Dickens's reputation, since in it Zabel reviews criticism of the previous half-century to explain how biography can help illuminate the sources of an artist's creativity. With that as his premise, Zabel proceeds to offer a highly critical account of the "deflationary and anti-Victorian bias" (5) of much work done since the novelist's death. He is particularly hard on Gladys Storey, whose *Dickens and Daughter* (1939), a work about the novelist and Ellen Ternan, he considers "ill-written, ill-documented, frankly amateurish" (5). But he is equally critical of Edmund Wilson, Humphry House, and F. R. Leavis, all of whom he says "repudiated the folkloristic approach" (5), and of T. A. Jackson and Jack Lindsay for recklessly pursuing Marxist and Freudian ideology. Zabel suggests that Una Pope-Hennessy, Hesketh Pearson, Ada Nisbet, and of course Edgar Johnson are the most credible of recent Dickens critics. He is convinced that "where biographical research aids the restitution of this larger and greater Dickens it makes a radical contribution to criticism and to something more — to an understanding of the vital sources out of which the genuine art of the modern novel has emerged" (13). His call for a sensible, scholarly re-examination of Dickens's life and reputation based on earlier discoveries, suggests that for him at least, biography still matters much in the criticism of the fiction.

In these years when formalism dominated critical practice, commentary on Dickens's novels appears frequently in examinations of themes common among a number of writers. A sampling of such studies from the 1950s and 1960s reveals remarkable agreement among scholars that Dickens is a master at his craft. For example, in *Poor Monkey: The Child in Literature* (1957) Peter Coveney observes there was "no other major English novelist whose achievement was so closely regulated by a feeling for childhood" (71). He explains how this sense of empathy for children influenced all of Dickens's writing. Coveney suggests, however, that earlier critics were wrong to accuse Dickens of remaining attached to childhood, or of creating scenes of excessive pathos by exploiting children in his fiction. Rather, Dickens used the child as a means of bringing home his stinging social criticism. In another thematic study, Ellen Moers's *The Dandy: Brummel to Beerbohm* (1960), Dickens is classified as "anti-Dandaical," even though he was himself given to dandyism in dress and demeanor. Moers suggests Dickens makes a conscious attack on dandyism in several later novels which strike out against what the dandy stood for: snobbery, unconcern for social injustice, support for a "do-nothing government" (231), and a "want of earnestness" (234).

Although he never published a book on Dickens, the noted American critic Douglas Bush did make a brief contribution to the Dickens Industry in "A Note on Dickens's Humor," published first in Robert Rathburn's collection *From Jane Austen to Joseph Conrad* (1958) and reprinted in Bush's own collection *Engaged and Disengaged* (1966). Bush suggests that, while the hostile reaction of Mario Praz "appears to be something of an anachronism," it would be worthwhile to treat with respect the Dickens whom critics of earlier generations admired, "an unsophisticated, erratic, inspired genius who gave his enormous public what it wanted." This Dickens was celebrated as a humorist, a side of his multifaceted personality Bush appreciates, and one he thinks is being lost on critics who see "the new Dickens" as "a highly conscious and developing artist, a sophisticated molder of symbolic patterns, a savage analyst of society" (82). Included in Rathburn's volume, however, is an essay by George Ford on *Bleak House* in which Ford concludes, much as Edmund Wilson did nearly two decades earlier, that Dickens was a man at odds with his age.

By far the most influential book on Dickens published after Johnson's biography appeared was J. Hillis Miller's *Charles Dickens: The World of His Novels* (1958). It was the first book by the man who would become one of the founders of the American school of deconstruction. Intended as a challenge to Humphry House's *The Dickens World*, the book reveals glimpses of the methodology that would make Miller one of the most controversial figures in critical studies. Miller believes it is a false dichotomy to claim one must see a novelist as either a product of his age or as independent from it — in Dickens's case, the first position being that of critics such as Gissing, Chesterton, and House, the second that of more recent critics such as Edmund Wilson and others who classify Dickens as a symbolist alienated from the world in which he lived and worked. Miller suggests there is a third way to view the relationship between a work of literature and its author, not as a "mere symptom or product of preexistent psychological condition, but as the very means by which a writer apprehends and in some measure, creates himself" (viii). Rather than viewing the novels as mirrors of Victorian society, Miller sees them as "autonomous works of art." His role as critic, he says, is to "assess the specific quality of Dickens's imagination in the totality of his works, to identify" the novelist's "view of the world which is unique" to him (viii).

By reading Dickens's works as manifestations of the author's perception of the world, Miller says, it is possible to come to some understanding of his "unique personality and vital spirit" (viii). To make his point, Miller examines six novels that deal in some way with what he calls "the search for a true and viable identity" (x). While he acknowledges there are other themes in Dickens, this one lends itself particularly well to his analysis because it lets him demonstrate how the novelist's imagination grew over time. The "world" of the Dickens novels is "the totality of all things as they are lived in by all human beings collectively." The "concrete embodiment of this totality" for Dickens is "the great modern commercial city," which is characterized by its "multitudinousness" (xv). Miller contends Dickens's attempts to capture this quality explain his methodology:

"The special quality of Dickens's imagination is his assumption that he can get behind the surface [of reality] by describing all of it bit by bit" (xvi). When every relationship, however obscure and hidden, is revealed, Dickens feels he will have created "a true likeness, an authentic image of the world" (xvi). For this reason Miller believes *Bleak House* is a key novel in the Dickens canon, because in it the novelist attempts for the first time "to synthesize in a single complex whole the familiar and the romantic, the objective facts of all the life of the age, and his own dreamlike apprehension of those facts as they appeared when transposed within the interior regions of his imagination" (159).

That statement reveals Miller's belief about the nature and function of novels. They do not reflect the real world; rather, they expose a world created from the real world by the imagination of the novelist. Each is "the transformation of the real world of Dickens's experience into an imaginary world with certain special qualities of its own, qualities which reveal in their irreplaceable way Dickens's vision of things" (328). Following through on his analysis, Miller says that in the novels he has examined, "the adventures of the protagonist are essentially attempts to understand the world," become integrated into it, and by doing so to "find a real self" (328–29). Just as Dickens's protagonists simultaneously change their world and are changed by it in their attempts to define their selves, so the novelist changes — and creates — the world he brings into being by writing about it.

Miller's book was immediately hailed for its contribution to Dickens studies. In his *South Atlantic Quarterly* review (1958), Lionel Stevenson called it a work of major importance, displaying wide-ranging scholarship and sound analysis and insight. Not everyone agreed, though. Some found it arrogant that in his first published book Miller felt he could ignore the work of others, although Miller suggests he has done so in order to "achieve a maximum concentration on Dickens himself" (xi). That disclaimer did not seem to satisfy Sylvère Monod, who astutely identified one source of Miller's theoretical superstructure in the work of Belgian critic Georges Poulet, and thinks it unfortunate Miller disregarded "some fairly broad facts" — including "all the biographical data of criticism" (360). Kathleen Tillotson admitted it was a "courageous and perceptive" undertaking, but one where both the methodology and conclusions are "vulnerable at several points" (442). Edgar Johnson complained that in his zeal to pursue the questions of identity raised in the novels, Miller "ignores other almost equally significant strands in Dickens's richly counterpointed structure" ("In a World They Never Made" 17). Additionally, Johnson says, whatever one makes of Miller's argument, "one defect cannot be passed over in silence": Miller's "linguistic convolutions" that "sometimes continue for pages," seriously hampering readers from comprehending an analysis "rich in creative insight" (18). In fact, it is against methodologies like Miller's that C. B. Cox protests in "In Defence of Dickens" (1958), an *apologia* for the kind of criticism that does not approach the novelist's work too narrowly. Cox believes "modern critics often fail to do justice to Dickens" (86) because they structure their critiques along preconceived ideological lines. Cox laments especially their failure to appreciate "the underlying effects of Dickens's humour" (87). He argues in part for a return to Chesterton's vision, because it reveals Dickens's delight in the varieties of human experience and the "gusto with which he enjoys the folly of his characters" (99). Cox's remonstrations notwithstanding, what can be said with certainty is that *Charles Dickens: The World of His Novels* had an influence on the course of Dickens studies matched by few books and surpassed by none.

Yet examples of what might be called in retrospect "traditional criticism" continued to appear without any notable reference to the incipient new theory of reading that Miller was proposing. Arthur Wilson, for instance, proclaims in "The Great Theme in Charles Dickens" (1959) that, like all great writers, Dickens "had developed for himself a philosophy of life with which he colors his writing." That philosophy, emerging from Dickens's nostalgic longing for the simpler life of the eighteenth century and revealed in all his novels, is that "nothing short of love" will allow humankind "to conquer evil in the world," and only "mutual respect among men alone can preserve the innate dignity of the human body, mind, and soul to which every individual is entitled under God" (456–57). In *The Theory of the Novel in England* (1959), a book dependent on theories of fiction developed by Henry James and E. M. Forster, Richard Stang cites passages from Dickens's correspondence and other writings to explain how the novelist developed his own theory of fiction. Stang concludes Dickens felt novelists should have a vision of society as it should be, and should present this vision in such a way that readers might understand the possibilities for transforming their current world into a better one. Stang gives Dickens great credit for being a thoughtful, conscious artist rather than a mere scribbler pandering to the reading public. By contrast, in his textbook-like survey of fiction *The English Novel: A Panorama* (1960) Lionel Stevenson suggests Dickens stumbled on plot and social criticism almost by accident; nevertheless, he too is quick to praise virtually every novel in the Dickens canon.

In 1959, Monroe Engel still found it necessary to complain in *The Maturity of Dickens* that the novelist has as yet earned only what he calls the "uneasy esteem" of critics who provide a "fluent recital of his faults and limitations" before making "a very limited declaration of his greatness" (ix). He acknowledges that his specific target is Mario Praz — whose negative assessment of Dickens seems something of an anomaly at this point in the critical history of the novelist. An admirer of Edmund Wilson, Engel says "the crucial aspect of Dickens's achievement is the absolute continuity of his commitments and materials" and "the astonishing range and development of that continuity" (x). Engel's chronological examination of the Dickens canon stresses the novelist's mastery of the multiplot novel and his ability to deal with both public and private themes. Concentrating on the later fiction, Engel paints Dickens as a dark visionary who manages to reconcile his personal life with the public life he tried to lead once he had become successful. Finding the causes of social ills were more profound and difficult than he had ever imagined, in his middle years Dickens developed a "single coherent and hellish vision of society." Thus, Engel says, whereas early works sound an optimistic note that social ills might be cured someday, Dickens eventually resigns himself to attacking social injustice while recognizing that "man's basic suffering" is "beyond the power of money or legislation to relieve"; it is "a pervasive and blighting spiritual disorder" (189).

As the foregoing discussion of Miller, Cox, Arthur Wilson, Stang, Stevenson and Engel illustrates, the diversity in approaches to reading the novelist was becoming more marked. By the end of the century, however, Wilson's nostalgic, turn-of-the-century critique was decidedly passé, and critics like Cox were swimming upstream in their plea for a reversal of critical focus. Even Stang and Engel were practicing a form of critical inquiry that would be categorized as decidedly traditional and old-fashioned within less than two decades. It was becoming ever more clear that J. Hillis Miller's approach to reading Dickens would shape attitudes of the next generation of scholars.

Works Cited

Aldington, Richard. "The Underworld of Young Dickens." *Four English Portraits, 1801–1851*, 147–89. London: Evans, 1948.

Allen, Walter. *The English Novel: A Short Critical History.* London: Phoenix House; New York: Dutton, 1954; Harmondsworth, England: Penguin, 1958.

———. *Six Great Novelists: Defoe, Fielding, Scott, Dickens, Stevenson, Conrad.* London: Hamish Hamilton, 1955.

Baker, Joseph E., ed. *The Reinterpretation of Victorian Literature.* Princeton, NJ: Princeton UP, 1950.

Boege, Fred W. "Point of View in Dickens." *PMLA* 65 (March 1950): 90–105.

Booth, Bradford. "Form and Technique in the Novel." In *The Reinterpretation of Victorian Literature,* edited by Joseph Baker, 67–96. Princeton, NJ: Princeton UP, 1950.

Bush, Douglas. "A Note on Dickens's Humor." In *From Jane Austen to Joseph Conrad; Essays Collected in Memory of James T. Hillhouse,* edited by Robert C. Rathburn and Martin Steinmann, Jr., 82–91. Minneapolis: U of Minnesota P, 1958. Reprinted in *Engaged and Disengaged.* Cambridge, MA: Harvard UP, 1966.

Butt, John E. "Charles Dickens: His Tragedy and Triumph." *Nineteenth Century Fiction* 8 (September 1953): 151–53.

Butt, John E., and Kathleen Tillotson. *Dickens at Work.* London: Methuen, 1957.

Church, Richard. *The Growth of the English Novel.* London: Methuen, 1951.

Churchill, R. C. "Dickens, Drama and Tradition." *Scrutiny* 10 (April 1942): 358–75. Reprinted in *The Importance of Scrutiny,* edited by Eric Bentley. New York: Stewart, 1948.

Coveney, Peter. "The Child in Dickens." *Poor Monkey: The Child in Literature,* 71–119. London: Rockliff, 1957. Reprinted in *The Image of Childhood.* Baltimore: Peregrine, 1967.

Cox, C. B. "In Defense of Dickens." *Essays and Studies* 11 (1958): 86–100.

Darwin, Bernard. "Return to Dickens." *St. Martin's Review* (January 1940): 30–33.

Davis, Robert G. "The Sense of the Real in English Fiction." *Comparative Literature* 3 (Summer 1951): 200–217.

Engel, Monroe. *The Maturity of Dickens.* Cambridge, MA: Harvard UP; London: Oxford UP, 1959.

Evans, B. Ifor. *A Short History of English Literature.* Harmondsworth, England: Penguin, 1940.

Fielding, Kenneth J. Review of Ada Nisbet, *Dickens and Ellen Ternan. Review of English Studies* n.s. 5 (July 1954): 322–25.

Ford, George H. "Self-Help and the Helpless in *Bleak House.*" In *From Jane Austen to Joseph Conrad,* edited by Robert C. Rathburn and Martin Steinmann, Jr., 92–105. Minneapolis: U of Minnesota P, 1958.

Gerould, Gordon H. *The Patterns of English and American Fiction: A History.* Boston: Little, Brown, 1942.

Grubb, Gerald G. "Dickens and Ternan." *Dickensian* 49 (June 1953): 121–29.

House, Humphry. *All in Due Time.* London: Hart-Davis, 1955.

———. *The Dickens World.* London: Oxford UP, 1941.

Johnson, Edgar. "Ada Nisbet's *Dickens and Ellen Ternan.*" *Nineteenth Century Fiction* 7 (March 1953): 296–98.

———. *Charles Dickens: His Tragedy and Triumph.* 2 vols. New York: Simon and Schuster; Toronto: Musson, 1952. London: Gollancz, 1953.

———. "Dickens and the Spirit of the Age." *Bibliotheca Bucnellensis* 4 (1966): 1–13. Reprinted in *Victorian Essays: A Symposium,* edited by Warren D. Anderson and Thomas D. Clareson, 28–42. Kent, OH: Kent State UP, 1967.

———. "In a World They Never Made." *Saturday Review* 41 (30 August 1958): 17–18.

———, ed. *Letters of Charles Dickens to Angela Burdett-Coutts 1841–1865.* London: Cape, 1953.

———. "The Scope of Dickens." *Saturday Review of Literature* 35 (29 November 1952): 13–14, 44–48.

———. "Turning Tides." *Virginia Quarterly Review* 31 (Autumn 1955): 644–48.

Johnson, Edgar, and Eleanor Johnson, eds. *The Dickens Theatrical Reader.* Boston: Little, Brown, 1964.

Kettle, Arnold. *An Introduction to the English Novel.* 2 vols. London: Hutchinson House, 1951–53.

Leavis, F. R. *The Great Tradition.* London: Chatto & Windus, 1948.

———. "The Novel as Dramatic Poem (1): *Hard Times.*" *Scrutiny* 14 (Spring 1947): 185–203. Reprinted as *"Hard Times:* An Analytic Note." *The Great Tradition.* London: Chatto & Windus, 1948.

Lindsay, Jack. *Charles Dickens: A Biographical and Critical Study.* London: Dakers; New York: Philosophical Society, 1950.

Mansbridge, Albert. "Munitions of the Spirit." *St. Martin's Review* (January 1940): 34–37.

Maugham, W. Somerset. "Charles Dickens." *Atlantic Monthly* 182 (July 1948): 50–56. Reprinted as "Preface." *David Copperfield.* London: J. C. Winston, 1948. Reprinted as "Charles Dickens and *David Copperfield.*" *Ten Novels and Their Authors.* London: Heinemann, 1954.

Miller, J. Hillis. *Charles Dickens: The World of His Novels.* Cambridge, MA: Harvard UP, 1958. Reprint, Bloomington: Indiana UP, 1969; Cambridge, MA: Harvard UP, 1974.

Moers, Ellen. "Dickens." *The Dandy: Brummel to Beerbohm,* 215–50. London: Secker & Warburg; New York: Viking, 1960.

Monod, Sylvère. "J. Hillis Miller's *Charles Dickens: The World of His Novels.*" *Nineteenth Century Fiction* 13 (March 1959): 360–63.

Mottram, R. H. "A Tonic for the Times." *St. Martin's Review* (January 1940): 27–30.

Nisbet, Ada B. *Dickens and Ellen Ternan*. Berkeley: U of California P, 1952.

Noyes, Alfred. "The Value of Dickens, Here and Now." *Dickensian* 35 (June 1939): 189–93. Reprinted as "Dickens." *Pageant of Letters*. New York: Shead, 1940.

O'Connor, Frank [Michael O'Donovan]. "Dickens: The Intrusion of the Audience." *The Mirror in the Roadway: A Study of the Modern Novel*, 70–82. New York: Knopf, 1956.

Pearson, Hesketh. *Dickens: His Character, Comedy, and Career*. New York: Harper, 1949.

Pope-Hennessy, Una. *Charles Dickens, 1812–70*. London: Chatto & Windus, 1945.

Praz, Mario. "Charles Dickens." In *The Hero in Eclipse in Victorian Fiction*, translated by Angus Davidson, 140–88. London, New York: Oxford UP, 1956.

Pritchett, V. S. "*Edwin Drood*." *New Statesman* 27 (February 1944): 143. Reprinted in *The Living Novel*. London: Chatto & Windus, 1946.

———. "The Rebel." *New Statesman and Nation* (16 February 1946): 124.

Stang, Richard. "Bulwer and Dickens — The Attack on Realism." *The Theory of the Novel in England 1850–1870*, 19–29. New York: Columbia UP; London: Routledge & Kegan Paul, 1959.

Stevenson, Lionel. "Dickens' Dark Novels, 1851–7." *Sewanee Review* 51 (Summer 1943): 398–409.

———. *The English Novel: A Panorama*. Boston: Houghton Mifflin; London: Constable, 1960.

———. Review of J. Hillis Miller, *Charles Dickens: The World of His Novels*. *South Atlantic Quarterly* 58 (Summer 1959): 478–79.

Storey, Gladys. *Dickens and Daughter*. London: F. Muller, 1939.

Symons, Julian. *Charles Dickens*. New York: Roy; London: Barker; Toronto: McClelland and Stewart, 1951.

Tillotson, Kathleen. *Novels of the Eighteen-Forties*. London: Oxford UP, 1954.

———. Review of J. Hillis Miller, *Charles Dickens: The World of His Novels*. *Modern Language Notes* 75 (May 1960): 439–42.

Trilling, Lionel. "The Dickens of Our Day." *A Gathering of Fugitives*, 41–48. Boston: Beacon P, 1956; London: Secker & Warburg, 1957.

———. "*Little Dorrit.*" *Kenyon Review* 15 (Autumn 1953): 577–90. Reprinted as "Introduction." *Little Dorrit.* New Oxford Illustrated Dickens. London: Oxford UP, 1953. Reprinted in *The Opposing Self: Nine Essays in Criticism.* New York: Viking, 1955.

Van Ghent, Dorothy. "The Dickens World: A View From Todgers'." *Sewanee Review* 58 (Summer 1950): 419–38.

———. *The English Novel: Form and Function.* New York: Holt, 1953.

Wagenknecht, Edward. "White Magic." *Cavalcade of the English Novel,* 173–268. New York: Holt, Rinehart and Winston, 1943.

Warner, Rex. "On Reading Dickens." *The Cult of Power,* 21–38. London: J. Lane, 1946.

Wilson, Angus. "Dickens and the Divided Conscience." *The Month* 189 (May 1950): 349–60.

Wilson, Arthur H. "The Great Theme in Charles Dickens." *Susquehanna University Studies* 6 (April–June 1959): 422–57.

Zabel, Morton D. *Craft and Character: Texts, Methods, and Vocation in Modern Fiction.* New York: Viking, 1957.

5: Dickens and Mainstream Academic Criticism (1960–1969)

IN SURVEYING THE STATUS of Dickens studies in 1961, Steven Marcus suggested that Edmund Wilson's claim made twenty years earlier that Dickens was the greatest dramatic writer in England since Shakespeare "could be advanced today without much fear of anyone's turning a hair" (278). Despite the occasional carping attack on Dickens's technical merits, by the 1960s he was accorded primacy of place among Victorian novelists both as an artist and a chronicler of society. Scholarship celebrating the many aspects of his creative genius appeared regularly. To supplement this original work, George Ford and Lauriat Lane's *The Dickens Critics* (1961) provided for the first time in a single volume a selection of essays representing the most influential criticism on Dickens published to date. The two scholars boasted excellent credentials for such work; Ford had published *Dickens and His Readers* in 1955, and Lane's "Dickens' Archetypal Jew" had appeared in *PMLA* just three years before *The Dickens Critics* was issued. Unfortunately, space limitations and some copyright problems prevented Ford and Lane from making the volume truly first-rate; for example, Wilson's "The Two Scrooges" is omitted, and many other commentaries are excerpted. Nevertheless, there was now one book to which interested scholars might turn to learn what Masson, Fitzjames Stephen, Ruskin, Lewes, James, Chesterton, Shaw, Santayana, Orwell and others had to say about Dickens. They could sample the work of Jack Lindsay, Morton Zabel, Edgar Johnson, and J. Hillis Miller. Lane's lengthy introduction provides a guide through the maze of Dickensian criticism, offering sound judgments about both the insights of critics and their motives.

In the same year the *Review of English Literature* issued a special number dedicated to Dickens. Guest editor John Butt assembled essays on Dickens's language, his humor, his relationship with the editor Francis Jeffrey, and many of the novels. Ironically, the selection most often cited and reprinted turned out to be British novelist Angus Wilson's, which begins with the assertion that "to examine the heroes and heroines of Dickens is to dwell on his weaknesses and failures" (3). The importance of the special issue for Dickens studies, though, lies in Butt's observations in his "Editorial" prefacing the collection. In 1961 Dickens criticism is a healthy industry, he observes, but much remains to be done, as opinions continue to vary widely about the value of individual novels, and definitive texts for many are not yet available. Over the next four decades the latter problem would begin to be corrected, but if Butt thought scholars would come to consensus on any one of Dickens's novels, he was sure to be disappointed with what developed during the next half-century.

The Dickens Critics was only one of several anthologies of criticism that appeared in the 1960s. Suddenly it became fashionable for publishers to issue collections of previously published essays on important literary figures, and volumes on Dickens were prominent among such books. Martin Price's *Dickens: A Collection of Critical Essays* (1967) reprints commentaries from preceding decades, including work by established critics such as Dorothy Van Ghent, Barbara Hardy, George Ford, John Bayley, W. J. Harvey, Steven Marcus, J. Hillis Miller, and Kathleen Tillotson, as well as essays by two men not often associated with Dickens criticism, W. H. Auden and Lionel Trilling. Price claims in his introduction that readers will find these selections represent a wide spectrum of critical approaches because, like Shakespeare, Dickens "confounds critical dogmatism" (1). In *Dickens: Modern Judgments* (1968), A. E. Dyson collects sixteen essays by a number of the most influential Dickens critics of the 1940s and 1950s, both British and American, including Angus Wilson, Steven Marcus, J. Hillis Miller, Kathleen Tillotson, Edgar Johnson, Humphry House, Monroe Engel, and Mark Spilka. Commentaries by Lionel Trilling and British novelist Graham Greene are included as well. This eclectic collection is bound together by the essayists' notion that Dickens is a great novelist — perhaps the greatest England has produced. Dyson summarizes the prevailing attitude about Dickens in what almost appears as a challenge to readers and critics of the 1960s and the future: "Dickens seems to me one of the supreme tests of literary taste. If readers have a theory of literature which will not accommodate him, so much the worse for their theory; if they have an outlook on life which is offended by him, so much the worse for themselves" (27).

The change in critical opinion from vilification or dismissal to unqualified admiration was not so simple, of course. A. O. J. Cockshut's *The Imagination of Charles Dickens* (1961), published early in the decade, is an interesting blend of psychological analysis, social commentary, and formalist criticism that offers some intriguing insights that would not be acknowledged by other critics for some time to come. Author of an earlier uncomplimentary article on Dickens in *Twentieth Century* (1957), Cockshut again offers an enigmatic assessment of the novelist's achievement, initially posing the questions, "How did a man with such a coarse mind become a master of his art? And how was it possible, in the nineteenth century, to be a best-seller and a true classic at the same time?" (11). Cockshut begins by positing that what others have criticized — Dickens's "melodramatic bias, his sympathy with popular taste" — are actually indispensable elements of his genius (9). He also asserts that biographical interpretations have no place in his work. Yet when he examines Dickens's work as a social reformer, he claims it was a characteristic of his personality "to be angry" (50). Cockshut reveals Dickens had a fascination for prisons, which became "emblematic of the whole problem of suffering" (48), and for crowds, partly because he was a born actor who loved to play for large audiences and partly because he saw their importance in influencing the justice system.

On the technical side, Cockshut considers the fiction both as works of art and as social commentary, concentrating on ways Dickens uses humor and excessive detail for thematic purposes. He is particularly taken with Dickens's ability to employ techniques of symbolism, but his conclusion about the way Dickens came to master the technique reveals just how firmly Cockshut refuses to recognize any sophistication in the novelist. Because Dickens was already obsessed with many social institutions and phenomena in the literal sense, Cockshut says, as he developed his powers as a novelist, things such as prisons, crowds, money, squalor and violence "become symbols of their own accord." In this, Cockshut concludes, Dickens "had an advantage as a lowbrow, for it is very commonplace ideas like these that are inexhaustible. If his obsession had been less ordinary, his imaginative development might not have been so formidably complete" (184).

Cockshut's latent negativism notwithstanding, if one can believe John Gross and Gabriel Pearson, the revolution in Dickens studies begun two decades earlier had finally taken hold. Their collection *Dickens and the Twentieth Century* (1962) provides a snapshot of critical opinion during those twenty years after a full-scale revaluation began — although Kenneth Fielding suggests in his review of the volume that it really just shows "the common reader's grounds for regarding Dickens as a great novelist have now come to be accepted by contemporary students and critics" (45). In separate introductions Gross and Pearson outline reasons for the transformation in Dickens's reputation. Pointing out that the two leaders of the revolution did not agree in their final assessment of Dickens — George Orwell called him "the old-fashioned radical, not very intelligent" but valuable for the anger he displays toward injustice (x), while Edmund Wilson found him consistently "subversive and uncomfortable" (ix) — Gross says the novelist is really among the "great masters of expressionism" (xiv). Pearson points out how the Dickens of 1960 is no longer "the popular Chestertonian Dickens" (xix), but he complains that many modern assessments fail to capture his complex nature and his mastery of the genre in which he worked. Believing it is no longer necessary to justify Dickens's place as a major novelist, Gross and Pearson offer no "startling new view of Dickens," but instead collect essays that are "typically mid-century and post-revolutionary." That is, the essays are intended to "pose questions about Dickens's mind" to determine how his thinking influenced his art and attempt to "anchor Dickens more firmly in the world in which he lived" (xxiii–xxiv). That is exactly what Pearson had done in his 1957 article "Dickens and His Readers," in which he claims Dickens was able to "make his private conflicts and compulsions public" in a way that stirred "the imaginative depths of a vast national audience" (52).

Yet in the same volume two essays challenge the growing acceptance of Dickens's artistic ability. One is Angus Wilson's oft-cited commentary on Dickens's "weaknesses and failures" (3). Much of Wilson's argument seems derived from critical opinion of decades gone by, but the fact that these attitudes were still being expressed makes it clear there was still room for disagreement in the Dickens Industry. Additionally, the trend to view Dickens as a symbolist is called into question by no less a critic than William Empson, who writes in "The Symbolism of Dickens" that "critics tend to evoke symbolism, by a very worthy impulse, when they know that something about the story has been found absurd but none the less feel that the effect on the whole is good" (14). In the case of Dickens, he goes on to say, many aspects of his novels that contemporary critics consider symbolic are merely theatrical, a technique commonplace in Victorian literature and not modern at all.

Also appearing in 1962 was *Dickens and Crime*, the first book by a young scholar who would become one of the most distinguished figures in the Dickens Industry for four decades. Philip Collins completed his doctoral work at Cambridge, where attitudes toward Dickens were being shaped by the Leavises, so his decision to specialize in Dickens studies seems in retrospect fairly courageous. Collins secured a teaching position in 1947 and began publishing on Dickens during the 1950s. His 1961 article "The Significance of Dickens's Periodicals" is indicative of the kind of careful scholarship that would characterize his career. In the preface to *Dickens and Crime* Collins claims that to date little had been done to establish Dickens within the context of Victorian society, citing Humphry House's *The Dickens World* as a notable exception. Collins believes this approach is much needed, especially in light of recently published work such as J. Hillis Miller's *Charles Dickens: The World of His Novels* (1958), which was in part a direct rebuttal of House's work. Collins is critical of Miller, claiming he willfully "misapprehend[s] passages from the novels, through failing to control his reactions to them by an historical awareness of what they could have meant to their author and his original readers" (viii). Collins takes as his central premise the idea that Dickens had an extraordinary, lifelong interest in crime, a hot topic among the Victorians and one that played to Dickens's personal proclivities. With that in mind, Collins examines the penal systems in place during Dickens's lifetime and the changes those systems underwent, especially with respect to reforms in punishment and incarceration, to explain how Dickens used this information in his novels throughout his career.

A year later, Collins followed this well-received study with a kind of companion volume, *Dickens and Education* (1963), designed to "show what Dickens wrote and did about education, not only as a novelist but also as a journalist, editor, public man, philanthropist, and parent; and to relate this on the one hand to the schools and educational ideas of his time, and on the other to the ethos and qualities of his fiction" (vi). Collins was not the first to write a book about the novelist's lifelong interest in education. John Manning's *Dickens on Education* (1959) had approached the topic sociologically, however, attempting to provide a comprehensive assessment of Dickens's views by first discussing nineteenth-century education practices before offering some assessment of Dickens's approach to them in his fiction. Collins is interested in showing how Dickens transformed what he saw and read into art. Further, he recognizes Dickens's limitations as an educational reformer and acknowledges that sometimes he was simply not well informed on the topic. Collins also admits Dickens did not accomplish much in the way of real reform, but finds the novelist used his knowledge of educational issues to create fiction that calls attention brilliantly to the social ills he perceived.

Collins's two volumes continue the tradition of British criticism that examines the relationship of the author to the world in which he lived and worked. Later in his career, Collins wrote a new entry on Dickens for the *New Cambridge Bibliography of English Literature* (1969), and provided an essay about Dickens's attachment to London for William Sharpe and Leonard Wallock's collection *Visions of the Modern City* (1987) in which he looks at Dickens's changing perceptions of the city as London itself changed over forty years.

Two studies published in the same year as Collins's *Dickens and Education* highlight the divergent paths Dickens critics were pursuing in the 1960s. Like the work of Collins, Ivor Brown's *Dickens in His Time* (1963) capitalizes on the interest in the relationship between Dickens and the world in which he lived and from which he drew inspiration for his fiction. Brown covers topics such as politicians, prisons, travel, lodgings, education, religion, city life, and America, and concludes with a chapter on the significance of Christmas, noting how important both the idea and the celebration of this holiday were to Dickens and his Victorian contemporaries. By contrast, Earle Davis's *The Flint and the Flame: The Artistry of Charles Dickens* (1963) explores Dickens's use of the literary tradition, especially his borrowings; his special reliance on farce, melodrama, sentimentality, and the Gothic; and his supposed debt to Wilkie Collins in his later years. Davis argues that Dickens's greatest contribution to literature is his development of "the panoramic or telescopic novel" (viii), a mode of writing fiction directly opposite that espoused by Henry James. Davis finds Dickens at his best in the dark novels of his later years, "building most of his late novels around a central purpose [some form of social criticism] and organizing all his sequences and techniques to move his purpose forward" (16). Dickens's "new concept of fictional artistry," Davis argues, "was a view of the broad-scale panoramic novel unified by a central purpose, developed by a number of revolving plots, and distinguished by suffusing symbolism" (16). This new art form provided a vehicle for the novelist to "comment on the world and all the worlds that follow the Victorian Age" (310). Ultimately, Davis concludes, Dickens is more than a commentator; he is also a prophet.

Certainly anyone following the publication of articles about Dickens in scholarly journals would not have been surprised at the appearance of Mark Spilka's *Dickens and Kafka: A Mutual Interpretation* (1963). Elements of the book had appeared in *Comparative Literature, Critical Quarterly, Minnesota Review, American Imago*, and elsewhere. Spilka's book provides an extended reading of works by both writers, arguing that the comparison helps reveal their artistic powers and illuminate themes that might otherwise be missed or misunderstood. The psychological foundation for his study lies in his assumption that Dickens and Kafka were obsessed with the problem of the child in both domestic and larger social settings. The childlike perspective that dominates their best fiction gives readers insight into the psychological and social complexities of living in a bureaucratic society. Spilka argues that Dickens suffered from "the absence of significant adult life" (23), so he used his fiction to gain control and bring order to his existence. Spilka believes Dickens's grotesque comedy becomes a means of dealing with a dehumanizing society. For him Dickens is a dark novelist, more in the vein of Melville, Hawthorne, and Faulkner than of Fielding or Smollett, models with whom he is normally associated.

The same kind of analysis by second-generation psychological critics can be seen in Leonard Manheim's "The Law as 'Father'" (1955) and "Thanatos: The Death Instinct in Dickens's Later Novels" (1966). The first follows up on suggestions made by Edmund Wilson that Dickens was consumed by oedipal aggression. In the second, Manheim claims humans are driven by competing impulses — *eros*, a life wish, and *thanatos*, a death wish. Manheim argues evidence of *thanatos* can be seen in many of the earlier novels as well as later ones. Another psychological critic of the 1960s, Taylor Stoehr, writes in *Dickens: The Dreamer's Stance* (1965) of the novelist's "literary manner," which he considers a form of "supernaturalism" relying on qualities outside the traditions of realism for effect (vii). Stoehr's analysis of language and rhetorical strategies demonstrates how Dickens writes in a manner akin to Freud's notion of dream work. He concentrates on Dickens's later novels, partly because they are considered his best and partly because these operate, he says, much like dreams, revealing symbolically what the dreamer cannot express directly. In the novels from *Bleak House* to *Edwin Drood* Stoehr sees a "hidden strand" beneath the surface plots (227). Inevitably, Stoehr argues, in each novel the hero suffers from some form of guilt for which he must atone. In following this dream method, Stoehr says, Dickens is mirroring a phenomenon common to the Victorians. Stoehr's own study is heavily reliant on psychological apparatus and terminology, and his specialized readings did not seem to catch on with other critics (even those practicing psychological criticism), as he is not cited often in subsequent studies of Dickens's fiction.

Some critics saw the need to offer a corrective check on the effusive criticism that had begun to dominate Dickens studies by the 1960s. Frederick Karl's long essay in *An Age of Fiction: The Nineteenth Century British Novel* (1964) celebrates Dickens's accomplishments but suggests the excessive praise Victorians had been receiving of late required tempering just as the previous decades of needless denigration had needed redress. Karl finds Dickens guilty of a willingness to compromise his vision of society and human relationships to satisfy a wide reading public that had specific demands of literature. Dickens's great gift, Karl says, was to unite the two major streams of English fiction, "Rousseauistic sentimental humanism" and "the opposing stream of realism" (12). Karl believes Dickens was "more moral critic than social or political commentator" (111), however, and that he consistently failed to recognize that "the institutions he opposed were simply the efforts of people to protect their 'minority interests'" (112). Karl finds it impossible to see Dickens as a Marxist, since he "shows little insight into public life as a whole" (113). Instead, he emerges in his early work as a kind of Quixotic figure, lashing out at ills that are sometimes more imagined than real. As he matured, Karl says, Dickens became increasingly concerned with "*power* [Karl's emphasis] and what it means in a society which professes democracy and justice and which practices the reverse" (132). Karl aligns himself with contemporary critics who believe Dickens's greatness lies in the later works, in which "the dark Dickens of the novels after *David Copperfield* heralds a counterthrust to Victorian optimism" (174). But Karl is not so willing to dismiss the early novels without an acknowledgement of their importance: Dickens could proceed to write "more weighty books upon which his serious reputation must ultimately rest" only after he had secured an audience by appealing to the public in the lighter works of his earlier period (174).

Among the more significant studies of Dickens produced during the 1960s is Steven Marcus's *Dickens: From Pickwick To Dombey* (1965). In some ways, Marcus's approach goes against the prevailing grain; while most critics during the period focused on Dickens's later works, Marcus attempts an "explanation of Dickens's development as a novelist through the first half of his career" (9). Marcus also insists one cannot understand Dickens's fiction without considering the novelist's life, because "that life is continually present in the novels, and undergoes successive transformations as Dickens, both as man and novelist, confronts its challenges" (10). With little in the way of introduction, Marcus launches into his study by examining the phenomenon of *Pickwick Papers,* a novel in which Dickens achieved "transcendence," a "representation of life" that "extends our awareness of the limits of our humanity" (17). Marcus focuses on this novel not only for its importance in revealing something of Dickens's artistry and vision, but also because, in his view, it vexes "the modern critical mind" by challenging "current preconceptions about the conditions and possibilities of greatness in literature" (20). Marcus stresses the historical significance of *Pickwick,* noting its originality in dealing with social events as well as social and moral attitudes. But he does not think Dickens consciously breaks with literary tradition in creating this novel, as some later critics have contended. Rather, Dickens simply did not know much about the tradition, and was in fact working *sui generis.*

Although in *Oliver Twist* Dickens is certainly interested in dealing with the problems caused by the Poor Laws, the novel is most valuable, Marcus thinks, for revealing the writer's "generic imagination" — an imagination "primarily employed in the dramatization of symbolization of abstract ideas" (63). In *Nicholas Nickleby* Dickens managed to combine the seriousness of purpose displayed in his second novel with the humor and vitality of the first. However, Marcus judges the next novel, *The Old Curiosity Shop,* Dickens's least successful, largely, he says, because he was preoccupied with the death of his sister-in-law Mary Hogarth and simply had no intellectual control over his materials. By contrast, he considers *Barnaby Rudge* a "vastly better novel than its reputation in any way suggests" (169–70), calling it "the last work of Dickens's apprenticeship to his art" (171). In this much maligned novel, Dickens was able to explore in some oblique way many of the problems of modern life. But it is with *Martin Chuzzlewit* that difficulties begin for critics. It is "the first novel of Dickens's maturity" (212), because in *Chuzzlewit* and every novel after it Dickens managed to combine "expansiveness and compactness" (214) into a single work. Both comic and serious at the same time, the novel presents an "elaborately balanced representation of society" (225) organized around the principal theme of selfishness. Its successor, *Dombey and Son,* is more subdued but no less powerful. In this novel, Marcus argues, Dickens achieves a clear focus on the problems with which he deals, skillfully using two principal images, the sea and the railroad, to embody conflicting values.

This summary of Marcus's commentary demonstrates how, even after nearly two decades that privileged the later novels, it was still possible for a skillful critic and careful reader to find in Dickens's early work much to praise. Marcus is also careful to explain how events of Dickens's life, especially his growing sense of restlessness, affected his career. Using *Dombey and Son* as a prime example, Marcus observes how fiction became a way for Dickens to express himself about the problems of change and development, both in individual lives and society as a whole. Marcus is no simplistic champion of the early work, as one might say of earlier critics. Instead, his sensitivity to language that produces strong, sympathetic readings of Dickens's first half-dozen works is coupled with a hardnosed view of his subject. "There is no writer in English," he acknowledges, "in whom the disparity between eminence and infirmity of style — and therefore of mind — is more dramatic and extreme" (139). Nevertheless, he concludes that even early in his remarkable career, Dickens exhibited the seeds of genius that would make him a writer to be reckoned with despite the many deficiencies formalists would find in his construction, and realists would discover in his portraits of everyday life.

Nowhere is the debate sharper between the proponents of Dickens as dark symbolist and those who cling to the image of him as a humorist and caricaturist than in Robert Garis's *The Dickens Theatre: A Reassessment of the Novels* (1965). Garis plants his flag firmly in the latter camp, almost immediately becoming a target for advocates of symbolic readings of the Dickens canon. The positive thesis Garis advances is that Dickens was principally a great performer who used the techniques of the stage in his fiction. He is theatrical too, Garis says, in his intent, overtly attempting to dazzle readers with "verbal devices" so they end up applauding the writer's performance no matter what the outcome of the story he tells (24). As a result, Garis concludes, there is no need for continuity in a Dickens novel — no need for careful, consistent plotting — because readers are focused on the performance of the writer rather than on story or its meaning. The novelist's theatricality makes him "largely exempt from the ordinary rules of literary procedure" and "largely exempt from, and ignorant of, and indeed hostile to the moral, intellectual, and emotional disciplines and habits which we accept as normal to serious concerns" (40). Dickens was never concerned about depicting the inner lives of characters, Garis says, nor did he "develop a fictional mode suitable for self-examination" (95). In fact, Garis suggests, when Dickens does try to depict people's inner lives, as in *Little Dorrit* and *Our Mutual Friend*, he is not particularly successful.

Curiously, the second and third segments of Garis's book, in which he offers close readings of some of Dickens's later novels, do not seem radically different from the commentaries he criticizes. Garis says as Dickens matured he developed a belief that Victorian society was "in the grip of a gigantic conspiracy" (97), and that people had willingly given themselves over to "the System" (98). But this analysis follows an opening broadside aimed at nearly the entire formalist establishment, and Garis leaves no doubt about his opinion of those who would turn Dickens into a precursor of the modern symbolist movement in fiction. In the first part of his study Garis insists "there is a Dickens problem" (1) that has led to "actual and grave distortion" of the novelist's canon resulting in "the widespread view, endorsed by some high authorities [a phrase that has the ring of sarcasm in context], that the most interesting and significant part of Dickens's work is that which can be regarded as seriously symbolic and prophetic" (3). Garis offers his work as a corrective to "this exciting but seriously misleading view" that he fears "may have already hardened into the new orthodoxy about this great and strange writer" (3). He writes with observable disdain for those who have discovered a symbolic pattern that allows them to dismiss the novelist's obvious failure as a realist. These critics claim for themselves, Garis says, a sophistication that sets them apart from ordinary readers — at least, he suggests (again with not-so-subtle sarcasm), "this is the optimistic way of understanding and forgiving the distortions of Edmund Wilson, Lionel Trilling, J. Hillis Miller, and others" (4). "I simply do not believe in the existence — now or in the middle of the nineteenth century — of the unknowing readers against whose insensitivity to Dickens's symbolism so much of the current criticism is triumphantly directed" (30).

In Garis's view, the kind of criticism being practiced by the new group of sophisticates is nothing more than "a mode of finding plausible ways of defending vested interests" (5), privileging "the most honored moral ideals in our culture," namely "disinterestedness" and "the sympathetic imagination" (37). There is no room for an intrusive author such as Dickens, so these critics must find a way to read the novels that eliminates Dickens the omnipresent performer consciously manipulating his characters before readers' eyes. As a result, Garis observes, modern criticism has produced many "'free' readings, for the discovery that [Dickens] is a symbolic novelist has apparently exempted his critics from even the most elementary standards of relevance" (13). Though he does not say so directly, Garis argues for a return to the kind of criticism practiced a century earlier, when character was prized over plot. "Were it not for the fashionable new readings of Dickens as a symbolic artist," he says, the novelist's plots would be acknowledged "as inert and without imaginative life" (87). It is small wonder that other critics would take umbrage at Garis's assault on their work. His book did receive favorable notice, however, in the widely circulated periodical *Commonweal*, where Bernard McCabe claims that it "points the way toward intelligently full and active participation in the novels" (247) after two decades of "more sophisticated" commentary in academic circles that had "transformed" Dickens into "the partner of Dostoevsky and Kafka" (244).

W. F. Axton's *Circle of Fire: Dickens's Vision and Style and the Popular Victorian Theater* (1966) is similar to Garis's book in that the author examines techniques of popular theater that Dickens adapted for his novels. But unlike Garis, who is often hostile toward his subject, Axton seems more concerned with trying to account for the principles of style Dickens employed throughout his career. Axton covers some of the same ground surveyed more than sixty years earlier by J. B. Van Amerongen in *The Actor in Dickens* (1926), a work promoting the same thesis but largely devoted to cataloging scenes from the novels that display elements of dramaturgy. By contrast, Axton demonstrates how the Victorian theater provides the source for much of what Dickens does in his fiction, as "the general spirit, idiom, or 'style'" of the drama "underwent a transmutation into the vernacular of prose fiction" in the hands of the novelist (ix).

The superstructure supporting the Dickens Industry underwent a major enhancement in 1965 when *Dickens Studies,* a new journal devoted to Dickens, was established in the United States. In his brief announcement introducing the publication, "Milestones along the Dover Road," editor Noel Peyrouton pays tribute to the *Dickensian,* which he says has for years done "yeoman's work" to promote Dickens studies (2). Feeling there is much yet to be done, however, Peyrouton says the new journal is designed to become "a vessel and a vehicle to help further promote Dickens scholarship" (2). *Dickens Studies* was intended as well to satisfy a "long felt need for an American periodical dedicated to serving a growing international community of Dickens students," one that would maintain "a proper and surely appropriate emphasis on contemporary criticism of the novels" while encouraging submissions "of an interdisciplinary nature" (2). Certainly the journal seemed well served by the Dickens community; its editorial board included Philip Collins, K. J. Fielding, Edgar Johnson, J. Hillis Miller, Sylvère Monod, Kathleen Tillotson, and Edward Wagenknecht. Unfortunately, Peyrouton was able to keep the journal alive for less than a decade. But his pioneering effort made it clear to American scholars that there was support for an American publication devoted exclusively to Dickens, and by the 1970s, more than one had arisen to replace *Dickens Studies.*

In 1965, Edward Wagenknecht restated his case for what he calls a sensible reading of Dickens's life and work, free from modernist cant. Combining material from his 1929 study with other work published during the previous three decades, Wagenknecht produced *Dickens and the Scandal-Mongers,* a collection of essays intended in part to sort out fact from rumor regarding such matters as Dickens's relationship with Ellen Ternan. Branding as anti-Dickens those who perpetuate and expand on stories about the novelist and his young actress friend, Wagenknecht repeats his claim that all evidence suggesting the relationship was anything but platonic is purely speculative. In addition to blasting literary historians, Wagenknecht again takes shots at a number of critics, particularly Edmund Wilson, whose Freudian study he calls "irresponsible both as criticism and as historical scholarship" (9). He is dismissive, too, of Marxist readings of Dickens, taking T. A. Jackson to task for suggesting the novelist had proletarian leanings. Less openly opinionated and certainly less controversial than Wagenknecht's book is Christopher Hibbert's *The Making of Charles Dickens* (1967). A professional biographer but not a Dickens scholar, Hibbert concocted a version of the author's life largely from Forster and Johnson. Intending his book for a popular audience — but vetted by scholars Madeline House and K. J. Fielding — Hibbert centers on the novelist's early life so he can show how Dickens transforms these experiences into fiction.

In addition to the steady stream of articles on Dickens appearing in scholarly journals, a number of books on Victorian literature published during the 1960s contain extensive commentary on his work and reputation. Among them is John Lucas's laudatory assessment of *Dombey and Son* in *Tradition and Tolerance in Nineteenth Century Fiction* (1966) in which he explains how the novel demonstrates Dickens's growing maturity in social criticism and argues for a disinterested and sympathetic reading of novels of social change regardless of their conformity with formalist critical standards. David Lodge takes a different approach to Dickens's work in *Language of Fiction: Essays in Criticism and Verbal Analysis of the English Novel* (1966). Despite its off-putting title, Lodge's highly readable account of the way prose writers employ language is aimed at establishing a theory of fiction parallel to that created by New Critics for poetry. In his reading of *Hard Times* he examines carefully rhetorical strategies Dickens employs in what Lodge calls his polemic against utilitarianism, asserting the work has mixed success in achieving its aims — success directly proportional to Dickens's control over the language he uses. Additionally, Lodge provides an intriguing explication of Dickens's use of fairy-tale motifs, noting how the novelist contrasts fairy-tale qualities of life against the harsh realities of life in Coketown. The issue of Dickens's use of the fairy tale would become the subject of two major studies within little more than a decade.

In 1967 the University of Notre Dame invited J. Hillis Miller to deliver a series of lectures on Victorian literature, which he published a year later as *The Form of Victorian Fiction* (1968). Interested in the function and limits of form, Miller concentrates on ways Victorian novelists, bound by conventions, nonetheless found ways to present a unique worldview that provides insight into human relationships. Selecting two Dickens novels as examples, *Oliver Twist* and *Our Mutual Friend*, he examines three issues "crucial to Victorian fiction: the question of time, the question of interpersonal relations, and the question of realism" (xii). At this point in his career, Miller had not moved completely into the world of deconstruction, but one can see him leaning toward those theoretical concerns in statements such as this one: "To move from the real Victorian society which Dickens was satirizing to the novel itself is to move into a lookingglass world of fictive language. This language constantly calls attention to the fact that it is language. Far from affirming the independent existence of what he describes, Dickens's narrative betrays in a number of ways the fact that fictional characters and their world are made only of words" (36).

Miller reprises his discussion of the three problems outlined above in an essay he contributed to Roy Harvey Pearce's collection, *Experience in the Novel* (1968), one of several anthologies of criticism published that year. Northrop Frye's essay in the same collection, "Dickens and the Comedy of Humours," also concerned with larger issues of literary theory, argues against those who wish to use the simplistic "realism vs. romanticism" dichotomy to judge Dickens's novels, which Frye says are "not realistic novels but fairy tales in the low mimetic displacement" (49) of characterization and action. In the same collection, Kenneth Fielding's "Dickens and the Past" provides a close textual analysis of *Little Dorrit* to demonstrate how Dickens's idea of the importance of the past helps shape the present in both fiction and life. The presence of essays with such widely varying perspectives in the same volume might suggest that the new methods of inquiry focused on Dickens's work were becoming accepted by mainstream critical audiences. On the other hand, a third collection published that year offers a different perspective. Maynard Mack and Ian Gregor's *Imagined Worlds: Essays on Some English Novels and Novelists in Honour of John Butt* (1968) includes two essays on Dickens: Kathleen Tillotson's detailed examination of the fourth number in the serial publication of *Dombey and Son* and Kenneth Fielding's reading of *Hard Times* as a touchstone for revealing Dickens's interest in educational reforms. These and other contributions in the volume suggest that British scholarship had been little affected by the movement toward critical theory taking hold in American universities.

Published in the same year, Herbert Sussman's *Victorians and the Machine: The Literary Response to Technology* (1968) explores ways the Victorians perceived and adapted to "changes in intellectual and emotional life" (vii) brought about by living in the first society dominated by technology. Sussman claims Dickens understood the nature of these changes and somehow managed to assimilate them into his artistic consciousness, using "complex technology" as a "symbol for the combination of industrial mechanization and mechanistic thought" that he saw "as the shaping principle of Victorian life" (41–42). Sussman believes Dickens appreciated what technology could do, but at the same time felt drawn to the simpler times that existed before mechanization began to rule everyday living. Sussman gleans from Dickens's novels references to and uses of technology, but he is principally concerned with ways Dickens uses these references symbolically. What makes Dickens better than others who wrote about the evils of mechanization was his focus on the psychological rather than the physical effects of the trend. "At the center of Dickens's work," Sussman concludes, is an "awareness that men are fated to coexist with the machine, but must ever work to preserve their emotional life from its deadening regularity" (75).

In yet another survey published in 1968, *The Victorian Debate: English Literature and Society 1832–1901,* Raymond Chapman fixes his critical gaze on ways Victorian literature highlights the major social and political issues with which the Victorians dealt. In 1968, Chapman feels comfortable writing that "no Victorian writer has equaled Charles Dickens in holding popularity as well as critical esteem" (101), a position that would hardly have been defensible thirty years earlier. Chapman's is a loving portrait, critical only indirectly, as when he observes that "towards the end of [Dickens's] life there was a tendency for his love of London to overrule his intellectual acceptance of the changes which had taken place" in the thirty years since he had begun writing (102). Chapman justifies Dickens's use of sentimentalist techniques by citing the novelist's need to reach a reading public "whose taste for fiction was but little developed" (109). He claims Dickens "was not really a lover of the rising cult of realism" (124). But in a prescient observation he says that, although he "truly hated oppression and injustice" (113), Dickens was at heart a conservative. In contrast to Chapman's extensive analysis, Masao Miyoshi has surprisingly little to say about Dickens in *The Divided Self: A Perspective on the Literature of the Victorians* (1969). Concerned with "ways in which Victorian men of letters experienced the self-division endemic to their times and gave expression to it in their writing" (ix–x), Miyoshi alludes to the novelist and his work throughout the study, but considers only a few novels in any detail. He argues Dickens had a "double vision" (269) of himself and his world that explains his frequent shifting from minute detail to cosmic commentary; it also accounts for his double plots and his heavy reliance on symbolism.

In 1968, Indiana University Press issued a two-volume set of *Uncollected Writings of Charles Dickens: Household Words 1850–1859.* The publication was the first major scholarly effort by Harry Stone, who would go on to become a significant voice in Dickens criticism for the next half century. Nearly a decade earlier, Stone had pronounced his admiration for Dickens's creative abilities in "Dickens and Interior Monologue" (1959), arguing that the novelist anticipated successors such as Joyce and Faulkner in amalgamating "into the mainstream of the English novel new and powerful modes of representing reality and experience" (65). Stone was also an avid collector of Dickens memorabilia and manuscripts; in 2003, when he donated his materials to California State University Northridge it was considered the finest private collection in the world. Stone's two volumes reprint not only dozens of essays — some for which Dickens is identified as the author for the first time — but also include appendixes containing variorum texts, biographical sketches of Dickens's various collaborators, instructions prepared by Dickens for those wishing to contribute to special Christmas numbers of the journal, and an index indicating dates of each issue. Stone's Introduction is actually a small monograph outlining Dickens's career as a journalist — a career that ran parallel to his work as a novelist. Stone describes Dickens's management style and outlines his working philosophy for *Household Words*. In the course of his discussion, he demonstrates the kind of close textual analysis that would characterize his work in the coming decades. Stone's Dickens is a writer conscious of both his mission and his methods, one given to experimentation that anticipates some of the more *avant garde* writers of the twentieth century, and at the same time a social reformer who never forgets that his readers need a touch of imagination to help improve their dreary lives.

The most distinguished twentieth-century French critic of Dickens, Sylvère Monod, had published a critical biography of the novelist in 1953, but it was available only in French for more than a decade. While the work attracted interest from those who could read the language, it was not until 1968, when Edward Wagenknecht arranged for an English translation of *Dickens the Novelist,* that Monod's study reached a wide English-speaking audience. Wagenknecht's rationale for supporting the project, explained in his introduction, is typical of his iconoclastic approach to Dickens. Monod is not an "old-line 'Dickensian,'" he says — not one of those amateurs Wagenknecht attacks in his own work on Dickens — but neither does he "adhere to the neo- or post-Wilsonian orthodoxy in Dickens criticism" (viii).

Monod writes in part as "a protest against the often expressed view that Dickens was a negligible craftsman" (xiii). Years before scholars like Kathleen Tillotson and John Butt began publishing studies of Dickens's craftsmanship, Monod had examined manuscripts of the novels in the Forster Collection at the Victoria and Albert Museum in London, and his descriptions of Dickens's working methods owe much to his careful comparison of various drafts with the finished novels. Monod believes that, even when forced to make adjustments and revisions to meet the demands of serial publication, Dickens constantly balanced pragmatic and aesthetic concerns in his fiction. The care with which Monod examines the summary sheets Dickens began preparing as outlines for his novels and with which he critiques the novelist's growing ability to construct scenes for effect make Monod's study one of the most valuable for understanding Dickens's composition process.

By the time the English version of Monod's book appeared in 1968, however, many of the charges the French scholar had made against earlier critics had been answered, because formalist criticism had already begun to recognize the artistry behind the novels. Nevertheless, Monod's study is one of the finest at explaining the care Dickens invested in shaping his fiction. Monod insists Dickens always "regarded his profession as an art" that involved "both moral and social responsibilities" (65). Using examples from the novels, from Dickens's correspondence, and from the work of Dickens's first major biographer John Forster, Monod creates a portrait of the novelist as a skilled artisan perfecting his craft as he matured.

Since one of his major themes is to refute the critical tradition that had painted Dickens as a careless composer, Monod is especially hard on Forster, whose *Life of Charles Dickens* he describes as being "richer in biographical information than in valid criticism" (217). Monod's own critical bias is to see as the best of Dickens those works that incorporate something of the novelist's own life into his fiction. No doubt that is why nearly one-fifth of his study is devoted to an examination of *David Copperfield*, which he calls a masterpiece of "psychological autobiography" (325). Every work after *Copperfield* is seen as an attempt to renew the inspiration that guided Dickens in composing that novel. Monod does not find much to measure up. He believes *Bleak House, Little Dorrit,* and *Our Mutual Friend* are certainly lesser achievements, although he examines their composition in great detail. He calls *Hard Times* and *A Tale of Two Cities* the "least Dickensian" of the novelist's works (448), dismissing them by saying that, while Dickens was "a very great novelist," he was "neither a great social writer nor a great historian" (456). By contrast, however, *Great Expectations* rises almost to the level of *Copperfield* in the Dickens canon, because in it Dickens recaptures the inspiration that made his first venture in psychological autobiography so successful.

Unlike Monod's detailed study, E. D. H. Johnson's *Charles Dickens: An Introduction to His Novels* (1969), part of the Princeton Studies in Language and Literature series, is intended as a guide for students, providing a brief account of Dickens's life and background information to help explain the fiction. Johnson offers a sketch of Dickens's relationship with his readers and provides some analysis of his technical skills in narration, characterization, and use of setting. Martin Fido's *Charles Dickens* (1968), also a brief sketch of Dickens's career followed by extracts from the novels, explains how the novelist dealt with matters such as comic action, comic dialogue, structure, symbolism, and social satire. Fido concentrates on the early work, arguing that the later, darker novels grew naturally from these comic roots. Similarly, George Wing's *Dickens* (1969), a brief monograph in the Writers and Critics series, includes a decidedly biased summary of the state of Dickens criticism to date. Wing begins with a critique of Gross and Pearson's volume, which he calls "one of those fashionable anthologies in which a different modern critic writes on each work from a chosen aspect" (91). Unfortunately, Wing says, "Chesterton is no longer a fashionable analyst of Dickens's fiction" (93). Instead, his loving and at times reverential approach has been replaced, Wing laments, by the criticism of Robert Graves, Aldous Huxley, and F. R. Leavis, all of whom share a pronounced "skepticism and disenchantment" about the novelist (93). Wing is even critical of Orwell and Wilson, who he says "opened up deadly lines of approach" to Dickens's works at the expense of the humor that characterizes so many of them (95). Wing pleads for a move away from the earnest, gloomy approach of postwar critics. Such was not to be the case, however, as critical studies being published contemporaneously with Wing's reveal.

Thematic studies published during the 1960s tended to elevate the later, darker novels as works of greater artistry and accomplishment. Quite a few were rather broad surveys of the Dickens canon, explaining some aspect of his craftsmanship or exploring a theme running through the novels. Not all were groundbreaking, of course. For example, in *Charles Dickens as a Serial Novelist* (1967) Archibald Coolidge claims to be extending work done earlier by Kathleen Tillotson and John Butt in accounting for the "vast cluster of Dickens's techniques" by explaining them as a by-product of serial publication (vii). While his approach may not have opened up new avenues for study, the work offered enough insight to merit praise from Kenneth Fielding in a *Dickensian* review. Frank Donovan also returns to an oft-discussed subject in *Dickens and Youth* (1968). Claiming "no other author wrote so extensively about youth in all its aspects" (2), Donovan excerpts liberally from the novels to illustrate how Dickens's decision to view the world through the eyes of children helped bring into sharp focus the good and bad qualities of Victorian society. Finally, Sylvia Jarmuth's *Dickens's Use of Women in his Novels* (1967) is particularly curious. Her approach is closer to that of William Dean Howells than to the feminists whose work was beginning to appear at this time. In her sweeping survey of Dickens's heroines, Jarmuth seems quite content to accept the idea that they are appropriately placed in subservient roles and that their treatment as objects to be desired or possessed warrants no criticism at all.

Less naïve but no less disconcerting is Ross Dabney's *Love and Property in the Novels of Dickens* (1967), a work that launches without introduction into commentary on the fiction, exposing ways Dickens's attitude toward love and property serve as an organizing principle throughout his career. Dabney notes how the two are frequently seen as opposing impulses in human behavior, creating dramatic tension in the works. Much of what Dabney offers, however, is an extended reading of the Dickens canon rather than any sharp critical commentary, and his decision not to reference any other critics might lead one to suspect he was consciously turning his back on traditional methods of scholarship as a form of subtle protest.

More scholarly and certainly more insightful, Grahame Smith's *Dickens, Money and Society* (1968) covers some of the same ground, but with considerably more critical acumen. Smith examines two aspects of Dickens that some critics have found incompatible: the novelist's interest in promoting a social reform agenda in his fiction and his concern for "total fictional form — complexity of plot, characterization, symbolism, use of language" (7). Smith argues against monolithic critics such as T. A. Jackson and against psychological critics who are, he suggests, too quick to attribute Dickens's accomplishments to some form of sickness. He also challenges readings like those of Humphry House, which in Smith's opinion turn Dickens into nothing more than a competent journalist. By contrast, Smith demonstrates how Dickens uses social criticism as "a thematic force that informs character, plot, and language with its unifying presence." In his best work, Smith says, "the aesthetic, the social, and the psychological are perfectly blended" (9–10).

Smith places himself squarely in the camp of the symbolist critics, organizing his study around a central image in Dickens's fiction: money. Moving back and forth between literary criticism and literary history, Smith links Dickens's career to the Victorian age to demonstrate how the novelist understood the social ills of his time. He detects a contradiction in Dickens that would receive considerably more attention in the coming decades. "One of the most difficult problems with Dickens," he observes, "is to separate the deeply revolutionary creative artist from the man who enjoyed and sympathized with so many aspects of his own culture" (56). Smith sees Dickens's career following a trajectory from a period of excessive optimism, when he thought it really was possible to solve all the world's problems, toward a sense of growing pessimism about society — and about his own life. In his conclusion, Smith finds himself compelled to grapple with the question that vexed British critics for decades: "Where is Dickens to be placed in the tradition of the English novel?" (194). Smith is willing to grant that George Eliot's *Middlemarch* may be the "defining touchstone of Victorian fiction" (194), but he considers Dickens the best among Victorian novelists for creating characters. In addition, "The worlds of the great novels of [Dickens's] last period are symbolic, transmutations of Victorian life; and within the novel as a whole, character, setting, and action are consistently imbued with symbolic meaning" (206). Because of the way his mind worked, Dickens's best fiction flowed naturally from his personal experiences, and this tendency demanded "a form that could encompass the public and private, the didactic and poetic" (213). Smith's work would receive immediate praise from reviewers and other critics, especially those who found merit in traditional humanistic studies that downplayed formalist principles. Before long, however, these formalist studies would be the "traditional" criticism against which a new breed of critics would rebel.

Works Cited

Axton, W. F. *Circle of Fire: Dickens's Vision and Style and the Popular Victorian Theater.* Lexington: UP of Kentucky, 1966.

Brown, Ivor. *Dickens in His Time.* London: Nelson, 1963.

Butt, John, ed. *Review of English Literature* 2 (July 1961). London: Longman's, 1961. Special Dickens Issue.

Chapman, Raymond. *The Victorian Debate: English Literature and Society 1832–1901.* London: Weidenfeld and Nicolson; New York: Basic Books, 1968.

Cockshut, A. O. J. *The Imagination of Charles Dickens.* London: Collins, 1961; New York: New York UP, 1962.

———. "Sentimentality in Fiction." *Twentieth Century* 161 (April 1957): 354–64.

Collins, Philip A. W. "Charles Dickens 1812–70." In *The New Cambridge Bibliography of English Literature.* Vol. 3, edited by George Watson, 779–850. Cambridge: Cambridge UP, 1969.

———. *Dickens and Crime.* London: Macmillan; New York: St. Martin's Press, 1962.

———. *Dickens and Education.* New York: St. Martin's; London: Macmillan, 1963.

———. "Dickens and the City." In *Visions of the Modern City: Essays in History, Art, and Literature,* edited by William Sharpe and Leonard Wallock, 101–21. Baltimore, MD and London: Johns Hopkins UP, 1987.

———. "The Significance of Dickens's Periodicals." *Review of English Literature* 2 (July 1961): 55–64.

Coolidge, Archibald C., Jr. *Charles Dickens as Serial Novelist*. Ames: Iowa State UP, 1967.

Dabney, Ross H. *Love and Property in the Novels of Dickens*. London: Chatto & Windus; Berkeley: U of California P, 1967.

Davis, Earle R. *The Flint and the Flame: The Artistry of Charles Dickens*. Columbia: U of Missouri P, 1963.

Donovan, Frank. *Dickens and Youth*. New York: Dodd, Mead, 1968.

Dyson, A. E., ed. *Dickens: Modern Judgments*. Toronto: Macmillan, 1968.

Empson, William. "The Symbolism of Dickens." In *Dickens and the Twentieth Century*, edited by John Gross and Gabriel Pearson, 13–15. London: Routledge and Kegan Paul, 1962.

Fido, Martin. *Charles Dickens*. London: Routledge & Kegan Paul, 1968.

Fielding, Kenneth J. "Dickens and the Past: The Novelist of Memory." In *Experience in the Novel*, edited by Roy H. Pearce, 107–31. New York: Columbia UP, 1968.

———. "Dickens as a Serial Novelist." *Dickensian* 63 (September 1967): 156–57.

———. Review of John Gross and Gabriel Pearson, *Dickens and the Twentieth Century*. *Dickensian* 59 (January 1963): 45–47.

Ford, George H., and Lauriat Lane, Jr., eds. *The Dickens Critics*. Ithaca, NY: Cornell UP, 1961.

Frye, Northrop. "Dickens and the Comedy of Humours." In *Experience in the Novel*, edited by Roy H. Pearce, 49–81. New York: Columbia UP, 1968.

Garis, Robert E. *The Dickens Theatre: A Reassessment of the Novels*. Oxford: Clarendon P, 1965.

Gross, John and Gabriel Pearson, eds. *Dickens and the Twentieth Century*. London: Routledge & Kegan Paul, 1962.

Hibbert, Christopher. *The Making of Charles Dickens*. London: Longmans, Green; New York: Harper & Row, 1967.

Jarmuth, Sylvia L. *Dickens's Use of Women in His Novels*. New York: Excelsior, 1967.

Johnson, E. D. H. *Charles Dickens: An Introduction to the Reading of His Novels*. New York: Random House, 1969.

Karl, Frederick R. *An Age of Fiction: The Nineteenth Century British Novel*. New York: Noonday Press of Farrar, Straus and Giroux, 1964.

Lane, Lauriat, Jr. "Dickens's Archetypal Jew." *PMLA* 73 (March 1958): 94–100.

Lodge, David. "The Rhetoric of *Hard Times*." *Language of Fiction: Essays in Criticism and Verbal Analysis of the English Novel*, 145–63. New York: Columbia UP; London: Routledge & Kegan Paul, 1966.

Lucas, John. "Dickens and *Dombey and Son:* Past and Present Imperfect." In *Tradition and Tolerance in Nineteenth-Century Fiction: Critical Essays on Some English and American Novels*, edited by David Howard, John Good, and John Lucas, 99–140. London: Routledge & Kegan Paul, 1966; New York: Barnes & Noble, 1967.

Manheim, Leonard F. "The Law as Father." *American Imago* 12 (Spring 1955): 17–23.

———. "Thanatos: The Death Instinct in Dickens's Later Novels." In *Hidden Patterns: Studies in Psychoanalytic Literary Criticism*, edited by Leonard and Eleanor Manheim, 113–31. New York: Macmillan, 1966.

Manning, John. *Dickens on Education*. Toronto: U of Toronto P, 1959.

Marcus, Steven. *Dickens: From Pickwick to Dombey*. New York: Basic Books; London: Chatto & Windus, 1965.

———. "The Lame, The Halt and the Blind." *New Statesman and Nation* 62 (1 September 1961): 278–79.

McCabe, Bernard. "Taking Dickens Seriously." *Commonweal* 82 (May 1965): 244–47.

Miller, J. Hillis. *The Form of Victorian Fiction: Thackeray, Dickens, Trollope, George Eliot, Meredith, and Hardy*. Notre Dame, IN: U Notre Dame P, 1968.

———. "Three Problems of Fictional Form: First-Person Narration in *David Copperfield* and *Huckleberry Finn*." In *Experience in the Novel*, edited by Roy H. Pearce, 21–48. New York: Columbia UP, 1968.

Miyoshi, Masao. "Broken Music: 1870." *The Divided Self: A Perspective on the Literature of the Victorians*, 265–78. New York: New York UP, 1969.

Monod, Sylvère. *Dickens the Novelist*. With an Introduction by Edward Wagenknecht. Norman: U of Oklahoma P, 1968.

Pearson, Gabriel. "Dickens and his Readers." *Universities and Left Review* 1 (Spring 1957): 52–56.

Peyrouton, Noel. "Milestones Along the Dover Road." *Dickens Studies* 1.1 (January 1965): 1.

Price, Martin, ed. *Dickens: A Collection of Critical Essays*. Englewood Cliffs, NJ: Prentice-Hall, 1967.

Review of English Literature. Special Dickens Number. 2 (July 1961). London: Longmans, 1961.

Smith, Grahame. *Dickens, Money, and Society*. Berkeley: U of California P, 1968.

Spilka, Mark. *Dickens and Kafka: A Mutual Interpretation*. Bloomington: Indiana UP, 1963.

Stoehr, Taylor. *Dickens: The Dreamer's Stance*. Ithaca, NY: Cornell UP, 1965.

Stone, Harry. "Dickens and Interior Monologue." *Philological Quarterly* 38 (January 1959): 52–65.

———, ed. *Uncollected Writings of Charles Dickens: Household Words 1850–1859*. 2 vols. Bloomington: Indiana UP, 1968; London: Allen Lane, Penguin Press, 1969.

Sussman, Herbert L. "The Industrial Novel and the Machine: Charles Dickens." *Victorians and the Machine: The Literary Response to Technology*, 41–76. Cambridge, MA: Harvard UP, 1968.

Tillotson, Kathleen. "New Readings in *Dombey and Son*." In *Imagined Worlds: Essays on Some English Novels and Novelists in Honour of John Butt*, edited by Maynard Mack and Ian Gregor, 173–82. London: Methuen, 1968.

Van Amerongen, J. B. *The Actor in Dickens: A Study of the Histrionic and Dramatic Elements in the Novelist's Life and Works*. London: Palmer, 1926; New York: D. Appleton, 1927. Reprint, New York: Haskell House Publishers, 1970.

Wagenknecht, Edward. *Dickens and the Scandal-Mongers: Essays in Defense and Criticism*. Norman: U of Oklahoma P, 1965.

Wilson, Angus. "The Heroes and Heroines of Dickens." *Review of English Literature* 2 (July 1961): 9–18. Reprinted in *Dickens and the Twentieth Century*, edited by John Gross and Gabriel Pearson. London: Routledge and Kegan Paul, 1962. Reprinted in *British Literature: Recent Revaluations*, edited by Shiv Kumar. New York: New York UP, 1968.

Wing, George D. *Dickens*. Writers and Critics Series. Edinburgh: Oliver and Boyd, 1969.

6: The Dickens Centenary and After (1970–1979)

BY THE TIME DICKENS had been dead a hundred years, it was possible for Philip Hobsbaum to write without equivocation that "The reputation of Charles Dickens is in no danger" (1). In fact, the centenary of Dickens's death was celebrated with public ceremonies, seminars, and innumerable publications. The tributes actually began a year early and continued for three years. In the summer of 1969, the editors of *Studies in the Novel* brought out a special issue on Dickens, collecting critical commentary from some of the current luminaries in Dickens studies and a few newer voices. The first of a number of essay collections, E. W. F. Tomlin's *Charles Dickens 1812–1870: A Centennial Volume* (1969) includes work by E. D. H. Johnson, Emlyn Williams, Ivor Brown, Harry Stone, and the novelist J. B. Priestley. Tomlin argues in an essay titled "Dickens's Reputation: A Reassessment" that, with the notable exception of Edmund Wilson, before 1950 the reading public were the real heroes of Dickens studies, keeping alive an interest in Dickens when critics found him unworthy of serious attention. Tomlin is probably correct in claiming that, at the moment of this centenary, "Dickens now enjoys a reputation among *critics* [Tomlin's emphasis] as an accomplished and conscious artist, far higher than ever before" (259). But Tomlin soars to heights of adulation often reserved for Shakespeare when he proclaims that "we may be confident that whatever men may be reading in another century, they will be reading Dickens" (263). While his reference to "men" is undoubtedly meant to be gender inclusive, by 1970 women — especially feminists — were reading Dickens in a decidedly different light, and many of them failed to find in the Victorian novelist the universal appeal Tomlin seems to take for granted.

In fact, in this year of tribute, the first salvo in a new attack on Dickens was fired — aimed not at his artistry but his ideology. The first really influential indictment of Dickens's treatment of women appeared in Kate Millett's *Sexual Politics* (1970), a seminal work in feminist literature. To be fair, Millett's commentary is not wholly derogatory. Writing about *Dombey and Son,* she calls the work "a nearly perfect indictment of both patriarchy and capitalism" and "virtually inspired by the phenomenon of prenatal preference" (89). On the other hand — and this is a rather notable qualifier — "Dickens did this without even relinquishing the sentimental version of women which is the whole spirit of Ruskin's 'Of Queen's Gardens,'" a work Millett holds up as the emblem of Victorian male attitudes toward women. Unfortunately, she concludes, "It is one of the more disheartening flaws in the master's work that nearly all the 'serious' women in Dickens's fiction" seem to be "insipid goodies carved from the same soap as Ruskin's queens" (90). This final judgment would condemn Dickens in the eyes of feminists, so much so that not even Michael Slater's later extensive analysis of Dickens's attitudes toward women would make much of a dent in the way he would be viewed by most feminist critics.

Millett's comments did not have immediate impact on the Dickens Industry, however, as most Dickens critics were still writing enthusiastically about his artistic achievements. *Dickens the Craftsman: Strategies of Presentation* (1970), assembled by Robert Partlow, is another centennial tribute in which all of the essays concentrate on ways Dickens manages the technical details in his fiction. Harry Stone examines the conscious patterning in the novels, Philip Collins explores Dickens's awareness of himself as an artist, Robert Patten discusses his techniques for constructing a story, Richard Stang analyzes his use of setting. Partlow says in his introduction that such a volume seems appropriate now that early criticisms of Dickens's craftsmanship have been rebuked. He argues that the work of Dickens critics during the period 1950–1970 "has not been to establish his artistry as a fact, but to document it" (xviii). Similarly, Michael Slater observes in his introduction to *Dickens 1970* (1970) that the novelist has finally been given his rightful place in the House of Fiction. The nine original essays in Slater's volume aim to achieve a balance in their exploration of important aspects of Dickens's achievement: three deal with his artistry, three with his social commentary, and three with what might be called human relationships. By contrast, Ian Watt's 1971 *The Victorian Novel: Modern Essays in Criticism* reprints excerpts, book chapters, and complete essays from noted scholars such as Kathleen Tillotson, Humphry House, John Butt, J. Hillis Miller, and Raymond Williams. Ada Nisbet and Blake Nevins's *Dickens: Centennial Essays* (1971) collects previously published essays from *Nineteenth Century Fiction* and a lecture delivered by J. Hillis Miller at a seminar sponsored by the William Clark Memorial Library at UCLA. Miller reprinted the same essay in *Charles Dickens and George Cruikshank* (1971), along with one by David Borowitz, his co-presenter in the lecture series at UCLA. And Joseph Gold issued one of the finest works of scholarship on Dickens, *The Stature of Dickens: A Centenary Bibliography* (1971).

The centenary also prompted the publication of materials not aimed exclusively at scholars but at students and the reading public that had always loved the novelist even when his critical reputation was at its nadir. Among the more commercially orientated publications, Martin Fido's

Charles Dickens: An Authentic Account of His Life and Times (1970) has the merit of containing high quality photographic reproductions and a text that, while derivative, is at least an accurate rendering of Dickens's biography. A. H. Gomme's *Dickens* (1971) in the Literature in Perspective series is designed to introduce readers to Dickens by placing him in his cultural setting. Angus Wilson's *The World of Charles Dickens* (1970) crosses the boundary between coffee-table books and serious scholarship, as its format is slightly oversized and contains numerous illustrations. A decade earlier in "Charles Dickens: A Haunting" (1960), Wilson had suggested that his "amateur" intrusions into Dickens criticism could be justified only as attempts to explain "Dickens's significance for the modern novelist" (101). But *The World of Charles Dickens* is clearly intended for a wider audience, if not for academe. Fortunately, Wilson's summary of Dickens's life is sound and his analysis of the fiction follows the line of critical inquiry he had previously explored, providing an evenhanded if somewhat dated assessment of Dickens's merits and deficiencies.

Of course, 1970 proved to be a banner year for the publication of important critical studies as well. For example, one of the major British critics of the Victorians, Barbara Hardy, collected her essays on Dickens in *The Moral Art of Dickens* (1970). Hardy had been publishing articles on Dickens for nearly two decades, and had prepared a slim volume, *Dickens: The Later Novels* (1968), for the Longman's Writers and Their Work series. Later Hardy would include previously published articles on Dickens in *Feeling in Victorian Fiction* (1985), a collection examining ways characters express affective feelings, and publish a brief introductory study, *Charles Dickens: The Writer and His Work* (1983). But *The Moral Art of Dickens* remains her major contribution to Dickens studies. Hardy begins by stating categorically that "the moral concern is especially conspicuous" in the novelist, at times even "a discursive intrusion into the virtual experience created by the art" (xi). She observes with disappointment the "trend of modern criticism" which tends "to blur the individuality of the artist and the work of art, by stressing those formal and theoretic qualities which most works of art hold in common" (xi). Further, she suggests critics like Dorothy Van Ghent and J. Hillis Miller have gone too far in stressing the symbolic qualities of Dickens's work at the expense of his social commentary. Hardy never wavers in her focus on Dickens as a social critic, though occasionally she finds him deficient in his assessment of Victorian society and especially of the women living in it.

Another important study appearing in 1970 was John Lucas's *The Melancholy Man: A Study of Dickens's Novels*, a philosophical examination in which Lucas describes Dickens as a version of Immanuel Kant's melancholy man, who by following his own instincts breathes "the noble air of freedom" (xi). Lucas argues that, increasingly frustrated by Victorian society, Dickens began casting around for ways to find the freedom he longed for, first looking to the past, and then to the pastoral tradition, to develop "an increasingly complex vision of the nature of freedom" (xi). He calls Dickens a greater mimetic novelist than George Eliot, and dismisses the negative criticism of G. H. Lewes and Henry James by asserting that Dickens's "method of showing human probabilities" is simply at odds with "their own calculations or judgments of the probable" (344). He even goes so far as to claim George Eliot "understands less about the social process than Dickens, just as she understands less about the nature of identity in social relationships" (344). Although Dickens has his share of faults, Lucas admits, significant ones occur only rarely. Taking a page from Goethe's criticism of Schiller, Lucas says that "before so great a man one should make one's criticisms on bended knees" (345). There are echoes of Chesterton and Gissing, too, in his claim that "We cannot apply to Dickens's novels terms invented for other novelists and expect to do him justice, or see how truly great he is" (344).

More reserved in his claims is Harvey Peter Sucksmith, whose *The Narrative Art of Charles Dickens* (1970) focuses on issues of craftsmanship and construction. Defining "narrative" broadly to mean "all of the art of the novel that is involved in telling the story" (vii), Sucksmith goes to manuscript sources to demonstrate the conscious concern Dickens exhibited in shaping his work. He examines rhetorical strategies, the use of language, and the novelist's concern for eliciting responses from readers, especially his use of irony and his attempts to generate sympathy. He also examines Dickens's efforts to structure his work and use rhetorical devices to create memorable characters.

Without question, however, the most important book on Dickens to appear in conjunction with the centenary was *Dickens the Novelist* (1970), the combined work of F. R. Leavis and Q. D. Leavis. Both had written about Dickens before. Q. D. Leavis had commented dismissively on him in *Fiction and the Reading Public* (1932) while her husband had relegated him to second-class status among England's novelists in *The Great Tradition* (1948). Both had left scattered comments and impressions of Dickens in other places, most notably in F. R. Leavis's 1962 essay on *Dombey and Son* in the *Sewanee Review*. The husband-and-wife team of Cambridge professors had always been careful, close readers of literary texts, but their insistence that a certain sense of high seriousness, or moral earnestness, be a major criterion for judging a writer's relative value had not always made their work popular with their contemporaries. The reaction among Dickensians to Leavis's exclusion of Dickens from the "great tradition" of the English novel had evoked multiple responses, most of them hostile. *Dickens the Novelist* is in part a revision of the Leavises' original estimate of the writer, in part an analysis of several novels that demonstrate Dickens's mastery of the art of fiction, and in part a stinging refutation of the critical tradition that had grown up during the twentieth century which, in their view, seriously distorts the sources of Dickens's genius.

As a study of Dickens's fiction, *Dickens the Novelist* is not very different from the kind of literary analysis one might find in the work of other British scholars. The Leavises state in their preface that their aim is to "enforce as unanswerably as possible the conviction that Dickens was one of the greatest of creative writers" and that "he developed a fully conscious devotion to his art." Further, they want to dispel the notion that his genius was confined to the realm of entertainment, so as to render any attempt to suggest limited intellectual capacity "obviously absurd" (ix). They approach the novels as critics, not as scholars, bringing together the tools of what might be called the humanist tradition with those of the New Critics. Careful, close readings of individual texts are combined with observations about the sociological and historical context that shaped the novels and that the novels in turn portray. They pore over Dickens to discover signs of moral earnestness. Rather than surveying all of Dickens's fiction, however, they concentrate on six major novels, examining them in chronological order to explain how Dickens developed his art. In every instance, though, the Leavises go out of their way to stress their appreciation for Dickens's technical skill and insight.

F. R. Leavis's lead essay on *Dombey and Son* argues it is the first of Dickens's novels to be "a providently conceived whole, presenting a major theme," his first real attempt to create an "elaborately plotted Victorian novel" (2). While writing *Dombey* Dickens "thought of himself with the conscious pride of responsibility as an artist, and with a developing earnestness pondered the claims of his art" (30). Q. D. Leavis makes a similar case for *David Copperfield,* exposing the care Dickens took in constructing his story. She also takes every opportunity to point out how critics such as Robert Garis and Ross Dabney are simply wrong in slighting this novel. In fact, in this chapter and elsewhere, Garis is seen as particularly villainous in his reading of the Dickens canon. F. R. Leavis reprises his assessment of *Hard Times* as a masterpiece, this time taking on critics who have been bold enough to disagree with him during the twenty years since the publication of *The Great Tradition*. He argues as well that, despite what some critics have said, in *Little Dorrit* Dickens again demonstrates "his genius as a novelist in a capacity for profound and subtle thought" (217). Claiming both George Eliot and Henry James owe a debt to Dickens for this novel, Leavis says "no one has surpassed Dickens in the treatment of Victorian snobbery" (257).

Q. D. Leavis begins her analysis of *Great Expectations* by first noting how difficult it has become for twentieth-century readers to approach the novel, "handicapped," as she believes, "by crass misdirections from contemporary Dickens specialists" (277). She is particularly hostile toward critics who insist the novel is some form of fairy tale. Far from it, she contends; it is instead "a great novel, seriously engaged in discussing, by exemplifying, profound and basic realities of human experience" (278). Part of the reason people misread the novel, she says, is that they simply do not understand Victorian culture and conventions. Once they do, they can see how intensely Dickens cared about people and society, and about ethical matters. Her reading of Pip's character has the suggestion of psychological analysis — without its attendant clinical vocabulary. Neither of the Leavises would ever acknowledge this, of course, since for them the greatest travesty of contemporary criticism has been the substitution of ill-informed psychological sleuthing for good, old-fashioned literary analysis.

What makes *Dickens the Novelist* most controversial, however, is not the careful if somewhat argumentative analysis of these six novels. Rather, it is the Leavises' attack on the critical establishment that had, since the 1940s, transformed Dickens from the hale-fellow-well-met humorist of Chesterton into the brooding, *angst-*filled, alienated social critic who by 1970 had become the darling of the contemporary literary establishment. The preface to *Dickens the Novelist* is one of the most stinging indictments of other academics ever to be published by anyone writing on Dickens, and hence bears attention by anyone interested in the history of Dickens criticism. A principal aim of their study, the Leavises announce almost immediately, is to "register specific protests against the trend of American criticism of Dickens, from Edmund Wilson onwards, as being in general wrong-headed, ill-informed," and "essentially ignorant and misdirecting" (ix). Of course, the Leavises had always aligned themselves with an earlier tradition of scholarship and criticism, a predilection that causes them to prefer, for example, John Forster's biography of Dickens "over modern, more 'correct' biographies, whether British or, still less acceptable, American" (ix) — including Edgar Johnson's, which they assert "cannot claim to have superseded or even to rival Forster's" (x). The attack on Wilson, however, may seem like something of a reversal, since F. R. Leavis had said in his 1942 *Scrutiny* review of *The Wound and the Bow* that "this is a book to recommend." Despite its being "typical of contemporary critical writing" in that Wilson is "preoccupied with explaining" Dickens's artistic development in terms of "private psychological tensions," Leavis says Wilson's account of the way Dickens deals with the Victorian social structure is "intelligent and illuminating," and that Wilson possesses "an educated mind, informed with good sense and a genuine interest in literature and civilization" (72).

While they find the "Marxizing and other ideologically-slanted interpretations" of Dickens have been "comparatively harmless" and now "a dead letter," they are vexed almost beyond words with "the echoes and elaborations of Edmund Wilson's theory of Dickens's art," which they believe reduces Dickens's artistry to "the volcanic explosions of a manic-depressive" (xiii). They are exasperated with those who claim to be literary critics but who are really nothing more than "amateur psychologists" spouting unsupported assumptions and theories whose "self-indulgent vapourings give no satisfaction to anyone but their perpetrators" (xiii). The Leavises are adamant in insisting that facts readily available about Dickens's life, his habits, and the environment in which he lived put the lie to such fantasies; critics and scholars need only to avail themselves of sources that would dispel their crazy notions. They are hopeful that what they consider a sane, substantiated, and carefully argued analysis, using techniques and terms from literary study rather than other disciplines, will rescue Dickens from the quagmire into which he and his works have been sunk by these misguided (mostly American) critics.

Of course, not all humanist critics of Dickens reacted so vehemently to the work of their predecessors. For example, H. M. Daleski says he was prompted to write *Dickens and the Art of Analogy* (1970) by a suggestion Steven Marcus made in *From Pickwick to Dombey* that Dickens had an analogical imagination. Daleski systematically pores through the fiction to explain how this quality aided Dickens in portraying the society with which he had a love-hate relationship throughout his life. Daleski uses his own overarching metaphor to study the novels, identifying Dickens's career with that of a skilled craftsman: in his apprenticeship he produced novels such as *Pickwick Papers* and *Oliver Twist,* as a journeyman *Martin Chuzzlewit* and *Dombey and Son,* and in his period as a master the great later novels such as *Bleak House, Little Dorrit, Great Expectations,* and *Our Mutual Friend.* Daleski's principal aim is to demonstrate the "rich resourcefulness of Dickens's art" and reveal "the existence of a Dickens who has tended to disappear from sight amid the subtleties of much modern criticism." Ultimately, his portrait is one of "a traditional Dickens who is pre-eminently concerned with money and love" (14). Despite his penchant to hearken back to the critics of an era before symbolism took center stage in studies of Dickens, Daleski does express a certain fondness for the work of Edmund Wilson, who he says initiated modern criticism of Dickens.

A. E. Dyson's centenary tribute, *The Inimitable Dickens: A Reading of the Novels* (1970), is a curious and even quirky study that reinforces many of the prejudices Americans have against British scholarship. There are no notes and no bibliography, but many cryptic allusions to work by other critics. Although Dyson is a knowledgeable scholar, his book is as much an appreciation as it is criticism. In some ways it seems closer to the work of late nineteenth-century critics or to Chesterton's commentary. In fact, Dyson challenges critics who think literary discourse should be impersonal or impartial. He begins with the premise that Dickens is somehow larger than life and has some special wisdom to impart to readers. "The celebration of life is a Dickens hallmark" (10) he asserts — a fact he thinks many modern critics overlook. He is emphatic in dismissing the notion (espoused, he claims, by Edmund Wilson) that Dickens was a victim of his manic-depressive personality. Proud of being a formalist, Dyson begins his assessment of Dickens's fiction by expressing his concern "with the organic structure of each novel, and with the terms of reading prescribed by itself." He follows with observations such as, "I doubt whether paragraphs of mere pudding could be found in any of the novels," and "I am certain that all of [the novels] are most subtly organized and knit through imagery and tone" (12). His claims to formalism notwithstanding, Dyson concentrates his discussion on an examination of Dickens's characters. Ultimately, Dyson's personal reading seems open to challenge by critics who do not share his enthusiasm.

The idea of Dickens-the-radical was alive and well in the centenary year, and plays a prominent role in the work of Raymond Williams, one of the most influential Marxist critics of his generation. Williams had touched on Dickens briefly in *Culture and Society* (1958), a sociological investigation into ways society changed in the nineteenth century, and had written a perceptive essay on problems in dealing with Dickens's social criticism in 1964. In *The English Novel: From Dickens to Lawrence* (1970) Williams places the mantle of Marxist theory over the Dickens canon, examining the novels as products of the social and political milieu in which they were written. The book is based on a series of lectures Williams delivered during the 1960s, and its style is reminiscent of criticism from the 1930s or 1940s, before the penchant for highly technical language began to dominate academic discourse. Studying Dickens as the first of a line of writers who shaped English fiction for nearly a century, Williams examines what he feels is the central theme of novels from the 1840s until the 1920s: "The exploration of community: the substance and meaning of community" (1). His thesis is that by the nineteenth century the notion that a community was "knowable" (16) was being called into question. Like any good Marxist, of course, Williams is really interested in the way fiction is influenced by class structure, specifically the decline of the landed gentry as prominent shapers of society and the attendant rise of the educated middle class.

In writing about Dickens, Williams feels compelled to deal with prior critics, especially proponents of formalism and aestheticism. He finds such approaches wanting because they fail to recognize that Dickens was writing "a new kind of novel"; through his plotting and characterization he is "uniquely capable of expressing the experience of living in cities" (31–32). Further, Williams says, Dickens is able "to dramatize those social institutions and consequences which are not assessable to ordinary physical observation" (34). In Dickens, the city is both a social fact and a human landscape. The novelist's linking of people and objects is a conscious strategy intended to call attention to the impact of city life on people. Exposing the novels through the lens of Marxism, Williams discovers that Dickens's method "relates very precisely to his historical period." As advances in mechanization made it possible to reshape the very structures of society, novelists such as Dickens found it necessary to deal with the "crisis of choice" — that is, how the world ought to be made (40–41). Williams makes similar judgments about Dickens in *The Country and the City* (1973), where he says Dickens had a love-hate relationship with the city, criticizing industrialism and mechanization but praising the vitality of the metropolis. In London Dickens was able to see "the common condition and destiny" that city life provided beneath the randomness that first strikes a viewer (154).

In *The English Novel: From Dickens to Lawrence* Williams leans heavily on passages from the novels that describe the city and its inhabitants, selecting those that highlight the growing depersonalization and division between classes. In assessing Dickens's achievement he takes a kind of *gestalt* approach: Dickens's consistently "deep and remarkable" (57) moral criticism of society transcends any of his individual attacks on money, chancery, family, or other specific components of the social order. In the final analysis, though, when he measures Dickens against Marx himself, Williams discovers the novelist and the political philosopher "had little in common" (50). Though they share a general sense that the human condition needed improvement, Dickens does not measure up to Marx in his critique of the evils of capitalism.

Two new journals devoted to Dickens studies were founded in the centenary year. *Dickens Studies Annual* was established at Southern Illinois University under the direction of Robert Partlow. Like *Dickens Studies*, which published its last issue in the same year, *DSA* was created to be an American counterpart to the *Dickensian*. Partlow notes in his Preface to the first issue that, in the twenty years prior to the launch of *DSA*, scholars had produced more than a hundred dissertations, twenty books, and hundreds of articles on Dickens. Surely, Partlow suggests, there is room for yet another publication devoted to the Victorian novelist. The editors at *DSA* also sought to provide a format for longer articles than those typically appearing in the *Dickensian,* whose rather small size and (at the time) staple-stitched binding limited the number of pages that could be published in each number.

In fact, in the same year, American scholars at a convention of the Modern Language Association agreed to start what was originally intended to be an adjunct publication to *DSA,* the *Dickens Studies Newsletter,* to promote communication among Americans working on Dickens. As Robert Partlow and Robert Patton mention in "To Our Readers," the initial entry in the newsletter, the quarterly publication was designed to complement but not compete with the *Dickensian,* whose "Notes and Activities" section focused almost exclusively on happenings in Britain. The aim of *DSN* was to collect information on works in progress, provide a quarterly bibliography of new publications on Dickens, and offer notice of recently published and forthcoming books. A "Letters to the Editor" section was to provide "housekeeping" information for Victorian scholars, providing, among other things, information on job vacancies. Robert Patten of Rice University was the first general editor, assisted by William Axton of the University of Louisville, who was to handle reviews. Production came under the supervision of Robert Partlow (who must have been quite busy with his editorial work on *Dickens Studies Annual* at the time); the bibliography section was compiled by Alan Cohen of the Southern Illinois University Library.

Like so many other scholarly publications, both *DSA* and *DSN* eventually migrated away from their original charters. *Dickens Studies Annual* continued under Partlow's editorship for seven years, but in 1977 he turned over the publication to a trio from New York University: Michael Timko, Fred Kaplan, and Edward Guiliano. At the same time, the focus of the journal was widened, and an explanatory subtitle added: "Essays on Victorian Fiction." In the case of *DSN,* the change was more gradual. By 1972 brief articles began to appear. Slowly but steadily articles, notes, and reviews began to nudge out informal communications, and in 1984 the journal was retitled *Dickens Quarterly.* The new editor, David Paroissien, found the change appropriate because, while he saw "no radical departure from the format that had earned *DSN* acceptance as a scholarly journal," the new title signified what he called an "evolution" to a journal that had wider audience appeal. By the mid-1980s the journal was devoted predominantly to publishing longer articles and reviews.[1]

Studies of Themes, Ideas, and Influences in the 1970s

The early 1970s were fruitful years for the production of new critical studies about Dickens. Among the most influential to appear was Alexander Welsh's *The City of Dickens* (1971). Welsh explores ways Dickens uses the city both literally and metaphorically, claiming that, as metaphor, the city "provides a context for values and purposes expressed by the English novel" (4). For him, Dickens's work is a kind of synecdoche for the entire Victorian age, reflecting its conflicting values. Throughout his work Welsh estalishes a constant comparison between Dickens's novels and Bunyan's *Pilgrim's Progress,* suggesting all of Dickens's fiction is somehow a representation of the progress made by people in cities like London toward the heavenly city where they all wish to live. Welsh's reading makes Dickens out to be more religious than most critics would tolerate, a fact Welsh himself acknowledges. His interest is not simply in Dickens, however; he is really intent on explaining how the Victorians in general viewed their lives in real cities and in the "city" where they hoped to reside for eternity.

Also appearing in 1971 was the first of what would be a series of distinguished studies of the Victorians by James Kincaid. In *Dickens and the Rhetoric of Laughter* Kincaid acknowledges that he is writing in the midst of the "dark-Dickens revolution" (1) that values the later, more somber novels. He insists, however, that sensitive readers should be able to appreciate both Dickens's seriousness and his humor. His study examines ways "our laughter is used" to "cement an involvement in the novel's themes and concerns" (1). The laughter generated by the humorous incidents is not a sidelight in the novels, but an integral device that illuminates important and often serious themes. Although most of the novels he examines are from the first half of Dickens's career, he includes intriguing discussions of what he calls the pivotal work in the Dickens canon, *David Copperfield,* and of two late novels, *Little Dorrit* and *Our Mutual Friend.* Kincaid argues against dividing Dickens's career, as J. Hillis Miller does, claiming that to appreciate Dickens one must see him as continuously developing. For Kincaid, Dickens is a conscious moral artist manipulating his readers gently as he exposes society's ills. Kincaid believes Dickens wants readers to laugh over the humorous scenes as much as he wants them to cry over sentimental passages or become angry at the injustices he portrays.

As Kincaid explores Dickens's humor, so Sylvia Bank Manning in *Dickens as Satirist* (1971) examines the characteristics of satire that appear in his novels. Manning is interested in Dickens's familiarity with the genre, and argues that, though his works cannot really be classified as satire, the tendency toward satire motivates much of his writing. She sees him experimenting with satiric techniques in the early novels, then offers readings of *Bleak House, Hard Times,* and *Little Dorrit* to explain how the mature Dickens makes use of satiric form. She argues further, however, that in novels following *Little Dorrit* the satire becomes ancillary to other social and moral concerns. Another study appearing just after Manning's work that also discusses Dickens's social criticism, Jean-Claude Amalric's *Studies in the Later Dickens* (1973), includes seven essays by scholars from Britain, France, and America that offer readings of the novels of Dickens's mature years, all stressing the division of his career at some point just before or after the publication of *David Copperfield.*

In *"Noah's Arkitecture": A Study of Dickens's Mythology* (1972) Bert Hornback, a disciple of J. Hillis Miller, undertakes to explain how Dickens transforms society in his fiction. Hornback views Dickens as a revolutionary standing outside society, offering a vision that is at once realistic (although exaggerated) and mythic — "an interpretation of this world in a universal context" (1). Hornback first locates the source of Dickens's discontent with society in his awareness of the evils of the class system. He then traces the growth of Dickens's awareness of this underlying problem through the early novels, with their focus on specific evils, to a comprehensive critique of society itself in the later ones. The "mythology" of his title, Hornback says, "is one of new beginnings, a Genesis mythology" (6) that Dickens uses as a means of structuring his social criticism. In this way, he offers a positive, not simply a negative view of the world, demonstrating that society is capable of being changed through love.

A year after publishing his bibliography of Dickens criticism, Joseph Gold joined the camp of humanist critics with *Charles Dickens: Radical Moralist* (1972). Basing his analysis on the work of Humphry House and George Orwell, who in his estimation published "the best essays ever written on Dickens" (1), Gold attempts to determine what kind of reformer Dickens actually was. Arguing that "one of Dickens's principal concerns and talents was the exploration of the psychology of behavior" (1), Gold divides the novelist's career into two phases. In the first, which Gold calls the "anatomy of society," Dickens tries to see how an individual can be integrated into the larger community; hence, the early novels contain repeated calls for social reform. In the second phase, dubbed by Gold the "Anatomy of Self," Dickens shows how individuals can find within themselves the answers to questions about meaning and human freedom regardless of how evil society has become. Gold insists, however, that "Dickens's work was, in its fundamental disposition, all of a piece," constituting a "unity of vision" extending from earliest to latest works (5). What makes Dickens distinguished among novelists, Gold argues, is his "visionary mind, able to grasp, by the power of its imagination, the possibility of some altered state of society and some better set of values than those which it encounters" (276). This portrait of Dickens as moral philosopher would be radical enough, but Gold goes even farther in claiming for the novelist a religious foundation for his social commentary. "The critics have wanted to regard this religious presence as sentiment or cliché or concession to social taste" (278), but this is not the case. Gold thinks Dickens relies on the notion of a Creator for his idea about the potential for achieving peace and harmony in the world. Not only does Gold celebrate Dickens for his religious leanings, he argues that the novelist's aproach to individual and social problems has value beyond the Victorian age. "Perhaps," Gold suggests, "we need Dickens today more than ever"

(7). Gold's judgment may have been affected by what he saw going on around him outside the walls of academe: the ugly war in Vietnam, the Cold War, the breakdown of traditional moral norms throughout the West, the threat of mass annihilation from nuclear weapons. Small wonder if he turned to Dickens for solace.

A second study appearing in the same year characterizing Dickens as a moralist and social reformer was Michael Goldberg's *Carlyle and Dickens* (1972). Goldberg's is not the first study to examine the relationship between the two writers; Samuel Davey did a cursory comparison in 1876, and James Pike provided a much more detailed study in a 1939 article "Dickens, Carlyle, and Tennyson." Goldberg's book is distinguished, however, by the systematic way he explores Dickens's fascination with the Sage of Chelsea and the influence Carlyle exerted on Dickens throughout the novelist's career. Traces of Carlylean thought appear as early as "A Christmas Carol," Goldberg says, and run through every subsequent work, to the point that "none of Dickens's last seven novels is without some mark of Carlyle's influence" (7). Goldberg believes Dickens found in Carlyle's writings a way of "comprehending the enormous complexity of society" and seeing "patterns of connectedness behind the breakdown of separate institutions" (6). But not only was Carlyle a force for shaping Dickens's social vision, Goldberg says; he also helped the novelist become a symbolist. Lest that point be taken out of context, however, Goldberg is quick to note that he believes Dickens never became the symbolist critics of the mid-twentieth century have made him out to be. He worries that post-Wilsonian interpretations of Dickens place too much stress on the novelist's modernity and alienation at the expense of his engagement with his own age. While there may be unconscious forces at work in Dickens, Goldberg is convinced the "part of Dickens's thinking that was consciously regulated, the main line of his social criticism, was directly influenced by Carlyle. His imaginative response to the Victorian world itself was also colored by his readings of Carlyle" (227). Surprisingly, thirteen years later Goldberg would take both writers to task for their views. In "Gigantic Philistines," a lecture delivered at the University of Santa Cruz and published in *Lectures on Carlyle and His Era* (1985) he accuses Dickens and Carlyle of being philistines, in that they lacked appreciation for art.

Presumably unaware of Goldberg's book, William Oddie the same year claims in the introduction to *Dickens and Carlyle: The Question of Influence* (1972) that his is the first full-length study of Carlyle's influence on the novelist. Oddie insists one must do more than cite Dickens's admiration for Carlyle to establish that influence — suggesting others have done little more than that. He begins by outlining Carlyle's stature during the nineteenth century, sketches the personal relationship between the two men, then examines in detail two novels in which he considers Carlyle's influence paramount, *Hard Times* and *A Tale of Two Cities*. He follows this with a wider look at issues both men cared about deeply: revolution and radicalism, the increasing mechanization of society, and the idea of history. Oddie concludes that "Carlyle's influence on Dickens's thinking was a forming and shaping one," although it did not operate as "a simple transference of ideas from one mind to another" (6). For Dickens, Carlyle was more of a catalyst than a mentor. At times, Oddie says, Dickens "misinterpreted" Carlyle to suit his own ends, and at times he even "ignored the essential parts" of Carlyle's message (154).

Throughout the 1970s, commentary on Dickens's work appeared in a number of studies dealing with broader topics. Douglas Hewitt's interesting guidebook *The Approach To Fiction: Good and Bad Novels* (1972) contrasts *Little Dorrit* with Anthony Trollope's *The Way We Live Now* and Thomas Love Peacock's *Crotchet Castle* to explain how novels should — and should not — be read. Classifying the three works respectively as a symbolic novel, a realistic novel, and a novel of ideas, Hewitt attempts to help readers appreciate each on its own terms. In *Season of Youth: The Bildungsroman from Dickens to Golding* (1974) Jerome Buckley makes what some would consider a startling claim regarding Dickens's fiction. "For all its objectivity of manner," he says, "*Great Expectations* comes closer than *Copperfield* to being a portrait of the author" (45). He considers this novel a great example of the *Bildungsroman* because "whatever was subjective in origin, the product of an acute self-knowledge has been assimilated to a beautifully controlled work of art" (46). Buckley's editorial project, *The Worlds of Victorian Fiction* (1975), includes three studies of Dickens's work, the most intriguing being Barbara Charlesworth Gelpi's assessment of Victorian autobiography, in which she argues that Dickens's method of retelling his life in *David Copperfield* was a model for supposedly real-life autobiographies of many Victorians, including Mill and Ruskin.

As had been the case in preceding decades, influence studies flourished during the 1970s. The new thrust in critical methodology, however, was not to try to demonstrate direct influence, but to look for subtle ways the work of one writer may have indirectly inspired others. Albert Guerard makes just such a point at the beginning of *The Triumph of the Novel: Dickens, Dostoevsky, Faulkner* (1976). "I have no desire to revive" American scholarship's century-long "obsession with influence," he asserts (3). Instead, Guerard stresses the fecundity of the three novelists' imagination, their ability to innovate within the genre, and their kinship in being "indisputably strange and disturbed men" (7). He describes Dickens as "the inventive fantasist and comic entertainer possessed with extraordinary narrative energy and creative power," not the "serious thinker and responsible social realist" that the Leavises would like him to be. Guerard relies on techniques of psychological criticism to identify the sources of Dickens's creative power — without falling back on another time-worn tradition in American criticism, the tendency to psychoanalyze the writer by extrapolating from his works.[2]

Of course, since the 1830s it had been fashionable to compare Dickens to Shakespeare. In 1965 Robert Fleissner had attempted what he described as a systematic study in *Dickens and Shakespeare: A Study in Histrionic Contrasts,* but the work was severely criticized by Philip Collins in a review for *Nineteenth-Century Fiction* (1967). However, in the 1975 American Philosophical Society lecture, later published as *A Kind of Power: The Shakespeare-Dickens Analogy* (1975), distinguished Shakespeare scholar Alfred Harbage takes up the issue once more. Although not a complete appraisal — it would be twenty years later before a truly comprehensive study would be published — Harbage suggests the influence of Shakespeare on Dickens was largely indirect. He finds parallels in their careers, stressing that each understood he was a professional entertainer who relied on popular support for his success. What they shared, in the view of Harbage and many others, was a special quality of imagination that permitted them to bring characters and scenes to life in their work.

Shifting Critical Methodologies

Two studies published in the 1970s focusing on the quality of Dickens's imagination illustrate some of the key differences between what might be called traditional criticism and the newer approaches to literary study ushered in by poststructuralists. John Carey's *The Violent Effigy: A Study of Dickens's Imagination* (1973), reprinted a year later under the jaunty title *Here Comes Dickens: The Imagination of a Novelist,* begins with the admonition that "Dickens is infinitely greater than his critics." Insistent that "Dickens is essentially a comic writer" (7), Carey complains that critics of the previous two decades have taken Dickens too seriously and tried to make him into something he never was. Contrary to the claims of the Leavises and the generation of American critics who consistently value the dark side of Dickens, Carey believes "we shall miss his real greatness if we persist in regarding him primarily as a critic of society." Dickens is markedly singular, Carey says, in his "inability to take institutions seriously" (8). Similarly, proponents of psychological realism who criticize Dickens for not revealing the inner lives of his characters present a "cramped" vision of the novelist (8). Carey is especially disappointed in critics like A. E. Dyson (*The Inimitable Dickens* 1970) who search deeply for hidden meanings, "as if great works of art were to be cherished, in the last resort, for whatever moral droppings can be coaxed from them" (10). The fault underlying all these approaches, Carey believes, lies in the predisposition to rank tragedy over comedy in the pecking order of literary greatness — a fault Carey attempts to correct in his reading of the Dickens canon.

Carey focuses on Dickens's imagination as it is applied to subjects such as violence, order, and humor. Employing as a central organizing device Dickens's lifelong fascination with corpses and effigies, he notes how the novelist uses these metaphorically and symbolically throughout his fiction to create a portrait of people and society that reveals much about human character. In Carey's judgment, Dickens is decidedly *not* modern, at least not in technique or vision; instead, he is the consummate humorist whose "imagination transforms the world" while his "laughter controls it" (175).

If Carey's work offers a traditional approach to analyzing Dickens's works, Garrett Stewart's *Dickens and the Trials of Imagination* (1974) is an example of the new kind of critical examination that would transform literary studies over the next generation. Interested in the way Dickens transposed ideas into "living prose" (xvi), Stewart takes as his subject "the distribution of Dickens's own fluid and buoyant imagination to the tributary intelligences both of his heroes and at times his villains," especially those who "fight to keep imagination alive in a sordidly real world." These characters, whom Stewart dubs "imaginists," are superior to ones who "have only words to live by, who cloak the vile hollows of their natures" in the "opaque and elaborate language" of rhetoric (xviii).

Stewart is exceptionally conscious of the critics who precede him, and a constant thread throughout his study is his attempt to set off his own readings from those of Carey and Kincaid. Balancing his appreciation for the comic side of Dickens with his acknowledgment that social criticism is an integral part of Dickens's artistry, Stewart engages in extensive, close readings of individual texts to demonstrate how the novelist creates characters whose ability to live as imaginists sets them apart from a society characterized by its "assault against imagination" (151). What comes through in his analysis is Stewart's genuine pleasure in reading Dickens and his appreciation for the novelist's comic genius — but not at the expense of recognizing the importance of the later, darker novels. Dickens's fiction, he says, is characterized by four distinct styles: the high comic, the satiric, the lyric, and the neurotic. All of these, Stewart says, are employed with great skill to demonstrate how those with imagination must struggle in a grim world.

Perhaps because he was among the first to write about Dickens using both the vocabulary and methodology of the new breed of literary theorists, Stewart was not immediately appreciated by mainstream Dickens critics. Reviewing his book in the *Dickensian,* Robin Gilmour not only challenged his conclusions about Dickens's career, but also questioned the style in which *Dickens and the Trials of Imagination* is written. The highly metaphoric and self-conscious presentation of critical commentary was not yet the accepted mode of scholarship in the early 1970s, but as it became more commonplace, Stewart's work became a more frequent touchstone against which future critics tested their own readings of individual novels and their overall approaches to the Victorian novelist.

Valentine Cunningham's *Everywhere Spoken Against: Dissent in the Victorian Novel* (1975) is one of those works that, like Stewart's, has as much to say about critical methodology as it does about the novelists whose works he examines. His strong opening statement is decidedly antiformalist: Novels, he argues "have had much more intercourse with society, with — to borrow the Marxist term — the economic and social base, than any other literary mode," and in Victorian novels those bonds are "clamorously obvious." Consequently, "the reader cannot avoid the consequences of a situation in which these novelists at any rate are blissfully unaware of the supposed autonomy of their art that is sometimes willed upon them by post-Jamesian criticism" (1–2). Describing as "heresy" the claims that Victorian novelists created a world independent of history (7), Cunningham focuses on ways writers such as Dickens dealt with dissent and dissenters. He is actually quite critical of Dickens for treating this subject lightheartedly, describing the novelist's attempts to satirize dissenters as signs of his "immaturity" and "failure of seriousness" (190). He faults Dickens for being "the most notorious of the novelists who are content with stereotypes of dissenters," frequently treating them as impious hypocrites (199). Nevertheless, understanding how Dickens viewed dissenters is important for social historians, Cunningham argues, because his influence was so pervasive that it contributed to the continuing distorted view of this religious group. Like Cunningham, in *Dickens and Charity* (1978) Norris Pope uses Dickens's life to explain why Dickens's methods of confronting social problems differed from those used by organized charities, especially religious groups. Pope's work is decidedly less grounded in new critical thought, and is largely a study of Dickens's reaction to and relationship with Evangelicals, for whom Pope says he had little sympathy.

Among the early feminist detractors, Françoise Basch argues in *Relative Creatures: Victorian Women in Society and the Novel 1837–1867* (1974) that most female characters in early Victorian novels are either caricatured or idealized, created simply to provide a means for a happy ending that culminates in marriage for the eligible hero. Relying heavily on Georg Lukács for her ideas about the relationship between realism and greatness in fiction, she argues Dickens fails in achieving greatness because he simply cannot portray women realistically. Basch finds few redeeming qualities in Dickens's women, whether single or married: "They explain neither the particularity or the complexity of human beings, nor the specific problems of a particular condition or profession" (151).

Perhaps fueled by Raymond Williams's extensive study of Dickens early in the decade, Marxist critics continued to show interest in him during the 1970s. In *Criticism and Ideology: A Study in Marxist Literary Theory* (1976), one of the early works in his distinguished and controversial career as a leading proponent of Marxist criticism, Terry Eagleton includes a chapter on Dickens that appeared originally as an essay in *New Left Review*. Eagleton admits he can be accused of providing a "partial and reductive reading" (7) but insists Dickens was tied to bourgeois ideology and conventions. Some of the novels, however, contain certain dissonances. Eagleton says these appear not in major characters, which are entirely conventional, but in peripheral figures, whose presence indicates the decentered nature of much of Dickens's fiction. But this is not enough to make Dickens a darling of the Marxists. Eagleton cites Dickens for a number of transgressions and shortcomings — most of which relate to the novelist's failure to provide an effective critique of society. For Eagleton and his Marxist colleagues, Dickens's novels may be interesting, but they do not rise to the level of great literature.

Traditional Criticism in the Late 1970s

By the mid-1970s traditional criticism of Dickens was gradually being challenged by new approaches based on theories of literature and language that made old-time Dickensians uncomfortable. In his introduction to *The Dickens Myth: Its Genesis and Structure* (1976) Geoffrey Thurley provides a somewhat biased snapshot of Dickens criticism at the start of the final quarter of the twentieth century. "Dickens has been revived," Thurley notes, "but the ceremony has been somewhat morbid." Critics "unable to shake off preconceptions about the nature of good fiction often irrelevant to Dickens" have tried instead "to show that he was really doing the same sorts of things as respectable realists." Beneath the surface praise of twentieth-century critics there lies "a radical ambivalence" (1). Thurley believes Dickens's art contains little realism, but "in many respects" is "qualitatively superior to the psychological realism of Tolstoy or George Eliot" (2). Hence, he is disappointed that so many critics simply misconstrue the novelist's methods and distort his artistry. He attacks Taylor Stoehr for creating "his own Dickens monster — a basically unhuman creature possessed of a brilliant faculty for telling his dreams" (3). He faults Robert Garis for similar treatment. "Charles Dickens is nowhere to be seen in *The Dickens Theatre*," Thurley complains, having been replaced by a "heartless gesticulating mime with no knowledge of himself or others" (4–5). He claims Harvey Sucksmith's book is a misguided attempt to turn Dickens into "a Jungian introvert" (5). Unfortunately, he says, American critics have not done the novelist any better service. By simply equating class with money, they overlook or oversimplify the complex social system at the root of Dickens's fiction. He is disappointed, too, that Marxist critics have been so harsh on Dickens for not being consistent in his critique of capitalism.

By contrast, Thurley celebrates the Leavises for holding on to "a conception of a human Dickens" (7) even if they do not always appreciate his genius. He ranks them with G. K. Chesterton as the best Dickens critics, because they understand Dickens's aims at exposing the evils of the class system. "The great universality of Dickens's work," Thurley says, lies in the novelist's ability to expose the anxieties that accompany the struggle for wealth, position, and affluence (25). "The persistent primal fantasy of Dickens's novels" — what Thurley calls "their myth" — directly reflects "the striving upward movement of modern society and the spiritual discomfort it brings with it" (27). Dickens's greatest distinction is to have been the first to lay bare these neuroses, and his attacks on capitalism remain relevant long after his death.

Despite the growing number of studies like those of Stewart, Basch, and Eagleton, formalists and social humanists still dominated Dickens studies during the decade. Norman Friedman, who had written about Dickens two decades earlier in "Versions of Form in Fiction — 'Great Expectations' and 'The Great Gatsby'" (1954), defends this approach to literature in *Form and Meaning in Fiction* (1975), reasserting the dictum that formal analysis "deals with meanings only in terms of the roles they play in the artistic whole." Friedman is upset with trends in criticism that consider novels to be "structure[s] of — and not simply containing — meanings," a fact he believes confuses the issue of interpretation (20). Friedman offers instead what he calls a "pluralistic" approach to fiction, demonstrating the many factors influencing "the author's choice and organization of his materials" (24). His point, made emphatically throughout this book, is that, far from being absent, authors are always present and always make conscious choices in selecting and organizing materials to produce specific effects on readers. Dickens's role as author is of primary importance to Duane DeVries as well. In *Dickens's Apprentice Years: The Making of a Novelist* (1976) DeVries focuses on Dickens's development during the period 1833–36, when he was working on materials for *Sketches by Boz*. His reliance on formalist principles is made evident by his acknowledgement of Percy Lubbock and E. M. Forster as his mentors.

In *The Confessional Fictions of Charles Dickens* (1977) Barry Westburg argues that, like Kierkegaard, Dickens understood the importance of achieving unity in the individual life. His Dickens is more concerned with "personal truth" than with "inherited cultural truths" (xiii). Consequently, Westburg finds the idea of growth through time and its impact on the human subject to be the central theme of the novelist's work, as this is the mode of confessional fiction. Westburg identifies three novels he finds overtly confessional: *Oliver Twist, David Copperfield,* and *Great Expectations.* These "radical probes into growth, time and life," Westburg says, serve as "keystones of Dickens's creativity" (xiv). Westburg's close readings demonstrate that Dickens advanced as an artist "most radically each time he posed development itself as a theme" (xvi).

With an eye toward answering the Leavises' objections to Dickens's being given too high a place in English letters, Robert Newsom sets out in *Dickens on the Romantic Side of Familiar Things: Bleak House and the Novel Tradition* (1977) to provide considerably more than a critique of a single novel. Newsom examines Dickens's mixture of the realistic and romantic traditions that the novelist himself claimed were woven into his fiction. By explaining how these operate in *Bleak House* and other novels, Newsom hopes to "bring Dickens back into the center of the tradition of the English novel and English literature," rather than leave him "on the outside of the tradition as an unassailable popular giant" (2). With similar intent, John Romano attempts to redirect nearly four decades of criticism about Dickens that had stressed his alienation from the society in which he lived and wrote by insisting in *Dickens and Reality* (1978) that the novelist is principally a realistic artist. His study provides a definition of the concept of realism that identifies formal characteristics and helps readers "recognize those distinctive gestures" by which a realistic novelist like Dickens helps signify "the world that lies beyond the farthest border of his power to portray" (7). Romano examines the novels thematically to demonstrate how Dickens is always referring to a world outside of his fiction.

George Worth is among those traditional critics who believe that Dickens's use of melodrama is a strength, not a weakness. His *Dickensian Melodrama: A Reading of the Novels* (1978) explains how theatrical techniques, specifically melodrama, influenced the production of the novels. Worth is convinced that no previous study has done justice to this aspect of Dickens's artistic achievement, despite the amount of criticism already available on the topic. As a result, he says, Dickens has been pilloried since 1838 for adopting a technique that was initially quite useful and ultimately essential to his success. Worth's real targets are Taylor Stoehr and Robert Garis, who use the term "melodrama" pejoratively. Worth believes that as Dickens evolved from a verbal sketch artist and aspiring dramatist into a novelist, he brought with him techniques that had served him well.

While critical analysis of the novels remained the major focus for Dickens scholars, several studies published during the 1970s focus on other aspects of his professional career. Gordon Spence concentrates on the nonfiction in *Charles Dickens as a Familiar Essayist* (1977). Taking examples from *Sketches by Boz* and comparing them to later publications from *The Uncommercial Traveler,* Spence is able to link Dickens to the tradition of social criticism that had characterized the familiar essay for two centuries. By reading Dickens's essays carefully, he argues, it is possible to gain further insight into his personality and interests. In *Victorian Novelists and Publishers* (1976) John Sutherland discusses Dickens's work as editor of *All the Year Round,* exploring his relationships with other writers whose work he serialized in the periodical. Dickens emerges as a careful reader and coach who, at the same time, could act with cool business sense to make sure circulation did not flag. Without calling him a co-author, Sutherland suggests Dickens influenced production of several novels by contemporaries through his suggestions — or other, more coercive tactics. But writers for *All the Year Round* were not the only people with whom Dickens collaborated, as Michael Steig demonstrates in *Dickens and Phiz* (1978). Steig argues Hablot Knight Browne, the most famous illustrator of Dickens's books, actually collaborated with him in creating a series of successful novels. Browne was, Steig says, "the very first interpreter of each of the novels he illustrated" (ix).

More detailed than Sutherland's study and more insightful than many done on the topic before or since, Robert Patten's *Charles Dickens and His Publishers* (1978) is one of the most exceptional works of scholarship on Dickens to emerge during the later decades of the century. Already established as an editor and authority on the illustrator George Cruikshank, Patten had most recently contributed a thoughtful essay, "A Surprising Transformation: Dickens and the Hearth" to U. C. Knoepflmacher and G. B. Tennyson's collection *Nature and the Victorian Imagination* (1977), in which he challenged conventional critical wisdom that the natural world played no significant role in Dickens's fiction. In *Charles Dickens and His Publishers* Patten collects records of the publishing history of Dickens's major work, including sales figures attesting to the novelist's popularity among his contemporaries and revealing something about his staying power with later audiences. Years before cultural critics made it fashionable (once again) to examine a novelist's work within the cultural context that led to its production, Patten was insisting that "the conditions of publishing" had "much to do with Dickens's career" (343). Patten puts forward a thesis that would have shocked the aesthetic critics of the mid-century: "That Dickens wrote for money should be at the very least a neutral fact," he asserts. "How it became possible for Dickens to write for money, on the other hand, takes us into the very heart of nineteenth-century culture, and into all the intimately reciprocal connections between the artist and his age" (344). Poring over the documentary evidence, Patten finds a Dickens who would have been both recognizable and admired by the more radical critics of the early century: "Working closely with a succession of enterprising publishers," he says, "Dickens democratized fiction" (343).

Another critic who continued to use traditional methodologies in the 1970s (and later) is Harry Stone. His *Dickens and the Invisible World: Fairy Tales, Fantasy, and Novel Making* (1979) is a major study of Dickens's use of the fairy-tale motif. Despite his claims in the introduction, however, Stone is not the first to write a book about Dickens's use of the fairy tale. Michael Kotzin's brief monograph *Dickens and the Fairy Tale* (1972) appeared before Stone's more extensive study on this topic. But to be fair to Stone, Kotzin relies heavily on articles Stone had published during the 1960s as the basis for his work. Stone's book is an examination of Dickens's use of the fairy tale as a structuring device for his novels. Stone considers not only traditional fairy tales but also the Gothic stories which thrilled Dickens as a youngster. He contends all of Dickens's novels owe a great debt to this tradition. In what might be seen as a reversal of the traditional way of viewing the trajectory of Dickens's career as a realist, Stone argues that in the early novels Dickens interpolates tales and characters from this tradition into novels intended to be more realistic. As he progressed in his career, the fairy tale became the structuring device. The reasons for this movement toward integration of fairy-tale and social commentary are clear. "By 1850," Stone says, "Dickens strongly and consciously associated the literature of childhood with the greatest of public ends," finding the fairy tale and associated legendary literature "potent instruments and incarnations of imaginative truth" (3–4). As he matured in his craft, Stone says, Dickens displayed a "growing ability to fuse the fanciful and the everyday and to achieve thereby a deeper sense of the *quidditas* and wonder of reality" (95). Further, these literary genres were often associated with oral tradition, and by extension the drama, so they appealed to Dickens's strong penchant as a performer. In this form, Stone argues, Dickens found he could convey life realistically while at the same time commenting on its deceptive exactitude and depicting its intricate mystery.

In 1979 Oxford University Press brought out a new biography of Dickens by the husband-and-wife team of Norman and Jeanne MacKenzie. If it did nothing else, the MacKenzies' *Charles Dickens: A Life* (1979) made it clear that not all Dickens biographies are of equal value. Despite being promoted by a major academic press, the book met with scathing reviews from Dickens scholars. Robert Newsom commented in *Dickens Studies Annual* that "both the scholar and general reader alike may safely leave [it] unopened" (268). Andrew Sanders, writing in the *Dickensian*, called it plodding and clichéd, failing to provide a good biography of the novelist or "any real perception of how his novels work" (44).

Signs of New Directions in Dickens Studies

By the late 1970s, the influence of J. Hillis Miller and European philosophers such as Jacques Derrida and Paul de Man was beginning to reshape Dickens studies in new and intriguing ways. In *Commissioned Spirits: The Shaping of Social Motion in Dickens, Carlyle, Melville, and Hawthorne* (1979), Jonathan Arac, one of the new generation of scholars who were beginning to reexamine nineteenth-century literature with the tools of poststructuralism, employs theories of language, text, and discourse to investigate nineteenth-century novelists' attempts to achieve a "narrative overview" of society (2). Arac focuses on ways Dickens and others employ techniques of plotting and linguistic strategies to structure the complex world from which they draw their fictions. Concurrently, he explores "the place of the institution of literature within society, and the powers and responsibilities of the writers within this institution" (4). Arac sees Dickens closely connected to the social milieu; in fact, he argues that the novelist's view of society paralleled that of many government and private agencies trying to survey the world, identify its ills, and propose improvements. Only late in his career, Arac suggests, did Dickens turn away from larger social themes to become a more private writer.

Among the more intriguing new approaches to Dickens was that of Maire Jaanus Kurrik. In *Literature and Negation* (1979), Kurrik employs the "criticism of negation" — a method for studying a text by examining not what it includes but "from the perspective of what it excludes, and in the cultural context that illuminates the exclusion" (x). Kurrik begins his critique by insisting that the demands made by Henry James, the Leavises, and David Cecil for "a more conscious intelligibility of structure and character" (163) should not be imposed on writers of genius. Dickens, he says, had the ability to produce a "gestalt form" that allows readers to "see a whole, a unity, a gestalt, which is far more than the sum of its parts because the gestalt overlooks the fragmented, varied, discrete and dispersed" (164). His own psychological readings rely heavily on competing theories of negation espoused by Hegel and Freud. In the end, though, he endorses earlier critics who have urged that Dickens's loose and baggy monsters be accepted as works of genius, filled with great insight into human nature.

Although his work has much in common with Alexander Welsh's *The City of Dickens* (1971), F. S. Schwarzbach's sociological and historical examination of Dickens's fiction, *Dickens and the City* (1979), goes beyond literary criticism to suggest something about the uses to which Dickens can be put in the twentieth century. Schwarzbach argues that urbanization is the most important phenomena of modern life; hence, because Dickens understood the city-as-idea so well, "to read Dickens is to read the imprint of the consciousness of an age" (4). Dickens was "moulded by and in turn helped to mould the sensibility of his culture," Schwarzbach says, "and of ours, as its inheritors" (29). His reading of the novels stresses the overriding notion that Dickens was driven by "creative and imaginative forces" to deal with the "complex psychological and fictional struggle" he and his Victorian contemporaries experienced "between a mythic vision of pastoral innocence and a hellish nightmare of urban experience" (213). Schwarzbach says Dickens's real merit lies in his ability to demystify the hellish landscape of the city.

Typical of the new, more self-reflective brand of criticism appearing late in the 1970s is Susan Horton's *Interpreting Interpreting: Interpreting Dickens's Dombey* (1979). Horton uses *Dombey and Son* as a base text for examining the many ways critics can read a work of fiction. She demonstrates that the novel is sufficiently complex to elude a full and definitive interpretation — that the meaning of *any* novel depends on the interpreter's angle of vision. Her real aim is not to critique Dickens, of course, but to attack critics who insist on a monolithic approach to literature. Those open to multiple approaches, she says, are likely to glean more from writers such as Dickens.

Criticism such as Horton's made sense to some, but made others just plain mad. In *Plot, Story, and the Novel* (1979) Robert Caserio strikes out at those he believes have been "stripping literature from its connections with what is allegedly nonliterary" (xiv), devaluing storytelling and elevating other literary qualities as the measures of talent and relevance. Caserio considers Dickens a master at telling a story, even though he can be illogical at times. Some minor flaws do occur, he concedes, when Dickens employs his storytelling for moral purposes. This rather Arnoldian approach would continue to inform the work of many in the Dickens Industry even as the poststructuralists began to assert their dominance on the critical scene.

Notes

[1] Actually, although there was no change in the journal's name, a similar evolution took place with the *Dickensian*, especially after Michael Slater became editor. Historians of academic publication might find interest in tracing the way journals evolve, since the pattern that *DSN* took toward becoming the *Dickens Quarterly* is not unique. The *Arnold Newsletter*, a publication founded in 1972 to serve Arnold scholars, metamorphosed into *The Arnoldian* in 1974, slowly began to concentrate on publishing articles rather than communications among Arnold scholars, and eventually emerged as *Nineteenth-Century Prose* in 1986, abandoning any pretext of serving only the small community of Arnold scholars. The prestigious quarterly *Nineteenth-Century Fiction* had its origins in the decidedly more modest *Trollopian*, founded in 1945 as a medium for exchange of information on Trollope and other Victorian novelists.

[2] The influence of Dickens on Dostoevsky has been the subject of several studies. Donald Fanger's earlier monograph, *Dostoevsky and Romantic Realism* (1965) offers a systematic examination of how Dickens influenced the Russian novelist. N. M. Lary takes virtually the same approach as Guerard in *Dostoevsky and Dickens: A Study in Literary Influence* (1973). Nearly twenty years later Michael Futrell covers the same ground in *Dostoevskii and Britain* (1995), again cautioning against efforts to assign too great a weight to Dickens's influence on Dostoevsky.

Works Cited

Amalric, Jean-Claude, ed. *Studies in the Later Dickens*. Montpellier, France: Université Paul Valery, 1973.

Arac, Jonathan. *Commissioned Spirits: The Shaping of Social Motion in Dickens, Carlyle, Melville, and Hawthorne*. New Brunswick, NJ: Rutgers UP, 1979.

Basch, Françoise. *Relative Creatures: Victorian Women in Society and the Novel, 1837–67*. Translated by Anthony Rudolf. London: Lane, 1974.

Buckley, Jerome H. "Dickens, David, and Pip." *Season of Youth: The Bildungsroman from Dickens to Golding*, 28–62. Cambridge, MA: Harvard UP, 1974.

———. *The Worlds of Victorian Fiction*. Cambridge, MA: Harvard UP, 1975.

Carey, John. *The Violent Effigy: A Study of Dickens's Imagination*. London: Faber and Faber, 1973. Rev. ed. London: Faber, 1991. Reprinted as *Here Comes Dickens: The Imagination of a Novelist*. New York: Schocken, 1974.

Caserio, Robert. *Plot, Story, and the Novel*. Princeton, NJ: Princeton UP, 1979.

Collins, Philip A. W. Review of Robert Fleissner, *Dickens and Shakespeare. A Study in Histrionic Contrasts*. *Nineteenth-Century Fiction* 21 (1967): 403.

Cunningham, Valentine. *Everywhere Spoken Against: Dissent in the Victorian Novel*. Oxford: Oxford UP, 1975.

Daleski, H. M. *Dickens and the Art of Analogy*. New York: Schocken, 1970.

Davey, Samuel J. "Charles Dickens." *Darwin, Carlyle and Dickens, With Other Essays*, 121–56. London: James Clark, 1876. Reprint, New York: Haskell House, 1971.

DeVries, Duane. *Dickens's Apprentice Years: The Making of a Novelist*. Totowa, NJ: Barnes & Noble, 1976.

Dyson, A. E. *The Inimitable Dickens: A Reading of the Novels*. London: Macmillan, 1970.

Eagleton, Terry. "Charles Dickens." *Criticism and Ideology: A Study in Marxist Literary Theory*, 121–56. London: Verso, 1976.

Fanger, Donald. *Dostoevsky and Romantic Realism: A Study of Dostoevsky in Relation to Balzac, Dickens, and Gogol*. Cambridge, MA: Harvard UP, 1965; reprint, Evanston, IL: Northwestern UP, 1998.

Fido, Martin. *Charles Dickens: An Authentic Account of His Life and Times.* London: Hamlyn, 1970.

Fleissner, Robert F. *Dickens and Shakespeare: A Study in Histrionic Contrasts.* New York: Haskell House, 1965.

Friedman, Norman. *Form and Meaning in Fiction.* Athens: U of Georgia P, 1975.

———. "Versions of Form in Fiction — *Great Expectations* and *The Great Gatsby.*" *Accent* 14 (Autumn 1954): 246–64.

Garis, Robert E. *The Dickens Theatre: A Reassessment of the Novels.* Oxford: Clarendon P, 1965.

Gilmour, Robin. Review of Garrett Stewart, *Dickens and the Trials of Imagination. Dickensian* 72.1 (January 1976): 39–40.

Gold, Joseph. *Charles Dickens: Radical Moralist.* London: Oxford UP, 1972.

———. *The Stature of Dickens: A Centenary Bibliography.* Toronto: U of Toronto P, 1971.

Goldberg, Michael. *Carlyle and Dickens.* Athens: U of Georgia P, 1972.

———. "Gigantic Philistines." *Lectures on Carlyle and His Era.* Santa Cruz: University Library, U of California P, 1985.

Gomme, A. H. *Dickens.* Literature in Perspective. London: Evans, 1971.

Guerard, Albert J. *The Triumph of the Novel: Dickens, Dostoevsky, Faulkner.* New York: Oxford UP, 1976.

Harbage, Alfred B. *A Kind of Power: The Shakespeare-Dickens Analogy.* Philadelphia: American Philosophical Society, 1975.

Hardy, Barbara. *Charles Dickens, The Writer and His Work.* Windsor, England: Profile Books, 1983.

———. *Dickens: The Later Novels.* Writers and Their Work 205. London: Longmans, Green, 1968.

———. *Forms of Feeling in Victorian Fiction.* London: Owen, 1985.

———. *The Moral Art of Dickens.* London: Athlone, 1970.

Hewitt, Douglas. *The Approach to Fiction: Good and Bad Novels.* London: Longmans, 1972.

Hobsbaum, Philip. *A Reader's Guide to Charles Dickens.* New York: Farrar, Straus, & Giroux, 1972.

Hornback, Bert G. *"Noah's Arkitecture": A Study of Dickens's Mythology.* Athens: Ohio UP, 1972.

Horton, Susan. *Interpreting Interpreting: Interpreting Dickens's Dombey.* Baltimore, MD: Johns Hopkins UP, 1979.

Kincaid, James R. *Dickens and the Rhetoric of Laughter*. Oxford: Oxford UP, 1971.

Kotzin, Michael C. *Dickens and the Fairy Tale*. Bowling Green, OH: Bowling Green UP, 1972.

Kurrik, Maire Jaanus. *Literature and Negation*. New York: Columbia UP, 1979.

Lary, N. M. *Dostoevsky and Dickens: A Study of Literary Influence*. London: Routledge & Kegan Paul, 1973.

Leavis, F. R. "An American Critic." *Scrutiny* 11 (Summer 1942): 72–73.

———. "*Dombey and Son*." *Sewanee Review* 70 (January-March 1962): 177–201.

———. *The Great Tradition*. London: Chatto & Windus, 1948.

Leavis, F. R., and Q. D. Leavis *Dickens The Novelist*. New York: Pantheon, 1970.

Leavis, Q. D. *Fiction and the Reading Public*. London: Chatto & Windus, 1932.

Lucas, John. *The Melancholy Man: A Study of Dickens's Novels*. London: Methuen, 1970.

Mackenzie, Norman and Jeanne Mackenzie. *Dickens: A Life*. Oxford: Oxford UP, 1979.

Manning, Sylvia Bank. *Dickens as Satirist*. London: Yale UP, 1971.

Miller, J. Hillis, and David Borowitz. *Charles Dickens and George Cruikshank*. Los Angeles: William Clark Memorial Library, 1971.

Millett, Kate. *Sexual Politics*. Garden City, NY: Doubleday, 1970.

Newsom, Robert. *Dickens on the Romantic Side of Familiar Things: Bleak House and the Novel Tradition*. New York: Columbia UP, 1977.

———. "Recent Dickens Studies." *Dickens Studies Annual* 9 (1981): 265–86.

Nisbet, Ada, and Blake Nevius, eds. *Dickens Centennial Essays*. Berkeley: U of California P, 1971.

Oddie, William. *Dickens and Carlyle*. London: Centenary, 1972.

Paroissien, David. "Editorial: Occasion, Chance, and Change." *Dickens Quarterly* 1.1 (March 1984): 1.

Partlow, Robert B. Jr., ed. *Dickens the Craftsman: Strategies of Presentation*. Carbondale and Edwardsville: Southern Illinois UP, 1970.

———. "Preface." *Dickens Studies Annual* 1, ix–x. Carbondale and Edwardsville: Southern Illinois UP, 1970.

Partlow, Robert B. Jr., and Robert Patten. "To Our Readers." *Dickens Studies Newsletter* 1.1 (March 1970): 1.

Patten, Robert. *Charles Dickens and His Publishers*. Oxford: Clarendon P, 1978.

———. "A Surprising Transformation: Dickens and the Hearth." In *Nature and the Victorian Imagination*, edited by U. C. Knoepflmacher and G. B. Tennyson, 153–70. Berkeley: U of California P, 1977.

Peyrouton, Noel. "Milestones Along the Dover Road." *Dickens Studies* 1.1 (January 1965): 1.

Pike, James S. "Dickens, Carlyle and Tennyson." *Atlantic Monthly* 164 (December 1939): 810–19.

Pope, Norris. *Dickens and Charity*. New York: Columbia UP, 1978.

Romano, John. *Dickens and Reality*. New York: Columbia UP, 1978.

Sanders, Andrew. Review of Norman and Jeanne MacKenzie, *Dickens: A Life*. *Dickensian* 76.1 (Spring 1980): 44–45.

Schwarzbach, F. S. *Dickens and the City*. London: Athlone, 1979.

Slater, Michael, ed. *Dickens 1970*. New York: Stein and Day, 1970.

Spence, Gordon. *Charles Dickens as a Familiar Essayist*. Salzburg: Institut for Englische Sprache und Literatur, 1977.

Steig, Michael. *Dickens and Phiz*. Bloomington: Indiana UP, 1978.

Stewart, Garrett. *Dickens and the Trials of Imagination*. Boston, MA: Harvard UP, 1974.

Stone, Harry. *Dickens and the Invisible World: Fairy Tales, Fantasy, and Novel Making*. Bloomington: Indiana UP, 1979.

Studies in the Novel 1.2 (Summer 1969). Charles Dickens Special Number.

Sucksmith, Harvey Peter. *The Narrative Art of Charles Dickens: The Rhetoric of Sympathy and Irony in His Novels*. London: Oxford UP, 1970.

Sutherland, John L. *Victorian Novelists and Publishers*. Chicago: U of Chicago P; London: Athlone, 1976.

Tomlin, Eric W. F., ed. *Charles Dickens 1812–1870: A Centenary Volume*. London: Weidenfeld and Nicolson, 1969.

Thurley, Geoffrey. *The Dickens Myth: Its Genesis and Structure*. New York: St. Martin's, 1976.

Watt, Ian, ed. *The Victorian Novel: Modern Essays in Criticism*. Oxford: Oxford UP, 1971.

Welsh, Alexander. *The City of Dickens*. Oxford: Oxford UP, 1971.

Westburg, Barry. *The Confessional Fictions of Charles Dickens*. Dekalb: Northern Illinois UP, 1977.

Williams, Raymond. *The Country and the City*. New York and London: Oxford UP, 1973.

———. *Culture and Society 1780–1950*, 92–97. London: Chatto & Windus, 1958.

———. *The English Novel: From Dickens to Lawrence*. New York and London: Oxford UP, 1970.

———. "Social Criticism in Dickens: Some Problems of Method and Approach." *Critical Quarterly* 6 (Autumn 1964): 214–27.

Wilson, Angus. "Charles Dickens: A Haunting." *Critical Quarterly* 2 (Summer 1960): 101–8.

———. *The World of Charles Dickens*. London: Secker & Warburg, 1970.

Worth, George J. *Dickensian Melodrama: A Reading of the Novels*. Lawrence: U of Kansas P, 1978.

7: Dickens in an Age of Theory I: New Theories, New Readings (1980–2000)

THE CHANGING TIDES IN LITERARY STUDY brought in a new wave of critics in the late 1960s and throughout the 1970s, and the agenda for Dickens studies was changed notably. New approaches to literature — deconstruction, new historicism, feminism, new psychological approaches to character and texts, and the rise of interdisciplinary studies of literary texts informed by new ideas of culture — signaled a sharp break from more conventional forms of criticism. While traditional biographical, historical, textual, formalist, and humanist studies continued to be published, such works competed for attention in the academic marketplace with those using new methodologies stressing the fluidity of texts, the "death of the author," the "situatedness" and historicity of knowledge, and the power relationships that underlie even the most seemingly benign works of literature.

The reaction of The Dickens Industry to these new approaches was mixed. It should not be surprising that a number of the most thoughtful and influential books on Dickens written during the last two decades of the century would be shaped by one theory or another, especially since one of the leaders of this new form of literary study in America was J. Hillis Miller, whose 1958 book on Dickens continued to be cited with greater frequency than any other critical work on the novelist. Nevertheless, there remained among the ranks of Dickens scholars (perhaps much more so than among those interested in other figures) a core of die-hard traditionalists who continued to read and write about Dickens as if Jacques Derrida, Jacques Lacan, Roland Barthes, the Russian formalists, the new historians, or even the feminists had never existed.

The following two chapters outline the impact of new critical theories on the Dickens canon, and the ongoing work of what have come to be called "traditional" or "conventional" critics in offering new readings of Dickens's fiction and journalism. One should recall, however, that the practices described as New Criticism or formalism, once considered avant garde, are now lumped together with older methodologies as "traditional." For ease of comparison, critical studies have been grouped around headings that suggest the major focus of individual books or articles. Of course, many scholars emerging from the universities in the 1970s and later were trained in a variety of theoretical approaches, and their work frequently reflects a blending of approaches to Dickens's work, defying strict categorization.

Studies of Language, Authorship, and the Representation of Reality

Peter Garrett's *The Victorian Multiplot Novel: Studies in Dialogical Form* (1980) is typical of new critical studies grounded in poststructuralist theory. His critique challenges the prevailing critical perception that multiplot novels have a "center" around which and from which other plots evolve and revolve. Using theoretical concepts developed by Russian literary theorist Mikhail Bakhtin, Garrett explains how the dialogical form accounts for many of the unresolved tensions readers feel in reading multiplot novels, including those by Dickens. Garrett highlights Dickens's use of shifting perspectives and multiple stories as a means of presenting a dramatic view of society in which opposites frequently remain unresolved. Focusing on *Bleak House, Little Dorrit,* and *Our Mutual Friend,* Garrett celebrates Dickens's conscious strategies to avoid being pinned down with respect to "meaning." "Where one perspective appears to gain control over one of Dickens's novels," Garrett says, "its basis of meaning is threatened. In a dialogical form, perspectives can have no independent value; they gain meaning only through the oppositions and tensions between them." Viewed in this light, "the most important form of freedom in Dickens's fiction is displayed not in his characters' self-determination but in the continuing play of perspectives that resists any monological resolution" (94). Garrett's is one of the best early studies to apply new critical methods and a new critical vocabulary to explain conundrums that have perplexed critics for decades.

How new theories drove re-examination of Dickens's work can be seen clearly in Susan Horton's *The Reader in the Dickens World* (1981). Horton looks across the Dickens canon to account for the anomalies previous critics have identified as the "energy" that comes through in reading Dickens's work. On one level, Horton's readings are subjective, but they are bolstered by reader-response theory and the trend promoting the integration of "the naïve appreciator" and "the scholar-critic" (2). Horton wishes to explain the presence of multiple modes of presentation in Dickens's work as a means of identifying the "origins and causes for our own rich responses to the Dickens world" (3). In a similar vein, the difficulties readers have with Dickens are outlined in Nancy Armstrong's perceptive essay "Dickens Between Two Disciplines: A Problem for Theories of Reading" (1982), in which she analyzes *Hard Times* to demonstrate the need for appreciating both the historical and literary contexts of a text.

The question of realism was among the subjects of particular interest to poststructuralists. In 1984 Chris Brooks wrote extensively about Dickens's novels in *Signs for the Times: Symbolic Realism in the Mid-Victorian World*, a study of what he calls "symbolic realism": an attempt to "give to the semantic connotations of the real a tangibility like that of physical reality itself" (3). Brooks examines eight novels to see how Dickens attempts to bridge the gap between what Brooks calls "self" and "world." Similarly, in *Society in the Novel* (1984) Elizabeth Langland argues that "Society in novels never simply replicates a world outside." Instead, a writer must "create a society consonant with the formal ends of the work itself," and because of this "the relationship between fictional society and the real world is not primarily a mimetic one but an evaluative one" (ix). Dickens, she says, is "aware of social injustices," but he is not one to offer "foolish sentimentality that the poor are happy in their poverty" (75). While portraying the evils of the social order, he permits his characters to transcend the society in which they live, thereby making himself at once "a trenchant social critic and a celebrator of human life and individual possibility" (76). In the fictionalized societies he creates, Dickens is always able to allow his characters to become free from social constraints. In this way, Langland says, he stands in opposition to novelists such as George Eliot, Henry James, or Thomas Hardy, all of whom insist that "the hampering, thread-like entanglements of social existence" determine character and morality (79).

Several books published in the 1980s approach the study of characterization from new perspectives. Thomas Docherty's *Reading (Absent) Character: Towards a Theory of Characterization in Fiction* (1983) is specifically aimed at refuting the conclusion of W. J. Harvey in *Character and the Novel* (1965) that "most great novels exist to reveal and explore character," a line Docherty quotes to set up his own argument (23). He considers as outmoded the idea that character creation is a purely mimetic device. To prove his point, Docherty draws examples from Dickens to explain how the novelist influences readers by character descriptions that are hardly true-to-life, but instead function as manipulative devices giving the novelist control over his narrative. Another assessment of Dickens's methodology in creating characters is provided by Michael Hollington in *Dickens and the Grotesque* (1984). Claiming his monograph is the first extended study of Dickens's use of the grotesque ironically "to undermine complacent fantasies of progress and utopia" (v), Hollington pays attention not only to the novels but to minor work as well. Grounded in theories of the grotesque developed by Wolfgang Kayser and Bakhtin, Hollington reveals Dickens's awareness that he was using the grotesque as a means of social criticism. A third view is offered by Robert Higbie, whose *Character and Structure in the English Novel* (1984) relies on the theoretical work of Vladimir Propp, Northrop Frye, Tzvetan Todorov, A. J. Greimas and others to examine ways novelists create intensely complex characters. His study culminates with Dickens, whose richness and detail, Higbie says, often defy simple categorization by any one theoretical approach. Challenging E. M. Forster's notion that only "round" characters can be interesting, Higbie argues that Dickens's characters, even those that border on caricature, are as fascinating as those of novelists classified as realists. What is particularly intriguing about Dickens's characters, Higbie says, is that so many are "unresolved"; they "tend to exist as ends in themselves," and "though they have implied tensions as conscious characters," they "do not exhibit an ability to resolve that tension" (122).

A decade after the appearance of *Dickens and the Trials of Imagination* (1974), Garrett Stewart published *Death Sentences: Styles of Dying in British Fiction* (1984) and contributed "Signing Off: Dickens and Thackeray, Woolf and Bennett" to William Cain's *Philosophical Approaches to Literature: New Essays on Nineteenth and Twentieth-Century Texts* (1984). In his book Stewart posits that death is the ultimate trial of the imagination. Calling death "the one inevitably fictional matter in prose fiction" (4), Stewart seeks to explain how writers deal with the subject, which he says requires a "specialized rhetoric of figural and grammatical devices" (7). He relies heavily on examples from Dickens's novels to define his terms for examining the phenomenon, largely he says because "Dickens was doubly a man of his epoch: obsessed by death, fascinated by its demands upon articulation" (56). In his essay Stewart suggests "fictional leave-taking becomes an investigation of the very authorizing impulse that gives a fiction leave to begin in the first place" (118). In Dickens, he says, the extent to which his fictional characters "wax authentic" is directly proportional to the extent to which the narrator — the authorial "I" — "becomes part of the fiction" (119–20).

In *Dickens and the Broken Scripture* (1985) Janet Larson applies the work of Derrida and Bakhtin to reassess ways Dickens employs biblical imagery in his novels. Several years earlier in *The Art of Allusion in Victorian Fiction* (1979) Michael Wheeler had pointed out how Dickens uses biblical imagery to create in the novel an apocalyptic vision that forces readers to confront "the four last things of eschatology: death, judgment, heaven and hell" (62). But Larson goes beyond Wheeler in her close examination of Dickens's texts. Determined to "weigh Dickens's biblical allusions in their fictional and historical contexts" (xii), she demonstrates that by the time Dickens wrote his later novels, "the Bible had become a paradoxical code that provides him with contradictory interpretations of experience" (3). Larson shows how "the Great Code," as William Blake had described the biblical accounts, had broken down and splintered, providing multiple and shifting meanings for writers and readers. Such an interpretation is a deconstructionist's dream, of course, and Larson exploits the techniques of semiotics to offer a "reasonably precise method of accounting for" the "contradictory attitudes and strategies" she finds in Dickens's use of biblical references. Unlike many late-century theorists, however, Larson refuses to become tied down by a single approach. She says she is forced to adopt "several angles of critical vision" in analyzing Dickens's work because his scriptural allusions take many forms, "slipping like the protean Dickens himself through the theorist's grids and classifications with wonderful dexterity" (44). Along the way, Larson provides a perceptive lesson in the religious controversies that gripped the Victorians and demonstrates how much Dickens was a man of his time in responding to them.

In her book on Dickens for the Harvester New Readings series, Kate Flint shows exceptional skill at incorporating the insights of contemporary literary theory to produce a reevaluation of the novelist. Beginning *Dickens* (1986) with the rather curious pronouncement that, "It is easy enough to enjoy reading Dickens" but "far less easy to try to write about his novels," Flint declares her wish to present "strategies of reading" that will help illuminate the Dickens canon (1). Rather than analyzing individual works, she looks at ways readers may connect with the texts and identifies problems they may discover when trying to understand and interpret them. She offers a method of diachronic reading to resolve some of the alleged inconsistencies that appear in the novels. She also explains how Dickens uses various narrative techniques and how he employs his fiction to effect social change.

Less ambitious, but no less adept at his craft, is Jeremy Hawthorn, whose *Bleak House* (1987) is a good example of how varying critical perspectives may be used to open up a single Dickens text. Hawthorn surveys the work of critics such as Edmund Wilson, J. Hillis Miller, John Carey, George Orwell, Robert Garis, Mark Spilka, Q. D. Leavis, Alexander Welsh, and Peter Garrett, revealing their different and often contradictory views about the novel. Hawthorn believes, however, that while two major approaches dominate criticism of *Bleak House,* one seeing it as an anatomy of Victorian society, the other as evidence of Dickens's ability to transcend historical boundaries, neither takes into account recent feminist criticism, which gives Dickens little credit for doing either task well. The extent to which critical perspective can shift meaning is also exhibited clearly in essays by Eiichi Hara and Christopher Morris. Hara's "Stories Present and Absent in *Great Expectations*" (1986) applies Barthes's eliding definitions of authorship to define other characters, such as Magwitch's authoring the story that Pip must live out. In "The Bad Faith of Pip's Bad Faith: Deconstructing *Great Expectations*" (1987) Morris applies the deconstructionists' concept of "vanishing," in which "the authorial establishment of some putative center" is simultaneously invalidated by concealing evidence. In this way, Morris exposes "fundamental contradictions," the various "aporia whose logical reconciliation seems impossible to articulate" (941).

Periodically a new work of literary criticism becomes an instant standard against which others are measured. D. A. Miller's *The Novel and the Police* (1988) is such a study. It is actually a collection of articles Miller published between 1981 and 1986, including two that feature explication of Dickens's fiction: a 1981 essay bearing the same title as his book, published in *Glyph*, and a 1983 article in *Representations*, "Discipline in Different Voices: Bureaucracy, Police, Family, and *Bleak House*." Miller examines various forms of social control that influence the production of literature. Following the insights of Foucault, Miller explores "the carcereal" — those unacknowledged forms of limitation and imprisonment that bind the individual subject (the person) even when he or she believes the self to be most free. He uses Dickens's *Bleak House* to demonstrate how Victorian novelists sought to impose social discipline on readers through choice of subject, theme, and selection of details. Here, Miller says, Dickens represents the concept of imprisonment extending far beyond the boundaries of penal institutions; the Court of Chancery, for instance, becomes a pervasive force imprisoning and disciplining individual lives throughout society. In his final chapter Miller proposes *David Copperfield* as central to the Dickens canon because in it Dickens gains control over and disciplines his own life story. In this highly theoretical discussion, Miller makes it clear that, like his contemporaries, Dickens was an advocate for "policing," not just institutionally but domestically, promoting restrictions on human behavior and thought while ostensibly railing against them.

In another book that is certainly not for the theoretically challenged, Audrey Jaffe uses Dickens's novels to explore a subject of profound importance to the study of fiction: the use of the omniscient narrator. *Vanishing Points: Dickens, Narrative, and the Subject of Omniscience* (1991) is an application of the theories of Derrida, Lacan, and Foucault to this technical device. Understanding how and why omniscient narration is used, Jaffe argues, gives some insight into the type of fictional world being created by the novelist. Victorian novelists, Dickens among them, loved to use this technique because it supported their mania for "scientific objectivity and the accumulation of knowledge" (8). At the same time, however, because the omniscient narrator can speak of what is most private about the characters in the tale, "omniscient narration is also in the business of constructing the knowledge that shapes Victorian ideology" (9).

Using five Dickens novels to test her thesis (*The Old Curiosity Shop, Dombey and Son, David Copperfield, Bleak House,* and *Our Mutual Friend*),

Jaffe elucidates an argument concerning the way knowledge is conveyed to or withheld from readers. Throughout her perceptive and exceptionally provocative study, Jaffe manages to "defamiliarize" the concept of the narrator (167) and call into question both the identity of the fictional speaker and the ideology behind that voice. Her conclusions not only reveal that Dickens was truly a man of his time — the gender-specific noun is used here intentionally — but they also support prevailing twentieth-century critical opinion about the Victorians: "Omniscient narration belongs to a series of cultural phenomena through which the gaze — and, more generally, knowledge itself — is coded as white, male, and middle class" (169). Jaffe would follow this longer work with a brief but intriguing assessment of Dickens's ideology in "Spectacular Sympathy: Visuality and Ideology in Dickens's *A Christmas Carol*" in a 1994 issue of *PMLA*, arguing his "ideological project" is to "link sympathy with business," thereby supporting the "commodity culture" in which he participated (255).

In *Secret Journeys: Theory and Practice in Reading Dickens* (1992) Nicholas Morgan speaks with admiration of the work of Derrida, the feminists, and the new historicists, but cautions that any critic wishing to make sense of the Dickens canon must possess "a well-grounded methodology and set of presuppositions" that is simultaneously flexible enough to deal with the novelist's "multifarious universe" (21). What seems strange, however, is that Morgan does not show any awareness of the significant advances in Dickens criticism since the 1940s — or else he is being disingenuous when he says that, since Chesterton's commentaries in the early decades of the twentieth century, nearly all Dickens criticism has focused on the biographical. His work, he claims, sets Dickens criticism on the correct path. If one can get by this rather tendentious assertion, one finds Morgan has much to offer in stressing the importance of readers' reactions to the novels and suggesting ways to limit the "free play" which some theorists have advocated in approaching a text. Morgan is old-school in insisting that the job of the critic is to assess a novel's value — by which he means its moral value. To him Dickens is a novelist who provides many clues by which readers are to judge the characters in his universe. Morgan is confident that, by helping readers become familiar with the world about which Dickens wrote, the critic can assist them in appreciating the lessons Dickens wished to convey in his fiction.

At a fairly early stage in the revolution in literary studies, Dickens's ability to represent urban life became a popular subject for theorists. Consciously departing from "the thematic approaches of Alexander Welsh and F. S. Schwarzbach," David Craig argues in "The Interplay of City and Self in *Oliver Twist, David Copperfield*, and *Great Expectations*" (1987) that in these novels Dickens "records his changing conception of the relationship between city and self." Concerns for self, Craig says, always condition acts of perception, including those of the city, and conversely, "the city encloses consciousness itself so that acts of consciousness are always shaped by their urban contexts" (17). Another of the more provocative new studies of the urban landscape, Richard Maxwell's *The Mysteries of Paris and London* (1992), demonstrates how different theoretical approaches can enrich one's reading of individual novels. Dickens is among the authors Maxwell discusses in this study of "the novel of urban mysteries," fiction written in the nineteenth century that tried to interpret the almost unintelligible phenomenon of the modern metropolis (ix). Ranging widely among the works of twentieth-century writers as diverse as de Man, Foucault, and Walter Benjamin, as well as those of turn-of-the-twentieth-century sociologist Georg Simmel to construct a theoretical framework for his analysis, Maxwell examines ways novelists used figurative language to make the chaotic modern city comprehensible. In addition to helping explain how Dickens understood city life in London, Maxwell places him within a larger, European tradition, seeing him as a contemporary of novelists throughout Europe who were confronting the transformations in society brought about by the burgeoning of urban life in the nineteenth century.

Natalie McKnight's *Idiots, Madmen, and Other Prisoners in Dickens* (1993) is a stimulating blend of Foucault and feminism, relying on both as the theoretical bases for examining the concepts of isolation, madness, and imprisonment in Dickens's works. McKnight considers Dickens a precursor to Foucault in recognizing the implications of the modern trend toward isolating social outcasts and attempting to restore them to normalized society. Like Foucault, Dickens saw the implicit power relationships between people in the mainstream and those on the fringes, and he understood the importance of language as a tool of power in maintaining the status quo. But as a man of his time he was blind to the imprisonment of women, reinforcing patriarchal notions about women's place in society. In the four novels she examines (*Nicholas Nickleby, Barnaby Rudge, Dombey and Son, Little Dorrit*), McKnight traces the novelist's growing sympathy for social outcasts. As Dickens got older and wiser, she says, he voices an ever stronger "distrust of institutionalization and normalization, advocating a greater openness to aberrancy, chaos, and irrationality" (129). At the same time, he "seems not to recognize the peculiar prisons Victorian women suffered," often playing "the jailer to female characters whom he constrains, subdues, and normalizes" (129–30).

Certainly the most extensive, and in many ways the most frustrating, Foucaldian study of Dickens's novels is Jeremy Tambling's *Dickens, Violence and the Modern State* (1995). As he had done in more abbreviated fashion in his 1986 article "Prison Bound: Dickens and Foucault," Tambling examines both the conscious and unconscious images of restriction, control, and imprisonment that characterize Dickens's later work. Ideas from Lacan, Julia Kristeva, Georges Bataille, Walter Benjamin and others are woven throughout Tambling's study. He concentrates on novels written after *Dombey and Son* because, he says, after 1848 people were able to see that the Chartist social and political reform movement had actually produced little of value — and little change — in England. Tambling finds Dickens's work changing as a result of that collective disillusionment, becoming a kind of crusade "against the forces of modernity which organize social and private life" (7). Tambling's political readings cast Dickens in the role of opponent to the organized State where violence is concealed under systems that promote order. The novelist is at his best when celebrating heterogeneity in a State that demands homogeneity. The only misfortune, Tambling notes along the way, is that Dickens tends to engender his images, perhaps unconsciously, making him less effective in breaking ties from the Victorian patriarchy than modern critics might wish.

As Tambling notes, whether one agrees with this highly charged assessment might depend on one's own critical "upbringing." He believes American critics are more prone to read Dickens in this way — and that they are in many ways better critics than their British counterparts, who are too concerned with the social background of the novels, while Americans tend to explore the sources of the creative process. Perhaps it is ironic, then, that Tambling ultimately judges Dickens to be a man of his time, adopting and adapting the language of nineteenth-century politics, science, and sociology. The central problem with Tambling's study, however, is not that he relies too much on contemporary theory, although as Laura Peters notes in her *Dickensian* review, Tambling's work is "not a book for the theoretically fainthearted" (46). Unfortunately, in melding the work of so many theorists and frequently eliding critical commentary with metaphoric description, Tambling becomes at times almost unintelligible. Though there may be significant insight in Tambling's work — and its appearance in numerous later studies suggests its impact — it is almost impossible to refute the observations of Trey Philpotts in the *Dickens Quarterly* that the work's effectiveness suffers immensely from "contorted language, puzzling syntax," and "just plain bad writing" (178).

Far less syntactically challenging is Brian Rosenberg's *Little Dorrit's Shadows* (1996), a study of characterization in Dickens. But this is not another exposition of what critics such as E. M. Forster and Henry James had in mind when they spoke of character — and certainly not the kind of source-hunting for originals that was done for decades after Dickens's death. Instead, Rosenberg challenges the work of theorists such as Hélène Cixous, Roland Barthes, and Tzvetan Todorov, who all question the idea that the conventional notion of character has any meaning. Considering "the way Dickens imagines character and the representation of character," identifying "stylistic, structural and imagistic habits" that mark his development of character, Rosenberg is also interested in the effect Dickens's characters have on readers (2). By applying what he calls the "revised representational approach" (11), Rosenberg believes modern critics can find in Dickens excellent examples of characters whose complexity defies the novelist's ability to represent them completely. It is in the absence of description as much as in what is said about fictional characters, he says, that readers are reminded of the "elusiveness and inscrutability" of human nature (13). Rosenberg thinks Dickens's characters seem real not because of their relationship to people outside the text, but because of the way they affect readers.

Editor John Schad introduces *Dickens Refigured: Bodies, Desires and Other Histories* (1996) by noting that all of the contributors to this volume are interested in what makes Dickens's work "so eccentric" (1). Several concentrate on the perceived division between the material and spiritual. Others examine the concept of desire, producing some highly sexual readings of Dickens's reticent surface texts. A third group explores the novels in relation to the historical contexts in which they were written and which they purport to represent. The fourth group focuses on characters and ideas existing at the margins of Dickens's narratives. Like them, Michael Peled Ginsburg is also interested in problems of narration in *Economies of Change: Form and Transformation in the Nineteenth-Century* (1996), posing the questions: "What does it mean that the work of an author, and indeed a particular text, articulates different economies of narrative? How is this related to the undeniable historical and cultural specificity of certain modes of narrative?" (138). Ginsburg looks at Dickens's use of central symbols and imagery in *Bleak House* and *Our Mutual Friend*, finding the novels to present two contrasting views: whereas *Bleak House* suggests the importance of "hoarding and inbreeding," *Our Mutual Friend* highlights the "recyclability of matter" (147).

In *Authorship, Ethics and the Reader: Blake, Dickens, Joyce* (1997) Dominic Rainsford pairs Dickens with two unlikely partners to discuss a concept of significant concern to theorists at the end of the twentieth century. David Simpson had done something similar fifteen years earlier in *Fetishism and Imagination: Dickens, Melville, Conrad* (1982), but his study of "the ethics of perception and representation" (xii) concentrates on Melville and addresses Dickens's work only briefly. Rainsford is more evenhanded in his exploration of the emotionally charged issue of ethics in fiction, demonstrating how authors impose their own moral codes on the events and characters they describe, expressing concern and "earn[ing] a special creditability for the role of the literary text as a vehicle for productive ethical debate through linking an implicit scrutiny of themselves, as authors and as human agents, to their analysis of the world around them" (3). Rainsford concentrates on Dickens's protagonists, especially Pip in *Great Expectations,* whom he considers the "most elaborated and convincing" (157) of Dickens's characters, to explain how Dickens carries out his "grave responsibility" as an originator of "public texts." He concludes Dickens is one of those rare novelists who demonstrates "an ethically motivated reluctance to deceive, and a hard-won critical self-awareness" (174), qualities that set him apart among practitioners in the genre.

In *Dickens, Novel Reading, and the Victorian Popular Theatre* (1998) Deborah Vlock returns to a topic often explored by Dickens critics, but seldom with the perceptivity and breadth of knowledge about the place of the theater in Victorian life. Her work displays throughout the influence of Foucault's theories of society. Interestingly, however, Vlock challenges the influential French historian and his American disciple D. A. Miller by claiming Dickens's novels were not intended to be part of the private experience that people in the nineteenth century came to value. Insisting the Victorians read novels, newspapers, and other forms of ostensibly private communication "through the lens of popular performance" (3), Vlock demonstrates how Dickens relied heavily on his first readers' familiarity and comfort with the theater, especially popular theater, to create memorable characters. She argues persuasively that, to appreciate Dickens fully, readers must become "active participants" attuned to "verbal patterns and relationships," with "other stories ringing in our ears." She is "convinced that he *was* [her emphasis] read in this way, and ought still to be read thus" (54). Only by becoming sensitive to the multiplicity of voices can readers engage fully in the experience Dickens creates in his prose. Vlock's survey of theatrical practices and her analysis of the many adaptations of Dickens's work for the stage not only help support her argument for reading with an eye toward the theater, but also make clear her important claim that "more than any of his contemporaries," Dickens was "a collective idea — public property in the most absolute sense" (11).

One of the best applications of theory to Dickens's works is Julian Wolfreys's *Writing London: The Trace of the Urban Text from Blake to Dickens* (1998). Like Alexander Welsh, F. S. Schwarzbach, and Richard Maxwell, Wolfreys examines ways Dickens and other nineteenth-century writers responded to the "experience" of the city — and how they "wrote" it. Specifically, Wolfreys wants to answer the questions, "How did they mediate its presence as a cultural and psychic force within which to situate their narratives?" (15), and how did their readers perceive the city as mediated in these texts? Acknowledging his debt to Derrida and Lacan, Wolfreys assumes the city can never be known or transcribed because it is more than a collection of streets and buildings. For him Dickens's London is not so much a place but an "event" (142) — a possibility for reading and writing. Wolfreys says "in writing London Dickens clearly opens up the fixed, essential and monumental to a questioning and destabilization, involving techniques which require the understanding of disparate multiplicities" (149). His Derridian conclusion is that "London for Dickens is a place of invention, rather than merely a reality," a "series of signals which suggest 'the idea that there is a reading event and that reading should take place'" (178).

Of course, given the tendency of poststructuralists to generate what have been called "playful" criticisms of canonical writers and texts, it should not be surprising that Dickens is the subject of at least one such work. John Glavin's *After Dickens: Reading, Adaptation and Performance* (1999) is less a critique of the novelist's work than an extended exhortation for readers to recreate and adapt Dickens's novels for themselves. Glavin challenges readers to put aside conventional readings and be "transgressive" in dealing with interpretations and texts. He insists novels must be revised by individual readers to maintain any form of meaning. Glavin goes so far as to encourage readers to treat Dickens's texts as subjects for their own performative recreations. Needless to say, such an approach was not welcomed by the mainstream. Even Grahame Smith, a critic well versed in contemporary theory, expressed serious reservations about Glavin's approach and his cavalier attitude toward the critical enterprise (*Dickensian* 61).

Feminism and Women's Studies

In writing about Dickens for the *Columbia History of the British Novel* (1994), John Kucich remarks that at this period in the history of criticism, "no other aspect of Dickens's work has drawn as much criticism as his portrayal of women" (392). To be sure, commentators had always expressed interest in Dickens's female characters. During the 1980s and 1990s, however, a number of important feminist studies highlighted the underlying dichotomies that characterized male writers' portraits of women, and Dickens's female characters underwent serious reevaluation. Kate Flint summed things up best in 1986: "Dickens's treatment of women," she observed, "has had a bad press" (112).

Initially some critics celebrated Dickens as a radical on the side of women in their struggle against the patriarchy. Among them is Richard Barickman, who argues in *Corrupt Relations: Dickens, Thackeray, Trollope, Collins, and the Victorian Sexual System* (1982) that Dickens offers "a complex, persistent, and radical critique of the Victorian system of sexual relationships" (vii). Dickens may have been personally conflicted about the roles women should play in society, but in his fiction he exposes the "persistent victimization at the heart of Victorian society" (viii), raising "issues of identity, power, freedom, and human fulfillment that ultimately call into question the whole system of sexual relationships in nineteenth-century England" (viii). In Barickman's judgment, Dickens manages to create women who begin to develop power within their given social roles, a condition that seemed threatening to the established patriarchy. Carol Senf takes a similar position in *"Bleak House:* Dickens, Esther, and the Androgynous Mind" (1983), arguing the Victorians' idea of separate spheres for men and women is mirrored in the narrative strategy Dickens employs. The "act of reading" actually "unites these two halves," allowing Dickens to highlight "the problems inherent in his culture's ideas of 'Separate Spheres'" and "illustrate the need for completeness" (26–27). But Virginia Blain argues in "Double Vision and the Double Standard in *Bleak House:* A Feminist Perspective" (1985) that the juxtaposition of two narrative voices actually sets up "a submerged dialectic between male and female viewpoints" (31). Unlike Senf, Blain finds Dickens in weak control of his materials, suggesting the text "carries inscribed within it a significance for a late twentieth-century female reader" that "it did not reveal to earlier critics or to the author himself" (31).

How Dickens dealt with female figures both real and imaginary is the subject of a major study by one of the most influential and knowledgeable Dickens critics of the century, Michael Slater. After completing his academic work at Oxford, Slater began his career as a lecturer at Birkbeck College, University of London, where he was also research assistant to the highly respected Victorian scholar Geoffrey Tillotson. In 1968 Slater became editor of the *Dickensian,* a position he held for nine years. In 1970 he edited a collection of essays for the centenary of Dickens's death and in 1978 published *Dickens on America and The Americans* (1978), a collection of excerpts from Dickens's letters, *American Notes,* and *Martin Chuzzlewit* reflecting the novelist's impressions of the United States.

Slater's articles and notes on Dickens are scattered throughout the pages of the *Dickensian* and other journals, but his first major analytical book on the novelist appeared in 1983 under the rather sweeping title *Dickens and Women.* Slater claims his book is the first major study of "Dickens's response to, and presentation of, one of the most fundamental aspects of human existence — femaleness in its myriad interrelationships and interactions with maleness" (xi). He divides his study into three major sections: the novelist's associations with the real women in his life, his portraits of female characters in his novels, and his concept of "woman" or idealized female nature. Reading Slater's book is like reading a detailed psychological biography of the novelist, as the focus throughout is on ways Dickens's relationships with his mother, his wife and her sisters, the actress Ellen Ternan, and others shaped not only his fictional portraits but also his ideas about what women were — or ought to be.

Slater is aware of recent trends in feminist criticism, observing at one point that he believes Kate Millett's comment in *Sexual Politics* regarding Dickens's treatment of women "oversimplifies Dickens's presentation of his female characters and his whole attitude toward the womanly" (244). Little of the ideology underlying feminist criticism seems to have permeated Slater's critical thinking; instead, he takes a more conventional approach that nevertheless leads him to some unflattering conclusions. "Female energy," Slater observes near the end of his study, "and the potential for passion in women's nature which he evidently believes is far greater than it is in men's, seems to make Dickens distinctly apprehensive" (354). Afraid of his own sexual nature, Slater says, Dickens displaced his concerns onto the women he depicted in his novels. Slater's account of the novelist's encounters with the real women in his life provides ample explanation for this phenomenon, as long as one accepts Slater's readings of these personal relationships.

Although Slater is no hero-worshiper, his traditional approach failed to appeal to the more radical feminist critics who simply would not accept his interpretation of Dickens's psychological crises. At times he seems protective of Dickens, especially in recounting his relationship with Ternan. As a result — an unfortunate result, perhaps — while Slater is politely acknowledged by subsequent critics who write about "Dickens and women," most give him little more than a polite nod before applying more radical feminist ideologies to their analysis of the novelist and his work.

In fact, most female critics have not been positive about Dickens's treatment of gender issues. Two examples from works devoted to larger cultural issues illustrate this point clearly. Mary Poovey's examination of *David Copperfield* in *Uneven Developments: The Ideological Work of Gender in Mid-Victorian England* (1988), a study of the way Victorian writers constructed the concepts of gender and gender differences, reveals that Dickens fulfills the role expected of him as a male writer in nineteenth-century England. Poovey looks at structural patterns imbedded in the novel and assumptions about identity and gender that shape the story. Establishing the limited roles that women could play was, in Poovey's view, a necessary function of the male writer in his role as shaper and preserver of the national character and identity. *Bleak House* figures prominently in Katherine Cummings's *Telling Tales: The Hysteric's Seduction in Fiction and Theory* (1991), a psychological reading of various seduction narratives "to discover how sexual and political events interrelate" (5). Cummings argues it is not only Esther's story that plays out the psychological pattern of seduction; the story told by the unnamed narrator is in its own way a tale of seduction. Both Poovey and Cummings paint Dickens as a man of his time, supportive of systems that allowed women to be oppressed by the patriarchy.

Although there are overtones of feminist criticism in Patricia Ingham's *Dickens, Women and Language* (1992), the book is really a study of the novelist's language as it is used to portray female characters. Ingham believes earlier attempts to understand Dickens's women, specifically John Carey's *The Violent Effigy* (1973) and Michael Slater's *Dickens and Women* (1983), promote "a spurious unity" to Dickens's portrayals of women by relating fictional women to "an archetypal figure in [Dickens's] life" (2). Ingham insists stereotypes and archetypes are never truly constant, because language is fluid, and meanings change from one generation to the next. Using the work of Victorian sociologist Sarah Stickney Ellis, Ingham shows how Dickens's language encodes certain Victorian stereotypes and conventions. Ranging across the novels, she locates several of the "types" identified by the Victorians themselves: nubile girls, fallen girls, "excessive females," passionate women, and mothers. Only in the language of the novels, Ingham says, can one find the real portraits of Dickens's women and discern his attitudes toward them; it is, in her view, fruitless to appeal to extra-literary sources.

From time to time feminism was linked with other approaches to suggest new ways of reading Dickens's fiction. For example, Deirdre David deftly combines feminist theory with the methodology of postcolonial studies in "Children of Empire: Victorian Imperialism and Sexual Politics in Dickens and Kipling," an essay in Antony Harrison and Beverly Taylor's collection *Gender and Discourse in Victorian Literature and Art* (1992). David had already published a sociological examination of *Our Mutual Friend* in *Fictions of Resolution in Three Victorian Novels* (1981), in which she demonstrates how this novel provides "a complex series of mediations between the social actuality" and the desires of predominantly middle-class readers to believe that "things need not be the way they were in that actuality" (ix). In "Children of Empire" David explains how Dickens is fully implicated in the era's imperialistic project. Her explication reveals how stereotypes about gender and gender differences reinforce the age's ideas about the natives of lands colonized by Britain — natives who were little more than savages, in the eyes of the Victorians.

Studies uniting feminism with psychological readings were particularly popular among feminist scholars during the final decades of the century. In "The Lost Self: Gender in *David Copperfield*," her contribution to Judith Spector's *Gender Studies: New Directions in Feminist Criticism* (1986), Margaret Myers uses psychological theory to argue that the novel is principally about construction of the self. She believes David is insistently identified with the feminine but simply cannot accept himself as incorporating both genders. Similar methodologies are also employed by Lynda Zwinger in her 1985 article "The Fear of the Father: Dombey and Daughter" and her book *Daughters, Fathers and the Novel* (1991), a study examining "the place of the fictional daughter as that place has been imagined in our literature" (5). In both studies, Zwinger explores the Victorians' prejudice against daughters embedded within the social system. Additionally, she argues *Dombey and Son* comes close to revealing a nasty important truth about such a world: "men don't like women, yet women seem to like men" (42) because they have to, in order to survive, using love as a weapon to get the status and security they need. Ultimately, "Love *is* power," Zwinger concludes, and "in our culture men (generally and generically) wield [power] and women ask for it. Any suggestion that the world might well be perceived differently is much too close to a radical re-creation for comfort" (45). Clearly, she suggests, Dickens would not have been comfortable with any situation but the status quo. Six years later, Hilary Schor would also deal with the image of the daughter in *Dickens and the Daughter of the House* (1999). Well versed in both Dickens criticism and contemporary feminist and gender criticism, Schor examines the figure of the daughter in Dickens's fiction as a reflection of the larger issue of the place of daughters in Victorian society, offering a provocative new angle on reading the novels as a window into that world. It certainly seems a different "world" than the "world of Dickens" Humphry House wrote about in 1941.

By the late 1980s it became customary for feminists to expose Dickens's essentially patriarchal and demeaning views of women. For example, in "'Great Expectations': Masculinity and Modernity" (1987) Carolyn Brown employs concepts of the modern from the work of Jürgen Habermas to explain "aspects of our history as constructing identities," especially "in constructing the speaking subject." What she discovers is that, while *Great Expectations* may be an account of the development of identity in the modern world, it is "also (to me) an extraordinary masculine world" (61). Along these same lines, in the very first sentence of "'Who is this in Pain?': Scarring, Disfigurement, and Female Identity in *Bleak House* and *Our Mutual Friend*" (1989) Helena Michie asserts that "Dickens's heroines, remarkable for their insubstantiality, inhabit the interstices of Victorian realism." The "female self" in Dickens, she continues later in the essay, "comes into being through illness, scarring, and deformity" (199). Her reading of the two novels uses a sophisticated blend of feminist psychology and close textual reading to explain how Dickens is able to give female characters a prominent role in spite of social strictures that tended to marginalize women.

Eventually, however, the monolithic antagonism with which many feminists attacked Dickens began to be challenged by other feminists who felt the novelist had been treated unfairly. Such is the position taken by editor Sally Minogue in *Problems for Feminist Criticism* (1990). She argues in her introduction to this collection of essays that there were both men and women writers who did not conform to feminist stereotypes and whose works can provide pleasure to readers of both genders. Minogue includes two essays on Dickens. In the first, "The Talkative Woman in Shakespeare, Dickens, and George Eliot," Barbara Hardy shows how Dickens uses the figure of the talkative woman, a typical misogynist device, in a way that frees these women from the strictures imposed on them by a patriarchal society. In the second, "'Wooman, Lovely Wooman': Four Dickens Heroines and the Critics," Sandra Hopkins explains how feminist criticism of the 1970s and 1980s has been little more than an assault on the novelist that tends to "homogenize the experience of reading a Dickens novel" (115). Ironically, she finds non-feminists such as Michael Slater supporting a view of Dickens which the feminists applaud in women writers but refuse to recognize in Dickens's work. Her own sympathetic analysis reveals how Dickens is more in line with feminist ideals than some critics are willing to acknowledge. Helene Moglen's insightful "Theorizing Fiction/Fictionalizing Theory: The Case of *Dombey and Son*" (1992) also suggests Dickens is capable of seeing the injustices done to women in Victorian society, calling his novel "an integrated, gender-based analysis of the pietistic assumptions of bourgeois idealism" in which he shows how "social failure is built into the epistemological and ontological structures" of the society Dombey represents (159).

Similarly, in *Daughters of the House: Modes of the Gothic in Victorian Fiction* (1992) Alison Milbank claims to be going "against the grain" in testing "the accuracy of feminist criticism of Victorian fiction" (1), by suggesting feminists have misunderstood Dickens. Challenging feminists on the notion that only women were without power in the patriarchal society of the Victorians, Milbank says Dickens was acutely aware "that men as well as women are cut off from the sources of power and the dominant discourse of society" (4). She finds Dickens using what she calls the "female Gothic plot," a device borrowed from Ann Radcliffe and others in which "the patriarchal order is revealed as malignant and in need of replacement" (11). Milbank claims when Dickens engages directly with public issues, he "most fully follow[s] the 'female' Gothic tradition," combining in his heroines "the prisoner who must escape and the mediator of spiritual and social vision" (16).

Not all gender studies at the end of the century were grounded in feminist ideology. David Holbrook's *Charles Dickens and the Image of Woman* (1993) is a psychological study in the vein of those Holbrook had done on women in the works J. M. Barrie, Shakespeare, C. S. Lewis, George MacDonald, and D. H. Lawrence. Holbrook looks for symbolic uses of women in Dickens's work. In his estimate, Dickens was a good Victorian in being repulsed by the Freudian "primal scene." As a result, there is in his fiction a recurrence of women associated with murder, a phenomenon highlighting the novelist's need "to re-experience the intensity of infantile fantasy for psychic purposes of his own" (4). In the novels, Holbrook says, Dickens displays decidedly contradictory attitudes toward women, sometimes exhibiting respect, even veneration, but at other times associating them with death and destruction. The underlying cause of Dickens's deep-seated fear of women, Holbrook concludes, must be some undocumented trauma with his mother. This kind of psychologizing reminds one of the 1920s and 1930s, when Freudian ideology dominated critical practice.

However, two books appearing late in the decade offer a more conventional feminist reading of the Dickens canon. In *Marital Power in Dickens's Fiction* (1996) Rita Lubitz describes a representative number of marriages in Dickens's novels to explain the functioning of power relationships. Lubitz tends to stick close to the texts and refrains from offering sweeping conclusions, but does suggest that when love and respect overcome the dominant power relationship, marriages can be successful. In *Professional Domesticity in the Victorian Novel: Women, Work, and Home* (1998), Monica Cohen includes chapters on *Great Expectations* and *Little Dorrit* in which she challenges long-held notions (supported, she argues, by Dickens) of the home as a place of rest, arguing that the polarization of "home" and "office," or public space, is actually a false dichotomy. Following leading feminist critics such as Mary Poovey and Isobel Armstrong, whose work represents the home as "a profession, as vocational work" (9), Cohen claims Dickens and other male novelists misunderstood and trivialized the nature of women's role and importance in society.

In the same year, however, Brenda Ayres offered an eloquent defense of Dickens in *Dissenting Women in Dickens' Novels* (1998). Building on the work of Alison Milbank and Barbara Hardy, Ayres approaches the novels from a feminist perspective but challenges many other feminist readings. Typically, as Ayres notes, Victorian fiction "often served as a vehicle for ideological modification," indoctrinating people to accept the patriarchal concept of the ideal woman (5). But Dickens is different; Ayres finds him inherently contradictory on the subject of women, overtly supporting the dominant ideology but altering and distorting it repeatedly. As a result, she says, "Dickens's women are anything but stereotypical" (7). Her careful reading of texts shows where these distortions occur, highlighting the subversive nature of Dickens's work. Her concluding chapter is actually a bibliographical essay outlining the variety of opinions held by critics regarding Dickens's female characters. For her own part, Ayres does not seem to mind taking on her feminist colleagues who are generally less kind to Dickens than she is.

Mary Lenard also challenges the typical feminist view of Dickens in *Preaching Pity: Dickens, Gaskell, and Sentimentalism in Victorian Culture*

(1999). Her exploration of Dickens's work links him with other nineteenth-century writers customarily dubbed "sentimental," arguing that Dickens's sentimentality is actually part of a larger design intended to transform public opinion. She portrays Dickens as a careful strategist using feminized language and the kinds of emotion associated with women writers to oppose what she terms the "masculinized discourse of Utilitarianism and laissez-faire capitalism" (77). But Lenard claims Dickens was uncomfortable being associated too closely with these women, and took a number of defensive strategies to distance himself from them, including assertions that they were plagiarizing his work. His insistence on originality was, in Lenard's view, a ploy that allowed him to claim his own "cultural space," excluding "the female social reform writers who shared it with him by discrediting them" (93).

Relative to other writers, comparatively little has been written about Dickens by critics specializing in "queer theory" or "gay studies." One notable exception is Eve Kosofsky Sedgwick. Her groundbreaking study of male relationships depicted in fiction, *Between Men: English Literature and Male Homosocial Desire* (1985), includes chapters on *Our Mutual Friend* and *Edwin Drood*. Stressing the power relationships present in Victorian society, she concentrates on exposing the interaction between the Victorians' homophobia and their attitudes toward class, race, and gender. Her close reading of these two Dickens novels reveals that, beneath the surface level of the text, Dickens is preoccupied with male homophobia and homosexuality. Borrowing from psychological critics, she describes *Our Mutual Friend* as "*the* English novel that everyone knows is about anality" (163) because it focuses on the dust heaps — piles of excrement. *Edwin Drood*, she says, is on one level "a novel about the homosexual panic of a deviant man" (199). Sedgwick asserts Dickens made use of the Gothic tradition, especially in his later novels, as a means of evoking the terror he sees in homosexuality. Such readings may be controversial, but they stand as compelling testimony to the complexity of Dickens's texts.

Psychological Criticism

By the 1980s, psychological critics writing about Dickens had begun to supplement Freudian analysis with approaches developed by post-Freudians such as Jacques Lacan. A good example of the new forms of psychological criticism is Thomas Hanzo's "Paternity and the Subject in *Bleak House*," in *The Fictional Father: Lacanian Readings of the Text* (1981). Interested in "the theory of the father in narrative" as described by Lacan (2), Hanzo uses Lacan's reinterpretation of Freud's Oedipus theory to offer a provocative psychological reading in which, on a subliminal level, the drama of incest is played out between Esther and John Jarndyce. Though consistent in his own analysis, Hanzo relies so heavily on technical language that his argument is sometimes hard for non-specialists to follow — a characteristic he shares with a number of his contemporaries whose work is modeled on Lacan. In contrast to Hanzo's work, Diane Sadoff employs a Freudian approach to Dickens in *Monsters of Affection: Dickens, Eliot, and Brontë on Fatherhood* (1982), a book assembled from previously published articles including "Storytelling and the Figure of the Father in *Little Dorrit*" that had appeared in *PMLA* (1980). Sadoff says Dickens's "narrative project," as she calls his canon, "takes as its central metaphor the primal scene. His novels track down the father's sexual and violent rape or wrong as narrative origin, deny the hero could have been conceived by that sinful figure, structurally and surreptitiously kill the father, and proceed to engender the hero as subject with language" (3).

Catherine Bernard's "Dickens and Victorian Dream Theory" is interesting in its own right as an analysis of Dickens's ideas about the nature and origins of dreams. Bernard makes a convincing case that Dickens, who was familiar with nineteenth-century theories of the supernatural and nineteenth-century psychology, actually pre-dates Freud in his recognition of the importance of recurrent dreams. Perhaps more intriguing, however, is the fact that Bernard's essay is included in James Paradis and Thomas Postlewait's *Victorian Science and Victorian Values: Literary Perspectives* (1981), a book published by the New York Academy of Sciences — a heartening sign that the hard boundaries between disciplines of study were starting to be crossed.

Like many practitioners of post-Freudian criticism, Karen Chase expresses in *Eros and Psyche: The Representation of Personality in Charlotte Brontë, Charles Dickens, and George Eliot* (1984) an interest in Dickens and others as authors responsible for "the fictive representation of personality" and especially the "inner lives" of characters (1). She concentrates on explaining how Victorian novelists give structure to emotion as they struggle to respond to demands of the emerging science of psychology. Her discussion of Dickens outlines his methodology for expressing the "complex representation of personality" (38), defending him against charges made by earlier critics that his characters are not complex. She sees Dickens telescoping his characters for effect, being content to "contract the expressive range" of his fictional men and women, "letting them dramatize aspects rather than wholes" (135). This conscious strategy allows him to present "the self" as "a vigorously bounded part which achieves significance only by entering a pattern of relations" (135). Chase suggests Dickens understood that the Self could be defined only in relationship to the Other, signifying he was more modern in his psychological insight than other critics have acknowledged.

Also interested in the concept of self, Lawrence Frank sets out in *Charles Dickens and the Romantic Self* (1984) to demonstrate how Dickens uses "those Romantic conceptions of the self emerging after, and in response to, the deconstructing skepticism of a David Hume and the recently triumphant science of life, biology" (4). Like so many studies done at this time, Frank's contains a lengthy introduction outlining the theoretical premises from which he launches his analysis of Dickens's fiction. He then examines Dickens's debt to the Romantics for his conception of the self. The self is "a construct, a compelling fiction," Frank says, and the lines "between fiction and autobiography are blurred (as Freud was to discover that the lines between fiction and case histories were blurred)" (16). In this view of the self, real men and women — and, Frank says, fictional characters in Romantic novels — "become the novelists of themselves by imaginatively creating the self upon which each acts" (16). Intent on exploring "the pilgrimage of being" upon which Dickens's characters so often embark (29), Frank provides careful readings of six novels to demonstrate how both Freudian psychology and the more recent theories of scholars such as Foucault regarding the construction of the self can help explain what is going on with Dickens's major characters.

The blending of psychological approaches is evident as well in Ned Lukacher's *Primal Scene: Literature, Philosophy, Psychoanalysis* (1986), a highly theoretical work grounded in Freud, Heidegger, and Walter Benjamin. Like Lacan and Derrida, Lukacher is eager to explore questions "concerning the possibility of a deconstructive theory of history" (13), and like them concludes history is "not the human subject — whether defined as an individual, a class, or a species — but rather the intertextual process itself" (13). His assessment of Dickens is built on the premise that the author's literary text has been either "forgotten" or "misconstrued" by Freudians in pursuit of "the spirit of Absolute Knowledge" (14). Lukacher believes the "primal scene" is not merely sexual; instead it is any scene from childhood "in which the repetitive and ambivalent character of a recollected scene figures more prominently than its sexual content" (330). For Dickens, Lukacher says, the "primal scene" was his experience as a child in the streets of London. He suggests the novelist "staged and restaged a memory/construction of his childhood experience in each of his works." For Dickens "the art of novel-writing is analogous in every respect to a psychoanalyst engaged in a lifelong self-analysis" (276).

In his final chapter, Lukacher makes clear how Benjamin's work helps reinterpret Dickens — and also reveals Lukacher's decidedly Marxist take on him. Claiming something in the novelist's unconscious drove him to express his personal primal scene, Lukacher sees a link between Dickens's obsession with taking long walks and his creative ability. Both walking and writing were compulsive, and the walks helped Dickens maintain his ties to the city in which the scene originally occurred. For this reason, the economic conditions Dickens witnessed would have weighed heavily on his mind as he wrote. Lukacher's argument regarding the tendency to rely too heavily on Freudian interpretation is reinforced in Douglas Steward's "Anti-Oedipalizing *Great Expectations:* Masochism, Subjectivity, Capitalism" (1999). Steward demonstrates that in *Great Expectations* Dickens anticipates twentieth-century neo-Freudians' arguments "against interpreting everyone's life experience in terms of the Oedipal conflict's family drama" (29).

In fact, during the 1980s one of the more intriguing alternative theories of psychology being applied to Dickens's work at this time was Third Force Psychology. The concept had been developed by German psychologist Karen Horney, although American psychologist Abraham Maslow had coined the rather catchy name. Horney had formulated an alternative to Freud's theories regarding personality, arguing that it is not necessary to go back to childhood to understand adult behavior. The theory was attractive to critics interested in psychological approaches to literary study, since it provided a way to get around the problem of having to extrapolate (or make up) information about the early lives of complex fictional characters whose whole history exists inside novels. The most notable proponent of the application of Third Force psychology to literary studies, Bernard J. Paris, writes in the preface to *Third Force Psychology and the Study of Literature* that applying Horney's psychological methods helps readers see such characters, "however remote their period or culture, as human beings who are very much like ourselves" (13). Patricia Eldredge's essay in the volume, a reprint of her 1981 article in *The Literary Review*, applies Horneyean principles to explore "the mystery of self-alienation" in *Bleak House* (136). Eldredge argues that in Esther Summerson, Dickens is consciously promoting "the fantasy of self-effacing innocence" (154) — a fantasy exposed by Horneyean analysis as inadequate for achieving real personal growth and self-actualization. Paris himself applies Horneyean analysis to Dickens's work in *Imagined Human Beings: A Psychological Approach to Character and Conflict in Literature* (1997). Paris focuses on the character of Pip, who he says is not the redeemed adult recounting past transgressions but instead is a troubled individual whose perceptions require careful analysis. Paris's reading challenges past accounts without inventing motives for which there is no textual support. As with most psychological criticism, the focus is on character analysis rather than theme, but Paris explains how Pip's character reveals social themes in which Dickens was most interested.

Christine van Boheemen's *The Novel as Family Romance: Language, Gender, and Authority from Fielding to Joyce* (1987) is yet another psychological study melding the theories of Lacan and Freud with those of

Derrida and Foucault to examine representative novels as "a confirming mirror of subjectivity" (ix). She argues the concept of the self was challenged by materialism and science, both of which brought into question the notion of permanency in the subject (person). Focusing on *Bleak House*, van Boheemen draws interesting parallels between Dickens's novel and Darwin's texts to show how the self is threatened. Through Esther's quest for identity, she says, Dickens manages to suggest a way of giving life meaning in an increasingly purposeless world.

Where van Boheemen focuses on character, Gwen Watkins concentrates on the novelist himself in *Dickens in Search of Himself: Recurrent Themes and Characters in the Work of Charles Dickens* (1987). Watkins explores what she considers Dickens's split personality and the dominance of his unconscious in so much of his best work. She relies on the writing of psychiatrists for evidence to support her claim that Dickens's deprived childhood was a formative experience affecting his writing in ways he did not even imagine. In Watkins's view, Dickens was a child whose self, or personality, never became unified. Rather than examining individual novels in depth, however, Watkins looks for hidden psychological themes that cross over from work to work; these, she argues, offer evidence of Dickens's complex personality.

In contrast to Watkins, however, Alexander Welsh argues forcefully in *From Copyright to Copperfield* (1987) that critics are misguided when they place too much stock in the incidents of Dickens's childhood as having deep-seated, unconscious psychological impact on him. Welsh wants to "shift attention from the formative years of Dickens's childhood to his mature development, from the family romance to his writing career, and from the claim of originality to his creative use of other literature" (1). Focusing on three works he considers pivotal to the Dickens canon — *Martin Chuzzlewit, Dombey and Son,* and *David Copperfield* — Welsh demonstrates how the young novelist worked consciously to perfect his craft and develop his identity as a novelist. The events that shaped him were those that had professional impact — the trip to America, for example — because they allowed him to transform older forms of literature, which he copied as models early in his career, into his own work. In the three novels he examines, Welsh finds Dickens projecting himself, both positively and negatively, onto characters in the books as a means of testing out his own identity.

In *Repression in Victorian Fiction* (1987) John Kucich also refutes psychological theories of creativity, making a compelling case that Dickens is always in control of his materials. Kucich establishes early in his book that he is not using the term "repression" as Freud did, but rather as the "cultural decision" he says nineteenth-century novelists and readers made "to value silence or negated feeling over affirmed feeling" (3). Kucich wants to see how acts of repression become libidinal acts, "forms of luxuriously self-descriptive and autoerotic experience" (3). He challenges notions that such forms of repression were simply demanded by bourgeois Victorian social norms, or that repression was used as a simplistic act of rebellion against the norms of the patriarchy. He believes the process is much more complex, and that it has a productive role in shaping identity. Employing the theories of Foucault and the Frankfurt School, Kucich shows exceptional awareness of the critical tradition and of the novelists on whom he focuses, including Dickens, whose works appear to be much more sophisticated than they seem to those who would accuse him of having "divided sensibilities" (20). Instead, Dickens uses repression (in the way Kucich defines the term) as a conscious strategy for having his characters achieve an integrated identity.

In some ways a throwback to the kind of psychological criticism practiced in the 1930s and 1940s, Morris Golden's *Dickens Imagining Himself* (1992) explores ways Dickens projects himself into his characters. Golden says in his introduction that "from the beginning" of his career "Dickens develops sides of himself in all the major figures in his moral and social spectrum, male and female, young and old" (4). Examining six novels written at points in the novelist's life "to which most of us pay special attention" (17), such as key birthdays, Golden looks for clues to establish what he calls "consanguinity" between the author and his characters. Less strident, perhaps, than his Freudian forebears, Golden is nevertheless convinced one can learn much about the writer by examining his characters with some attention to the parallels between their adventures and those experienced by Dickens himself. Though he is insistent his interest lies in opening "avenues of criticism toward the novels, toward the art rather than the artist" (251), his focus on Dickens's self-absorption and self-consciousness makes this work more psychobiographical than critical.

Near the end of the century Carolyn Dever revisited Dickens's fictionalization of his problematic relationship with his mother in *Death and the Mother from Dickens to Freud* (1998). Dever is intrigued by the fact that in Victorian fiction this important, formative figure is frequently absent or inadequate. After introductory chapters describing the cultural context in which Victorian fiction was produced, Dever examines several novels that "undermine a protagonist's efforts to construct an identity, to consolidate a life story" (xiii). Dever demonstrates how this prevailing narrative of the absent mother led eventually to Freud's ideas about the role of the mother in sexual development of the mature individual.

Although he also employs Freudian methodology, Robert Higbie takes a more subtle approach in *Dickens and Imagination* (1998). Acknowledging his debt to precursors such as Edwin Eigner, Fred Kaplan, Harry

Stone, and Garrett Stewart, Higbie revisits a subject that had occupied critics of Dickens and other Victorians as well: What did "imagination" mean? How did it differ from fantasy, and from reality? Specifically, how did Dickens use "imagination," and why did he feel compelled to do so? Higbie finds the answer to the last question in psychology, constructing a reading of the Dickens canon that focuses on the struggle of the novelist to strive for an Object of Desire while acknowledging the ultimate futility of achieving Desire completely. Higbie explains how the Romantic notion of the imagination was transformed by the Victorians, noting ways the opposition of imagination and reality played a key role in the creation of both poetry and fiction in the nineteenth century. His readings of Dickens's novels highlight the many ways Dickens used the tension between these opposites to suggest the possibility of a better world than the one in which he lives. The driving passion to create such an ideal world, Higbie says, comes from Dickens's own feelings of abandonment by his parents — once again emphasizing the importance of the novelist's humiliating experience in Warren's blacking factory. Higbie selects from the novels incidents that highlight tensions between the real and ideal, then explains how imagination allows both the novelist and his readers to see the harsh, unchanging realities of this world while entertaining the notion that things could, of course, be better.

Finally, the psychological as well as sociological dimensions of Dickens's treatment of orphans is the focus of Baruch Hochman and Ilja Wachs's *Dickens: The Orphan Condition* (1999). Hochman and Wachs suggest Dickens's career demonstrates his lifelong attempt to master the vision inherent in the "orphan condition," which they define as "the clash between the orphan's wish to accommodate to the received world and the fury-driven compulsion to attain restitution for abandonment" (11). Concentrating on five of the novels (*Oliver Twist, David Copperfield, Bleak House, Little Dorrit, Great Expectations*), they argue Dickens's cotinuous critique of society can best be understood when viewed through the lens of the orphan, who is frequently abandoned and abused.

Marxist, New Historicist, and Sociological Readings

Just how radical was Dickens in his critique of society? It seems in every generation at least one critic undertakes to answer that question, using some form of socialist or Marxist theory to analyze his novels. During the final decades of the twentieth century, the technique was elevated to a fine science by a number of scholars using tools of New Historicism, with its socialist theoretical bias, and Marxist scholars influenced by Raymond Williams and Terry Eagleton. Generally, their assessments reversed the tendency of earlier Marxists who embraced Dickens, finding instead that beneath the veneer of socialist outrage beat the heart of a dyed-in-the-wool conservative who, despite his strident attacks on the social order, was quite content with the status quo.

Igor Webb's *From Custom to Capital: The English Novel and the Industrial Revolution* (1981) is an early attempt at New Historicist criticism. Specifically interested in works dealing with the Industrial Revolution, Webb asserts categorically that any novel written between the late eighteenth century and the middle decades of the nineteenth was affected by this phenomenon. Webb considers Dickens and other mid-century novelists heavily immersed in their own age, writing to their contemporaries about contemporary problems. In *Hard Times,* Webb says, Dickens tries to find some way for individuals to accommodate themselves within the new, industrialized society. Like Webb, Catherine Gallagher demonstrates in a 1980 *Arizona Quarterly* article her interest in ways fiction changed as novelists became engaged in the Condition of England question, a debate spurred by the turmoil arising from significant social, economic, and political changes in the country brought on by the Industrial Revolution and democratic movements in America and France. Gallagher includes a revision of her article in *The Industrial Reformation of English Fiction* (1985), using *Hard Times* to explain how "the discourse over industrialism led novelists to examine their assumptions of their literary forms" (xi). Like other novelists, Gallagher says, Dickens learned to "create coherence by reconciling social and familial needs in the industrial novel" (xii).

In a relatively early New Historicist revision of ideas about Dickens's popularity, "The Moment in *Pickwick* or the Production of a Commodity Text" (1984), N. N. Feltes challenges notions put forward by earlier literary historians like George Ford and Robert Patten about Dickens's early popularity, claiming instead that changes in book production had as much to do with his success as any inherent genius he might have possessed. After explaining how the publishing industry had transformed itself into yet another exploitative industry in Britain, Feltes concludes that, "Produced in the capitalist mode of production and drawing forth a mass bourgeois audience," *Pickwick Papers* became "the first commodity-text" (209). Additionally, the novel promoted a capitalist ideology to readers ready to accept it. Feltes continued his Marxist critique of Dickens and other Victorians in a series of articles, most notable among them "Realism, Consensus, and 'Exclusion Itself': Interpellating the Victorian Bourgeois" (1987), in which he applies principles developed by Michel Pêcheux and Louis Althusser to explain how societies create fictions of realism based on ideological presuppositions.

However, James M. Brown claims in *Dickens: Novelist in the Market Place* (1982) that "what gives Dickens's mature fiction its essential character is the fact that in his role as novelist Dickens was both imaginatively obsessed and artistically inspired by the market nature of everyday social life," while at the same time "acutely conscious of his own economic standing in the literary market" (166). Brown cautions against reading novels simply as sociological texts — the approach he sees Humphry House using in *The Dickens World* (1941). While class ideology is important as a mediating factor in Dickens's treatment of social institutions, Brown admits, so is literary convention. He believes Dickens employs descriptions of social conditions for artistic purposes, not simply to report on them.

Examining the later works, Brown concludes Dickens was essentially a realist, deeply concerned about society. This stand put Brown at odds with John Carey, who makes the opposite point in *The Violent Effigy* (1973). But Brown insists Dickens "was no conscious proto-Marxist" either, as others had argued. Dickens offers social criticism, Brown says, without grounding it in a particular theory. "The critical nature of Dickens's novelistic reflection of society implies not merely an observation" he says, "but an imaginative judgment" (17). Brown sees Dickens employing a single controlling metaphor in his later fiction, viewing society as "one huge market-place" (23). Dickens attempts to expose the emptiness of mid-Victorian social behavior, which he sees as "conditioned by a degraded market-place logic" (23).

Brown demonstrates his reliance on Marxist critic Lucien Goldman at several points. Nevertheless, he notes how difficult it has been for left-wing critics to embrace Dickens fully, because the novelist does not seem to endorse revolution even though he identifies serious problems in his society. Brown sees Dickens's vision of society darkening as he grew older, but believes the novelist retained his bourgeois tendencies even while criticizing social ills. Although Dickens could criticize middle-class values, Brown says, he never rose above or descended below his own class to enter imaginatively into the worlds of the higher and lower social orders.

The most sustained Marxist reading of the novelist's work produced in the late twentieth century is Steven Connor's *Charles Dickens* (1985). Terry Eagleton, editor for the Rereading Literature series in which Connor's book appeared, praises Connor for dismissing both traditional humanist approaches — the "realist criticisms" that Eagleton says "measure the text against a covertly ideological version of what counts as psychological complexity, moral value, and narrative credibility" — and the aesthetic approach that purports to read novels as "structures of symbolic meaning" but which is really, in Eagleton's view, "quite as normative as its humanistic counterpart" (iv). By contrast, Connor "treats characters, events, and relations as functions of certain controlling systems of signification" (iv–v).

Actually, Connor seems more interested in debunking earlier critical readings of Dickens than in offering new readings himself. Predictably, as

Eagleton observes, Connor discovers that "encompassing all the particular signifying structures" with which the novelist works "is nothing less than the capitalist mode of production itself, by which Dickens's novels are increasingly haunted" (v). Like many of the new breed of Marxist critics, Connor relies heavily on poststructuralist theory for his critical vocabulary and methodology. Consequently, he pays close attention to the text, and his analysis of individual passages reveals much about what is happening at the margins as well as in the dominant narrative. Connor reveals the deep structures inherent in Dickens's novels, offers ways to deconstruct the work, and comments on the relationship between "self" and "system," explaining how the individual is always located within social systems and forced to operate within them.

His final chapter, "Reading in History," provides some provocative suggestions on ways to bridge the gap between traditional critics' demand for stable meaning and the poststructuralists' insistence on "absolute openness" (160). His solution is, of course, Marxist. By restoring "a sense of the historical context of texts," he says, it becomes possible "to understand the particular historical reasons for particular instabilities of meaning" (160). Interestingly, Connor believes that, to fully appreciate Dickens, it is necessary to overcome the embarrassment modern critics have felt in discussing the very idea of the author. "The sense of an author (who need in no way overlap with the real, historical author)," he cautions, "is nevertheless extremely important in Dickens's novels" (166). Dickens is eager to "establish an immediate, indeed an imaginary relationship" between the author and the audience, which Connor interprets as evidence of Dickens's need for control (167). Dickens was constantly seeking closure, fixing meaning as a means of communicating with and controlling his readers. But he never fully succeeded, and that, Connor argues, is what makes the novels great. "The greatness of Dickens's texts lies in the fact that they are so persistently haunted within themselves by all kinds of textual openness." In the drive to "establish closure and fixity, they comply with certain ideological imperatives of the Victorian period." But there are simply too many "loose ends [that] contradict the narrative of the unity of the self and the transparency of language," allowing the novels to be seen as "distanc[ing] themselves from the ideologies which they inhabit" (171).

Badri Raina argues in *Dickens and the Dialectic of Growth* (1986) that, taken as a whole, the Dickens canon presents a portrait of an artist who "urgently aspired to the substantive fruits of the bourgeois culture that surrounded him" while at the same time "intensely" despising the "living expressions of bourgeois Victorian insensitivity" (13). Reading the evolution of Dickens's vision of society as a dialectic in which old ideas from earlier works were tested, challenged, and discarded for newer ones, Raina provides an analysis of the major novels that highlights their connectedness. He is not afraid to challenge received opinion about Dickens, nor to take on critics whom he feels have been wrong in their readings of the novels. At times reading Raina is like sitting in on a symposium in which all the major Dickens critics, past and present, have gathered for a brief chat. Of course, Raina as moderator gets the last word, and he uses it to drive home his thesis that the Dickens canon is evidence of the growth and change of a major artist who struggled to reconcile his conflicted attitudes toward his society.

In *The Politics of Story in Victorian Social Fiction* (1988), which deals with ways novelists respond to social change, Rosemarie Bodenheimer discusses *Oliver Twist* and *Hard Times* as illustrations of social problem novels that "set themselves in a dramatic way to the task of giving fictional shape to social questions that were experienced as new, unpredictable, without closure" (4). These novels, Bodenheimer argues, give readers insight into the middle-class response to troublesome questions. She sees Dickens valuing "temporality, memory, continuity, and loyalty" over the forces of determinism (167). The real target of Dickens's anger is not "industrialization itself" but "the production of social discourse about it" (190). Echoes of Foucault can be heard in her final pronouncement on the novel. "When *Hard Times* works at its best," she says, "it works as a fiction that liberates life stories from the rhetorical spells cast by antihistorical fictions of power" (207).

Pam Morris, a new voice in Marxist studies emerging in the 1990s, published her first critique of Dickens in 1991 by combining the formalist principles of Bakhtin with newer theories of self and society developed by Althusser and Lacan. In *Dickens's Class Consciousness: A Marginal View* (1991), a political reading of Dickens's novels, she relies on Bakhtin's idea of the novel as a dialogical form engaged in "polemical relations with dominant voices of its era" and the "experience of marginalization" of both class and gender (ix). Following Bakhtin's methodology, Morris shifts "critical focus" from the central characters "toward those who exist at the margin of the text" (14), relying on insights from Althusser and Lacan to determine how each of these figures attempts to create a sense of self in a repressive system. Some sense of her approach — and her critical style — can be gleaned from her introduction: "The texts" of Dickens's novels must "be released from the mystifying totality of a 'corpus' created by the individual 'genius' of their author, Charles Dickens. They need to be repositioned as material, discursive elements." Instead of privileging the "author as unified autonomous individual, we need to see a socially constituted system" (2). Morris admits her reading follows what she considers the groundbreaking study by the Leavises, who recognized that Dickens's later works "showed an ever-increasing awareness of the oppressive influence of social structures" (3).

New Historicists' interest in exploring the novelist's relationship to his age has produced some of the best insights into the novels, but their emphasis on exposing Dickens's "reactionary" ideology and his (sometimes unconscious) support of the prevailing power structure has created a portrait that more traditional Dickensians have found disconcerting. Like so many other new theorists, the New Historicists often reach out widely to incorporate the work of formalists and Marxists, as well as sociologists and historians who have described the inherent assumptions underlying literature. In "Dickens and the New Historicism" (1986) Roger D. Sell provides a succinct explanation of this new approach to the novels, making a strong case that the Victorian public was far from homogeneous. Dickens had to respond to many constituencies to achieve popularity. Following that line of reasoning Sell challenges the notion that the novels possess any real unity, noting "it now seems far less easy to attribute such unity to Dickens's novels, than twenty or thirty years ago" (67). Rather than search for such aesthetic principles, Sell says, the New Historian is more interested in how Dickens's novels "have functioned and can still function as interactive social discourse" (67). Of course, as Sell admits, "everybody has always appropriated Dickens for their own purposes" (78), and he does the same in making the novelist a dancer to the public's tune. Joseph Childers, also interested in ways fiction can be historicized, offers in "History, Totality, Opposition: The New Historicism and *Little Dorrit*" (1989) a model for conducting New Historicist analysis of a Dickens novel.

Less obvious, perhaps, than Sell and Childers but no less concerned about historicizing texts, Ian Duncan argues in *Modern Romance and Transformations of the Novel: The Gothic, Scott, and Dickens* (1992) that the novel emerged as the dominant literary form of the century because it relied on elements of the romance to "offer a panoramic and historical imitation of the life of the people, and something more: a criticism of life" (2). Taking this rather Arnoldian view, Duncan links Dickens with his predecessor Sir Walter Scott as heroes — "the author as hero," he calls each of them at one point (18) — men who became national figures in their own right, independent of their literary works. A disciple of Northrop Frye and Frederic Jameson, Duncan concentrates on genre but is willing to challenge his mentors when their theories do not seem to fit the facts as he sees them. For example, he points out an essential difference between Dickens and Scott in their use of romance. Scott "historicized romance as the form of a difference from modern life," he says, while Dickens, "reproducing that difference," would empty the romance of "its historical, collective charge to make it ontological and individual" (15).

Throughout his analysis of Dickens's novels, Duncan insists Dickens was consciously intent on being "present" to readers in and through his work. "In forging a unified identity of author as public figure, Dickens's writing insists upon itself as the idiom of a personal presence. It is always 'Dickens' who speaks to us" (193). Nevertheless, Dickens had great reverence for Scott, and in many ways wanted to emulate his career. That is why, Duncan argues, he was continually struggling to write a historical novel modeled on Scott's work. *Barnaby Rudge* is a failure, he notes, because it is Dickens's "oedipal struggle" to break free from Scott's influence; the novel was "necessary" but at the same time "arduous and ultimately barren" (232). But Dickens triumphs in *Dombey and Son,* where he manages to transform Scott's techniques of integrating romance and history into his own brand of "historical novel" — one that focuses on the present. "*Dombey and Son* is a revolutionary narrative," Duncan concludes, in which "we read about the overthrow of a dynasty" (252). On the thematic level, Dickens had finally achieved what Scott had tried to do in all his historical works: offer an object lesson for the present by illuminating the past. Dickens manages to offer his lesson by focusing on the present and giving it the sense of historical dimension.

Gail Turley Houston manages to combine New Historicist and feminist methodologies quite comfortably in her intriguing study *Consuming Fictions: Gender, Class, and Hunger in Dickens's Novels* (1994). Like most New Historicists, Houston is concerned with ways Dickens deals with the consumer society in which he lived. Specifically, however, she sees his concerns with hunger and satiation reflected in his descriptions of eating as being reflective, metaphorically, of the society's consumer mentality. Interested in what she calls "Dickens's conflicting attitudes about gender-based codes of consumption" (xi) — and class-based codes as well — she manages to weave in discussions of eating disorders and other maladies the Victorians saw in women. Houston believes these are emblematic of the diseases of Victorian society itself.

Mary Poovey, another critic who manages to meld her expertise in feminist criticism with New Historicist analysis, demonstrates in "Reading History in Literature: Speculation and Virtue in *Our Mutual Friend*" (1993) that deconstruction is simply a new brand of formalism. Insisting that "literature and literary criticism do not exist in a formalist vacuum" but instead are "inevitably concerned with politics" (42), she contends a work of literature "can alert the reader to the network of connotations and associations to which the language of the literary text" belongs (43). To appreciate fully the significance of any literary text, it must be positioned within the "historically specific discussions in which it participated" (47). In reading *Our Mutual Friend* Poovey looks at "the complex of financial, ethical, and legal questions introduced by the apparently limitless opportunities provided by new forms of capital organization and investment" (48). She sees the novel as Dickens's response to the threats posed by these new systems, especially in the domestic sphere. Amassing considerable detail from other nineteenth-century sources, she demonstrates how Dickens's novel contributed to the debate on the value of these new systems in light of their impact on race and gender relations as well as economic relations among individual and classes. She uncovers some of the contradictions in the novel — contradictions of which Dickens may have been unaware — providing a better sense of how the novelist understood and reacted to his own times while simultaneously being caught up in them too closely to be totally outside the structures and conventions of his age.

A third feminist who turned to historical and contextual studies of Dickens, Anny Sadrin, offers a new approach to the idea of inheritance in *Parentage and Inheritance in the Novels of Charles Dickens* (1994). Sadrin, a protégée of Sylvère Monod, had published a feminist reading of *Bleak House* in 1992. In her book she examines Dickens's heroes from the standpoint of their "inheritance" in both the economic and ontological senses. "Inheriting the father's name and the father's property is crucial in determining the ontological status" of all of Dickens's heroes, Sadrin says, calling such inheritance "a necessary step toward self-knowledge, self-definition, and self acceptance" (x). In her estimation, Dickens conceived "the relationship between man and property as the secular manifestation of some ontological pilgrimage" (4). Sadrin is critical of her predecessors who had not noticed the importance of bequests and other forms of passing down an inheritance — literally or figuratively — which she sees as central to Dickens's novels from *Oliver Twist* to *Our Mutual Friend.*

Three other studies illustrate how critics interested in literature's relationship to economics contributed to Dickens studies during this period. In *Circulation: Defoe, Dickens, and the Economies of the Novel* (1988) David Trotter says Dickens anticipates the development of social science. Reading the novels through the lens of "economics," that is, the practice of trade, which serves as his central metaphor, Trotter demonstrates how Dickens positions individuals within the urban landscape. Suvendrini Perera's *Reaches of Empire: The English Novel from Edgewater to Dickens* (1991) is one of the earliest postcolonial studies of Dickens's work. In a study of the way imperial ideology shaped the novel as a literary form, Perera examines two of Dickens's novels, *Dombey and Son* and *Edwin Drood,* to demonstrate how "a cosmic system with imperial trade at its center" (62), such as that in *Dombey and Son,* exposes ways in which colonialism slowly yet inexorably affected not only the English economy but English novelists. Long before colonialism became an overt topic for writers like Kipling and Conrad, Perera argues, novelists found it increasingly more difficult to marginalize colonies and colonial peoples in their work, ultimately being forced to confront the impact of colonialism on British economy and culture much earlier than might have been thought. Finally,

Jeff Nunokawa's *The Afterlife of Property: Domestic Security and the Victorian Novel* (1994) also focuses on issues of commodification. Despite his highly specialized vocabulary, Nunokawa offers a thoughtful and intriguing analysis of *Little Dorrit* and *Our Mutual Friend* to explain how Dickens dealt with the "reach of market forces" (4) into the domestic sphere.

In *Critical Theory and the Novel: Mass Society and Cultural Criticism in Dickens, Melville, and Kafka* (1994), an analysis of Dickens's methods for dealing with the problems of writing for a mass audience and with political issues, David Suchoff relies heavily on the philosophical findings of the Frankfurt School, specifically Walter Benjamin and Theodor Adorno, to explain how Dickens helped shape a "liberal-modernist paradigm" for the social novel (3). Suchoff criticizes those who suggest Dickens was alienated from Victorian society, contending instead that he was frequently conducting a "dialectical engagement" with "the industrial culture of his age," critiquing the materialistic and imperialist society of Victorian England (3). Andrew Miller's *Novels Behind Glass: Commodity, Culture, and Victorian Narrative* (1995) makes use of narratology, feminism, and social history to examine ways novelists deal with the problem of the increasing commodification of their society. "Among the dominant concerns motivating mid-Victorian novelists was a penetrating anxiety," he says, "that their social and moral world was being reduced to a warehouse of goods and commodities, a display window in which people, their actions, and their convictions were exhibited for the economic appetites of others" (6). Miller believes *Our Mutual Friend* best exemplifies the struggle between home life and the public world. Citing key biographical evidence of Dickens's mania for order in his own homes, Miller exposes tensions between the tendency for order and "an urban landscape composed of the detritus sloughed off in the heat of capitalist transformation" (120). In no other work, Miller argues, does Dickens represent so dramatically the differences between private and public spaces — and private and public values.

Four essays on Dickens's novels are included in editors John Jordan and Robert Patten's *Literature in the Marketplace: Nineteenth-Century British Publishing and Reading Practices* (1995), a collection dealing with cultural history and the economics of book production. J. Hillis Miller's "Sam Weller's Valentine" demonstrates how much Dickens depended on his audience to be "streetwise" in understanding terms he used as a kind of short-hand, in this case the commercialization of Valentine's Day. Patten explains in "Serialized Retrospection in *Pickwick Papers*" how serialized fiction affected its readers. Jonathan Rose contributes his ideas on methods historians have employed to determine how Dickens's first readers reacted to his work in "How Historians Study Reader Response; Or, What Did Jo Think of *Bleak House*?" In the most intriguing of the contributions, "Dickens in the Visual Market," Gerald Curtis discusses ways novels were marketed using visual aids — illustrations and advertisements — to a readership that valued the art of seeing as much as the pleasure of reading. Dickens's relationship with his readers is also the subject of Helen Small's "A Pulse of 124: Charles Dickens and a Pathology of the Mid-Victorian Reading Public" (1996). Small links Dickens's efforts to build readership for his novels among the various social classes in England with contemporary political efforts to develop and extend the franchise. She notes that efforts to create a common class, whether for readership or voting, exposed underlying tensions between public and private spheres of life so important to the Victorians. Reading, traditionally a private activity, was brought into the public domain by Dickens, whose efforts were seen as a threat to conservatives intent on preserving the social status quo.

More extensive than Sell's brief study published a decade earlier, William J. Palmer's *Dickens and New Historicism* (1997) employs the theoretical work of Foucault, Hayden White, and Dominick LaCapra to explain how Dickens develops his own philosophy of history. Claiming Dickens "'decenters' the portrayal of history in his fiction" (4), Palmer says that "in every one of his novels, Dickens questions the accuracy of history, redefines history from new perspectives, and critiques from below the accepted power relationships of the master texts of history" (13). Palmer believes Dickens shares with New Historicists the belief that the history of oppressed peoples is "resistant" to the "act of construction" (14), comfortable in the idea that such history is decentered, multivalent, and at times chaotic. Palmer believes New Historicism has much to offer as a means of reading Dickens, since it can help enlighten readers about his motives — by which Palmer means his aims as a social reformer. To read Palmer is to find a Dickens close to the one described by Thomas Jackson in *Charles Dickens: The Progress of a Radical* (1937), or the one whose work George Bernard Shaw considered more radical than *Das Kapital*.

Another exceptionally good study making use of contemporary theories of history and sociology to explain the relationship between Dickens's life and writings and demonstrate how social constraints influenced the production of his fiction is Catherine Waters's *Dickens and the Politics of the Family* (1997). Relying on Foucault and Jacques Donzelot, author of *Policing of Families* (1977), Waters examines what she calls "the ideology of family life" in Dickens's fiction (12). Her aim is to explain what she identifies as the "puzzling gap" between Dickens's reputation as a champion of the happy home and hearth and the presence in his novels of so many "fractured families." To do so she explores his work in the "context of the discourses which helped to formulate narrative definitions of the family in the nineteenth century" (16). Her readings of several novels and a number of Christmas stories focus on power relationships within the family. She concludes that Dickens was constantly crossing boundaries between public and private spheres, ostensibly upholding "the role of the nineteenth-century novel in the formation of cultural values" (205) while at the same time subtly questioning and subverting those values. Another disciple of Foucault and D. A. Miller, Gareth Cordery, suggests in "Foucault, Dickens, and David Copperfield" (1998) that if one listens to "the silences" in Dickens's semiautobiographical novel, "the narrative which emerges from the surface *bildungsroman* is very different from" the one traditionally accepted by conventional critics. "While the surface story traces the disciplining of David's emotions," the narrative found in the silences "tells of a different kind of disciplining, one that subjects David to a variety of social norms, rule, and regulations" (71).

Finally, two books published during the 1990s collect the best thinking of postmoderns past and present. First, the wide range of theoretical approaches to Dickens developed during the twentieth century is represented in Steven Connor's *Charles Dickens* (1996) in the Longman Critical Readers series. Connor brings together essays and excerpts by deconstructionists, Foucaldians, Marxists, feminists, practitioners of gender studies, and psychological critics. He includes as well Mikhail Bakhtin's influential "Heteroglossia in the Novel: *Little Dorrit*," published in Russian in 1935 but not widely known in Anglo-American circles until the 1970s. Connor's introduction provides a succinct summary of the critical problems Dickens has posed since the mid-nineteenth century, noting how the theorists of the late twentieth century have overturned many of the structuralist and symbolist approaches that had themselves replaced the once highly respected moral criticism promoted by Dickens's contemporary Matthew Arnold.

The second collection, *Dickens, Europe and the New Worlds* (1999), gathers papers originally prepared for presentation at a 1996 conference. Edited by Anny Sadrin, these essays attempt to place Dickens within a wider European context, thus extending Dickens studies beyond their traditional Anglo-American perspective. Five of the essays deal with Dickens's relationship to the Continent, specifically France and Italy. Two others concentrate on his American connections, while three examine his contacts with other colonial areas. Others examine the concept of "otherness," "the uncanny," and "science," all displaying the impact of critical theory on Dickens studies in the late twentieth century. A half-dozen look at Dickens's impact on the modern world and the reciprocal impact of the modern world on current perceptions of Dickens and his work. Informed by the best new scholarship, these studies point the way to the future of Dickens criticism in the twenty-first century.

Works Cited

Armstrong, Nancy. "Dickens Between Two Disciplines: A Problem for Theories of Reading." *Semiotica* 38 (1982): 243–75.

Ayres, Brenda. *Dissenting Women in Dickens's Novels: The Subversion of Domestic Ideology.* Westport, CT: Greenwood, 1998.

Barickman, Richard. *Corrupt Relations: Dickens, Thackeray, Trollope, Collins, and the Victorian Sexual System.* New York: Columbia UP, 1982.

Bernard, Catherine A. "Dickens and Victorian Dream Theory." In *Victorian Science and Victorian Values: Literary Perspectives,* edited by James Paradis and Thomas Postlewait, 197–216. New York: New York Academy of Sciences, Vol. 360, 1981. Reissued New Brunswick, NJ: Rutgers UP, 1985.

Blain, Virginia. "Double Vision and the Double Standard in *Bleak House*: A Feminist Perspective." *Literature and History* 11.1 (Spring 1985): 31–46.

Bodenheimer, Rosemarie. *The Politics of Story in Victorian Social Fiction.* Ithaca, NY and London: Cornell UP, 1988.

Boheemen, Christine van. *The Novel as Family Romance: Language, Gender, and Authority from Fielding to Joyce.* Ithaca, NY: Cornell UP, 1987.

Brooks, Chris. *Signs for the Times: Symbolic Realism in the Mid-Victorian World.* London: Allen & Unwin, 1984.

Brown, Carolyn. "'Great Expectations': Masculinity and Modernity." *Essays and Studies* 40 (1987): 60–74.

Brown, James M. *Dickens: Novelist in the Market Place.* London: Macmillan, 1982.

Carey, John. *The Violent Effigy: A Study of Dickens's Imagination.* London: Faber and Faber, 1973. Rev. ed. London: Faber, 1991. Reprinted as *Here Comes Dickens: The Imagination of a Novelist.* New York: Schocken, 1974.

Chase, Karen. *Eros and Psyche: The Representation of Personality in Charlotte Brontë, Charles Dickens, and George Eliot.* New York: Methuen, 1984.

Childers, Joseph W. "History, Totality, Opposition: The New Historicism and *Little Dorrit.*" *Dickens Quarterly* 6 (September 1989): 150–57.

Cohen, Monica. *Professional Domesticity in the Victorian Novel.* Cambridge: Cambridge UP, 1998.

Connor, Steven. *Charles Dickens.* Oxford: Blackwell, 1985.

———, ed. *Charles Dickens.* Longman Critical Readers, London: Longman, 1996.

Cordery, Gareth. "Foucault, Dickens, and *David Copperfield.*" *Victorian Literature and Culture* 26.1 (1998): 71–85.

Craig, David M. "The Interplay of City and Self in *Oliver Twist*, *David Copperfield* and *Great Expectations*." *Dickens Studies Annual* 16 (1987): 17–38.

Cummings, Katherine. *Telling Tales: The Hysteric's Seduction in Fiction and Theory.* Stanford, CA: Stanford UP, 1991.

Curtis, Gerald. "Dickens and the Visual Market." In *Literature in the Marketplace: Nineteenth-Century British Publishing and Reading Practices*, edited by John O. Jordan and Robert L. Patten, 213–49. Cambridge: Cambridge UP, 1995.

David, Deirdre. "Children of Empire: Victorian Imperialism and Sexual Politics in Dickens and Kipling." In *Gender and Discourse in Victorian Literature and Art*, edited by Antony H. Harrison and Beverly Taylor, 124–42. DeKalb: Northern Illinois UP, 1992.

———. *Fictions of Resolution in Three Victorian Novels.* London: Macmillan, 1981.

Dever, Carolyn. *Death and the Mother from Dickens to Freud.* Cambridge: Cambridge UP, 1998.

Docherty, Thomas. *Reading (Absent) Character: Towards a Theory of Characterization in Fiction.* Oxford: Clarendon P, 1983.

Donzelot, Jacques. *Policing of Families.* Paris: Éditions de Minuit, 1977. Translated by Robert Hurley. New York: Pantheon, 1979.

Duncan, Ian. *Modern Romance and Transformations of the Novel: The Gothic, Scott, and Dickens.* Cambridge; New York: Cambridge UP, 1992.

Eagleton, Terry. "Editor's Preface." *Charles Dickens*, by Steven Connor, iv–v. Oxford: Blackwell, 1985.

Eldredge, Patricia R. "The Lost Self of Esther Summerson: A Horneyean Interpretation of *Bleak House*." *Literary Review* 24.2 (Winter 1981): 252–78. Reprinted in *Third Force Psychology and the Study of Literature*, edited by Bernard J. Paris, 136–55. Rutherford, NJ: Fairleigh Dickinson UP, 1986.

Feltes, N. N. "The Moment of *Pickwick*, or the Production of a Commodity Text." *Literature and History* 10 (Autumn 1984): 203–17.

———. "Realism, Consensus, and 'Exclusion Itself': Interpellating the Victorian Bourgeois." *Textual Practice* 1.3 (Winter 1987): 297–308.

Flint, Kate. *Dickens.* London: Harvester, 1986.

Frank, Lawrence. *Charles Dickens and the Romantic Self.* Lincoln: U of Nebraska P, 1984.

Gallagher, Catherine. "*Hard Times* and *North and South*: The Family and Society in Two Industrial Novels." *Arizona Quarterly* 36.1 (1980): 70–95.

———. *The Industrial Reformation of English Fiction: Social Discourse and Narrative Form, 1832–1867.* Chicago: U of Chicago P, 1985.

Garrett, Peter. *The Victorian Multiplot Novel: Studies in Dialogical Form*, 23–51. New Haven, CT and London: Yale UP, 1980.

Ginsburg, Michael Peled. *Economies of Change: Form and Transformation in the Nineteenth-Century Novel*. Stanford, CA: Stanford UP, 1996.

Glavin, John. *After Dickens: Reading, Adaptation, and Performance*. Cambridge: Cambridge UP, 1999.

Golden, Morris. *Dickens Imagining Himself: Six Encounters with a Changing World*. Lanham, MD: UP of America, 1992.

Hanzo, Thomas A. "Paternity and the Subject in *Bleak House*." In *The Fictional Father: Lacanian Readings of the Text*, edited by Robert Con Davis, 27–47. Amherst: U of Massachusetts P, 1981.

Hara, Eiichi. "Stories Present and Absent in *Great Expectations*." *ELH* 53.3 (Fall 1986): 593–614.

Hardy, Barbara. "The Talkative Woman in Shakespeare, Dickens, and George Eliot." In *Problems for Feminist Criticism*, edited by Sally Minogue, 15–45. London: Routledge, 1990.

Harvey, W. J. *Character and the Novel*. Ithaca, NY: Cornell UP, 1965.

Hawthorn, Jeremy. *Bleak House: An Introduction to the Variety of Criticism*. London: Macmillan, 1987.

Higbie, Robert. *Character and Structure in the English Novel*. Gainesville: UP of Florida, 1984.

———. *Dickens and Imagination*. Gainesville: UP of Florida, 1998.

Hochman, Baruch and Ilja Wachs. *Dickens: The Orphan Condition*. Rutherford, NJ: Fairleigh Dickinson UP, 1999.

Holbrook, David. *Charles Dickens and the Image of Woman*. London: New York UP, 1993.

Hollington, Michael. *Dickens and the Grotesque*. London: Helm, 1984.

Hopkins, Sandra. "'Wooman, Lovely Wooman': Four Dickens Heroines and the Critics." In *Problems for Feminist Criticism*, edited by Sally Minogue, 109–44. London: Routledge, 1990.

Horton, Susan. *The Reader in the Dickens World*. Pittsburgh, PA: U of Pittsburgh P, 1981.

Houston, Gail Turley. *Consuming Fictions: Gender, Class, and Hunger in Dickens's Novels*. Carbondale: Southern Illinois UP, 1994.

Ingham, Patricia. *Dickens, Women & Language*. London: Harvester, 1992.

Jaffe, Audrey. "Spectacular Sympathy: Visuality and Ideology in Dickens's *A Christmas Carol*." *PMLA* 109 (1994): 254–65.

———. *Vanishing Points: Dickens, Narrative, and the Subject of Omniscience*. Berkeley: U of California P, 1991.

Jordan, John O. and Robert L. Patten, eds. *Literature in the Marketplace: Nineteenth-Century British Publishing and Reading Practices*. Cambridge: Cambridge UP, 1995.

Kucich, John. "Charles Dickens." In *Columbia History of the British Novel*, edited by John Richetti et al., 381–406 New York: Columbia UP, 1994.

———. *Repression in Victorian Fiction: Charlotte Brontë, George Eliot, and Charles Dickens*. Berkeley: U of California P, 1987.

Langland, Elizabeth. *Society in the Novel*. Chapel Hill: U of North Carolina P, 1984.

Larson, Janet L. *Dickens and the Broken Scripture*. Athens: U of Georgia P, 1985.

Lenard, Mary. *Preaching Pity: Dickens, Gaskell, and Sentimentalism in Victorian Culture*. New York: Peter Lang, 1999.

Lubitz, Rita. *Marital Power in Dickens's Fiction*. New York: Peter Lang, 1996.

Lukacher, Ned. "Dialectical Images: Benjamin/Dickens/Freud." *Primal Scene: Literature, Philosophy, Psychoanalysis*, 275–336. Ithaca, NY and London: Cornell UP, 1986.

Maxwell, Richard. *The Mysteries of Paris and London*. Charlottesville: UP of Virginia, 1992.

McKnight, Natalie. *Idiots, Madmen, and Other Prisoners in Dickens*. New York: St. Martin's, 1993.

Michie, Helena. "'Who is this in Pain?': Scarring, Disfigurement, and Female Identity in *Bleak House* and *Our Mutual Friend*." *Novel* 22 (1989): 199–212.

Milbank, Alison. *Daughters of the House: Modes of the Gothic in Victorian Fiction*. New York: St. Martin's, 1992.

Miller, Andrew H. "Rearranging the Furniture of *Our Mutual Friend*." *Novels Behind Glass: Commodity, Culture, and Victorian Narrative*, 119–58. Cambridge: Cambridge UP, 1995.

Miller, D. A. "Discipline in Different Voices: Bureaucracy, Police, Family, and *Bleak House*." *Representations* 1 (February 1983): 58–79.

———. "The Novel and the Police." *Glyph: Johns Hopkins Textual Studies* 8, 127–47. Baltimore, MD: Johns Hopkins UP, 1981.

———. *The Novel and the Police*. Berkeley: U of California P, 1988.

Miller, J. Hillis. "Sam Weller's Valentine." In *Literature in the Marketplace: Nineteenth-Century British Publishing and Reading Practices*, edited by John O. Jordan and Robert L. Patten, 93–128. Cambridge: Cambridge UP, 1995.

Minogue, Sally, ed. *Problems for Feminist Criticism.* London: Routledge, 1990.

Moglen, Helene. "Theorizing Fiction/Fictionalizing Theory: The Case of *Dombey and Son.*" *Victorian Studies* 35 (1992): 159–84.

Morgan, Nicholas H. *Secret Journeys: Theory and Practice in Reading Dickens.* Cranbury, NJ: Associated UP, 1992.

Morris, Christopher D. "The Bad Faith of Pip's Bad Faith: Deconstructing *Great Expectations.*" *ELH* 54.4 (Winter 1987): 941–55.

Morris, Pam. *Dickens's Class Consciousness: A Marginal View.* London: Macmillan, 1991.

Myers, Margaret. "The Lost Self: Gender in *David Copperfield.*" In *Gender Studies: New Directions in Feminist Criticism,* edited by Judith Spector, 120–32. Bowling Green, OH: Popular P, 1986.

Nunokawa, Jeff. *The Afterlife of Property: Domestic Security and the Victorian Novel.* Princeton, NJ: Princeton UP, 1994.

Palmer, William J. *Dickens and New Historicism.* New York: St. Martin's, 1997.

Paris, Bernard J. *Imagined Human Beings: A Psychological Approach to Character and Conflict in Literature.* New York: New York UP, 1997.

———. "Introduction." *Third Force Psychology and the Study of Literature,* 11–22. Rutherford, NJ: Fairleigh Dickinson UP, 1986.

Patten, Robert. "Serialized Retrospection in *The Pickwick Papers.*" In *Literature in the Marketplace: Nineteenth-Century British Publishing and Reading Practices,* edited by John O. Jordan and Robert L. Patten, 123–42. Cambridge: Cambridge UP, 1995.

Perera, Suvendrini. *Reaches of Empire: The English Novel from Edgewater to Dickens.* New York: Columbia UP, 1991.

Peters, Laura. Review of Jeremy Tambling, *Dickens, Violence and the Modern State. Dickensian* 93.2 (Summer 1997): 145–46.

Philpotts, Terry. Review of Jeremy Tambling, *Dickens, Violence and the Modern State. Dickens Quarterly* 13.3 (September 1996): 176–78.

Poovey, Mary. "Reading History in Literature: Speculation and Virtue in *Our Mutual Friend.*" In *Historical Criticism and the Challenge of Theory,* edited by Janet Levarie Smarr, 42–80. Urbanna-Champlain: U of Illinois P, 1993.

———. "The Man-of-Letters Hero: *David Copperfield* and the Professional Writer." *Uneven Developments: The Ideological Work of Gender in Mid-Victorian England,* 89–125. Chicago: U of Chicago P, 1988.

Raina, Badri. *Dickens and the Dialectic of Growth.* Madison: U of Wisconsin P, 1986.

Rainsford, Dominic. *Authorship, Ethics and the Reader: Blake, Dickens, Joyce.* London: Macmillan; New York: St. Martin's, 1997.

Rose, Jonathan. "How Historians Study Reader Response; Or, What Did Jo Think of *Bleak House*?" In *Literature in the Marketplace: Nineteenth-Century British Publishing and Reading Practices,* edited by John O. Jordan and Robert L. Patten, 195–212. Cambridge: Cambridge UP, 1995.

Rosenberg, Brian. *Little Dorrit's Shadows: Character and Contradiction in Dickens.* Columbia: U of Missouri P, 1996.

Sadoff, Diane. *Monsters of Affection: Dickens, Eliot, and Brontë on Fatherhood.* Baltimore, MD: Johns Hopkins UP, 1982.

———. "Storytelling and the Figure of the Father." *PMLA* 95 (March 1980): 234–45.

Sadrin, Anny, "Charlotte Dickens: The Female Narrator of *Bleak House.*" *Dickens Quarterly* 9 (June 1992): 47–57.

———. *Parentage and Inheritance in the Novels of Charles Dickens.* Cambridge: Cambridge UP, 1994.

———, ed. *Dickens, Europe and the New Worlds.* London: Macmillan, 1999.

Schad, John, ed. *Dickens Refigured: Bodies, Desires and Other Histories.* Manchester, England: Manchester UP, 1996.

Schor, Hilary. *Dickens and the Daughter of the House.* Cambridge UP, 1999.

Sedgwick, Eve Kosofsky. *Between Men: English Literature and Male Homosocial Desire,* 180–200. New York: Columbia UP, 1985.

Sell, Roger D. "Dickens and the New Historicism." In *The Nineteenth-Century British Novel,* edited by Jeremy Hawthorn, 63–80. London: Edward Arnold, 1986.

Senf, Carol A. "*Bleak House:* Dickens, Esther, and the Androgynous Mind." *Victorian Newsletter* 64 (Fall 1983): 21–27.

Simpson, David. *Fetishism and Imagination: Dickens, Melville, Conrad.* Baltimore, MD: Johns Hopkins UP, 1982.

Slater, Michael. *Dickens and Women.* London: Dent, 1983.

———, ed. *Dickens on America and the Americans.* Austin and London: U of Texas P, 1978.

Small, Helen. "A Pulse of 124: Charles Dickens and a Pathology of the Mid-Victorian Reading Public." In *The Practice and Representation of Reading in England,* edited by James Raven, Helen Small, and Naomi Tadmor, 263–90. Cambridge: Cambridge UP, 1996.

Smith, Grahame. Review of John Glavin, *After Dickens: Reading, Adaptation and Performance. Dickensian* 96.1 (Spring 2000): 60–61.

Steward, Douglas. "Anti-Oedipalizing *Great Expectations:* Masochism, Subjectivity, Capitalism." *Literature and Psychology* 45.3 (1999): 29–50.

Stewart, Garrett. *Death Sentences: Styles of Dying in British Fiction.* Cambridge, MA: Harvard UP, 1984.

———. *Dickens and the Trials of Imagination.* Cambridge, MA: Harvard UP, 1974.

———. "Signing Off: Dickens and Thackeray, Woolf and Beckett." In *Philosophical Approaches to Literature: New Essays on Nineteenth and Twentieth-Century Texts,* edited by William E. Cain, 117–39. Lewisburg: Bucknell UP, 1984.

Suchoff, David. *Critical Theory and the Novel: Mass Society and Cultural Criticism in Dickens, Melville, and Kafka.* Madison: U of Wisconsin P, 1994.

Tambling, Jeremy. *Dickens, Violence and the Modern State.* London: Macmillan, 1995.

———. "Prison-bound: Dickens and Foucault." *Essays in Criticism* 36 (January 1986): 11–31.

Trotter, David. *Circulation: Defoe, Dickens, and the Economies of the Novel.* New York: St. Martin's, 1988.

Vlock, Deborah M. *Dickens, Novel Reading, and the Victorian Popular Theatre.* Cambridge: Cambridge UP, 1998.

Waters, Catherine. *Dickens and the Politics of the Family.* Cambridge: Cambridge UP, 1997.

Watkins, Gwen. *Dickens in Search of Himself: Recurrent Themes and Characters in the Work of Charles Dickens.* London: Macmillan, 1987.

Webb, Igor. *From Custom to Capital: The English Novel and the Industrial Revolution.* Ithaca NY: Cornell UP, 1981.

Welsh, Alexander. *The City of Dickens.* Oxford: Oxford UP, 1971.

———. *From Copyright to Copperfield.* Cambridge, MA and London: Harvard UP, 1987.

Wheeler, Michael. *The Art of Allusion in Victorian Fiction.* London: Macmillan, 1979.

Wolfreys, Julian. *Writing London: The Trace of the Urban Text from Blake to Dickens.* London: Macmillan; New York: St Martin's, 1998.

Zwinger, Lynda. *Daughters, Fathers and the Novel: The Sentimental Romance of Heterosexuality.* Madison, WI and London: U of Wisconsin P, 1991.

———. "The Fear of the Father: Dombey and Daughter." *Nineteenth-Century Fiction* 39.4 (March 1985): 420–40.

8: Dickens in an Age of Theory II: The Persistence of Traditional Criticism (1980–2000)

BY THE 1980S, WHAT HAD BEEN CALLED New Criticism in the 1920s and 1930s had become the conventional way of approaching literature, and ideologies of the aesthetic critics, the moderns, and their formalist disciples — once considered radical — had been superseded by new ways of examining works of fiction. Nevertheless, textual studies, biographies, and various forms of formal and aesthetic analysis continued to be published, and Dickensians of every critical persuasion kept up a lively dialogue that on occasion extended beyond the covers of books and journals.

In 1981, Murray Baumgarten, John Jordan, and Edwin Eigner established The Dickens Project at the University of California Santa Cruz. Their aim was to promote a different kind of study than that found in typical graduate schools. Funded by the University of California system and engaging scholars from many other campuses, the organizers set out not only to promote scholarship but also to provide opportunities for people to "experience" Dickens and his world. For more than twenty-five years the Project has supported the Dickens Universe, a week-long celebration during which scholarly work shares the limelight with recreations of Victorian England. What the Dickens Project has done quite well is to recreate the kind of community of Dickens lovers that existed in England in the late nineteenth and early twentieth centuries — the community that had created the Dickens Fellowship nearly a century earlier.

Biographical Studies and Overviews

Despite the attractions of deconstruction and other theories stressing the independence of texts, interest in Dickens's personal and professional life remained high, and a number of new studies supplemented earlier work or retold Dickens's story for a new generation. Some were highly specialized, such as Jane Cohen's *Charles Dickens and His Original Illustrators* (1980) and Michael Allen's *Charles Dickens's Childhood* (1988). Cohen provides brief biographical sketches of the men who illustrated Dickens's novels and Christmas books, discussing the novelist's involvement with them in preparing his works for publication. Allen mines published biographies and original source documents to create a portrait of the novelist's early years. His narrative stresses the importance of Dickens's father, whose life is presented in some detail.

Many might have assumed Edgar Johnson's biography of Dickens would remain the standard for nearly a century, as Forster's had. In less than forty years, however, two new major biographies virtually superseded Johnson's work. The first to appear, Fred Kaplan's *Dickens* (1988), is representative of trends in biographical studies in the late twentieth century. Half the length of Johnson's book, it is principally a character study in which Kaplan attempts to identify the sources of Dickens's particular genius, supplementing what Kaplan calls Johnson's "somewhat innocent" (11) examination that glosses over some of the novelist's least admirable personal traits. As a corrective, Kaplan reads the fiction as an outgrowth of personal experience and psychological forces that drove Dickens to live and write as he did.

Kaplan had prepared himself well for his task, producing earlier work on Dickens including *Dickens and Mesmerism* (1975), in which he combines biographical study and critical analysis to explore the novelist's fascination with this subject. In 1977 Kaplan became one of the editors of *Dickens Studies Annual*. Three years later he edited Dickens's 1855 memoranda book, and over the years authored a number of articles on him.

Like the best modern biographers, Kaplan returns to primary sources to construct his narrative, relying on correspondence and diaries to paint his portrait of a frenetic, restless, and driven individual whose public personality belied his struggles with private demons that were often objectified in his fiction. For Kaplan, Dickens is the consummate performance artist, exhibiting in his life the exaggerated behaviors critics then and later would find unbelievable when recreated in his fiction. Expanding on Johnson's corrective commentary regarding Dickens's education, Kaplan stresses the many opportunities the novelist took to immerse himself in literature and history, explaining how this supposedly unlettered genius could incorporate so many suggestive allusions into his writing. The fiction is of special interest to him when he can show how it sprang from events in Dickens's life. In Kaplan's estimate, "All crisis was a spur" to Dickens's "creativity, all fiction a mirror of imaginative distortion in which the model of his own life became a portrait of his culture and his world" (429).

Kaplan sees Dickens as a man almost torn to pieces by an oppressive restlessness that fueled his creative genius but also drove him to engage in numerous forms of self-destructive behavior. The frantic pace of Dickens's life is made apparent throughout Kaplan's narrative, and if he does not describe the novelist's long walks in the kind of excruciating detail Johnson employs in his earlier biography, Kaplan is even more insistent on capturing the mania for theatrical performance that was a hallmark of Dickens's personality from his earliest adult years. He is sober in his assessment of Dickens's relationship with Ellen Ternan, refusing to take sides definitively on the question of whether the affair was consummated sexually, but admitting that to assume it was platonic requires an unusually high degree of naïveté. He does not gloss over Dickens's unreasonable behavior as a husband and father, but he does highlight the qualities that made him a determined businessman and a devotee of liberal causes.

Of course, in the critical climate of the late century, there is certainly enough in Kaplan to irritate virtually every group of literary theorists. Formalists would find fault with his readings of individual novels as autobiographical statements. Neo-Marxists would object to his assertion that Dickens really was a reformer at heart (although Kaplan does make it clear that the novelist retained, throughout his life, certain conservative tendencies that set him apart from the truly radical reformers of his day). His discussion of Dickens's constant involvement with the theater might initially appeal to those who considered Dickens a shallow poseur, but Kaplan makes a virtue of the novelist's theatricality. His balanced treatment of the women in Dickens's life and fiction — and his assertion that Catherine Dickens may have indeed been dull and unsuited for marriage to the novelist — is sure to antagonize feminists. And the fact that he links inextricably the author and his works makes his whole approach anathema to critics who believe that texts exist independent of the people who produced them. To all of these, Kaplan provides an answer in the preface to the 1998 re-issue of his biography. "Like culturally self-assured cannibals," he says, "we put Dickens into our particular contemporary pot, bring the water to a boil, and then help ourselves to those parts that entice our palates" (11). By implication, Kaplan wants his work to be regarded as a kind of Arnoldian attempt to see Dickens clearly, and to see him whole.

The reviews of Kaplan's work were still appearing in scholarly journals when another major biography appeared, Peter Ackroyd's *Dickens*.[1] Published in England in 1990 and a year later in the United States, this postmodern assessment reflects the age in which it was written. Ackroyd posits at the outset that Dickens saw reality as a reflection of his fiction. Further, he asserts that the psychological trauma Dickens suffered as a child was the shaping force for all his creative work. Born to a careless father and a neglectful mother, Dickens used fiction as a means of expelling his inner demons. Although Ackroyd does not seem directly influenced by Foucault, he nevertheless finds the image of the prison central to Dickens's work, insisting the novelist was constantly trying to escape the various prisons in which he found himself. Reading the events of his life in this light, Ackroyd claims the reading tours that seemed to exhaust Dickens actually gave him a sense of release — and provided him a way to further his clandestine relationship with Ellen Ternan.

Ackroyd brings to biography some of the same techniques that made him a successful novelist, creating suspense throughout his narrative and turning Dickens into a character that readers alternately pity or judge. To Ackroyd Dickens is a kind of Peter Pan figure who simply does not want to grow up, using his novels as a way of fantasizing to escape from the family and job responsibilities that imprison him. The biography is light on critical analysis, but when Ackroyd offers commentary, it is usually to point out parallels between the author and his characters. Ackroyd reads virtually every novel autobiographically, explaining how one character after another is transformed into an alter ego for their creator.

Perhaps the most unusual aspect of Ackroyd's work is his disdain for conventional forms of scholarship. He includes no notes acknowledging his sources, opting instead to place at the end of the text long, descriptive explanations about materials he used to prepare each chapter. Additionally, he inserts between chapters several intercalary sections (another postmodernist technique) that provide a contrapuntal commentary on the main narrative. Even more contemporary is his claim that he is creating his subject as he writes about him. Nevertheless, it seems clear from the general tenor of the work that Ackroyd is not simply being playful, but is trying to make sense of Dickens and convey his insights to a late-twentieth century audience.

Apparently Ackroyd's "take" on Dickens spoke to his own contemporaries. Within a decade his book became the most quoted source for information about the novelist's life and motivations. The novelist Jane Smiley made it her principal reference for her study of Dickens in 2002. Perhaps, too, the popularity of Ackroyd's *Dickens* was the impetus for the BBC to sponsor a kind of companion volume, *Dickens: Public Life and Private Passion,* which Ackroyd published in 2002. This book, printed on glossy paper and filled with photos and illustrations, is an abbreviated portrait of the novelist intended for readers who might not want to tackle Ackroyd's thousand-page biography.

Decidedly less ambitious than Ackroyd's lengthy tome, Brian Murray's *Charles Dickens* (1994) is a summary account intended as an introduction for students and general readers. Relying heavily on Ackroyd for biographical details, and on other critics for much of his analysis, Murray concentrates on explaining the complexity of Dickens's fiction and the inability of critics to categorize him as an advocate for one cause or another. His readings of individual novels show how Dickens went through three phases during which his interests shifted from the conflict of good vs. evil to an examination of what Murray calls the "facts of life" and finally to a concern for money and mystery. "Dickens's novels are not particularly hard to understand," Murray says. "They deal with themes and situations fundamental to great literary works — and to great myths —

that cross cultures and centuries" (185). This conclusion puts him at odds with several critical movements: the moderns of the late nineteenth and early twentieth century who first dismissed the novelist as conventional and sentimental, the mid-century formalists who found his work deep and complex, and the postmoderns who consider him closely tied to his imperialist and materialist times.

Perhaps even better than Murray's account, Grahame Smith's *Charles Dickens: A Literary Life* (1996) fulfills its aims as a tale of Dickens's career while bringing to bear some of the best insights of contemporary cultural studies on the production of his novels. Smith attempts to explain Dickens's achievement by examining the major fiction in the context of his career as a professional writer. He considers the novels not simply the artistic expressions of private feelings, but rather as constructs influenced by the novelist, his publisher, his readers, and the literary, social, and moral conventions of the age. To Smith Dickens is something of a composer and conductor — an analogy that emphasizes the collaborative nature of novel production in the nineteenth century (and probably ever since). Seeing Dickens in this way, Smith says, helps explain how he could combine "the solitariness of writing fiction with a commitment to communal activity" and reveal "the inextricable nature of the connections between the private and the public in his life and his work" (9).

Rather than proceed on strictly chronological lines, Smith examines in turn those factors that shaped his work: the role of his publishers, Dickens's own reading, the influence of periodical publication, the impact of the theater and other forms of popular entertainment, and demands of the public on novelists in general and Dickens in particular once he had become popular. Smith also takes account of the status of social institutions against which Dickens railed so frequently. Convinced that "Dickens's professional career is interesting in its own right" (159), Smith devotes his final chapter to an analysis of *Great Expectations,* explaining how all the forces impinging on the novelist were harnessed to produce one of his greatest works. Smith's insightful analysis demonstrates how external forces helped "shape [the novels] artistically through the medium of Dickens's imagination" (178).

Shorter biographical studies were published as well. Catherine Peters's *Charles Dickens* (1998) in the Pocket Biographies series is a readable if highly derivative work, providing little criticism but offering a sense of the novelist's accomplishments. Unfortunately, Norrie Epstein's *The Friendly Dickens* (1998), a chatty and whimsical account of his life, provides only superficial analysis, and some of her distortions give the narrative the faint ring of those early coffee-table studies that presented Dickens as a convivial *bon vivant.*

Dickens's love-hate relationship with the United States continued to attract critical attention. In *Charles Dickens's Quarrel with America* (1984) Sidney Moss carefully chronicles details of Dickens's visits, even providing schedules of his travels and his reading, in order to make the case that the fault for the novelist's "argument" with America is largely one-sided. Dickens did not make any real attempt to understand the American character, Moss asserts. Although Moss drew praise from Michael Slater in a *Dickensian* review, Jerome Meckier resented Moss's mischaracterization so strongly that he undertook his own book on the subject. *Innocent Abroad: Charles Dickens's American Engagements* (1990) is Meckier's extended refutation of Moss, blending new analysis of old material with insights gained from new sources such as the diary of Annie Fields, wife of Dickens's American publisher. Meckier finds plausible explanations for what others have described as initial hostility on Dickens's part. What really happened, he says, is that Dickens underwent "a nasty formative experience" on his first tour in 1842 that turned the visit into "a voyage of self-discovery" (1). Expecting to find Utopia, Dickens learned the sad truth that "no place at home or abroad can succeed in illustrating the perfectibility of the species without a prior improvement in human nature" (239). The lesson, in Meckier's view, made Dickens's subsequent novels better. The "bitter disappointment" he experienced in 1842 became "the impetus for Dickens's deceptively simple call for personal, inward formation as a prerequisite" for lasting social change (239).

Thematic and Critical Analysis Focused Principally on Dickens

Continuing a trend begun in the 1940s, scholars during the 1980s and 1990s turned out dozens of critical monographs on specific themes or characteristics that highlight Dickens's achievements. S. J. Newman's *Dickens at Play* (1981) is a good example of this kind of work. Newman is concerned principally with the development of Dickens's comic imagination, which he considers both an aesthetic and a moral quality. He ascribes the curious development of this attribute to Dickens's "discontent with, and evasion of, unity" (3). Newman shows special affection for the early, comic Dickens over the tragic, alienated figure, but suggests at the same time that the comic mask allowed Dickens to be truly subversive.

It took a surprisingly long time for the editors at Twayne to bring out a volume on Dickens in their English Authors series. Although books on most major figures had appeared in the 1960s and 1970s, Harland Nelson's *Charles Dickens* was not published until 1981. Additionally, unlike most books in the series, Nelson's is not a comprehensive survey of the novelist's career. Instead, Nelson approaches his subject topically, concentrating on Dickens's work practices, his relationship with his audience, and the methods he used for publication. All of these, Nelson says, influenced Dickens in choosing subjects and composing his plots. In a very insightful central chapter Nelson deals with Dickens's rhetoric, noting how the structure of his novels is carefully worked out, and argues further that his use of imagery, symbol, and other technical devices is similarly well planned, demonstrating Dickens's conscious artistry. Selecting *Bleak House* for extended analysis, Nelson explains how Dickens employs the various techniques of fiction to offer a critique of society and deal with the theme of individual salvation.

Like Nelson, in *"The Hero of My Life": Essays on Dickens* (1981) Bert Hornback concentrates on a single novel, in this case *David Copperfield*, to illustrate the qualities he says make Dickens great. Hornback admits in the preface that his study contains no "properly definable critical focus" (xi) — meaning it is not based on a particular theoretical approach, thus putting him at odds with an emerging critical tradition that has scant use for both his methods and conclusions. In fact, Hornback believes it is his role to develop his own methodology rather than acquiesce to the popular trend of applying one theory to all of literature, "as though a poststructuralist socket-wrench or whatever were the ideal tool to use on everything" (xi). His five essays on Dickens's most autobiographical novel explain what he thinks are the most important themes, repeated in novels that follow. "From *David Copperfield* on," Hornback says, "Dickens the artist has as his goal the creation of human wisdom" (x). This personal, text-oriented approach emphasizes Dickens's role as a creator and his constant awareness that a novel can be a vehicle for instruction.

If there is a distinguishing characteristic about many of the thematic and technical studies done in the 1980s and 1990s, it is their narrow focus. Mark Lambert admits as much about his work in the introduction to *Dickens and the Suspended Quotation* (1981). He playfully describes his work as being more like an examination of plankton rather than of whales. Lambert is interested in a stylistic device he finds characteristic in Dickens's novels: the use of interruptions in characters' speeches. He claims this technique affects the way readers view these characters and eventually leads readers to understand larger issues with which Dickens deals. One might accuse Lambert of overkill, but it is not possible to ignore his ability to read the text closely. His conclusion reveals something about Dickens's conscious artistry: "behind these pages is an author who never lets up but is courting and wooing his audience anew in almost every paragraph" (115). Dickens's relationship to his audience is also at the core of Nancy K. Hill's *A Reformer's Art: Dickens's Picturesque and Grotesque Imagery* (1981), a study of the novelist's use of visual imagery for moral purposes. Hill finds Dickens creating a "visual aesthetic that would alter his readers' perceptions of the world around them" (2). Like the eighteenth-century illustrator William Hogarth, Dickens uses grotesque imagery for its shock value to get readers' attention and influence their views on social issues. In another narrowly focused work, Deborah Thomas admits *Dickens and the Short Story* (1982) is not an exhaustive study of Dickens's work in this genre, but rather an assessment of "the general question of the reason for the recurring presence of such stories in the larger context of Dickens's art" (2). The short stories sometimes became places for experimentation, allowing Dickens to try out techniques of characterization or theme that he would later exploit in his longer fiction. Thomas contends a familiarity with the short stories enriches readers' appreciation for Dickens.

Although he claims to be filling a gap in Dickens scholarship, Dennis Walder actually picks up on the work of earlier critics in *Dickens and Religion* (1981). Walder asserts the influence of Dickens's religious beliefs have not been studied systematically, possibly because the novelist often presents them obliquely or obscurely. Dickens believed the religious impulse was central to human nature, Walder insists, and for readers to really appreciate his work it is necessary to understand Dickens's feelings regarding the role religion played in life. Walder examines each novel to see what Dickens has to say about religious issues, and also sketches the few real-life encounters Dickens had with organized religion. Walder admits that "Dickens was not a religious novelist; nor were any of his novels *primarily* religious in intention or effect" (15). But he insists that Dickens was a pious man who promoted piety in his novels.

Dickens's covert religious tendencies also emerge in the exceptionally fine "close and affectionate reading" (xiii) of the novels by Andrew Sanders, who succeeded Michael Slater as editor of the *Dickensian* in 1978. Revisiting the topic of Dickens's lifelong interest in death and dying, in *Charles Dickens: Resurrectionist* (1982) Sanders focuses on five novels in which death figures prominently both as a plot device and as a major theme. Like many critics before and after him, Sanders acknowledges that the death of Dickens's sister-in-law Mary Hogarth prompted in the novelist an almost morbid fascination with death, especially the death of young people. Unlike most other critics, however, Sanders does not see Dickens overworking the death of children and young adults simply to milk his audience's sympathies. Instead, he believes Dickens is intensely aware of the prevalence of such deaths in his society and extremely sensitive to the pain they cause. Sanders suggests that as Dickens's career advanced, he evolved an idea about death that was "resurrectionist" — that is, death came to be seen as a phase of life, a passageway to eternal life. Such an overtly Christian reading of Dickens's works is unusual, as most critics have dismissed Dickens's views on Christianity as murky and ill-formed.

Sanders argues persuasively, however, that the novelist's simple belief in the essentials of Christian doctrine, despite his unwillingness to "proclaim it from the housetops" (xi), serves as a source of solace and inspiration in his exploration of one of life's great mysteries.

In another narrowly focused but adeptly argued study, *Excess and Restraint in the Novels of Charles Dickens* (1981), John Kucich articulates the "special kind of tension between energy and limits" in Dickens's work (1). At the outset Kucich makes clear his intention to focus on aesthetic, not sociological, matters. He is conscious, too, of avoiding both the ahistorical traps of New Criticism or structuralism, "totalities whose ultimate goal is a hypostatized balance of forces, one whose significance lies entirely in an internal logic of coherence" (2). Kucich parts company with many postmodernists, though, by insisting that Dickens's novels are linked to a real world outside of them and have a moral dimension as well. Kucich would continue his work on Dickens over the next decades, producing among other studies a fine analysis of Dickens's rhetoric, "Dickens's Fantastic Rhetoric: The Semantics of Reality and Unreality in *Our Mutual Friend*" (1985). In this essay he suggests that the "specialness of Dickens's prose" resides in its "combination of two very different kinds of rhetoric," one used in workmanlike fashion to carry his story and meaning forward, the second consisting of "language that exuberantly wastes itself, flaunting its freedom from such an economical, reductive, and reasonable relation to meaning" (168).

Two collections of essays issued in the early 1980s became handy reference texts for those wishing to get a snapshot of the range of Dickens criticism. Wendell Stacy Johnson's *Charles Dickens: New Perspectives* (1982) is an eclectic collection of materials published during the first heyday of modern criticism of Dickens, making the collection "new" only because it updated one issued by Prentice Hall, Johnson's publisher, fifteen years earlier. Johnson's rationale for selecting essays is to stress Dickens's role "as a reporter and social critic, and at the same time, as an imaginative genius" (5). Like Johnson's collection, Robert Giddings's *The Changing World of Charles Dickens* (1983) is a potpourri drawn together to explain how changes in social conditions, technology, politics, and other areas of life influenced Dickens as a writer. The eleven essays cover predictable topics, such as David Trotter's assessment of Dickens's use of metaphor in shaping ideas about social progress and David Craig's examination of the crowd in his fiction. But there are also more unusual ones, like David Edgar's "Adapting *Nickleby*," a commentary on the Royal Shakespeare Company's stage production of the novel.

Allan Grant's *A Preface to Dickens* (1984) challenges new historical and cultural approaches to critical study by asserting at the outset that "the writer of genius transcends his own time" and "great literature, therefore, is always contemporary" (ix). Grant claims other critics have overemphasized the importance of Dickens's childhood experiences and the contemporary Victorian scene. He believes Dickens owes his greatest debt not only to the eighteenth-century novelists he read, but especially to Shakespeare and the English Romantic poets. Nevertheless, Grant devotes half his study to explaining how Dickens learned about human nature from observing contemporary society. A second reactionary study is Graham Hough's essay on *Bleak House* in Nicholas Boyle and Martin Swales's *Realism in European Literature* (1986). Hough takes a stand against the growing influence of poststructuralists who treat texts as self-contained and language as exclusively self-reflexive. He contends Dickens uses language to create a sense of reality so that in his work "we see through the language to the life behind it" (67). Finally, Jerome Meckier argues in *Hidden Rivalries in Victorian Fiction* (1987) that nineteenth-century British fiction is "a honeycomb of intersecting networks" in which novelists "rethink and rewrite other novels as a way of enhancing their own credibility" (2). Among the tasks Meckier takes on is a reconciliation of competing claims by critics such as Humphry House, who celebrates Dickens as a reporter of Victorian society, and J. Hillis Miller, who sees Dickens as an inventor of his own world. At the same time, Meckier challenges postmodern notions of literature, which he claims distort the Victorian novel. He admits texts frequently refer to other texts, but he insists that they also refer to a world "out there," independent of the closed loop of language others have claimed is the sole reality of fiction.

While those employing conventional methodologies tended to be less critical of Dickens than proponents of various postmodern theories, even in this camp discordant voices sometimes emerged. Myron Magnet's *Dickens and the Social Order* (1985), an assessment of Dickens's political philosophy, begins by acknowledging openly that Dickens was essentially a conservative. Interested in "Dickens's understanding of the nature and function of society," Magnet explores a phenomenon he finds in both the early and late Dickens: the concern for "human aggression" and the neutralizing force of civilization on this individual human trait (5). His study concentrates on two novels that have not often received extended attention, *Nicholas Nickleby* and *Barnaby Rudge,* the latter presenting Dickens's "deeply meditated philosophy" that stresses the importance of society as the "chief defense against aggression" (51). Magnet's readings of *American Notes* and *Martin Chuzzlewit* provide a fresh perspective on Dickens's attitudes toward America. Positing that Dickens had a political interest in the United States, Magnet explains why the novelist was deeply disappointed in what he found there. Magnet thinks Dickens appreciated the appeal of liberalism but recognized that "since men, plentifully endowed by nature with instincts of violence and aggression, get tamed and humanized by society, then society's civilizing work ought to be done as well and as fully as possible" (202). This meant that not only are education and charity important, so is enforcement of social norms.

On a somewhat lighter note, Paul Schlicke's *Dickens and Popular Entertainment* (1985) examines Dickens's attitudes toward forms of entertainment in Victorian England and his conception of himself as an entertainer. Schlicke sees the novelist "rooted in the traditions of the past" because these highlight "old communal patterns" of society, serving as "a locus for the spontaneity, selflessness and fellow-feeling which lay at the heart of his moral conviction" (7). Schlicke argues persuasively that "Dickens's role as a popular entertainer contributes significantly to the development of his art" (12). Moving freely between description of the social context and commentary on the novels, Schlicke demonstrates how forms of entertainment achieve thematic significance in Dickens. Schlicke would continue to write about Dickens, publishing articles in *Dickens Quarterly, Dickens Studies Annual,* and *Theatre Notebook.* His commentary in the *Oxford Readers' Companion to Dickens* (1999) on contemporary trends in Dickens criticism, discussed in the introduction to this book, is a valuable resource for those wishing to understand the status of Dickens studies in the last quarter of the twentieth century. A second critic looking to the world of popular entertainment for clues to Dickens's genius, Edwin Eigner, asserts in the introduction to *The Dickens Pantomime* (1989) that it is possible to understand Dickens's creative imagination "in terms of pantomime conventions" (x). He claims Dickens was quite familiar with the three-hundred-year-old tradition that stressed theatricality and stock characters, and made use of it frequently as both an organizing device and a method of characterization.

The premise of Juliet McMaster's *Dickens the Designer* (1987), a study of Dickens's visual imagination, is that Dickens "saw himself as an artist in a visual mode" akin to Hogarth (xi). Because Dickens was constantly examining the relationship between the visible world and the inner world of the spirit, "there is a consonance between appearance and essence" in a Dickens novel "that pertains more usually in the visual than in the verbal arts" (3). Physique, gesture, and appurtenance are intended to convey information about character. McMaster gleans from the novels examples of Dickens's use of these traits, demonstrating how a critic finely attuned to the text can offer sensitive and sensible readings that highlight the importance of imagery in revealing the moral sense of Dickens's fiction. She employs her sophisticated critical vocabulary to affirm and extend the conclusions about Dickens made by earlier critics such as Chesterton and Orwell, who happily acknowledge the moral quality of Dickens's novels and the primacy of character in his works.

One of the recurrent critical issues scholars have tackled repeatedly has been the claim that Dickens was an undisciplined genius. This opinion was accepted by many Victorian critics and embellished by modernists who reveled in pointing out the formlessness of Dickens's novels. From time to time refutations to these charges have appeared, especially during the 1950s and 1960s when proponents of the "dark Dickens" found symbolic unity in his work. In 1987 two critics once again attempted to put an end to debate about the novelist's craftsmanship. Harry Stone's massive *Dickens's Working Notes for his Novels* (1987) — "oversize" is the classification libraries give it — contains facsimiles of Dickens's notes for every novel after *Pickwick Papers* (which *was* constructed rather haphazardly, as Stone admits in his introduction), and transcriptions that make sense of Dickens's difficult handwriting. In a brief but convincing introduction, Stone describes Dickens's practice for drafting his work, observing that the notes can be used "to verify a meaning, document an intention, underscore a motif, trace a genesis, buttress a reading, clarify a relationship, examine the creative process, or study Dickens's imagination" (xix). One of the most important uses is in helping critics understand "how Dickens concentrates on structure and long-range planning" (xv). Graham Daldry's *Charles Dickens and the Form of the Novel* (1986) concentrates more on the finished products. Daldry argues that by examining the genres of Dickens's works and the structure employed in individual novels, one can see the developing tensions in narrative art that led to what we now call modernism.

In the introduction to *Dickens and Other Victorians* (1988) editor Joanne Shattock says "the world of Dickens Studies, by virtue of its central subject, can never remove itself entirely from the social, cultural, and political milieu in which the books were written" (xi). Following critical principles espoused by Philip Collins, to whom the volume is dedicated, the contributors "determinedly place their texts in the wider context of nineteenth-century thought and culture" (xii). George Levine writes on the influence of nineteenth-century science on *Little Dorrit,* Sylvère Monod on Dickens's view of children in *Sketches by Boz,* Andrew Sanders on the sources for *A Tale of Two Cities,* Graham Storey on links between the novelist's letters and his fiction, and U. C. Knoepflmacher on Dickens's complex attitudes toward women. The two most intriguing essays, however, diverge a bit from an examination of individual works: John Sutherland analyzes nineteenth-century social fiction sparked by Dickens's success, while K. J. Fielding speculates on the meaning of the phrase "The Dickens World."

In *The Dickens Aesthetic* (1989) and its companion volume *Dickens on Literature: A Continuing Study of His Aesthetic* (1990), Richard Lettis examines the fiction, nonfiction, and especially the letters to see what

Dickens has to say about painting, architecture, sculpture, drama, dramatic readings, music, and poetry. Lettis reveals that Dickens had studied the sister arts much more carefully than early critics had recognized, and had formulated an idea about the nature and function of art that he applied systematically in his fiction. Lettis believes Dickens's view was essentially Romantic: for art to be great it had to evoke emotions, imitate life, refrain from sentimentality, and be carefully crafted, whatever the medium. Above all, Lettis says, Dickens thought great art should be affirming — an attitude that would not earn him any favor with subsequent generations that preferred irony to enthusiasm.

Others who return to the much-discussed subject of Dickens's imaginative powers include Mildred Newcomb, whose *Imagined World of Charles Dickens* (1989) proposes a theory of imagination that informs Dickens's creative efforts and creates a single, coherent myth uniting individual works. Identifying recurrent images, Newcomb constructs what she calls "the total allegory" contained in the fiction (187). In her view, the Dickens canon can be read as a continuous web of works that tells a consistent story: that of "a nineteenth-century Everyman" who responds to the challenges of modern life with "an infectious faith in life itself" (184–85). Like Tennyson's Arthur in *Idylls of the King*, he "emerges from the mists, travels steadily along the road or river in a series of changing figures he carries with him, and in due time passes back into the mists" (185). One might think, after reading Newcomb, that there had been no poststructuralist revolution in literary criticism. Her work is reminiscent of those studies of the 1950s, 1960s, and 1970s that concentrate on the literary text as if it were a self-contained world of intertwined situations and symbols that reveal something about universal human experience.

So, too, might one wonder at seeing Doris Alexander's *Creating Characters with Charles Dickens* appear in 1991 rather than a century earlier, but its publication offers a curious insight into the manifold approaches to critical inquiry that Dickens's work continued to inspire. Alexander is interested in ferreting out the originals on which a number of Dickens characters are based. Hers is not simply an exercise in discovering who among real-life Victorians served as models for Dickens. Rather, she focuses on the creative process that drove the novelist to transform the essential features of an individual's personality into a fictional character. While Alexander makes use of psychological tools not available to Dickens's first admirers, the absence of references to three decades of philosophical and literary theories of characterization make her work seem naïve.

In 1992 John Lucas, author of the influential *The Melancholy Man: A Study of Dickens's Novels* (1970), published *Charles Dickens: The Major Novels* (1992) in which he cites *Dombey and Son, David Copperfield, Bleak House, Little Dorrit, Great Expectations,* and *Our Mutual Friend* as

Dickens's greatest achievements. In his early novels, Lucas argues, Dickens was gaining confidence in dealing with the contemporary scene. These later works, his masterpieces, are all aimed at revealing weaknesses in both social and human relationships; they also expose problems in Victorian society that lead to individual unhappiness. Lucas claims Dickens had a deeply held belief in the efficacy of communities, and his concern for social health and individual happiness lies at the root of his creative genius. Additionally, he says, Dickens had an unusual ability to focus on a theme and carry out his vision of society through characterization and story.

Two years later Harry Stone brought out another major study, *The Night Side of Dickens* (1994), in which he examines three aspects of Dickens's literary career he thinks had not been adequately documented: his interest in cannibalism, his fascination with violent passions, and his belief in some form of necessity driving human activity. Stone provides close readings of individual texts, comparing them carefully with biographical information to demonstrate how Dickens's "dark side" emerges from texts that are often comical on the surface. Stone's major interest is in Dickens's strange fascination with cannibalism, which turns up quite often in his work as a metaphor rooted, Stone believes, in the abandonment and resentment Dickens felt toward his mother for allowing him to be demeaned when he was a child. Stone's speculations lead to some interesting readings of the novels, especially *David Copperfield, Great Expectations, Bleak House,* and *Our Mutual Friend.*

Stone is at his best when demonstrating how Dickens transforms his own experience into fiction. This he does quite well in the sections on cannibalism and on the passions. In these sections biographical readings are strengthened by Stone's careful analysis of Dickens's letters and non-fiction, as he demonstrates ways the novelist expresses his *angst* over his relationships with his wife and Ellen Ternan. Stone goes so far as to suggest that until he met Ternan, Dickens was incapable of describing love with any sense of verisimilitude. After he had separated from Catherine and taken up with Ellen, Stone says, Dickens created a series of tormented lovers who must represent what the novelist himself was feeling in his personal life. While Stone's readings of individual novels are provocative, his most significant contribution may be his analysis of two shorter works he calls keys to understanding the dark side of Dickens's character, "The Bride's Chamber" and *George Silverman's Explanation*. His discussions of these works are models of what traditional critics continued to contribute to Dickens scholarship at a time when others were engaged in theoretical analysis.

In the 1990s a number of traditional studies focusing on Dickens's treatment of family matters appeared. Frances Armstrong's *Dickens and the Concept of Home* (1990), examines the novelist's use of the home in his fiction. She shows how Dickens employs conventional views of the home prevalent in Victorian England while not fully accepting them. For Dickens, the home was never "a place of permanent retreat" (151). His view was constantly evolving; as his career progressed, he came to believe that a "loss of faith in the home" could become, "in some miraculous way, a source of power" (152). In *Dickens and the Grown-Up Child* (1994) Malcolm Andrews takes what he calls a "metaphysical-historical" perspective on Dickens's work (2), exploring what the concept of childhood meant for him. After explaining the notions Dickens inherited from the eighteenth century, Andrews suggests that, especially in the novels of the 1840s, Dickens creates the figure of the grown-up child as an attempt to reconcile the competing demands of childhood and maturity.

Comparative Studies

The practice of comparing Dickens with other writers began almost as soon as *Sketches by Boz* appeared. Certainly the majority of comparative criticism focused on Dickens's relationship with other English writers. However, in the early 1980s it suddenly became fashionable to point out Dickens's influence on American novelist William Faulkner. Both Merritt Moseley in "Faulkner's Dickensian Humor in *The Sound and the Fury*" (1981) and Linda Kauffman in "The Letter and the Spirit in *Hard Times* and *The Sound and the Fury*" (1981) look for evidence of influence in Faulkner's most celebrated novel, while Geraldine LaRocque searches for the same kind of indebtedness in "*A Tale of Two Cities* and *Absalom, Absalom!*" (1982). In *The Novel in England and Germany* (1981) H. R. Klieneberger compares Dickens's achievement to that of his German contemporary Wilhelm Raabe. Klieneberger explains how Raabe was heavily influenced by Dickens, especially in handling subjects such as gender relations, anti-Semitism, and the aristocracy. Even in the area of characterization Dickens had an influence, Klieneberger says, at least early in Raabe's career.

John Reed's *Dickens and Thackeray: Punishment and Forgiveness* (1995) is reminiscent of the scholarship that characterized Dickens studies in the 1960s and 1970s — the period when Reed established himself as a Victorian scholar with a fine book on Tennyson's *Idylls of the King* (1969), followed by a sweeping study of the period, *Victorian Conventions* (1975). After completing a second extensive analysis of the Victorians' mindset, *Victorian Will* (1989), Reed turned his attention to two of the period's greatest novelists. In dealing with Dickens's and Thackeray's attitudes toward punishment and forgiveness, Reed acknowledges he may be employing "a somewhat discredited humanistic approach to literature." While many critics "may have lost their faith in literary texts as vehicles for message," Reed makes sure his readers know he does not share that view. "There can be little doubt that many texts, especially before the twentieth century, were intended to bear such messages" (xiv). Yet Reed demonstrates throughout his study an awareness of the work of contemporary critics, using their ideas to support his own case when relevant, dismissing them gently when he thinks they are wrong. Openly rejecting the postmodern notion of the "death of the author," Reed insists Dickens is one of the most conscious and present authors ever to write for readers he hoped to influence. He believes Dickens has an essentially Christian outlook regarding punishment and forgiveness, though not one linked to organized religion. Reed discovers Dickens developing a darker vision as his career progressed. Problems of evil are resolved more simply and completely in the early novels than in later works, which are "heavy with a sense of accumulated guilt" (289).

Reed's major premise is that the moral struggle underlying Dickens's handling of good and evil works not only thematically but structurally, binding together novels others have described as poorly constructed but which Reed believes are integrated by their focus on the problems of human behavior. He says Dickens is "not shy about asserting his moral opinions" (300). Unwilling to let his good characters direct punishment on his villains, Dickens emphasizes "the tendency for the wicked to create their own punishments" (301). His intricate plots suggest to Reed "a pattern of retribution that extends beyond the novel's text and encompasses it." This technique, coupled with "repeated patterns of retribution" that "reinforce the larger pattern in the novel" as a vehicle for moral instruction, create "a redundance [*sic*] of moral information that insures the successful transmission of the fundamental moral message of the literary work" (301). The patterns of coherence are visible to anyone who is willing to look for them — and they can be found with little effort, Reed argues, unless one intentionally misreads Dickens by ignoring or denying "the language's contextual meaning" (301).

Finally, in *Shakespeare and Dickens: The Dynamics of Influence* (1996) Valerie Gager does what Robert Fleissner promises but fails to deliver in his 1965 book on the relationship between the two writers. Her very impressive piece of traditional scholarship is not simply a compilation of parallel passages, but a study of "the infinite variety of ways in which Dickens uses Shakespeare for his own creative purposes" (18). Aware of but not enslaved by poststructuralist commentary, Gager concentrates on ways Shakespeare influenced Dickens not only in creating characters but also in developing themes. She refutes earlier assertions that Dickens was a sloppy interpreter of Shakespeare, and argues persuasively that Dickens drew many of his notions about Shakespeare from nineteenth-century stage productions of his work, not from the texts of his plays.

Thematic Study and Critical Analysis Including Commentary on Dickens

Even when Dickens was not the principal focus of a critical study, discussions of his work appeared frequently in studies of the nineteenth-century novel published in the 1980s and 1990s. The attempt to maintain the place established for him by critics of the preceding three decades is nowhere more prominent than in Robert Polhemus's *Comic Faith: The Great Tradition from Austen to Joyce* (1980). In a clear refutation of Leavis, Polhemus claims nineteenth-century comic fiction performs many roles that religion performed in earlier centuries. Linking the comic novel of the nineteenth century with the work of Chaucer, Shakespeare, and its eighteenth-century predecessors, he insists the public demand for humor and the traditional happy ending did not stand in the way of the novelist's ability to write with serious moral purpose. In commenting on *Martin Chuzzlewit*, Polhemus calls Dickens a master of the "comedy of expression" (88), using language as a weapon to impose his vision on the world.

The novelist Vladimir Nabokov is similarly enthusiastic about Dickens in his *Lectures on Literature* (1980). No doubt Nabokov developed an affinity for Dickens early in his life, since his father, the elder Vladimir Nabokoff, had published a series of articles under the title "Charles Dickens: A Russian Appreciation" that ran in the *Dickensian* in 1912. For years after arriving in America the younger Nabokov taught at Cornell, lecturing on a number of writers, including Dickens, whom he ranks with Jane Austen as the greatest English novelists. His reverence for Dickens is undisguised. "If it were possible," he writes, "I would like to devote the fifty minutes of every class meeting to mute meditation, concentration, and admiration of Dickens" (64). Yet his work is not blindly exhortative. With the precision of a fellow practitioner, Nabokov comments on Dickens's handling of characterization and theme, his use of literary devices, and his skill at plotting — the only talent Nabokov has the temerity to criticize. Nabokov's homage is mirrored in several studies published at the same time, including Donald Stone's *The Romantic Impulse in Victorian Fiction* (1980). Calling Dickens an "instinctive Romantic" (250), Stone finds him aptly suited to his age's "new Romantic sense of the author as sage, as hero, as inspired genius, as magician imaginatively competing with reality rather than merely reflecting it" (2). He traces the influence of Romanticism on Dickens, suggesting it was the reason his art became "a combination of realism and romanticism, of observation filtered through the spectacles of romance" (253).

A number of more traditional sociological studies of Victorian fiction published at this time feature work on Dickens. In *The Idea of the Gentle-*

man in the Victorian Novel (1981) Robin Gilmour explores "ways in which the idea of the gentleman helps to focus — in the society and in its literature — the experience of the Victorian middle class" between 1840 and 1880 (2). In a chapter on *Great Expectations* Gilmour explains how the tension in this work arises from Dickens's own conflicted status; he was not born a gentleman, but wanted desperately to be one, and was therefore "deeply involved in the process of social evolution" (107). Because in 1860 he had just left his wife, Dickens could "appreciate the irony of his own disappointed great expectations" and was therefore able to recognize "the irony of the larger cultural pattern into which these expectations fell" (111). Gilmour is careful to avoid turning the novel into autobiography, however, instead claiming Pip's story is "representative of early nineteenth-century experience" in his "exaggerated allegiance to the concept of refinement" (123). "In its historical depth, social range, and psychological penetration," Gilmour concludes, "*Great Expectations* is the most complex and satisfying fictional examination of the idea of the gentleman in the Victorian period" (143).

Janice Carlisle's *The Sense of an Audience* (1981), another study of relations between Victorian writers and their readers, asserts that mid-Victorian novelists wrote with a moral purpose. Carlisle attempts to answer the question: "How did the novelist's sense of moral responsibility to his audience affect the narrative form of his art?" (2). She writes appreciatively of Dickens's ability to present his moral vision to his first readers, claiming Dickens saw fiction as a means of making his readers cognizant of the grim realities of life while simultaneously alerting them to the potential for social improvement. Carlisle sees herself working in the critical tradition of Juliet McMaster and W. J. Harvey, who also link morals and aesthetics in their studies of Victorian novelists. Her reference to McMaster is interesting because in the same year Carlisle's book appeared, Juliet McMaster and her husband Rowland McMaster published a collection of essays, *The Novel from Sterne to James* (1981), in which they focus on "novelists' concern with the relation of life to language" (vii). These are not simply reminiscent of scholarship done during the heyday of formalist criticism — they are actually reprinted, virtually unchanged, from the journals in which they originally appeared in the 1950s and 1960s. The McMasters' work suggests something about the trend among some Dickens critics to keep alive the humanist tradition in the face of poststructuralist reinterpretations.

Not everyone writing at this time, however, was an admirer. Laurence Lerner, whose first critical work also appeared decades earlier, likewise resisted the siren song of poststructuralist theory, but his assessment of Dickens is less like the McMasters' and more closely akin to that of the Leavises. Lerner is convinced that great literature must possess *gravitas,* and in his view Dickens does not exhibit that quality. In his 1982 study *The Literary Imagination: Essays on Literature and Society*, he examines ways writers work as social critics. Lerner finds Dickens representative of a kind of philistinism that characterized Victorian thinking. "The arts, the intellect, and the religious life are almost totally absent from Dickens's conception of happiness" (186). Lerner goes so far as to claim Dickens was actually sympathetic toward ideas of progress, including mechanization.

Barry Qualls was much more appreciative of Dickens's abilities. In *The Secular Pilgrims of Victorian Fiction* (1982) he reads novels by Dickens and others in light of writings by Carlyle, Bunyan, and Francis Quarles, hoping his analysis will allow modern readers to experience fiction in the way the Victorians did, "as representations of and visionary responses to life as it was — as both novels and books of life" (xi). Qualls argues that Carlyle's works provide "the best critical medium for looking at Dickens's novels" (85). The darkening vision Dickens exhibits in his later works reflects his growing Carlyle-like revulsion with the bestiality he sees all around him. Analyzing the novelist's use of images such as shipwrecks, labyrinths, prisons, and dunghills, Qualls demonstrates that Dickens was "essentially an emblematic artist" (89) linked to Bunyan, Hogarth, the fairy tale tradition, and the Bible. Yet Dickens, he says, transforms and secularizes emblems that formerly had religious overtones. Three years later, Thomas Vargish examined the work of Dickens, Charlotte Brontë, and George Eliot in *The Providential Aesthetic in Victorian Fiction* (1985), a study explaining how the "providential habit of mind" (ix) shaped many novels of the period. He claims many literate Victorians believed the action of God's will in the world was of paramount concern, and the loss of this belief among later generations has affected their view of Victorian literature. Vargish demonstrates how the idea of God's interaction with the world helps explain some of the coincidences in Dickens's work, and accounts in part for the poetic justice with which so many novels close.

Two studies published in 1986 also explore Dickens's work in the context of larger issues common to Victorian fiction. In *Representation and Revelation: Victorian Realism from Carlyle to Yeats* (1986), John McGowan explores ways Victorians "tried to connect mind with word." He argues the Victorians were constantly striving to identify a "'reality' that exists prior to and independent of any thought and speech" in order to "guarantee literature's ability to represent that reality" (1). Acknowledging the influence of Foucault's ideas about the representation of reality, McGowan examines the work of Dickens and others to identify strategies for representing the world outside of themselves. However, his readings of Dickens's novels are based more on close textual analysis than on theoretical presuppositions, and his ideas seem to be shaped more by his interest in seventeenth- and eighteenth-century philosophers' influence on

Victorian ideas than by Foucault's observations. Steve Cohan's *Violation and Repair in the English Novel* (1986), an extended study of "the construction of experience as a journey into selfhood" (3), includes discussions of both *Bleak House* and *Great Expectations* to illustrate how Dickens employs the "paradigm of experience," wherein "innocence must be challenged by reality if characters are to achieve selfhood" (5). In Dickens's case, Cohan argues, the innocent child is forced to learn how to identify with the adult world in order to achieve maturity.

In "The Galvanic World: Carlyle and the Dickens Monster" in his provocative study *In Frankenstein's Shadow* (1987), Chris Baldick employs his considerable insights as a social critic to explain how Dickens is influenced by the Frankenstein myth. Baldick sees Dickens following Carlyle's lead in creating grotesques and reversing the roles of people and objects. Carlyle's "galvanic world" is "absorbed into Dickens's morbid humor, his distinctive anatomy of melancholy" (107). Dickens projects in his fiction a "nightmare world" in which "animation of the apparently inanimate is a key characteristic" (108). Baldick offers numerous examples from Dickens's fiction to show how monsters are created by a society that does not value humanity or human wholeness. Dickens's most compelling technique, Baldick says, is his use of synecdoche, which "tends to dismember any sense of human wholeness and to offer us a world composed of detachable organs" (108). Even heroes such as Pip share with Frankenstein's monster the sense of being merely a composite of parts.

Although relatively few scholars have written extensively on Dickens's knowledge or use of science, George Levine does so in his major study *Darwin and the Novelists* (1988). Concerned with ways Victorian novelists absorbed Darwin's ideas, Levine identifies similarities between the fictional world Dickens creates and the one Darwin describes. Levine thinks Dickens admired Darwin and was not horrified by his theories. On the contrary, he embraced science as a means of "help[ing] dispel superstition and ancient prejudice and habit" (123). As an intelligent layman, Dickens eagerly followed contemporary developments, although his interest may be more evident in his nonfiction than in the novels. Levine provides a reading of *Little Dorrit* as a Darwinian novel, explaining how Dickens addresses the implications of scientific concepts of thermodynamics and evolutionary biology in what Levine calls "the most religious of Dickens's novels," one that confronts directly "the unredeemed secularity of human society" (155).

Bleak House is one of the principal works Clyde Ryals uses in *A World of Possibilities: Romantic Irony in Victorian Literature* (1990) to explain his theory of Romantic Irony, a concept he says comes from the Germans and is not often applied to English literature. Ryals defines the work of Romantic Irony as "an arabesque, a mixture of styles, modes and genres" that "avoids closure and determinate meaning as it deconstructs the invented historical world that it pretends to offer." By its nature reflexive, it is at the same time "distrustful of its own linguistic medium" and is "permeated by a sense of play" (13). Despite the highly theoretical nature of his introductory comments, Ryals offers a reading of the novel that accounts for its elusive qualities without overbearing jargon and heavily allusive language. He considers it a turning point in Dickens's career, the last one in which the author sees some hope for change in the corrupt society he portrays. At the same time, Ryals says, Dickens achieves a careful balance between optimism and pessimism, leaving his ultimate meaning indeterminate.

Even such time-tested topics as Dickens's use of sentimentality were revisited in the 1990s. Building on the work of Fred Kaplan (*Sacred Tears,* 1987) and on his own previously published work in Don R. Cox's *Sexuality and Victorian Literature* (1984), in *"Here a Captive Heart Busted": Studies in the Sentimental Journey of Modern Literature* (1993) Howard Fulweiler treats seriously and positively the development of sentimentality in nineteenth-century literature. Fulweiler sees sentimentality as "not simply an excess of emotion or feeling. Instead it consists in focusing upon individual emotions or fresh experiences and transforming them into generalized notions or 'ideas'" (5). Far from being exclusively the province of hacks, it is instead "a commonplace in the work of the greatest artists of the eighteenth and nineteenth centuries," including Dickens, a writer of "power, depth, and intellectual substance" (6). Although he appears to be swimming upstream against the critical currents of the late twentieth century, Fulweiler argues forcefully that not only was it conceivable to be serious and sentimental, but it was also possible for a Victorian novelist to be serious and popular, as Dickens was. To ignore the serious nature of Dickens's sentimentality is to miss a major reason for his effectiveness.

The crossover or disciplines among scholars proved particularly beneficial to Dickens studies at the end of the century. Josephine Guy makes him a major focus of *The Victorian Social-Problem Novel* (1996), an examination of fiction's influence in shaping ideas about history. Guy's principal interest is in theories of history, so it is not surprising she pays some attention to *Hard Times*, a novel she says has received more critical attention than any other work in the genre. Guy admits the novel is often denigrated as poor art and considered atypical by critics, who first complained that it presented stereotypes and later that it exposed Dickens's unabashed sympathy for the middle classes rather than the poor. Guy emphasizes the impact of social problems on individuals rather than classes; from this perspective, she finds Dickens's novel both appealing and enlightening. Her favorable reading stresses Dickens's focus on the conflict between "economic man" and "moral man." Although she thinks Dickens clearly favors the latter, she does not find him optimistic about this view of human nature trumping its adversary. At best, she says, *Hard Times* gives one a sense of "qualified pessimism — that the moral basis of human nature is exceptionally vulnerable" (136).

In 1998 Murray Baumgarten joined with H. M. Daleski to edit *Homes and Homelessness in the Victorian Imagination,* a collection of essays originally delivered as papers at a conference at the Hebrew University in Jerusalem titled "Homes and Homelessness in Dickens and the Victorian Imagination." Nearly half of the twenty essays in the volume focus on Dickens, who in the editors' view practically invented the concepts of "home" and "homelessness" in *Oliver Twist* and continued to refine them in subsequent novels. *David Copperfield* is the subject of two intriguing essays. In the first one Robert Polhemus explains the importance of home for children — and child wives. In the second Patrick McCarthy argues that David is essentially unlike other heroes of *Bildungsroman* novels precisely because he sees domestic bliss as "the genesis, nurturer, and goal of the enlightened will" (58). Two essayists try out ideas about Dickens that would be developed into longer studies within a few years: Efraim Sicher examines the values Dickens ascribes to the concept of home in *Bleak House,* while Baruch Hochman looks at the issue of homelessness as a metaphor for what he calls the "orphan condition." All of the essayists, and especially the editors, see themselves as participating in a larger cultural enterprise, arguing that Dickens's ideas can serve as a springboard for discussions about nineteenth- and twentieth-century attitudes toward the concept of home and the problems of homelessness.

Dickens at the Movies

Dickens's novels have enjoyed a long if somewhat limited popularity among movie makers, but in the 1980s the number of adaptations seemed to grow exponentially. Concurrently, a body of serious, sustained scholarship on screen adaptations of his work began to emerge. Michael Klein and Gillian Parker's *The English Novel and the Movies* (1981) contains essays on three movies adapted from Dickens novels: Brian Desmond Hunt's 1951 *A Christmas Carol,* George Cukor's 1935 version of *David Copperfield,* and David Lean's 1946 *Great Expectations.* The essays discuss the relationship between different media, and highlight changes required by transformation of one form into the other. In *The Lives and Times of Ebenezer Scrooge* (1990) Paul Davis traces the evolution of the character from his initial appearance in "A Christmas Carol" in 1843 to the 1988 film adaptation *Scrooged,* starring comedian Bill Murray. Davis's scholarly examination of the way this character is remodeled attests to the appeal of the original figure and suggests something about the demands of audiences at various times in history.

The success of film versions of *A Christmas Carol* underscores the general premise of Michael Pointer's *Charles Dickens on the Screen* (1996). "Although Dickens has the reputation of having remained fresh and modern," Pointer says, "this is due less to his written style than to the astonishing characterization in his books that has proved so attractive to cinema and television" (2). Beginning with the earliest cinematic efforts in 1897, he examines virtually every adaptation produced in the past hundred years, indicating how closely directors and screenwriters follow Dickens's original stories and explaining why they took the liberties they did.

* * *

The honor of having the "last word" on Dickens in the twentieth century has been reserved for two former editors of the *Dickensian*, both of whom published books in 1999 that offer a decidedly traditionalist approach to Dickens's fiction. Michael Slater's *An Intelligent Person's Guide to Dickens* (1999) is in some ways a portrait-in-miniature of what traditional thematic studies have been all about. Slater attempts to get at what he calls basic Dickensian values, reading the novelist as if he has something to offer in his own right — and in the words he chooses to use, not adaptations the reader supplies. Slater deals competently with topics such as "fancy," "innocence," "responsibility and earnestness," "progress," "home," and "faith," providing his readers a way to appreciate what Dickens is up to in his fiction. In *Dickens and the Spirit of the* Age (1999) Andrew Sanders looks back at the Victorians in light of the twentieth century's preoccupation with modernism. While not claiming Dickens should be classified as modern, Sanders finds in him the genesis of the modern novelist who was, at the same time, representative of the age in which he lived. Dickens expresses the spirit of his age, Sanders says, because "he was free from many of the anti-urban, anti-populist, anti-commercial prejudices of his literary predecessors and their latter-day progeny" (14). Sanders considers issues such as the Victorians' political and technological enterprises, the urbanization of the country, the new definitions of social class and social mobility, and the Victorian era's "dynamic sense of its distinction from, and currency with, the preceding century" (4). Viewed from these perspectives, the Dickens canon stands collectively as a testament to the age whose characteristics are captured in the fiction. Sanders believes that while "Dickens should not be viewed exclusively as the quintessential writer of his day," he is unquestionably "the most representative Victorian writer and the novelist who, it seems to me, most merits our continuing and informed critical attention in the twenty-first century" (13).

Notes

[1] A version of this discussion of Ackroyd's biography appeared in *Magill's Literary Annual 1992* (Englewood Cliffs, NJ: Salem Press, 1992), 170–73.

Works Cited

Ackroyd, Peter. *Dickens,* London: Minerva, 1990.

———. *Dickens: Public Life and Private Passion.* London: Hydra, 2002.

Alexander, Doris. *Creating Characters with Charles Dickens.* University Park: Penn State UP, 1991.

Allen, Michael. *Charles Dickens's Childhood.* London: Macmillan, 1988.

Andrews, Malcolm. *Dickens and the Grown-Up Child.* London: Macmillan, 1994.

Armstrong, Frances. *Dickens and the Concept of Home.* Ann Arbor, MI: UMI Research P, 1990.

Baldick, Chris. "The Galvanic World: Carlyle and the Dickens Monster." In *Frankenstein's Shadow: Myth, Monstrosity and Nineteenth Century Writing,* 103–20. Oxford and New York: Oxford UP, 1987.

Baumgarten, Murray and H. M. Daleski, eds. *Homes and Homelessness in the Victorian Imagination.* New York: AMS Press, 1998.

Carlisle, Janice. *The Sense of an Audience: Dickens, Thackeray, and George Eliot at Mid-Century.* Athens: U of Georgia P, 1981.

Cohan, Steve. *Violation and Repair in the English Novel: The Paradigm of Experience from Richardson to Woolf.* Detroit, MI: Wayne State UP, 1986.

Cohen, Jane. *Charles Dickens and His Original Illustrators.* Columbus: Ohio State UP, 1980.

Cox, Don Richard, ed. *Sexuality and Victorian Literature.* Knoxville: U of Tennessee P, 1984.

Daldry, Graham. *Charles Dickens and the Form of the Novel: Fiction and Narrative in Dickens's Work.* Totowa, NJ: Barnes & Noble, 1986.

Davis, Paul. *The Lives and Times of Ebenezer Scrooge.* New Haven, CT: Yale UP, 1990.

Eigner, Edwin. *The Dickens Pantomime.* Berkeley: U of California P, 1989.

Epstein, Norrie. *The Friendly Dickens.* New York: Viking, 1998.

Fulweiler, Howard W. *"Here a Captive Heart Busted": Studies in the Sentimental Journey of Modern Literature.* New York: Fordham UP, 1993.

Gager, Valerie L. *Shakespeare and Dickens: The Dynamics of Influence.* Cambridge: Cambridge UP, 1996.

Giddings, Robert, ed. *The Changing World of Charles Dickens*. Totowa, NJ: Barnes & Noble, 1983.

Gilmour, Robin. *The Idea of the Gentleman in the Victorian Novel*. London: Allen & Unwin, 1981.

Grant, Allan. *A Preface to Dickens*. London and New York: Longman, 1984.

Guy, Josephine M. *The Victorian Social-Problem Novel*. London: Macmillan, 1996.

Hill, Nancy K. *A Reformer's Art: Dickens's Picturesque and Grotesque Imagery*. Athens: Ohio UP, 1981.

Hochman, Baruch, and Ilja Wachs. *Dickens: The Orphan Condition*. Rutherford, NJ: Fairleigh Dickinson UP, 1999.

Hornback, Bert G. *"The Hero of My Life": Essays on Dickens*. Athens: Ohio UP, 1981.

Hough, Graham. "Language and Reality in *Bleak House*." In *Realism in European Literature*, edited by Nicholas Boyle and Martin Swales, 50–67. Cambridge: Cambridge UP, 1986.

Johnson, Wendell Stacy, ed. *Charles Dickens: New Perspectives*. Englewood Cliffs, NJ: Prentice-Hall, 1982.

Kaplan, Fred, ed. *Charles Dickens's Book of Memoranda*. New York: New York Public Library, 1981.

———. *Dickens: A Biography*. London: Hodder & Stoughton, 1988; reprint, Baltimore, MD: Johns Hopkins UP, 1998.

———. *Dickens and Mesmerism: "The Hidden Springs of Fiction."* Princeton, NJ: Princeton UP, 1975.

———. *Sacred Tears: Sentimentality in Victorian Literature*. Princeton, NJ: Princeton UP, 1987.

Kauffman, Linda. "The Letter and the Spirit in *Hard Times* and *The Sound and the Fury*." *Mississippi Quarterly: The Journal of Southern Culture* 34.3 (Summer 1981): 299–313.

Klein, Michael, and Gillian Parker, eds. *The English Novel and the Movies*. New York: Ungar; 1981.

Klieneberger, H. R. *The Novel in England and Germany: A Comparative Study*. London: Wolff, 1981.

Kucich, John. "Dickens's Fantastic Rhetoric: Semantics of Reality and Unreality in *Our Mutual Friend*." *Dickens Studies Annual* 14 (1985): 167–90.

———. *Excess and Restraint in the Novels of Charles Dickens*. Athens: U of Georgia P, 1981.

Lambert, Mark. *Dickens and the Suspended Quotation*. New Haven, CT and London: Yale UP, 1981.

LaRocque, Geraldine E. "*A Tale of Two Cities* and *Absalom! Absalom.*" *Mississippi Quarterly: The Journal of Southern Culture* 35.3 (Summer 1982): 301–4.

Lerner, Laurence. *The Literary Imagination: Essays on Literature and Society.* Totowa, NJ: Barnes & Noble, 1982.

Lettis, Richard. *The Dickens Aesthetic.* New York: AMS Press, 1989.

———. *Dickens on Literature: A Continuing Study of His Aesthetic.* New York: AMS Press, 1990.

Levine, George. "*Little Dorrit* and Three Kinds of Science." *Darwin and the Novelists: Patterns of Science in Victorian Fiction*, 153–76. Cambridge, MA and London: Harvard UP, 1988.

Lucas, John. *Charles Dickens: The Major Novels.* New York: Penguin, 1992.

Magnet, Myron. *Dickens and the Social Order.* Philadelphia: U of Pennsylvania P, 1985.

McGowan, John P. *Representation and Revelation: Victorian Realism from Carlyle to Yeats.* Columbia: U of Missouri P, 1986.

McMaster, Juliet. *Dickens the Designer.* Totowa, NJ: Barnes & Noble, 1987.

McMaster, Rowland, and Juliet McMaster. "Dickens and the Horrific." *The Novel from Sterne to James: Essays on the Relation of Literature to Life*, 37–53. Totowa, NJ: Barnes & Noble, 1981.

Meckier, Jerome. *Hidden Rivalries in Victorian Fiction.* Lexington: UP of Kentucky, 1987.

———. *Innocent Abroad: Charles Dickens's American Engagements.* Lexington: UP of Kentucky, 1990.

Moseley, Merritt. "Faulkner's Dickensian Humor in *The Sound and the Fury.*" *Notes on Mississippi Writers* 13.1 (1981): 7–13.

Moss, Sidney P. *Charles Dickens's Quarrel With America.* Troy, NY: Whitson, 1984.

Murray, Brian. *Charles Dickens.* New York: Continuum, 1994.

Nabokoff, Vladimir. "Charles Dickens: A Russian Appreciation." *Dickensian* 8 (June 1912): 145–48; (July 1912): 173–76; (August 1912): 201–4.

Nabokov, Vladimir. "*Bleak House* (1852–3)." In *Lectures on Literature*, edited by Fredson Bowers, 62–124. New York: Harcourt, Brace, Jovanovich, 1980.

Nelson, Harland S. *Charles Dickens.* Boston: Twayne, 1981.

Newcomb, Mildred. *The Imagined World of Charles Dickens.* Columbus: Ohio State UP, 1989.

Newman, S. J. *Dickens at Play.* New York: St. Martin's, 1981.

Peters, Catherine. *Charles Dickens.* Gloucestershire, England: Sutton, 1998.

Pointer, Michael. *Charles Dickens on the Screen: The Film, Television, and Video Adaptations.* Metuchen, NJ: Scarecrow Press, 1996.

Polhemus, Robert M. *Comic Faith: The Great Tradition from Austen to Joyce.* Chicago and London: U of Chicago P, 1980.

Qualls, Barry V. *The Secular Pilgrims of Victorian Fiction: The Novel as Book of Life.* Cambridge: Cambridge UP, 1982.

Reed, John R. *Dickens and Thackeray: Punishment and Forgiveness.* Athens: Ohio UP, 1995.

———. *Perception and Design in Tennyson's Idylls of the King.* Athens: Ohio UP, 1969.

———. *Victorian Conventions.* Athens: Ohio UP, 1975.

———. *Victorian Will.* Athens: Ohio UP, 1989.

Ryals, Clyde de L. *A World of Possibilities: Romantic Irony in Victorian Literature.* Columbus: Ohio State UP, 1990.

Sanders, Andrew. *Charles Dickens: Resurrectionist.* London: Macmillan, 1982.

———. *Dickens and the Spirit of the Age.* Oxford: Clarendon P, 1999.

Schlicke, Paul. *Dickens and Popular Entertainment.* London: Allen & Unwin, 1985.

———, ed. *Oxford Reader's Companion to Dickens.* Oxford: Oxford UP, 1999.

Shattock, Joanne, ed. *Dickens and Other Victorians: Essays in Honour of Philip Collins.* London: Macmillan, 1988.

Slater, Michael. *An Intelligent Person's Guide to Dickens.* London: Duckworth, 1999.

Smiley, Jane. *Charles Dickens.* New York: Viking, 2002.

Smith, Grahame. *Charles Dickens: A Literary Life.* New York: St. Martin's, 1996.

Stone, Donald D. *The Romantic Impulse in Victorian Fiction.* Cambridge, MA and London: Harvard UP, 1980.

Stone, Harry. *Dickens's Working Notes for his Novels.* Chicago: U of Chicago P, 1987.

———. *The Night Side of Dickens.* Columbus: Ohio State UP, 1994.

Thomas, Deborah. *Dickens and the Short Story.* Philadelphia: U of Pennsylvania P, 1982.

Vargish, Thomas. *The Providential Aesthetic in Victorian Fiction.* Charlottesville: UP of Virginia; 1985.

Walder, Dennis. *Dickens and Religion.* London: Allen and Unwin, 1981.

9: The Future of Dickens Studies: Trends in the Twenty-First Century

REVIEWING DICKENS CRITICISM in 2003, Frederick Karl observed that "if the present sampling of recent critical and scholarly books on Dickens is any indication of what is happening and what is yet to come, Dickens studies are more than alive and well; they have turned their subject into an iconic figure, the prose Shakespeare" (610). As Karl suggests, all signs point to continuing strength, even growth, in the Dickens Industry. Books and articles continue to appear every year as a new crop of Dickens scholars revisits the novels, stories and the journalism to find some hitherto undiscovered nugget of wisdom about Dickens's artistry or social concerns, or to apply new theories to works not yet deconstructed, historicized, or scrutinized through the lens of gender or culture. What directions such studies might take can be surmised from a brief survey of criticism written during the first years of the new millennium.

Surveys and Biographies

Dickens scholars celebrated the millennium by issuing a number of retrospectives and surveys that attempt to define Dickens — the man, his work, and the industry that has grown up around both — for a new generation. One of the first of such books to appear was Robert Newsom's *Charles Dickens Revisited* (2000) in the Twayne's English Authors series. Twenty years earlier Harland Nelson had produced a study of the novelist focused on issues important to undergraduate students. By contrast, Newsom's book is targeted more at other scholars, and on the first page he announces his willingness to engage with contemporary theory. "The very idea of the 'author' has come under such close critical scrutiny," he notes, "that we may at the outset ask whether even so prominent a figure as Dickens can safely escape the critical phenomenon known as 'the death of the author'" (1). Noting that, despite current critical trends, scholars writing on Dickens continue to stress biographical and contextual issues, Newsom concentrates on key themes he sees emerging from Dickens's novels. Central among these is the tension between the novelist's public and private selves, which leads Newsom to a discussion of the idea of the integrity of the self — a significant concern for postmodernists. Throughout his commentary Newsom expresses continuing interest in "the relations between the author and his culture" (20) and the nature of the middle class in the nineteenth century.

Rod Mengham's *Charles Dickens* (2001), prepared for the British Council's Writers and their Work series, contains a brief review of Dickens's concern with urban life, childhood, authority and rebellion, control and repression, money, and especially questions of identity. Meant as an introduction to the novelist and his work, Mengham's volume is limited in critical analysis, though his insistence that Dickens was constantly using his fiction to try to understand himself — as witnessed by his repeated attempts at fictional autobiography — suggests critics are still enamored with the notion of Dickens as a Romantic. Another survey, Robert Sirabian's *Charles Dickens: Life, Work, and Criticism* (2002), is further testimony to the eagerness of publishing companies to profit by the continuing popularity of Dickens's work in the classroom. Intended for high-school and college students, Sirabian's book contains a brief biography, critical commentary on the novels, and an annotated bibliography. Similar in organization and scope is Elizabeth James's *Charles Dickens* (2004), part of the British Library Writers Lives series aimed at high-school students in Britain, a work heavily illustrated to get students more accustomed to visual stimulation engaged in the text — which, fortunately, displays sound scholarship. Not wanting to miss this continuing market for "new" materials on Dickens, Chelsea House Publishing — the trade name for another great literary industry headed up by Yale University Professor Harold Bloom — continues to publish new titles focusing on Dickens and his work, aimed at students as young as middle-school age. Donna Dailey's *Charles Dickens* (2005), a slim volume in the "Who Wrote That?" series targeting sixth through twelfth grades, covers the same ground as Sirabian and James in what could be considered the limits for twenty-first century young readers — a mere 112 pages. This title is but one of a half-dozen issued in the last decade by Chelsea House specifically aimed at introducing students to Dickens, ranging from general assessments in their Bloom's Classic Critical Views series prepared for the high-school market to an updated collection of essays for Bloom's Modern Critical Views.

While she relies heavily on other biographies for information about Dickens's life, in *Charles Dickens* (2002) Jane Smiley manages to bring her own considerable knowledge of the writer's craft to her assessment of Dickens. The Pulitzer Prize winner writes appreciatively of Dickens's care in applying his literary skills to both the social problems of his day and perennial moral and personal issues. She recognizes that he was, in twenty-first century parlance, something of a commodity: "If we see Dickens as the first true celebrity of the popular arts," she says, "we also can see him as the first person to become a 'name brand'" (26). He was "more than a self-made man"; he was "a self-made phenomenon" (27). He took advantage of his celebrity to promote causes dear to him. But like so many celebrities before and after, he found it difficult to live constantly in the public eye. He was only too human, Smiley reminds readers in her sympathetic descriptions of the novelist's dealings with friends and family. She sees a pattern in Dickens's personal behavior, especially as he became disenchanted with his wife, "more familiar in our divorce culture than it was in Dickens's time — a man filled with conflicting passions, resentments, and needs transfers his allegiance from one object to another" (149). Smiley's interpretations of the novels reveal her familiarity with the demands of writing fiction, explicating themes often propounded but seldom so well expressed. The strength of Smiley's volume lies in its lively, jargon-free descriptions of the novelist and his work. Her assessment suggests the traditional humanist approach can still be practiced in an age when theory-based readings are certain to continue to dominate Dickens studies.

Postmodern Criticism in the New Millennium: A Sampling

Studies published during the first five years of the twenty-first century shows the indisputable influence of postmodernism on Dickens studies, as a new generation of critics revisited subjects examined years before by their predecessors. A good example of how older work was being revised by critics using new approaches is John Bowen's *Other Dickens: Pickwick to Chuzzlewit* (2000), a reprise of Steven Marcus's 1965 study *From Pickwick To Dombey*. Retracing the same ground Marcus covers, Bowen uses the tools of poststructuralist literary theory to determine why critics have found it hard to explain the continuing popular appeal of Dickens's early novels, which had never regained the privileged status they had enjoyed until the 1940s. Bowen is less interested in discovering a pattern of artistic development in Dickens's career than in exposing the many forms of experimentation in these early works. Writing in the self-reflexive style of late twentieth-century criticism, he celebrates rather than criticizes the paradoxes and contradictions in Dickens's work.

Dickens's techniques of characterization continue to draw attention from scholars like Alex Woloch, whose *The One vs. the Many: Minor Characters and the Space of the Protagonist in the Novel* (2003) includes an analysis of *Great Expectations* as one of several examples of how novelists consciously choose to present and delimit minor characters, apportion space to figures who perform various functions in the narrative, and organize texts to eliminate these characters from the story when they have served their function. Dickens's novel provides evidence of ways "crucial formal breakthroughs in fictional characterization, and character-space, are intertwined with the aesthetics of social realism" (20). Woloch offers a fruitful method for examining Dickens's fiction that helps account for his artistry and gives the lie to E. M. Forster's reductive descriptions of characters as "flat" or "round."

Dickens remains a major subject for Victorian cultural studies specialists, especially those interested in the intersections of literature and nineteenth-century life — and "afterlife." In *Charles Dickens* (2002), a critical survey prepared for the Palgrave Critical Issues series, Lyn Pykett is concerned with "'Charles Dickens' as a cultural and critical site: a site not only for the formation and definition of the novel in the nineteenth century, but also for twentieth century theorizations (and contestations) of the novel" (3). Andrew Dowling's *Manliness and the Male Novelist in Victorian Literature* (2001) examines Dickens's efforts to create a portrait of the manly novelist. Although positive attributes of masculinity may have seemed "natural" and "self-evident" (ix) to the Victorians, Dowling believes the concept was always one "in crisis" (ix) as ideas of masculinity vacillated between the positive portrait of the strong, moral figure representing order (and power) and the frightening picture of the "demonized male other" (3) who terrorized society. Within this cultural framework, Dowling sees Dickens as less secure psychologically about his position in society than his public persona might have suggested.

Dickens's understanding and depiction of city life remains a fascinating subject for critics as well. Fortunately, the problems of obfuscation that plagued Jeremy Tambling's *Dickens, Violence, and the Modern State* (1995) are largely absent from his 2001 study of the novelist, *Lost in the American City: Dickens, James and Kafka*, even though his readings of these three novelists are based on the theoretical work of Benjamin, Foucault, and others. As in his earlier study, Tambling makes Dickens's reaction to prisons a central focus of his analysis, but in *Lost in the American City* he is less ambitious in surveying all of Dickens's work and more provocative in examining key texts — principal among them *American Notes* — to see how the novelist reacts to the growing dominance of urbanization as a condition of modern life. Claiming that the American city was essentially different from its European counterpart, Tambling traces Dickens's early visit to America by reading closely (and at times imaginatively) the anecdotes Dickens compiled in his 1842 travelogue and the novel that followed, *Martin Chuzzlewit*. Dickens found the American city a truly frightening place, Tambling asserts, and he argues persuasively that as the novelist grew older he began to see similar qualities in his beloved London. In *Lost in the American City,* Tambling himself manages to escape from the prison-house of theory to provide a culturally sensitive, interdisciplinary analysis of the way Dickens and two other novelists confronted issues of modernity.

Like Tambling's work, Efraim Sicher's *Rereading The City, Rereading Dickens* (2003) and Alan Robinson's *Imagining London 1770–1900* (2004) complement studies by Alexander Welsh (1971), F. S. Schwarzbach (1979), Richard Maxwell (1992), and Julian Wolfreys (1998). Robinson's is a more sweeping look at the way artists and writers try to "make sense of the social transformations" occurring in the city throughout the nineteenth century (xiv). Sicher's interdisciplinary examination attempts to resolve difficulties critics have had in applying the term "realistic" to Dickens's work. Claiming the novels "relate to ideological and literary debates in mid-Victorian England," Sicher insists they be examined "in their intellectual as well as artistic context" (xi). He examines not only the aesthetic aspects of Dickens's imaginative productions, but the economic dimensions as well, demonstrating how the growth of consumer culture and changes in gender relations affected the production of works about London. At the heart of his argument is the idea that "representation in Dickens's novels was conflicted by the tension between the cultural constructs of the landowning classes and those of a new urban middle class," between "a literature based on a declining patronage and a new mass reading public," and between "the aesthetics of the Romantics and the political debates of a railway age and an industrialized economy" (23). Sicher sees Dickens's writing as "a generic act of resistance to the ideological assumptions embedded in the representation of the city," in the process "radically rereading the city" and "testing the possibility of change" (32). To do full justice to the novelist's vision of society, Sicher supplements his analysis of Dickens's novels with discussions of contemporary art, journalism, political discourse, medical practice, and poetry. Sicher uses the work of his predecessors wisely, challenging monolithic readings such as Jeffrey Tambling's in *Dickens, Violence and the Modern State* (1995).

Early in his career, Sicher notes, Dickens demonstrated a unique ability "to reread the landscape of the city, with its multiple signs and codes, its din and babble" (45). Dickens's great insight is his understanding that no description can be comprehensive and accurate. He knew the so-called "omniscience of the panoramic view" practiced by others in describing the city was not adequate for capturing its complex nuances (76). As a result, Dickens sought to describe the complexity of city life by making "unseen connections between different parts of the city," penetrating its "secret mysteries" (80). His response to the city reflects "a sense of exile and longing in the mutable and amorphous confusion of a rapidly changing metropolis" (67). Not dismayed, Dickens responds to the growing mechanization and depersonalization of urban life by offering an alternative "vision of mutual responsibility and benevolence" (87).

In a study related to the work of Tambling, Robinson and Sicher, Lisa Rodensky employs the insights of Foucault, J. Hillis Miller, and D. A. Miller in *The Crime in Mind: Criminal Responsibility and the Victorian Novel* (2003) to assess Dickens's imaginative vision of the criminal mentality. In addition to providing a cogent assessment of *Oliver Twist*, she extends the earlier work of Christopher Dahl (1981) by discussing the reasons for Sir James Fitzjames Stephen's animosity toward Dickens. Stephen considered Dickens a danger, Rodensky says, because he was influential among his readers but woefully uninformed about the law. In examining the novel, Rodensky pays close attention to the dramatically realized relationships between "character" and "conduct" in the principal criminals, Sikes, Nancy, and especially Fagin, explaining the meaning of those key terms for Dickens and his contemporaries.

The twelve essays in Suzy Anger's collection *Knowing the Past: Victorian Literature and Culture* (2001) are organized around a pair of central questions: Can contemporary critics understand what the Victorians knew of themselves and *their* past? Are there lessons to be learned from understanding their viewpoint? Three essays in the volume center on Dickens. Mary Poovey uses *Hard Times* to explain her epistemological model for understanding the Victorians, suggesting Dickens was ahead of his time in dealing with social problems. Bruce Robbins reads *Great Expectations* as a "narrative of the emerging social welfare state" (21), and claims critics of the twenty-first century engage with such issues not simply because Dickens wrote about them but because they are relevant to the present generation. Finally, Rosemarie Bodenheimer reexamines *David Copperfield* to show how poststructuralist readings of the novel erroneously assume critics of the late twentieth and twenty-first centuries have greater understanding of the past than those who lived through it. Cleverly Bodenheimer points out that much of what twentieth-century critics cite as repressed meanings — ideas such as class oppression, for example — were obvious to Dickens's contemporaries as well. She argues that the postmodern generation should give Dickens more credit than he normally receives for being aware of social issues now recognized as important.

New Historicists and Marxists are also well represented in the most recent criticism of Dickens. In "Literature, Nation, and Revolution: *A Tale of Two Cities*" (2000), Richard Allen offers suggestions for interpreting Dickens's tale of the French Revolution in light of events that had taken place closer to the date of the novel's publication, such as the Indian Mutiny of 1857 and the emergence of the new genre of detective fiction. Episodes like these, Allen argues, influenced the novelist as he constructed his tale that turned revolution into a kind of exotic tale of mystery. Examining the growth of modern economics in the nineteenth century in *Fiction, Famine, and the Rise of Economics in Victorian Britain and Ireland*

(2003) Gordon Bigelow exposes "the relationship between economics and other forms of social discourse and description" (8). He sees *Bleak House* as Dickens's most sustained analysis of the economic situation, noting parallels between the plight of the individual consumer in the marketplace and the central characters in the novel who are dealing with the English courts. In *The Marxian Imagination: Representing Class in Literature* (2003) Julian Markels, building on the theories of Raymond Williams, Louis Althusser, Frederic Jameson, Stephen Resnick, and Richard Wolff, turns on its head the central premise of Lionel Trilling's *The Liberal Imagination* (1950) in order to "identify a literary imagination that abstracts a political master narrative" (11). Although in *Hard Times* Dickens ultimately fails to deal head-on with labor issues — a fact that clearly disappoints Markels — in *Little Dorrit* he provides a coherent analysis of the class struggle. Pam Morris's examination of the Victorians' efforts to develop or thwart an inclusive society, *Imagining Inclusive Society in Nineteenth-Century Novels: The Code of Sincerity in the Public Sphere* (2004), uses examples from Dickens to reveal how the growing interaction of the social classes within a single cultural milieu worked to homogenize society, especially during the middle decades of the century. Morris claims that Dickens's novels are part of "a distinctive and ambitious political tradition of fiction, a tradition that consciously and responsibly participates in public debates and contention" (5).

Although known for his Marxist critiques of fiction, in his commentary on Dickens in *The English Novel* (2005) Terry Eagleton takes a slightly different approach. Interested in questions of identity and the construction of the self, Eagleton presents Dickens as a conflicted artist whose novels "move ambiguously" between a "view of the self as a set of shifting impressions, and a more traditional belief in identity as a stable continuity over time" (148). Eagleton characterizes Dickens as an urban novelist "not just because he writes about the city, but because he writes about it in an urban kind of way" (145), mimicking the hectic pace of city life in his style and using caricature to make his people stand out. He actually defends Dickens from charges that his characters lack complexity, calling his brand of "grotesque realism [a] stylistic distortion in the service of truth" (149).

While Eagleton's Marxist ideological prejudices are somewhat muted in this study, they emerge in statements such as, "It would not be ideologically acceptable for Dickens to end his novels on a tragic note, since the Victorians, like the governing classes today, regarded gloom as socially subversive" (156). The pleasure of Dickens's novels comes from the "anxiety and disorientation" that is contrasted with "the comic exuberance of a still buoyant middle class, one which is in the process of transforming the face of the earth" (155). Eagleton finds there is "a good deal of the brisk modernizer about Dickens." He is a "fairly middle-of-the-road, progressively minded middle-class Victorian," Eagleton says. When compared to George Eliot or Hardy, he seems "strikingly uninterested in ideas." Yet, despite his "animus against the gentry" he displays "a very English weakness for the English gentleman" and a "typical middle-class fear of the mob" (157).

Eagleton applauds Dickens's reformist tendencies, but does not see him offering practical solutions to social problems. Especially in the later novels, Eagleton says, Dickens uses various social systems as unifying devices, exposing people's mutual interdependence by relying on coincidence to reveal the hidden links between them. Eagleton concludes with enigmatic praise for Dickens, whom he calls "both a serious novelist and a great entertainer." While not intellectually gifted or psychologically subtle, he is unusually perceptive about the urban landscape. On the other hand, "Dickens was no revolutionary, though he was an ardent, tireless reformer." His views, Eagleton concludes, are "fuzzily libertarian" at times, but he also feared "the kinds of forces that might have *really* transformed the society he was trying to change." Unfortunately, Eagleton notes with a certain sadness, the society Dickens describes in his later fiction "is so thoroughly false and dehumanized" that it would have required much more radical change than Dickens would approve (162).

Postcolonial criticism of Dickens may be particularly strong in the coming decades if the collection of essays in *Dickens and the Children of Empire* (2000) is any indication. Edited by Wendy Jacobson, the volume includes work by distinguished Anglo-American critics such as James Kincaid, Murray Baumgarten, and Grahame Smith. Other essays are by critics from countries that were once colonies of the British Empire. All promote the theme Jacobson discusses in her introduction, that in Dickens "the empire was there to provide the impoverished [in England] with a not altogether desirable option" for economic advancement. All of the contributors read Dickens's work "on the periphery," looking for repressed narratives within the larger context of his novels. Among the more intriguing ones is Robert Lougy's discussion of *Martin Chuzzlewit*, which reminds readers that the United States was once considered by the British as "colonial," not much different from Africa or India. The essayists are not only interested in how Dickens viewed the Empire, but also in how "the Empire" viewed Dickens. A number of them suggest ways literary education influenced colonial peoples, creating "a myth of a benevolent home country." Jacobson insists that an awareness of colonial perspectives on the novels forces one "into a different relationship with Dickens's novels if his Eurocentric vision is not shared" (9). Collectively these essays offer a fresh perspective on Dickens himself, one that makes him seem more arrogant, less universally humanitarian, and more limited in his view of what constitutes humanity.

Grace Moore employs a similar approach to the fiction in *Dickens and Empire: Discourses of Class, Race and Colonialism in the Works of Charles Dickens* (2004), a well-argued and insightful study of Dickens's lifelong interest in and engagement with issues of colonization and racial discrimination. Moore ranges widely across the Dickens canon, placing her readings of individual works into the larger context of Victorian literature and culture to explain how matters of empire shaped Dickens's fiction and how his ideas shaped public perceptions. Moore traces a pattern of growth in the novelist's attitude, showing how Dickens first saw the colonies as a dumping ground for characters he wanted to save. But as he progressed in his career, Dickens began to focus on the effects of imperialism on the Victorians at home and on the peoples being colonized. Moore is neither a blind apologist for Dickens nor a detractor ready to write him off as a racist without considering the complexity of his responses to Britain's imperialist attitudes. Instead, she sees Dickens struggling to differentiate between ideas of race and class in his fiction and nonfiction, sometimes in step with his age, sometimes its fiercest critic.

Publications during the early years of the new century also indicate that feminist criticism will remain strong and productive. Relying on the tools of traditional historical and literary criticism as well as insights provided by New Historicism and feminism, in *The Spectacle of Intimacy: A Public Life for the Victorian Family* (2000) Karen Chase and Michael Levenson explain how, in his early work, Dickens creates a fantasy of idyllic family life that is constantly being challenged and shattered. Their careful counterpointing of biographical information with details from the fiction confirms what other writers have argued for some time: that Dickens's "affirmation" of domestic bliss is often "shadowed by insecurity" (86). Their commentary would be followed up in the next several years by others examining Dickens through the lens of feminism, including Catherine Robson's *Men in Wonderland: The Lost Girlhood of the Victorian Gentleman* (2001), a work employing recent research into studies of childhood and masculinity to trace "the intimate relationship between middle-class men and little girls in nineteenth-century British culture" (3). She shows how in *The Old Curiosity Shop* Little Nell is a figure of monumental importance for understanding how male authors "construct girlhood" (3), and how Dickens's displacement of Nell from "the privileges of bourgeois domesticity" (75) puts an exceptionally heavy symbolic burden on the character. Concentrating on the relationship between Nell and the various adult males with whom she comes in contact, Robson exposes a world populated by men only too ready to take advantage of this girl.

Elizabeth Campbell's *Fortune's Wheel: Dickens and the Iconography of Women's Time* (2003) is at once a study of a popular classical and medieval image that had fallen out of favor by the nineteenth century and an analysis of Dickens's novels from a feminist perspective. Relying on theorists such as Julia Kristeva and Gerda Lerner, Campbell explains how the image of fortune's wheel is inextricably bound up in Dickens's treatment of women and "women's time," which was perceived as different from men's time, the former being cyclical and the latter more linear. Noting how Dickens revitalized the image for his Victorian contemporaries, Campbell demonstrates how "the image of Fortune's wheel accrues tragic significance over the course of Dickens's career" and "becomes the controlling vision of his mature novels" (204). Further, she argues the image of the wheel becomes a descriptor for the structure of Dickens's major works, standing in opposition to the dominant Victorian "idea of progress" in which time was a measure of the advancement of civilization. Her provocative readings of novels such as *The Old Curiosity Shop*, *Bleak House*, and especially *Great Expectations* demonstrate how Dickens's concern with women came to dominate his fiction. Dickens found his own life increasingly governed by women, Campbell notes, and his novels increasingly reflect his recognition that "the era of men's time is over and women have gained full control in both the pubic and private spheres" (203). If one accepts Campbell's argument, it is easy to see why so many critics have reluctantly concluded Dickens was, after all, something of a misogynist.

Britta Zangen's strong feminist leanings guide her study of Victorian novelists in *Our Daughters Must Be Wives* (2004), an analysis of ways Dickens and others portray young, unmarried women in their fiction. Arguing that the novel was a vehicle for establishing social norms rather than simply reflecting them, Zangen offers an extensive summary of the place of women in Victorian society before exploring ways Dickens helped shape attitudes regarding The Woman Question. Unfortunately, her brief survey of all fifteen of his novels is little more than a catalog of the marriageable women appearing in these works.

Briefer pieces also suggest the direction feminists and gender studies critics may take in discussing Dickens's work. For example, Mary Armstrong makes use of ideas from Foucault and Eve Kosofsky Sedgwick in "Multiplicities of Longing: The Queer Desires of *Bleak House* and *Little Dorrit*" (2004) to discover in these novels examples of "eroticized prehomosexual same-sex relations between women" (60). James Simmons's brief commentary on *Great Expectations*, "No Expectations at All," in *Women in Literature: Reading Through the Lens of Gender* (2003), demonstrates how conventional Dickens was in his view of women. Simmons suggests the novel is emblematic of the full Dickens canon. As his article appears in a book intended to help teachers guide discussions of literature, its implications for future feminist studies of Dickens seem clear.

Natalie Bell Cole, author of a number of insightful essays grounded in contemporary theory, demonstrates in "Amen in a Wrong Place" (2004) that, viewed in light of new theoretical perspectives, there may still be something worthwhile to say about Dickens's understanding and use of religion. Published in Jude V. Nixon's *Victorian Religious Discourse: New Directions in Criticism* (2004), Cole's essay is proof that a careful reading of the novels and nonfiction, especially *The Uncommercial Traveler*, reveals additional insight into Dickens's struggle to understand religious issues that were driving Church practices in his time. Taking a slightly different tack in *The Scriptures of Charles Dickens* (2004), Vincent Newey studies ways Dickens reflects and responds to the *angst* of his era. Using *A Christmas Carol* as his paradigmatic text, Newey explains how Dickens modifies the traditional Puritan story of guilt and reformation into a new social gospel in which characters bear closer resemblance to existential heroes than to their seventeenth-century forebears. Tracing the pattern through *Oliver Twist, David Copperfield, Great Expectations,* and *Our Mutual Friend,* Newey employs the theoretical work of philosopher Louis Althusser as a foil for his own position that Dickens's subjects are not only struggling to establish a sense of self but also to develop a way of working in and for society. Newey claims the novels he examines "all promulgate ideological schemes yet, in various ways and degrees, open them to interrogation." Even ideas of gender are challenged, prompted by what — in Newey's view, at least — is Dickens's "intuitive apprehension of the hidden psychology of women" (10). In several ways, Newey says, Dickens's works are filled with tensions that at times support and other times undercut the dominant ideology informing them. As a result, the "totemic figure of the socialized self is shadowed, disruptively, as a rival center of significance, by its raw, non-conforming, experiencing counterpart, the individual who lives to struggle and struggles to live" (20). In all his works, Newey says, Dickens searches for a way to "preserve, or reconstitute, spiritual and moral values in an increasingly secular world" (18).

Traditional Criticism

Alongside this body of work informed by new theories of reading and culture, more traditional scholarship and textual studies continue to appear. Goldie Morgentaler's *Dickens and Heredity: Like Begets Like* (2000), a sociological and historical study in the vein of Philip Collins and Humphry House, explores the novelist's fascination with the way personality traits are passed on to children. After providing a lengthy introduction explaining the Victorians' ideas regarding heredity, Morgentaler examines Dickens's novels to see how he employs these notions. She believes Dickens generally subscribed to the idea that positive qualities may be inherited but negative ones tended to be *sui generic* in characters, thereby mitigating the force of evil in the world. Also interested in reading Dickens work in the humanist tradition, A. O. J. Cockshut suggests in "Children's Death in Dickens: A Chapter in the History of Taste" (2000) that Dickens was far from being excessively morbid about this subject, but was simply acting as a writer influenced heavily by the times in which he worked. Dickens was not striving to treat such tragedies sentimentally. Rather, he recognized that "the deaths of children arouse the strongest emotions and may lead to the deepest questionings." Therefore, when he writes of such deaths, Dickens "brings us face to face with our own deepest convictions. Not everyone can bear this," and as a consequence, readers find such scenes deeply disturbing (152). And while the popularity of personal readings may have waned during the second half of the twentieth century, these have not disappeared. For example, Bernard Schilling's *The Rain of Years: Great Expectations and the World of Dickens* (2001) contains no notes or bibliography; it is simply an attempt by someone familiar with Dickens's novels to explain how an individual work fits within the canon.

Perhaps the most extensive traditional critique published early in the new millennium is that by David Parker, curator of the Dickens House on Doughty Street in London for more than two decades. In *The Doughty Street Novels* (2002) Parker demonstrates his deep love for the novelist as well as his exceptional familiarity with the tradition of Dickens criticism. Interested in the creative process, Parker takes issue with Roland Barthes's notion that "writing makes an author," claiming instead that "books are made by authors" (xii). Hence it is important to understand what prompted a novelist like Dickens to write what he did, in the way he did. Parker believes that by looking at "what was happening to the man" one gains insight into the books (5). Dickens's "domestic life helped to shape his fiction," Parker says, and "his instinct for fiction helped to shape his domestic life" (11). Reviewing the novelist's career during the years he lived on Doughty Street in London, Parker finds "circumstantial pomp was something he sought both in literary style and domestic environment. And he sought to subvert it in both" (27). This thesis leads Parker to explore the ramifications for Dickens's fiction of the three great crises in his life — his time at Warren's blacking house, his unsuccessful courtship of Maria Beadnell, and the death of his sister-in-law Mary Hogarth. Parker's assessments, informed by prior criticism but largely independent of them, reveal the conscious artistry behind Dickens's early performances. He sees in the plotting, characterization, and thematic unity of *Pickwick Papers, Oliver Twist,* and *Nicholas Nickleby* "a novelist in control of his art, just as he was of his life" (213). And though, like the best of modern Dickensians, Parker acknowledges the faults of *Barnaby Rudge,* he still believes "we can detect a discriminating artist at work" (213) even at this early stage of his career.

More focused studies have also appeared. In *Dickens's Villains: Melodrama, Character, Popular Criticism* (2001) Juliet John takes on the critical tradition that has dismissed Dickens's villains as melodramatic caricatures, suggesting instead that they are "frequently the site of tensions and paradoxes which surround the attempt to marginalize the psychic underpinning" of the melodramatic world Dickens seems on the surface to support (11). Claiming the continued reliance on biography as a means of interpreting the novelist's work is "warped" and "damaging," John promotes a view of Dickens as a skilled craftsman and consummate artist who used the melodramatic form for subversive purposes. Tore Rem also investigates Dickens's use of melodrama in *Dickens, Melodrama, and the Parodic Imagination* (2002), but sees it as the subject for parody in the novels, offering a reappraisal that celebrates the comic elements of Dickens's fiction without denying his achievements as a social satirist. Ann Gaylin's *Eavesdropping in the Novel from Austen to Proust* (2002) analyzes a technique employed by Dickens and others as a means of communicating important information. Her principal concern, however, is to explore readers' reactions to the activity of eavesdropping, explaining how awareness of this activity helps them make judgments about characters, situations, and novelists. And once again Dickens's use of Shakespeare is examined, this time by Robert Sawyer in *Victorian Appropriations of Shakespeare* (2003). Sawyer claims Dickens "reproduced Shakespeare more often on the page in his novels than on stage" (117) — an obvious acknowledgment of Dickens's frequent appearances in dramatic productions. Sawyer seems more interested, however, in demonstrating how Dickens played the father figure to family and friends than in examining the fiction.

Interest in the Gothic elements of Dickens's fiction continues to fascinate critics. Julian Wolfreys's "'I Wants to Make Your Flesh Creep': Notes toward a Reading of the Comic-Gothic in Dickens" (2000), offers intriguing insights into Dickens's use of the tradition. Like others employing the Gothic in the middle decades of the nineteenth century, "Dickens is less interested in bringing the foreign, gothic, other home" than in "finding it already at home, at the dinner table, locating the gothic *within* English humour" (37). Similarly, Peter Garrett's chapter on Dickens in *Gothic Reflections: Narrative Force in Nineteenth-Century Fiction* (2003) provides a sensitive reading of *Bleak House, Little Dorrit,* and other works. Not content simply to expose the Gothic elements in the novels, Garrett explains how these shape the narrative in Dickens's fiction.

Stanley Friedman's *Dickens's Fiction: Tapestries of Conscience* (2003) continues the traditional critical commentary that informed his earlier work on Dickens, focusing on the moral dimension of his fiction. Carefully exploring the literary techniques Dickens employs, Friedman explains how Dickens's fiction resembles "the popular Gothic architecture found in the homes of many wealthy Victorians" (9). He argues that the realism of surface detail causes readers to suspend their disbelief in an otherwise improbable story, while the inclusion of some fantastic detail may cause them to confront moral issues they "would prefer to avoid" (11). Through his exploration of literary technique, Friedman demonstrates how Dickens expresses his concern for the idea of "conscience" in both "the customary and the older senses" — that is, "offering guidance on how to behave and increasing our consciousness of the complexity of human life" (12). Dickens is a man with a purpose, Friedman says, who finds didacticism a high calling.

One area of study that had risen in popularity before the end of the twentieth century and seems to offer fruitful ground for further study is Dickens's nonfiction. To that end, John Drew, coeditor with Michael Slater of volume 4 of the Dent Uniform Edition of Dickens's journalism (2000), attempts in *Dickens the Journalist* (2003) to produce what he claims is the first comprehensive analysis of Dickens's journalistic writings as an independent body of literature. More limited studies had been done, of course, and in 2001 Matthew Bevis's "Temporizing Dickens," a study of the way Dickens's experiences as a parliamentary writer and newspaper reporter influenced his early work, had won the *Review of English Studies* essay prize. Ranging much wider across Dickens's career than Bevis, Drew offers a careful assessment of both original materials and critical articles about Dickens's journalism to determine the role Dickens played in highlighting concerns about contemporary society. After examining work Dickens published in the *Daily News* and *The Examiner*, as well as his editorial and original efforts in *Household Words* and *All the Year Round*, Drew concludes that "Dickens's claim to artistic excellence lay most in his spectacular straddling" of "two distinct art forms simultaneously" (188). Drew is aware that journalism is by its nature ephemeral and time-bound, and he insists that, for modern readers to appreciate its value, the work must be approached in its original context. He extends this admonition to all of Dickens's work, too, noting it would be wise to recognize not only that the nineteenth-century novelist was influenced by his age, but also that twenty-first century critics (and their predecessors) fall equally under the sway of the age in which they live and write.

Drew's 2003 study may be but the first in what could be a long list of critical studies of Dickens's journalism, and Drew may be largely responsible for increased attention to this aspect of Dickens's career. In 2006 Drew and David Paroissien, editor of the *Dickens Quarterly*, began "The Dickens Journal Online" (DJO), a project designed to create Internet-accessible facsimiles of Dickens's weekly magazines, *Household Words* and

All the Year Round, along with searchable indexes, lists of scholarship on the journals, and links to information about writers who contributed articles to these magazines. By 2012, the bicentennial of Dickens's birth, this compendium of source materials will be available at scholars' desktops — free of charge. What is particularly inspiring about this project is that, in an age where the marketplace seems to determine a product's value, "Dickens" is still a commodity deserving of subsidy by those who admire his life and love his work.

At the opposite end of the critical spectrum from works like Bevis's and Drew's are cultural studies such as Jay Clayton's *Dickens in Cyberspace: The Afterlife of the Nineteenth Century in Postmodern Culture* (2003). Where Drew is narrow but deep, Clayton is wide — but certainly not shallow. Clayton's title is a bit misleading, however, in that his book deals with a much broader topic than the work of a single novelist. But the shadow of Dickens hangs over every chapter in which Clayton examines the parallels between the Victorians and their postmodern great-great-great grandchildren. That is because, as Clayton says, in so many ways Dickens anticipated the age of the Internet and the deconstructed subject. He was a proponent of technology, a blatant self-promoter, and an experimenter who took advantage of the capitalist state while at the same time rebuking it for its excesses and social failings. While the title may "have a metaphoric dimension" (4), one central chapter, "Is Pip Modern? Or, Dickens at the Turn of the Millennium," directly examines the novelist's stature at the beginning of the twenty-first century. What Clayton discovers is that Dickens is everywhere. His novels may not be on everyone's bookshelves, but the presence of businesses named for his characters and scenes, the web sites devoted to discussion of his life and work, his continuing appearance in college and high-school syllabi, and his monumental influence on contemporary Christmas celebrations — contemporary but notable for their nostalgia for bygone days — are sure signs that "Dickens" is alive and well more than a century after Charles Dickens was laid to rest in Westminster Abbey.

As Clayton notes repeatedly, one way in which Dickens continues to be present is through film adaptations of his work. Therefore, a fruitful area for Dickens studies is sure to be the ways his novels have been adapted for the screen, and two studies published in 2003 confirm that interest in this topic is high. John Glavin's *Dickens on Screen* (2003) collects essays from noted Dickens scholars examining the novelist's impact on aspects of filmmaking. Grahame Smith's curious but intriguing *Dickens and the Dream of Cinema* (2003) provides a provocative analysis of the novelist as a precursor to the filmmakers of the twentieth century. Taking his cue from philosopher Walter Benjamin, who argued that great artists of one epoch imagine the epoch that will succeed them, Smith demonstrates how

Dickens prefigures much that would characterize the film industry of the twentieth century. The idea is not new, of course; the great Russian film director Sergei Eisenstein had made similar observations in an essay included in *Film Form: Essays in Film Theory* (1949) more than sixty years earlier. Not claiming a causative relationship between the novels and the films that would follow, Smith instead examines techniques of presentation and structure that suggest Dickens possessed a sense of consciousness that would be a necessary component for constructing movies. Smith looks at Dickens's preoccupation with visual entertainment in his own day and examines his obsession with the problems of presenting the complexities of city life. The book is quite different from most of the scholarship that established Smith's reputation among Dickens scholars, but it is indicative of the kind of work that has become increasingly common among twenty-first century critics.

Glavin's and Smith's studies also suggest something about the way Dickens will be present to "readers" of the twenty-first century. Film adaptations of Dickens's novels grew exponentially during the 1980s and 1990s, as both Hollywood and the British Broadcasting Company transormed nearly all of them into movies or television mini-series. These have been reproduced in various electronic forms (videotape, DVD, etc.), making them readily accessible to a generation accustomed to obtaining its information and entertainment visually. Hence there seems a strong possibility that Dickens will become known to millions not directly from the texts of his books, but from these existing visual interpretations, or new ones. What that does to our understanding of Dickens and the world about which he wrote is sure to be a subject for fruitful study.

* * *

As the survey of works in this chapter indicates, the future of the Dickens Industry looks bright. There seems no possibility of a decline in critical inquiry, at least not in the near term. The *Dickens Studies Annual, Dickens Quarterly,* and *Dickensian* numbers for 2006 are as large as any of the previous issues. The continuing presence of Dickens's novels in college and high-school classrooms guarantees a market for handbooks such as Donald Hawes's *Charles Dickens* (2007). Hawes supplements a brief biography and summary of the major works with commentary on background and themes, all informed by critical studies that have adjusted the focus of Dickens studies in the past decade. An even more significant work of this nature, David Paroissien's *A Companion to Charles Dickens,* was released in early 2008.

Major new studies recently published or in preparation demonstrate it is still possible to add directly to our knowledge of Dickens's life and work. Among those sure to figure prominently in any book on the Dickens Industry to be written twenty or thirty years from now will be Malcolm Andrews's *Charles Dickens and His Performing Selves* (2006), a fresh look at Dickens's career as a public performer whose readings of his own works was one of the earliest "interpretations" that shaped opinions of the novels among his contemporaries. Certainly the first major work to be discussed in a future study of Dickens criticism will be Michael Slater's biography, a 2008 release from Yale University Press. If his previous work is any guide, there is great likelihood that Slater will stand beside John Forster and Edgar Johnson as one of the great biographers of Dickens.

There is a danger, of course, that in a field where much has already been done, those who wish to make a name for themselves will have to resort to re-treading well-covered ground or write commentaries so tenuously connected to the Dickens canon that they make only slight contributions to the body of scholarship. To that end, Natalie McKnight's observation on Britta Zangen's *Our Daughters Must Be Wives* is worth pondering for its larger implications. "Newcomers" to the history of middle-class Victorian women "will learn much" from Zangen's book, she says in her *Dickens Quarterly* review, "and even veteran scholars would benefit from Zangen's thorough review and synthesis of important works in the field. Her analysis of the novels, however, offers little new ground for those familiar with existing criticism of Victorian fiction" (29). The implications for future publications on Dickens seem obvious. While it is often easy to weed out ill-conceived essays and monographs — much of that work is already being done by competent editors and readers for journals and publishing houses — how many other books and articles, perhaps well written and well argued, will simply repackage what has already been said, adding bulk but not depth to our inventory of studies on Dickens and his work?

Additionally, in recent years the field of Dickens studies has become cluttered with books providing summaries and syntheses rather than critical analysis. Of course, librarians like these because undergraduates find them a great source for boning up on an author, but such books often contain little to deepen our understanding of Dickens's artistry or ideology. Again, not all of these books are without merit — certainly Donald Hawes's fine new guidebook cited above is an example of one that can offer "newcomers," as McKnight calls them, an entry point into Dickens's work. There *is* a place for such books, but one wonders if their growing dominance in the field is a signal that fewer publishers, especially academic presses, are willing to invest in books with limited potential for sales. One can only hope that handbooks and guides will not squeeze out truly groundbreaking work that in the past bore the imprint of many publishing houses other than those at Oxford, Cambridge, Harvard, or Yale.

Of greater concern is the tendency, prevalent for more than century but perhaps more noticeable in recent decades, to take Dickens's work as grist for the mill of one or another critical theory that seems to be fashionable at the moment. I would hardly wish to suggest that theory-based criticism is inherently bad, and I am convinced the Dickens Industry is better for the work of some feminists, Marxists, and new historicists. The problem I have found in surveying much of the new theory-based approaches to Dickens is that too many of them are either attempts to pour old wine into new bottles, or examples of critical contortionism by practitioners who care little for a text except as it can be manipulated to suit their prejudices. A good bit of the "New Historical" criticism of Dickens seems little more than a politically charged reworking of the same materials one might have found half a century earlier in books by Humphry House or Richard Altick. On a related note, in a rather harsh critique of *Gender at Work in Victorian Culture* (2004), a study of (among other things) the concept of "manliness," *Dickens Quarterly* reviewer Chriss Loutitt accuses author Martin Danahay of chasing after a "boom topic" long after the market has been saturated (202). If the past is prologue to the future, we might expect to see quite a few studies that make their case for a "new look" at Dickens by applying arcane — and frequently obtuse — terminology to restate arguments already laid out in earlier critiques.

And yet . . . one need only recall that in his 1928 biography of Dickens, Ralph Straus made the definitive — and wrongheaded — pronouncement that he was going to offer little criticism about the novels because Gissing and Chesterton "have said all that it is necessary to say on the matter" (xiv). In the past eighty years since Straus's biography appeared, hundred of books and thousands of articles attest that there is yet more to say, as each generation discovers for itself what is important *to them*. With due deference to Keats, I think it is safe to say that if new critical theory and new critical practices have taught us anything of value, it is that the work of truly great artists will always have the capability to "tease us out of thought" — if not eternally, certainly for a very long time. I remain confident, then, that Dickens's works will continue to fascinate those who wish to learn something about the novelist and his age — and about ourselves and our age, and ages yet to come.

Works Cited

Allen, Richard. "Literature, Nation and Revolution: *A Tale of Two Cities.*" In *Literature and Nation: Britain and India, 1800–1990,* edited by Richard Allen and Harish Trivedi, 55–66. London: Open University, 2000.

Andrews, Malcolm. *Charles Dickens and his Performing Selves: Dickens and the Public Readings.* Oxford: Oxford UP, 2006.

Anger, Suzy, ed. *Knowing the Past: Victorian Literature and Culture.* Ithaca, NY: Cornell UP, 2001.

Armstrong, Mary A. "Multiplicities of Longing: The Queer Desires of *Bleak House* and *Little Dorrit.*" *Nineteenth Century Studies* 18 (2004): 59–79.

Bevis, Matthew. "Temporizing Dickens." *Review of English Studies: A Quarterly Journal of English Literature and the English Language* 52 (May 2001): 171–91.

Bigelow, Gordon. *Fiction, Famine, and the Rise of Economics in Victorian Britain and Ireland.* Cambridge: Cambridge UP, 2003.

Bodenheimer, Rosemarie. "Knowing and Telling in Dickens's Retrospects." In *Knowing the Past: Victorian Literature and Culture,* edited by Suzy Anger, 215–33. Ithaca, NY: Cornell UP, 2001.

Bowen, John. *Other Dickens: Pickwick to Chuzzlewit.* Oxford: Oxford UP, 2000.

Campbell, Elizabeth A. *Fortune's Wheel: Dickens and the Iconography of Women's Time.* Athens: Ohio UP, 2003.

Chase, Karen, and Michael Levenson. *The Spectacle of Intimacy: A Public Life for the Victorian Family.* Princeton, NJ: Princeton UP, 2000.

Clayton, Jay. *Dickens in Cyberspace: The Afterlife of the Nineteenth Century in Postmodern Culture.* New York: Oxford UP, 2003.

Cockshut, A. O. J. "Children's Death in Dickens: A Chapter in the History of Taste." In *Representations of Childhood Death,* edited by Gillian Avery et al., 133–53. Basingstoke, England: Macmillan; New York: St. Martin's, 2000.

Cole, Natalie Bell. "'Amen in a Wrong Place': Charles Dickens Imagines the Victorian Church." In *Victorian Religious Discourse: New Directions in Criticism,* edited by Jude V. Nixon, 205–34. Basingstoke, England: Palgrave Macmillan, 2004.

Dahl, Christopher C. "Fitzjames Stephen, Charles Dickens, and Double Reviewing." *Victorian Periodicals Review* 14.2 (Summer 1981): 51–58.

Dailey, Donna. *Charles Dickens.* New York: Chelsea House, 2005.

Dowling, Andrew. *Manliness and the Male Novelist in Victorian Literature*. Aldershot, England: Ashgate, 2001.

Drew, John M. L. *Dickens the Journalist*. London: Palgrave Macmillan, 2003.

Eagleton, Terry. *The English Novel: An Introduction*. Malden, MA: Blackwell, 2005.

Eisenstein, Sergei. *Film Form: Essays in Film Theory*. Translated by Jay Leyda. New York: Harcourt, Brace, 1949.

Friedman, Stanley. *Dickens's Fiction: Tapestries of Conscience*. New York: AMS Press, 2003.

Gardiner, John. *The Victorians: An Age in Retrospect*, 161–79. London: Hambledon & London, 2002.

Garrett, Peter K. "Dickens." *Gothic Reflections: Narrative Force in Nineteenth-Century Fiction*, 141–67. Ithaca, NY: Cornell UP, 2003.

Gaylin, Ann. *Eavesdropping in the Novel from Austen to Proust*. Cambridge: Cambridge UP, 2002.

Glavin, John. *Dickens on Screen*. Cambridge: Cambridge UP, 2003.

Hawes, Donald. *Charles Dickens*. London and New York: Continuum, 2007.

Jacobson, Wendy S., ed. *Dickens and the Children of Empire*. New York: Palgrave, 2000.

James, Elizabeth. *Charles Dickens*. British Library Writers Lives Series. New York and Oxford: Oxford UP, 2004.

John, Juliet. *Dickens's Villains: Melodrama, Character, Popular Culture*. Oxford: Oxford UP, 2001.

Karl, Frederick R. "Recent Dickens Studies." *Victorian Literature and Culture* 31.2 (2003): 593–611.

Kucich, John. "Charles Dickens." In *The Columbia History of the British Novel*, edited by John Richetti et al., 381–406. New York: Columbia UP, 1994.

Loutitt, Chriss. Review of Andrew Dowling, *Manliness and the Male Novelist in Victorian Literature* and Martin A. Danahy, *Gender at Work: Victorian Culture, Literature, and Masculinity*. *Dickens Quarterly* 23.3 (September 2006): 199–202.

Markels, Julian. *The Marxian Imagination: Representing Class in Literature*. New York: Monthly Review P, 2003.

McKnight, Natalie. Review of Britta Zangen, *Our Daughters Must Be Wives*. *Dickens Quarterly* 23.2 (June 2006): 127–29.

Mengham, Rod. *Charles Dickens*. Plymouth, England: Northcote House, 2001.

Moore, Grace. *Dickens and Empire: Discourses of Class, Race and Colonialism in the Works of Charles Dickens.* Aldershot, England: Ashgate, 2004.

Morgentaler, Goldie. *Dickens and Heredity: Like Begets Like.* London: Macmillan, 2000.

Morris, Pam. *Imagining Inclusive Society in Nineteenth-Century Novels: The Code of Sincerity in the Public Sphere.* Baltimore, MD: Johns Hopkins UP, 2004.

Newey, Vincent. *The Scriptures of Charles Dickens: Novels of Ideology, Novels of the Self.* Aldershot, Eng. and Burlington, VT: Ashgate, 2004.

Newsom, Robert. *Charles Dickens Revisited.* New York: Twayne, 2000.

Parker, David. *The Doughty Street Novels.* New York: AMS Press, 2002.

Poovey, Mary. "The Structure of Anxiety in Political Economy and *Hard Times.*" In *Knowing the Past: Victorian Literature and Culture,* edited by Suzy Anger, 151–71. Ithaca, NY: Cornell UP, 2001.

Pykett, Lyn. *Charles Dickens.* Critical Issues Series. London: Palgrave, 2002.

Rem, Tore. *Dickens, Melodrama, and the Parodic Imagination.* New York: AMS Press, 2002.

Robbins, Bruce. "How to be a Benefactor without any Money: The Chill of *Great Expectations.*" In *Knowing the Past: Victorian Literature and Culture,* edited by Suzy Anger, 172–91. Ithaca, NY: Cornell UP, 2001.

Robinson, Alan. *Imagining London 1770–1900.* London: Palgrave Macmillan, 2004.

Robson, Catherine. *Men in Wonderland: The Lost Girlhood of the Victorian Gentleman.* Princeton, NJ: Princeton UP, 2001.

Rodensky, Lisa. *The Crime in Mind: Criminal Responsibility and the Victorian Novel.* Oxford: Oxford UP, 2003.

Russell, Corinna, ed. *Lives of Victorian Figures I: Eliot, Dickens and Tennyson By Their Contemporaries.* London: Pickering & Chatto, 2003.

Sawyer, Robert. *Victorian Appropriations of Shakespeare: George Eliot, A. C. Swinburne, Robert Browning, and Charles Dickens.* Madison, NJ: Fairleigh Dickinson UP, 2003.

Schilling, Bernard N. *The Rain of Years: Great Expectations and the World of Dickens.* Rochester, NY: U of Rochester P, 2001.

Sicher, Efraim. *Rereading the City, Rereading Dickens: Representation, the Novel, and Urban Realism.* New York: AMS Press, 2003.

Simmons, James R., Jr. "No Expectations at All: Women in Charles Dickens's *Great Expectations* (1861)." In *Women in Literature: Reading through the Lens of Gender,* edited by Jerilyn Fisher and Ellen Silber, 124–26. Westport, CT: Greenwood, 2003.

Sirabian, Robert H. *Charles Dickens: Life, Work, and Criticism.* Toronto: York UP, 2002.

Slater, Michael and John Drew, eds. *'The Uncommercial Traveller' and Other Papers 1859–1870.* Dent Uniform Edition of Dickens's Journalism. Vol. 4. London: J. M. Dent, 2000.

Smiley, Jane. *Charles Dickens.* New York: Viking, 2002.

Smith, Grahame. *Dickens and the Dream of Cinema.* Manchester, England: Manchester UP, 2003.

Straus, Ralph. *Charles Dickens: A Portrait in Pencil.* London: Gollancz, 1928. Issued as *Charles Dickens: A Biography from New Sources.* New York: Cosmopolitan Books, 1928.

Tambling, Jeremy. *Dickens, Violence and the Modern State.* London: Macmillan, 1995.

———. *Lost in the American City: Dickens, James and Kafka.* Basingstoke, England: Palgrave, 2001.

Trilling, Lionel. *The Liberal Imagination.* Garden City, NY: Doubleday, 1950.

Wolfreys, Julian. "'I Wants to Make Your Flesh Creep': Notes toward a Reading of the Comic-Gothic in Dickens." In *Victorian Gothic: Literary and Cultural Manifestations in the Nineteenth Century,* edited by Ruth Robbins and Julian Wolfreys, 31–59. New York: Palgrave, 2000.

Woloch, Alex. *The One vs. the Many: Minor Characters and the Space of the Protagonist in the Novel.* Princeton, NJ: Princeton UP, 2003.

Zangen, Britta. *Our Daughters Must Be Wives: Marriageable Young Women in the Novels of Dickens, Eliot, and Hardy.* Frankfurt, Germany: Peter Lang, 2004.

Major Works by Charles Dickens

MANY OF DICKENS'S NOVELS FIRST APPEARED in serial form, issued monthly or weekly over a span of twelve to twenty months. The dates given below indicate the first publication of a novel as a complete book. Additionally, Dickens was prolific. He wrote fifteen novels, several nonfiction books, a half-dozen Christmas tales, a number of plays, and hundreds of sketches, essays, articles, letters, and notes both as a contributor to various periodicals and for those for which he served as editor. He was an equally prolific correspondent; more than twelve thousand of his letters are included in the Pilgrim Edition. The works listed below include his novels, the travel books, the Christmas tales, and the most useful collections of his journalism and letters. I have attempted to give the first date of publication and publisher's information, although in most cases the novels, nonfiction, and letters are available in multiple editions (some considerably more reliable than others). A more complete bibliography of Dickens's writings can be found in Paul Schlicke's entry in *The Cambridge Bibliography of English Literature,* volume 4, edited by Joanne Shattock (1999).

Sketches by "Boz." London: Macrone, 1836.

Pickwick Papers. London: Chapman & Hall, 1837.

Memoirs of Joseph Grimaldi. 2 volumes. London: Richard Bentley, 1838.

Oliver Twist. London: Richard Bentley, 1838.

Sketches of Young Gentlemen. London: Chapman & Hall, 1838.

Nicholas Nickleby. London: Chapman & Hall, 1839.

Sketches of Young Couples. London: Chapman & Hall, 1839.

Master Humphrey's Clock. London: Chapman & Hall, 1841.

The Old Curiosity Shop. London: Chapman & Hall, 1841.

Barnaby Rudge. London: Chapman & Hall, 1841.

American Notes for General Circulation. London: Chapman & Hall, 1842.

A Christmas Carol. London: Chapman & Hall, 1843.

Martin Chuzzlewit. London: Chapman & Hall, 1844.

The Chimes. London: Chapman & Hall, 1844.

The Cricket on the Hearth. London: Chapman & Hall, 1845.

The Life of Our Lord, Written for His Children. Written 1846–49. New York: Simon & Schuster, 1934.

Pictures from Italy. London: Bradbury & Evans, 1846.

The Battle of Life. London: Chapman & Hall, 1846.

Dombey and Son. London: Bradbury & Evans, 1848.

The Haunted Man. London: Bradbury & Evans, 1848.

David Copperfield. London: Bradbury & Evans, 1850.

A Child's History of England. 3 volumes. London: Bradbury & Evans, 1852–54.

Bleak House. London: Bradbury & Evans, 1853.

Hard Times. London: Bradbury & Evans, 1854.

Little Dorrit. London: Bradbury & Evans, 1857.

Reprinted Pieces. London: Bradbury & Evans, Chapman & Hall, 1858.

A Tale of Two Cities. London: Chapman & Hall, 1859.

The Uncommercial Traveler. London: Chapman & Hall, 1860.

Great Expectations. London: Chapman & Hall, 1861.

Our Mutual Friend. London: Chapman & Hall, 1865.

The Mystery of Edwin Drood. London: Chapman & Hall, 1870.

The Speeches of Charles Dickens. Edited by K. J. Fielding. Oxford: Clarendon Press, 1960.

The Letters of Charles Dickens. Pilgrim Edition. 12 volumes. Oxford: Clarendon Press, 1965–2002.

Uncollected Writings of Charles Dickens: Household Words 1850–59. 2 volumes. London: Allen Lane, 1968.

Complete Plays and Selected Poems. London: Vision, 1970.

The Dent Uniform Edition of Dickens's Journalism. 4 volumes. Columbus: Ohio State UP, 1994–2000.

Chronological List of Works Cited

1830s

Anon. Review of *Sketches by Boz*. *Metropolitan Magazine* 15 (March 1836): 77.

Hogarth, George. Review of *Sketches by Boz*. *Morning Chronicle* 20 (11 February 1836).

"Literary Examiner." *Examiner* no. 1456 (28 February 1836): 132–33.

Anon. Review of *Pickwick Papers*. *Metropolitan Magazine* 18 (January 1837): 6.

Buller, Charles. "The Works of Dickens." *London and Westminster Review* 29 (July 1837): 194–215.

Hayward, Abraham. Review of *Pickwick Papers* and *Sketches by Boz*. *Quarterly Review* 62 (October 1837): 484–518.

Lister, Thomas Henry. Review of *Sketches by Boz, Pickwick Papers, Oliver Twist*, and *Nicholas Nickleby*. *Edinburgh Review* 68 (October 1838): 75–97.

Ford, Richard. Review. *Quarterly Review* 64 (June 1839): 83–102.

1840s

Anon. Review of *Master Humphrey's Clock*. *Metropolitan Magazine* 30 (December 1840): 111.

"Charles Dickens and His Works." *Fraser's Magazine* 21 (April 1840): 381–400.

Hood, Thomas. Review of *Master Humphrey's Clock* and *The Old Curiosity Shop*. *Athenaeum* 7 (November 1840): 887–88.

"Modern Novels." *Christian Remembrancer* 4 (December 1842): 585–96.

"The Reception of Mr. Dickens." *United States Magazine and Democratic Review* (April 1842): 315, 320.

Croker, John Wilson. Review of *American Notes*. *Quarterly Review* 71 (March 1843): 502–28.

Blanchard, E. L. Review of *A Christmas Carol*. *Ainsworth's Magazine* 5 (January 1844): 86.

Horne, R. H. *A New Spirit of the Age*. 3 vols. London: Smith, Elder, 1844. Reprint, New York: Garland, 1986.

Thackeray, W. M. "A Box of Novels." *Fraser's Magazine* 29 (February 1844): 166–69.

Cleghorn, Thomas. "Writings of Charles Dickens." *North British Review* 3 (May 1845): 65–87.

Anon. Review of *The Cricket on the Hearth*. *Chambers's Edinburgh Journal* n.s. 5 (17 January 1846): 44–48.

Anon. Review of *Dombey and Son*. *Westminster Review* 47 (April 1847): 5–11.

Eagles, John. "A Few Words about Novels — a Dialogue." *Blackwood's Magazine* 64 (October 1848): 468–69.

Anon. Review of *The Haunted Man*. *Macphail's Edinburgh Ecclesiastical Journal* 6 (January 1849): 423–31.

Martineau, Harriet. *A History of England During the Thirty Years' Peace 1816–1846*. 4 vols. London: C. Knight, 1849. London: G. Bell, 1877–78.

Whipple, Edwin P. "Novels and Novelists: Charles Dickens." *North American Review* 69 (October 1849): 383–407.

1850s

"Charles Dickens and David Copperfield." *Fraser's Magazine* 42 (December 1850): 698–700.

Masson, David. "*Pendennis* and *Copperfield:* Thackeray and Dickens." *North British Review* 15 (May 1851): 57–89.

Anon. Review of *Bleak House*. *Bentley's Miscellany* 34 (October 1853): 372–74.

Brimley, George. Review of *Bleak House*. *Spectator* 26 (24 September 1853): 923–25.

Forster, John. Review of *Bleak House*. *Examiner* 8 (October 1853): 643–45.

———. Review of *Hard Times*. *Examiner* 9 (September 1854): 568–69.

Simpson, Richard. Review of *Hard Times*. *The Rambler* n.s. 2 (October 1854): 361–62.

Stothert, James Augustine. "Living Novelists." *The Rambler* n.s. 1 (January 1854): 41–51.

Stephen, James Fitzjames. "The Relation of Novels to Life." *Cambridge Essays*, 148–92. London: J. N. Parker, 1855.

Eliot, George [Marian Evans]. "The Natural History of German Life." *Westminster Review* 66 (July 1856): 55.

Taine, Hippolyte. "Charles Dickens: son talent et ses oeuvres." *Revue des Deux Mondes* n.s. 1 (1 February 1856): 618–47.

Bayne, Peter. *Essays in Biography and Criticism*, 363–92. First series. Boston: Gould and Lincoln, 1857.

Forsyth, William. "Literary Style." *Fraser's Magazine* 55 (March 1857): 260–63.

Hamley, E. B. "Remonstrance with Dickens." *Blackwood's Magazine* 81 (April 1857): 490–503.

Stephen, James Fitzjames. "License of Modern Novelists." *Edinburgh Review* 106 (July 1857): 124–56.

———. "*Little Dorrit*." *Saturday Review* 4 (July 1857): 15–16.

———. "Mr. Dickens as a Politician." *Saturday Review* 3 (January 1857): 8–9.

Whitman, Walt. "Charles Dickens." *Brooklyn Daily Times*, 6 May 1857.

Bagehot, Walter. "Charles Dickens." *National Review* 7 (October 1858): 458–86.

Stephen, James Fitzjames. "Mr. Dickens." *Saturday Review* 5 (May 1858): 474–75. Reprinted in Albert Mordell, ed., *Notorious Literary Attacks*. New York: Boni & Liveright, 1926.

Masson, David. *British Novelists and Their Styles: Being a Critical Sketch of the History of British Prose Fiction*. London: Macmillan; Boston: Gould and Lincoln, 1859. Reprint, Boston: W. Small, 1928.

Stephen, James Fitzjames. "*A Tale of Two Cities*." *Saturday Review* 8 (17 December 1859): 741–43.

1860s

Ruskin, John. *Unto this Last*. *Cornhill Magazine* 2 (August 1860): 159.

Anon. Review of *Great Expectations*. *Saturday Review* 12 (20 July 1861): 69.

Dallas, E. S. Review of *Great Expectations*. *The Times* (17 October 1861): 6.

Whipple Edwin P. "*Great Expectations*." *Atlantic Monthly* 8 (September 1861): 380–82.

Oliphant, Margaret. "Sensation Novels." *Blackwood's Edinburgh Magazine* 91 (May 1862): 564–84.

Anon. Review of *Dr. Marigold's Prescriptions*. *Saturday Review* 20 (16 December 1865): 763–64.

Anon. Review of *Our Mutual Friend*. *London Review* (28 October 1865): 467–68.

Anon. Review of *Our Mutual Friend*. *Saturday Review* 20 (11 November 1865): 612–13.

Dallas, E. S. Review of *Our Mutual Friend*. *The Times* (29 November 1865): 6.

James, Henry. "*Our Mutual Friend.*" *Nation* 1 (December 1865): 786–87. Reprinted as "The Limitations of Dickens." *Views and Reviews*. Boston: Ball, 1908.

Anon. Review of *Our Mutual Friend*. *Westminster Review* n.s. 29 (April 1866): 582–85.

Whipple, Edwin P. "The Genius of Dickens." *Atlantic Monthly* 19 (May 1867): 546–54.

Hutton, R. H. "Mr. Dickens's Moral Services to Literature." *Spectator* 42 (17 April 1869): 474–75.

Stott, George. "Charles Dickens." *Contemporary Review* 10 (January 1869): 203–25.

1870s

MacKenzie, Robert Shelton. *Life of Charles Dickens*. Philadelphia: T. B. Peterson, 1870.

Sala, George Augustus. *Charles Dickens*. London: Routledge, 1870.

Kent, Charles. *Charles Dickens as a Reader*. London: Chapman & Hall, 1872. Reprint, New York: Haskell House, 1973.

Lewes, George Henry. "Dickens in Relation to Criticism." *Fortnightly Review* 17 (February 1872): 141–54.

Forster, John. *The Life of Charles Dickens*. London: Chapman & Hall, 1872–74. Boston: Osgood, 1875. Reprint, London: Palmer, 1928.

Pierce, Gilbert. *A Dickens Dictionary*. Boston: Osgood, 1872.

Davey, Samuel J. "Charles Dickens." *Darwin, Carlyle and Dickens, With Other Essays*, 121–56. London: James Clark, 1876. Reprint, New York: Haskell House, 1971.

Whipple, Edwin P. Review of *Hard Times*. *Atlantic Monthly* 39 (March 1877): 353–58.

Dickens, Charles. *The Letters of Charles Dickens*. Edited by Mary Dickens and Georgina Hogarth. 2 vols. London: Chapman & Hall, 1879.

1880s

Watt, James C. "Dickens." *Great Novelists: Scott, Thackeray, Dickens, Lytton*, 163–218. Edinburgh: Macniver and Wallace, 1880.

Ward, Adolphus W. *Charles Dickens*. English Men of Letters Series. London: Macmillan, 1882.

Dickens, Mary. *Charles Dickens by His Eldest Daughter.* London: Cassell, 1885. Reprinted as *My Father as I Knew Him.* London: Roxburghe Press, 1897; reprint, New York: Harmon & Irwin, 1928.

Stephen, Leslie. "Dickens, Charles." *Dictionary of National Biography.* 1885 ed. Vol. 5, 925–37. London: Smith, Elder, 1908.

Kitton, Frederic G. *Dickensiana: A Bibliography of the Literature Relating to Charles Dickens and his Writings.* London: Redway, 1886.

Marzials, Frank T. *Life of Charles Dickens.* London: W. Scott, 1887.

1890s

Henley, William E. "Dickens." *Views and Reviews: Essays in Appreciation,* 1–8. London: David Nutt, 1890. London: David Nutt; New York: Scribner's Sons, 1906.

Kitton, Frederic G. *Charles Dickens, By Pen and Pencil.* London: F. T. Sabin, 1890.

Howells, William Dean. *Criticism and Fiction.* New York: Harper; London: Osgood, 1891. Reprinted in *Criticism and Fiction and Other Essays by W. D. Howells,* edited by Clara M. and Rudoph Kirk. New York: New York UP, 1959.

Oliphant, Margaret. *The Victorian Age of English Literature.* London: Tait, 1892.

Saintsbury, George. *Miscellaneous Essays.* London: Percival, 1892.

McCarthy, Justin. "Dickens and Thackeray." *A History of Our Times.* Rev. ed. Vol. 2. New York: Lovell, Coryell & Co., 1894.

Harrison, Frederic. "Charles Dickens." *Forum* 18 (January 1895): 545–53. Reprinted as "Dickens's Place in Literature." *Studies in Early Victorian Literature,* 128–44. London: E. Arnold, 1895.

Howells, William Dean. "Dickens." *My Literary Passions,* 88–103. New York: Harper, 1895.

Saintsbury, George. "Charles Dickens." *Corrected Impressions: Essays on Victorian Writers,* 117–37. London: Heinemann, 1895.

Hutton, Laurence. "Charles Dickens, 1812–1870." In *Library of the World's Best Literature, Ancient and Modern.* Vol. 8, edited by Charles Dudley Warner, 4625–88. New York: R. S. Peale and J. A. Hill, 1896–99.

Saintsbury, George. "Dickens." *A History of Nineteenth Century Literature 1780–1895,* 145–50. New York: Macmillan, 1896.

———. *Essays on English Literature.* London: Rivington, Percival, 1896.

Howells, William Dean. "My Favorite Novelist and His Best Book." *Munsey's Magazine* (April 1897). Reprinted in *Criticism and Fiction and Other Essays by W. D. Howells,* edited by Clara M. and Rudolph Kirk, 97–100. New York: New York UP, 1959.

Kitton, Frederic G. *The Novels of Charles Dickens: A Bibliography and Sketch.* London: E. Stock, 1897.

Shorter, Clement. *Victorian Literature: Sixty Years of Books and Bookmen.* New York: Dodd, Mead, 1897. Reprint, New York: Bart Franklin, 1970.

Gissing, George. *Charles Dickens: A Critical Study.* London: Blackie, 1898. Reprinted in *Collected Works of George Gissing on Charles Dickens,* edited by Pierre Coustillas. Vol. I. Surrey, England: Grayswood, 2004.

Saintsbury, George. *A Short History of English Literature.* London: Macmillan, 1898.

Cross, Wilbur L. "The Realistic Reaction (Dickens)." *The Development of the English Novel,* 168–96. New York: Macmillan, 1899.

Kitton, Frederic G. *Dickens and his Illustrators.* London: Redway, 1899.

1900s

Kitton, Frederic G. *The Minor Writings of Charles Dickens: A Bibliography and Sketch.* London: E. Stock. 1900.

Howells, William Dean. "The Earlier Heroines of Charles Dickens." *Harper's Bazaar* 33 (September 1900): 1192–97. Reprinted in *Heroines of Fiction.* Vol. 1. New York: Harper, 1901.

———. "Heroines of Dickens's Middle Period." *Harper's Bazaar* 33 (September 1900): 1287–92. Reprinted as "Heroines of Charles Dickens's Middle Period." *Heroines of Fiction.* Vol. 1. New York: Harper, 1901.

———. "Later Heroines of Dickens." *Harper's Bazaar* 33 (October 1900): 1415–21. Reprinted as "Dickens's Later Heroines." *Heroines of Fiction.* Vol. 1. New York: Harper, 1901.

Kitton, Frederic G. *Charles Dickens, His Life, Writings and Personality.* London: T. C. and E. C. Jack, 1902.

Matz, Bertram W. *Charles Dickens: The Story of His Life and Writings.* London: Dickens Fellowship, 1902.

Swinburne, Algernon C. "Charles Dickens." *Quarterly Review* 196 (July 1902): 20–39. Reprint, with additions as *Charles Dickens.* Edited by T. Watts-Dunton. London: Chatto & Windus, 1913. Reprinted in *Swinburne as Critic,* edited by Clyde K. Hyder, 223–42. London: Routledge & Kegan Paul, 1972.

Chesterton, G. K., and Frederic G. Kitton. *Charles Dickens.* London: Hodder & Stoughton, 1903.

Kitton, Frederic G., ed. *The Poems and Verses of Charles Dickens.* London: Harper, 1903.

Meynell, Alice. "Charles Dickens as a Man of Letters." *Atlantic Monthly* 91 (January 1903): 52–59.

Dawson, William J. *The Makers of English Fiction.* London: Hodder & Stoughton; Toronto: F. H. Revell, 1905.

Fitzgerald, Percy. *The Life of Charles Dickens, as Revealed in his Writings.* 2 vols. London: Chatto & Windus, 1905.

Chesterton, G. K. *Charles Dickens.* London: Methuen, 1906. Reprinted as *Charles Dickens: A Critical Study.* London: Dodd, Mead, 1913. Reprinted as *Charles Dickens: The Last of the Great Men.* New York: The Press of the Readers Club, 1942.

Compton-Rickett, Arthur. "Charles Dickens: The Humorist." *Personal Forces in Modern Literature,* 143–85. London: Dent, 1906. Reprint, New York: AMS Press, 1970.

Milne, James. "How Dickens Sells: He Comes Next to the Bible and Shakespeare." *Book Monthly* 3 (August 1906): 773–76.

Saintsbury, George. "Dickens." In *Cambridge History of English Literature.* Vol. 13, edited by A. W. Ward and A. R. Waller, 303–39. Cambridge: Cambridge UP, 1907–16.

Williams, Mary. *The Dickens Concordance.* London: F. Griffiths, 1907. Reprint, New York: Haskell House, 1970.

Jackson, Holbrook. "Charles Dickens." *Great English Novelists,* 215–54. London: Grant Richards, 1908.

More, Paul Elmer. "The Praise of Dickens." *Shelburne Essays,* 22–44. 5th series. New York: Putnam, 1908.

Pugh, Edwin. *Charles Dickens: The Apostle of the People.* London: New Age Press, 1908. Reprint, New York: Haskell House Publishers, 1971.

Stephen, Sir Leslie. "Dickens, Charles." *Dictionary of National Biography.* Vol. 5, 925–37. London: Smith, Elder, 1908.

Burton, Richard. "Dickens." *Masters of the English Novel: A Study of Principles and Personalities,* 175–94. New York: Henry Holt, 1909.

Chesterton, G. K. "Dickensian." *Tremendous Trifles,* 96–103. London: Methuen, 1909.

Philip, Alexander J. and W. L. Gadd. *A Dickens Dictionary.* New York: Dutton, 1909. 2nd ed., revised and enlarged. London: Simpkin, Marshall, 1928.

1910s

The Bookman Extra Number. *Charles Dickens*. London: Hodder & Stoughton, 1910.

Canning, Albert S. *Dickens and Thackeray Studied in Three Novels*. London: T. F. Unwin, 1911. Reprint, New York: Kennikat, 1971.

Kitton, Frederic G. *The Dickens Country*. London: A. and C. Black, 1911.

Walters, J. Cuming. *Phases of Dickens: The Man, His Message, and His Mission*. London: Chapman & Hall, 1911. Reprint, New York: Haskell House Publishers, 1971.

Wilkins, W. Glyde. *Charles Dickens in America*. London: Chapman & Hall, 1911.

Benson, Arthur C. "Charles Dickens." *North American Review* 195 (March 1912): 381–91.

Biron, H. C. "The Plots of Dickens." *National Review* 59 (May 1912): 514–23.

Bookman. Extra Number: *Charles Dickens*. London: Hodder & Stoughton, 1912. Reprint, 1914.

Cross, Wilbur L. "The Return to Dickens." *Yale Review* 2 (October 1912): 142–62.

Ellis, Stewart M. "Dickens and Forster." *Chambers Journal* (January 20, 1912). Reprinted in *Mainly Victorian*, 80–88. London: Hutchinson, 1925.

Figgis, Darrell. "Praise of Dickens." *Nineteenth Century* 71 (February 1912): 274–84; *Living Age* 272 (March 1912): 524–32. Reprinted in *Studies and Appreciations*. London: Dent, 1912.

Lehmann, R. C. *Charles Dickens as Editor*. London: Smith, Elder, 1912.

Meynell, Alice. "Notes of a Reader of Dickens." *Dublin Review* 150 (April 1912): 370–84. Reprinted as "Dickens as Man of Letters." *Hearts of Controversy*. London: Burns and Oates, 1917. Reprinted in *Living Age* 69 (May 1912): 461–69.

Nabokoff, Vladimir. "Charles Dickens: A Russian Appreciation." *Dickensian* 8 (June 1912): 145–48; (July 1912): 173–76; (August 1912): 201–4.

Van Dyke, Henry. "The Good Enchantment of Charles Dickens." *Scribner's Magazine* 51 (June 1912): 656–65. Reprinted in *Companionable Books and Their Authors*, 656–65. London: Hodder & Stoughton, 1912.

Chesterton, G. K. *The Victorian Age in Literature*. London: Williams & Norgate, 1913. Reprint, London: Oxford UP, 1966.

Fitzgerald, Percy. *Memories of Charles Dickens*. London: Simpkin, Marshall, Hamilton, Kent & Co., 1913.

Fyfe, Thomas A. *Who's Who in Dickens*. London: Hodder & Stoughton, 1913.

Saintsbury, George. *The English Novel*. London: Dent, 1913.

Shaw, George Bernard. "Introduction." *Hard Times*. London: Waverley Book Co., 1913. Reprinted in Dan H. Laurence and Martin Quinn, eds. *Shaw on Dickens*. New York: Frederick Ungar, 1985.

Walker, Hugh. "Dickens and Thackeray." *The Literature of the Victorian Era*, 660–706. Cambridge: Cambridge UP, 1913.

Phelps, William L. "Dickens." *Essays on Books*, 178–91. New York: Macmillan, 1914.

Shaw, George Bernard. "On Dickens." *Dickensian* 10 (June 1914): 150–51. Reprinted in *The Bookman* Extra Number (1914). 103–4.

Ley, J. W. T. "Dickens and Our Allies." *Dickensian* 11 (November 1915). 285–90.

Powys, John C. "Dickens." *Visions and Revisions*, 119–31. New York: Shaw, 1915. Reprint, London: Macdonald, 1955.

Leacock, Stephen. "Fiction and Reality: A Study of the Art of Charles Dickens." *Essays and Literary Studies*, 159–88. London: John Lane, 1916.

Phelps, William L. *The Advance of the English Novel*. New York: Dodd, Mead, 1916.

Burton, Richard. *Charles Dickens: How to Know Him*. Indianapolis: Bobbs-Merrill, 1919.

Crotch, W. Walter. "The Decline — and After!" *Dickensian* 15 (July 1919): 121–27.

———. *The Secret of Dickens*. London: Chapman & Hall, 1919. Reprint, New York: Haskell House, 1972.

Dark, Sidney. *Charles Dickens*. London: T. Nelson, 1919. Reprint, New York: Haskell House, 1975.

Ley, J. W. T. *The Dickens Circle: A Narrative of the Novelist's Friendships*. London: Chapman & Hall; New York: Dutton, 1919.

Phillips, Walter C. *Dickens, Reade and Collins: Sensation Novelists*. New York: Columbia UP, 1919. Reprint, New York: Russell and Russell, 1962.

1920s

Chesterton, G. K. *Charles Dickens Fifty Years After*. London: Methuen, 1920.

Elton, Oliver. "Charles Dickens." *Survey of English Literature: 1830–1880*, 194–221. Vol. 2. London: E. Arnold, 1920. Rev. and reprinted in *Dickens and Thackeray*. London: E. Arnold, 1924.

Lubbock, Percy. *The Craft of Fiction*. London: J. Cape, 1921.

Santayana, George. "Dickens." *Dial* 71 (November 1921): 537–49. Reprinted in *Soliloquies in England and Later Soliloquies*. New York: Scribner, 1922. Reprint, Ann Arbor: U of Michigan P, 1967.

Murry, John Middleton. "The Dickens Revival." *Times* 19 (May 1922): 16.

Zweig, Stefan. "Charles Dickens." Translated by Kenneth Burke. *Dial* 74 (January 1923): 1–24. Reprinted in *Three Masters*. Translated by Eden and Cesar Paul. New York: Viking, 1930.

Gissing, George. *Critical Studies of the Works of Charles Dickens*. New York: Greenberg, 1924.

———. *The Immortal Dickens*. Edited by B. W. Matz. London: Palmer, 1925; reprint, New York: Haskell House, 1965.

Quiller-Couch, Sir Arthur T. *Charles Dickens and Other Victorians*. Cambridge: Cambridge UP, 1925.

Weygandt, Cornelius. *A Century of the English Novel*. New York: The Century Co., 1925.

Woolf, Virginia. "*David Copperfield.*" *Nation and Athenaeum* 37 (August 1925): 620–21. Reprinted in *The Moment and Other Essays*. London: Hogarth, 1947. Reprinted in *Collected Essays*. Vol. 1. London: Hogarth, 1966.

Cason, Clarence E. "Charles Dickens in America Today." *Literary Digest International Book Review* 4 (September 1926): 603–7.

Ley, J. W. T. "History of the *Dickensian*." *Dickensian* 22 (January 1926): 11–22, 121–29.

Mordell, Albert, ed. *Notorious Literary Attacks*. New York: Boni & Liveright, 1926.

Rainey, Lillian F. "Dickens Up To Date." *Century* 3 (February 1926): 504–6.

Van Amerongen, J. B. *The Actor in Dickens: A Study of the Histrionic and Dramatic Elements in the Novelist's Life and Works*. London: Palmer, 1926; New York: D. Appleton, 1927. Reprint, New York: Haskell House Publishers, 1970.

Williams, Orlo. *Some Great English Novels: Studies in the Art of Fiction*. London: Macmillan, 1926.

Belloc, Hillaire. "Dickens Revisited." *New Statesman* 28 (January 1927): 444–45.

Eliot, T. S. "Wilkie Collins and Dickens." *Times Literary Supplement* (4 August 1927): 525–26. Reprinted in *Selected Essays, 1917–1932*. New York: Harcourt, Brace, 1932; new ed., 1950.

Forster, E. M. *Aspects of the Novel*. London: E. Arnold, 1927.

Galsworthy, John. "Six Novelists in Profile." *Castles in Spain and Other Screeds*, 201–35. New York: Scribner, 1927. Reprinted in *Candelabra*. New York: Scribner, 1933.

Kidd, H. H. "Is Dickens Still A Hero?" *South Atlantic Quarterly* 26 (July 1927): 280–89.

Chesterton, G. K. "The Popularity of Dickens." *Spectator* 141 (November 1928): 43–44. Reprinted in *Sidelights on New London and Newer York*. New York: Dodd, 1932.

Dickens, Sir Henry F. *Memories of My Father*. London: Gollancz, 1928; New York: Duffield, 1929.

Muir, Edwin. *The Structure of the Novel*. London: L. and V. Woolf, 1928; New York: Harcourt, Brace, 1929.

Straus, Ralph. *Charles Dickens: A Portrait in Pencil*. London: Gollancz, 1928. Issued as *Charles Dickens: A Biography from New Sources*. New York: Cosmopolitan Books, 1928.

Chesterton, G. K. "On *Edwin Drood*." *Generally Speaking*, 261–67. New York: Dodd, Mead, 1929.

Maurois, André. "The Philosophy of Dickens." *Forum* 81 (January 1929): 54–59.

Wagenknecht, Edward. *The Man Charles Dickens: A Victorian Portrait*. Boston: Houghton Mifflin, 1929. Rev. ed., Norman: U of Oklahoma P, 1966.

1930s

Ford, Ford Madox. *The English Novel: From the Earliest Days to the Death of Joseph Conrad*. London: Lippincott, 1930.

Huxley, Aldous. "The Vulgarity of Little Nell." *Vulgarity in Literature*, 54–59. London: Chatto & Windus, 1930. Reprinted in *Music at Night and Other Essays*. London: Chatto & Windus, 1931.

Walters, J. Cuming. "'Biting' Critics." *Dickensian* 26 (Autumn 1930): 282–85.

Chesterton, G. K. "On Dickens and After." *Come to Think of It*, 250–60. New York: Dodd, Mead, 1931.

Beach, Joseph W. *The Twentieth Century Novel*. New York: Century, 1932.

Chesterton, G. K. "The Great Gusto." In *The Great Victorians*, edited by H. J. and Hugh Massingham, 163–71. London: Nicholson and Watson; New York: Doubleday, Doran, 1932. Reprinted in *A Handful of Authors*, edited by Dorothy Collins. London: Sheed and Ward, 1953.

Laski, Harold. "In Praise of Dickens." *Daily Herald* (24 December 1932).

Leavis, Q. D. *Fiction and the Reading Public*. London: Chatto & Windus, 1932.

Lovett, R. M. and H. S. Hughes. *The History of the Novel in England*. Boston: Houghton Mifflin, 1932.

Osborne, Charles. *Letters of Charles Dickens to the Baroness Burdett-Coutts*. New York: E. P. Dutton, 1932.

Sitwell, Sir Osbert. *Dickens*. London: Chatto & Windus, 1932. Reprint, New York: Haskell House, 1973.

Collins, Norman. "Charles Dickens." *The Facts of Fiction*, 155–65. New York: Dutton, 1933.

Darwin, Bernard. *Dickens*. London: Duckworth; New York: Macmillan, 1933. Reprint, New York: Haskell House, 1973.

Edgar, Pelham. *The Art of the Novel from 1700 to the Present Time*. New York: Macmillan, 1933. Reprint, New York: Russell & Russell, 1965.

Leacock, Stephen. *Charles Dickens: His Life and Work*. London: Davies, 1933; New York: Doubleday, Doran, 1934.

Livingston, Flora, ed. *Charles Dickens's Letters to Charles Lever*. Cambridge, MA: Harvard UP, 1933.

Cecil, Lord David. "Charles Dickens." *Early Victorian Novelists*, 27–63. London: Constable, 1934; Indianapolis, IN: Bobbs-Merrill, 1935. Reprinted in *Victorian Novelists: Essays in Revaluation*. Chicago: Chicago UP, 1958.

Kingsmill, Hugh [Hugh Kingsmill Lunn]. *The Sentimental Journey: A Life of Charles Dickens*. London: Wishart, 1934; New York: William Morrow, 1935.

Maurois, André. *Dickens, His Life and Work*. Translated by Hamish Miles. London: J. Lane, 1934.

Wagenknecht, Edward. "Review of Recent Dickens Literature." *Virginia Quarterly Review* 10 (July 1934): 455–59.

Cruse, Amy. "Dickens." *The Victorians and Their Reading*, 151–73. Boston: Houghton Mifflin, 1935. Issued as *Victorians and Their Books*. London: G. Allen and Unwin, 1935.

Wright, Thomas. *The Life of Charles Dickens*. London: H. Jenkins, 1935.

Baker, Ernest A. *The Age of Dickens and Thackeray*. Vol. 7 of *The History of the English Novel*. London: H. F. and G. Witherby, 1936.

Straus, Ralph. *Dickens: The Man and the Book*. London: Nelson, 1936.

Jackson, Thomas A. *Charles Dickens: The Progress of a Radical*. London: Lawrence & Wishart, 1937; New York: International, 1938. Reprint, New York: Haskell House, 1971.

Dexter, Walter, ed. *The Letters of Charles Dickens*. 3 vols. London: Nonesuch Press, 1938.

Powys, John C. "Dickens." *Enjoyment of Literature*, 321–41. New York: Simon and Schuster, 1938.

———. *Pleasures of Literature*, 321–41. London: Cassell, 1938.

Sitwell, Sir Osbert. "Dickens and the Modern Novel." *Trio: Dissertations on Some Aspects of National Genius*, 1–45. London: Macmillan, 1938.

Boas, Guy. "Charles Dickens To-day." *Blackwood's Magazine* 245 (March 1939): 314–26.

Christie, O. F. *Dickens and His Age*. London: H. Cranton, 1939. Reprint, New York: Phaeton P, 1974.

Noyes, Alfred. "The Value of Dickens, Here and Now." *Dickensian* 35 (June 1939): 189–93. Reprinted as "Dickens." *Pageant of Letters*. New York: Shead, 1940.

Pike, James S. "Dickens, Carlyle and Tennyson." *Atlantic Monthly* 164 (December 1939): 810–19.

Storey, Gladys. *Dickens and Daughter*. London: F. Muller, 1939.

1940s

Darwin, Bernard. "Return to Dickens." *St. Martin's Review* (January 1940): 30–33.

Evans, B. Ifor. *A Short History of English Literature*. Harmondsworth, Eng.: Penguin, 1940.

Orwell, George. "Charles Dickens." *Inside the Whale*, 9–85. London: Gollancz, 1940. Reprinted in *Critical Essays*. London: Secker & Warburg, 1946; *Dickens, Dali and Others*. New York: Reynal and Hitchcock, 1946; *A Collection of Essays*. New York: Doubleday, 1954; *Collected Essays*. London: Secker & Warburg, 1961.

Wilson, Edmund. "Dickens: The Two Scrooges." *New Republic* 102 (March 1940): 297–300, 339–42. Reprinted, revised and enlarged, in *The Wound and the Bow: Seven Studies in Literature*. Boston: Houghton, Mifflin, 1941. Reprinted in *Eight Essays*. New York: Doubleday, 1954.

Bevington, Merle Mowbray. *The Saturday Review 1855–1868: Representative Educated Opinion in Victorian England*. New York: Columbia UP, 1941. Reprinted New York: AMS Press, 1966.

House, Humphry. *The Dickens World*. London: Oxford UP, 1941.

Churchill, R. C. "Dickens, Drama and Tradition." *Scrutiny* 10 (April 1942): 358–75. Reprinted in *The Importance of Scrutiny*, edited by Eric Bentley. New York: Stewart, 1948.

Gerould, Gordon H. *The Patterns of English and American Fiction: A History.* Boston: Little, Brown, 1942.

Leavis, F. R. "An American Critic." *Scrutiny* 11 (Summer 1942): 72–73.

Stevenson, Lionel. "Dickens's Dark Novels, 1851–7." *Sewanee Review* 51 (Summer 1943): 398–409.

Wagenknecht, Edward. *Cavalcade of the English Novel*, 173–268. New York: Holt, Rinehart & Winston, 1943.

Pritchett, V. S. "*Edwin Drood.*" *New Statesman* 27 (February 1944): 143. Reprinted in *The Living Novel*. London: Chatto & Windus, 1946.

Rantavaara, Irma. *Dickens in the Light of English Criticism.* Helsinki, Finland. 1944.

Pope-Hennessy, Una. *Charles Dickens, 1812–70.* London: Chatto & Windus, 1945.

Pritchett, V. S. "The Rebel." *New Statesman and Nation* (16 February 1946): 124.

Warner, Rex. "On Reading Dickens." *The Cult of Power*, 21–38. London: J. Lane, 1946.

Leavis, F. R. "The Novel as Dramatic Poem (1): Hard Times." *Scrutiny* 14 (Spring 1947): 185–203. Reprinted as "*Hard Times:* An Analytic Note." *The Great Tradition*. London: Chatto & Windus, 1948.

Aldington, Richard. "The Underworld of Young Dickens." *Four English Portraits, 1801–1851*, 147–89. London: Evans, 1948.

Leavis, F. R. *The Great Tradition.* London: Chatto & Windus, 1948.

Maugham, W. Somerset. "Charles Dickens." *Atlantic Monthly* 182 (July 1948): 50–56. Reprinted as "Preface." *David Copperfield*. London: J. C. Winston, 1948. Reprinted as "Charles Dickens and *David Copperfield.*" *Ten Novels and Their Authors*. London: Heinemann, 1954.

Eisenstein, Sergei. *Film Form: Essays in Film Theory.* Translated by Jay Leyda. New York: Harcourt, Brace, 1949.

Pearson, Hesketh. *Dickens: His Character, Comedy, and Career.* New York: Harper, 1949.

1950s

Baker, Joseph E., ed. *The Reinterpretation of Victorian Literature.* Princeton, NJ: Princeton UP, 1950.

Boege, Fred W. "Point of View in Dickens." *PMLA* 65 (March 1950): 90–105.

Booth, Bradford. "Form and Technique in the Novel." In *The Reinterpretation of Victorian Literature*, edited by Joseph Baker, 67–96. Princeton, NJ: Princeton UP, 1950.

Chesterton, G. K. "A Tale of Two Cities." *The Common Man*. New York: Sheed & Ward, 1950.

Lindsay, Jack. *Charles Dickens: A Biographical and Critical Study*. London: Dakers; New York: Philosophical Society, 1950.

Rouse, H. Blair. "Charles Dickens and Henry James: Two Approaches to the Art of Fiction." *Nineteenth Century Fiction* 5 (September 1950): 151–57.

Van Ghent, Dorothy. "The Dickens World: A View From Todgers'." *Sewanee Review* 58 (Summer 1950): 419–38.

Wilson, Angus. "Dickens and the Divided Conscience." *The Month* 189 (May 1950): 349–60.

Church, Richard. *The Growth of the English Novel*. London: Methuen, 1951.

Davis, Robert G. "The Sense of the Real in English Fiction." *Comparative Literature* 3 (Summer 1951): 200–217.

Kettle, Arnold. *An Introduction to the English Novel*. 2 vols. London: Hutchinson House, 1951–53.

Symons, Julian. *Charles Dickens*. New York: Roy; London: Barker; Toronto: McClelland & Stewart, 1951.

Johnson, Edgar. *Charles Dickens: His Tragedy and Triumph*. 2 vols. New York: Simon and Schuster; Toronto: Musson, 1952. London: Gollancz, 1953.

———. "The Scope of Dickens." *Saturday Review of Literature* 35 (29 November 1952): 13–14, 44–48.

Nisbet, Ada B. *Dickens and Ellen Ternan*. Berkeley: U of California P, 1952.

Boege, Fred W. "Recent Criticism of Dickens." *Nineteenth Century Fiction* 8 (December 1953): 171–87.

Butt, John E. "Charles Dickens: His Tragedy and Triumph." *Nineteenth Century Fiction* 8 (September 1953): 151–53.

Grubb, Gerald G. "Dickens and Ternan." *Dickensian* 49 (June 1953): 121–29.

Johnson, Edgar. "Ada Nisbet's *Dickens and Ellen Ternan*." *Nineteenth Century Fiction* 7 (March 1953): 296–98.

———, ed. *Letters of Charles Dickens to Angela Burdett-Coutts 1841–1865*. London: Cape, 1953.

Leavis, Q. D. "A Note on Literary Indebtedness: Dickens, George Eliot, Henry James." *Hudson Review* 8 (Autumn 1955): 423–28.

Trilling, Lionel. "*Little Dorrit.*" *Kenyon Review* 15 (Autumn 1953): 577–90. Reprinted as "Introduction." *Little Dorrit.* New Oxford Illustrated Dickens. London: Oxford UP, 1953. Reprinted in *The Opposing Self: Nine Essays in Criticism.* New York: Viking, 1955.

Van Ghent, Dorothy. *The English Novel: Form and Function.* New York: Holt, 1953.

Allen, Walter. *The English Novel: A Short Critical History.* London: Phoenix House; New York: Dutton, 1954; Harmondsworth, Eng.: Penguin, 1958.

Fielding, Kenneth J. Review of Ada Nisbet, *Dickens and Ellen Ternan. Review of English Studies* n.s. 5 (July 1954): 322–25.

Friedman, Norman. "Versions of Form in Fiction — *Great Expectations* and *The Great Gatsby.*" *Accent* 14 (Autumn 1954): 246–64.

Tillotson, Kathleen. *Novels of the Eighteen-Forties.* London: Oxford UP, 1954.

Allen, Walter. *Six Great Novelists: Defoe, Fielding, Scott, Dickens, Stevenson, Conrad.* London: Hamish Hamilton, 1955.

Ford, George H. *Dickens and His Readers: Aspects of Novel Criticism Since 1836.* Princeton, NJ: Princeton UP, 1955. Reprint, New York: Norton, 1965.

House, Humphry. *All in Due Time.* London: Hart-Davis, 1955.

Johnson, Edgar. "Turning Tides." *Virginia Quarterly Review* 31 (Autumn 1955): 644–48.

———. "The Present State of Dickensian Studies." *Victorian Newsletter* 7 (April 1955): 4–9.

Manheim, Leonard F. "The Law as Father." *American Imago* 12 (Spring 1955): 17–23.

O'Connor, Frank [Michael O'Donovan]. "Dickens: The Intrusion of the Audience." *The Mirror in the Roadway: A Study in the Modern Novel,* 70–82. New York: Knopf, 1956.

Praz, Mario. "Charles Dickens." In *The Hero in Eclipse in Victorian Fiction,* translated by Angus Davidson, 140–88. London, New York: Oxford UP, 1956.

Trilling, Lionel. "The Dickens of Our Day." *A Gathering of Fugitives,* 41–48. Boston: Beacon P, 1956; London: Secker & Warburg, 1957.

Wilson, Angus. "Novels and Highbrows." *Encounter* 31 (April 1956): 75–77.

Butt, John E. and Kathleen Tillotson. *Dickens at Work.* London: Methuen, 1957.

Cockshut, A. O. J. "Sentimentality in Fiction." *Twentieth Century* 161 (April 1957): 354–64.

Coveney, Peter. "The Child in Dickens." *Poor Monkey: The Child in Literature*, 71–119. London: Rockliff, 1957. Reprinted in *The Image of Childhood*. Baltimore: Peregrine, 1967.

Johnson, Edgar. "Dickens and Shaw: Critics of Society." *Virginia Quarterly Review* 33 (Winter 1957): 66–79.

Pearson, Gabriel. "Dickens and his Readers." *Universities and Left Review* 1 (Spring 1957): 52–56.

Zabel, Morton D. *Craft and Character: Texts, Methods, and Vocation in Modern Fiction*. New York: Viking, 1957.

Bush, Douglas. "A Note on Dickens' Humor." In *From Jane Austen to Joseph Conrad*, edited by Robert C. Rathburn and Martin Steinmann, Jr., 82–91. Minneapolis: U of Minnesota P, 1958. Reprinted in *Engaged and Disengaged*. Cambridge, MA: Harvard UP, 1966.

Cox, C. B. "In Defense of Dickens." *Essays and Studies* 11 (1958): 86–100.

Fielding, Kenneth J. *Charles Dickens: A Critical Introduction*. London: Longmans, Green, 1958. 2nd ed. London: Longmans, Green, 1965.

Ford, George H. "Self-Help and the Helpless in *Bleak House*." In *From Jane Austen to Joseph Conrad*, edited by Robert C. Rathburn and Martin Steinmann, Jr., 92–105. Minneapolis: U of Minnesota P, 1958.

Johnson, Edgar. "In a World They Never Made." *Saturday Review* 41 (30 August 1958): 17–18.

Lane, Lauriat, Jr. "Dickens' Archetypal Jew." *PMLA* 73 (March 1958): 94–100.

Miller, J. Hillis. *Charles Dickens: The World of His Novels*. Cambridge, MA: Harvard UP, 1958. Reprint, Bloomington: Indiana UP, 1969; Cambridge, MA: Harvard UP, 1974.

Williams, Raymond. *Culture and Society 1780–1950*, 92–97. London: Chatto & Windus, 1958.

Engel, Monroe. *The Maturity of Dickens*. Cambridge, MA: Harvard UP; London: Oxford UP, 1959.

Manning, John. *Dickens on Education*. Toronto: U of Toronto P, 1959.

Monod, Sylvère. "J. Hillis Miller's *Charles Dickens: The World of His Novels*." *Nineteenth Century Fiction* 13 (March 1959): 360–63.

Spilka, Mark. "*David Copperfield* as Psychological Fiction." *Critical Quarterly* 1 (Winter 1959): 292–301.

Stang, Richard. "Bulwer and Dickens — The Attack on Realism." *The Theory of the Novel in England 1850–1870*, 19–29. New York: Columbia UP; London: Routledge & Kegan Paul, 1959.

Stevenson, Lionel. Review of J. Hillis Miller, *Charles Dickens: The World of His Novels. South Atlantic Quarterly* 58 (Summer 1959): 478–79.

Stone, Harry. "Dickens and Interior Monologue." *Philological Quarterly* 38 (January 1959): 52–65.

Wilson, Arthur H. "The Great Theme in Charles Dickens." *Susquehanna University Studies* 6 (April–June 1959): 422–57.

1960s

Fielding, Kenneth J., ed. *The Speeches of Charles Dickens.* Oxford: Clarendon P, 1960.

Moers, Ellen. "Dickens." *The Dandy: Brummel to Beerbohm,* 215–50. London: Secker & Warburg; New York: Viking, 1960.

Spilka, Mark. "Dickens's *Great Expectations:* A Kafkan Reading." In *Twelve Original Essays on Great English Novelists,* edited by Charles Shapiro, 103–24. Detroit, MI: Wayne State UP, 1960.

Stevenson, Lionel. *The English Novel: A Panorama.* Boston: Houghton Mifflin; London: Constable, 1960.

Tillotson, Kathleen. Review of J. Hillis Miller, *Charles Dickens: The World of His Novels. Modern Language Notes* 75 (May 1960): 439–42.

Wilson, Angus. "Charles Dickens: A Haunting." *Critical Quarterly* 2 (Summer 1960): 101–8.

Cockshut, A. O. J. *The Imagination of Charles Dickens.* London: Collins, 1961; New York: New York UP, 1962.

Collins, Philip A. W. "The Significance of Dickens's Periodicals." *Review of English Literature* 2 (July 1961): 55–64.

Ford, George H. and Lauriat Lane, Jr., eds. *The Dickens Critics.* Ithaca, NY: Cornell UP, 1961.

Marcus, Steven. "The Lame, The Halt and the Blind." *New Statesman and Nation* 62 (1 September 1961): 278–79.

Review of English Literature 2 (July 1961). London: Longmans, 1961. Special Dickens Issue.

Wilson, Angus. "The Heroes and Heroines of Dickens." *Review of English Literature* 2 (July 1961): 9–18. Reprinted in *Dickens and the Twentieth Century,* edited by John Gross and Gabriel Pearson. London: Routledge and Kegan Paul, 1962. Reprinted in *British Literature: Recent Revaluations,* edited by Shiv Kumar. New York: New York UP, 1968.

Collins, Philip A. W. *Dickens and Crime.* London: Macmillan; New York: St. Martin's Press, 1962.

Empson, William. "The Symbolism of Dickens." In *Dickens and the Twentieth Century,* edited by John Gross and Gabriel Pearson, 13–15. London: Routledge and Kegan Paul, 1962.

Ford, George et al. *Dickens Criticism: Past Present, and Future Directions.* Cambridge, MA: Charles Dickens Reference Center, 1962.

Gross, John and G. Pearson, eds. *Dickens and the Twentieth Century.* London: Routledge & Kegan Paul, 1962.

Leavis, F. R. "*Dombey and Son.*" *Sewanee Review* 70 (January-March 1962): 177–201.

Lukács, Georg. *The Historical Novel.* Translated by Hannah and Stanley Mitchell. London: Merlin Press, 1962.

Brown, Ivor. *Dickens in His Time.* London: Nelson, 1963.

Collins, Philip A. W. *Dickens and Education.* New York: St. Martin's; London: Macmillan, 1963.

Davis, Earle R. *The Flint and the Flame: The Artistry of Charles Dickens.* Columbia: U of Missouri P, 1963.

Fielding, Kenneth J. Review of John Gross and Gabriel Pearson, *Dickens and the Twentieth Century. Dickensian* 59 (January 1963): 45–47.

Spilka, Mark. *Dickens and Kafka: A Mutual Interpretation.* Bloomington: Indiana UP, 1963.

Johnson, Edgar, and Eleanor Johnson, eds. *Dickens Theatrical Reader.* Boston: Little, Brown, 1964.

Karl, Frederick R. *An Age of Fiction: The Nineteenth-Century British Novel.* New York: Noonday Press of Farrar, Straus & Giroux. 1964.

Nisbet, Ada. "Charles Dickens." In *Victorian Fiction: A Guide to Research,* edited by Lionel Stevenson, 43–55. New York: Modern Language Association, 1964.

Williams, Raymond. "Social Criticism in Dickens: Some Problems of Method and Approach." *Critical Quarterly* 6 (Autumn 1964): 214–27.

Fanger, Donald. *Dostoevsky and Romantic Realism: A Study of Dostoevsky in Relation to Balzac, Dickens, and Gogol.* Cambridge, MA: Harvard UP, 1965; reprint, Evanston, IL: Northwestern UP, 1998.

Fleissner, Robert F. *Dickens and Shakespeare: A Study in Histrionic Contrasts.* New York: Haskell House, 1965.

Garis, Robert E. *The Dickens Theatre: A Reassessment of the Novels.* Oxford: Clarendon P, 1965.

House, Madeline, and Graham Storey, eds. *The Letters of Charles Dickens.* 12 vols. Pilgrim Edition. Oxford: Clarendon Press, 1965–2002.

Marcus, Steven. *Dickens: From Pickwick to Dombey.* New York: Basic Books; London: Chatto & Windus, 1965.

McCabe, Bernard. "Taking Dickens Seriously." *Commonweal* 82 (May 1965): 244–47.

Muir, Edwin. "The Dark Felicities of Charles Dickens." *Essays on Literature and Society,* 206–14. Cambridge, MA: Harvard UP, 1965.

Peyrouton, Noel. "Milestones Along the Dover Road." *Dickens Studies* 1.1 (January 1965): 1.

Stoehr, Taylor. *Dickens: The Dreamer's Stance.* Ithaca, NY: Cornell UP, 1965.

Wagenknecht, Edward. *Dickens and the Scandal-Mongers: Essays in Defense and Criticism.* Norman: U of Oklahoma P, 1965.

Axton, W. F. *Circle of Fire: Dickens's Vision and Style and the Popular Victorian Theater.* Lexington: UP of Kentucky, 1966.

"The Clarendon Dickens: Aim to Present Text Readers Were Meant to See." *Bookseller* (8 October 1966): 1928–34.

Johnson, Edgar. "Dickens and the Spirit of the Age." *Bibliotheca Bucnellensis* 4 (1966): 1–13. Reprinted in *Victorian Essays. A Symposium,* edited by Warren D. Anderson and Thomas D. Clareson, 28–42. Kent, OH: Kent State UP, 1967.

Lodge, David. "The Rhetoric of *Hard Times.*" *Language of Fiction: Essays in Criticism and Verbal Analysis of the English Novel,* 145–63. New York: Columbia UP; London: Routledge & Kegan Paul, 1966.

Lucas, John. "Dickens and *Dombey and Son:* Past and Present Imperfect." In *Tradition and Tolerance in Nineteenth-Century Fiction: Critical Essays on Some English and American Novels,* edited by David Howard, John Good, and John Lucas, 99–140. London: Routledge & Kegan Paul, 1966; New York: Barnes & Noble, 1967.

Manheim, Leonard F. "Thanatos: The Death Instinct in Dickens's Later Novels." In *Hidden Patterns: Studies in Psychoanalytic Literary Criticism,* edited by Leonard and Eleanor Manheim, 113–31. New York: Macmillan, 1966.

Collins, Philip A. W. Review of Robert Fleissner, *Dickens and Shakespeare: A Study in Histrionic Contrasts. Nineteenth-Century Fiction* 21 (1967): 403.

Coolidge, Archibald C., Jr. *Charles Dickens as a Serial Novelist.* Ames: Iowa State UP, 1967.

Dabney, Ross H. *Love and Property in the Novels of Dickens.* London: Chatto & Windus; Berkeley: U of California P, 1967.

Fielding, Kenneth J. "Dickens as a Serial Novelist." *Dickensian* 63 (September 1967): 156–57.

Hibbert, Christopher. *The Making of Charles Dickens*. London: Longmans, Green; New York: Harper & Row, 1967.

Jarmuth, Sylvia L. *Dickens's Use of Women in His Novels*. New York: Excelsior, 1967.

Johnson, Edgar. "Dickens and the Spirit of the Age." In *Victorian Essays: A Symposium*, edited by Warren D. Anderson and Thomas D. Clareson, 28–42. Kent, OH: Kent State UP, 1967.

Price, Martin, ed. *Dickens: A Collection of Critical Essays*. Englewood Cliffs, NJ: Prentice-Hall, 1967.

Chapman, Raymond. *The Victorian Debate: English Literature and Society 1832–1901*. London: Weidenfeld & Nicolson; New York: Basic Books, 1968.

Donovan, Frank. *Dickens and Youth*. New York: Dodd, Mead, 1968.

Dyson, A. E., ed. *Dickens: Modern Judgments*. Toronto: Macmillan, 1968.

Fido, Martin. *Charles Dickens*. London: Routledge & Kegan Paul, 1968.

Fielding, Kenneth J. "Dickens and the Past: The Novelist of Memory." In *Experience in the Novel*, edited by Roy H. Pearce, 107–31. New York: Columbia UP, 1968.

Frye, Northrop. "Dickens and the Comedy of Humours." In *Experience in the Novel*, edited by Roy H. Pearce, 49–81. New York: Columbia UP, 1968.

Hardy, Barbara. *Dickens: The Later Novels*. Writers and Their Work 205. London: Longmans, Green, 1968.

Miller, J. Hillis. *The Form of Victorian Fiction: Thackeray, Dickens, Trollope, George Eliot, Meredith, and Hardy*. Notre Dame, IN: U of Notre Dame P, 1968.

———. "Three Problems of Fictional Form: First-Person Narration in *David Copperfield* and *Huckleberry Finn*." In *Experience in the Novel*, edited by Roy H. Pearce, 21–48. New York: Columbia UP, 1968.

Monod, Sylvère. *Dickens the Novelist*. With an Introduction by Edward Wagenknecht. Norman: U of Oklahoma P, 1968.

Smith, Grahame. *Dickens, Money, and Society*. Berkeley: U of California P, 1968.

Stone, Harry, ed. *Uncollected Writings of Charles Dickens: Household Words 1850–1859*. 2 vols. Bloomington: Indiana UP, 1968; London: Allen Lane, Penguin Press, 1969.

Sussman, Herbert L. "The Industrial Novel and the Machine: Charles Dickens." *Victorians and the Machine: The Literary Response to Technology*, 41–76. Cambridge, MA: Harvard UP, 1968.

Tillotson, Kathleen. "New Readings in *Dombey and Son*." In *Imagined Worlds: Essays on Some English Novels and Novelists in Honour of John Butt*, edited by Maynard Mack and Ian Gregor, 173–82. London: Methuen, 1968.

Collins, Philip A. W. "Charles Dickens 1812–70." In *The New Cambridge Bibliography of English Literature*. Vol. 3, edited by George Watson, 779–850. Cambridge: Cambridge UP, 1969.

Gold, Joseph. "Charles Dickens and Today's Reader." *English Journal* 58 (February 1969): 205–11.

Johnson, E. D. H. *Charles Dickens: An Introduction to the Reading of His Novels*. New York: Random House, 1969.

Miyoshi, Masao. *The Divided Self: A Perspective on the Literature of the Victorians*, 265–78. New York: New York UP, 1969.

Studies in the Novel 1.2 (Summer 1969). Charles Dickens Special Number.

Tomlin, Eric W. F., ed. *Charles Dickens 1812–1870: A Centenary Volume*. London: Weidenfeld & Nicolson, 1969.

Vann, J. Don. "A Checklist of Dickens Criticism, 1963–67." *Studies in the Novel* 1 (Summer 1969): 255–78.

Wing, George D. *Dickens*. Writers and Critics Series. Edinburgh: Oliver and Boyd, 1969.

1970s

Daleski, H. M. *Dickens and the Art of Analogy*. New York: Schocken, 1970.

Dyson, A. E. *The Inimitable Dickens: A Reading of the Novels*. London: Macmillan, 1970.

Fido, Martin. *Charles Dickens: An Authentic Account of His Life and Times*. London: Hamlyn, 1970.

Hardy, Barbara. "Dickens and the Passions." *Nineteenth-Century Fiction* 24 (March 1970): 449–66.

———. *The Moral Art of Dickens*. London: Athlone, 1970.

Leavis, F. R. and Q. D. Leavis. *Dickens The Novelist*. New York: Pantheon, 1970.

Lucas, John. *The Melancholy Man: A Study of Dickens's Novels*. London: Methuen, 1970.

Millett, Kate. *Sexual Politics*. Garden City, NY: Doubleday, 1970.

Partlow, Robert B. Jr., ed. *Dickens the Craftsman: Strategies of Presentation*. Carbondale and Edwardsville: Southern Illinois UP, 1970.

———. "Preface." *Dickens Studies Annual*, ix–x. Vol. 1. Carbondale and Edwardsville: Southern Illinois UP, 1970.

Partlow, Robert B. Jr., and Robert Patten. "To Our Readers." *Dickens Studies Newsletter* 1.1 (March 1970): 1.

Slater, Michael, ed. *Dickens 1970.* New York: Stein & Day, 1970.

Sucksmith, Harvey Peter. *The Narrative Art of Charles Dickens: The Rhetoric of Sympathy and Irony in His Novels.* London: Oxford UP, 1970.

Wall, Stephen, ed. *Charles Dickens.* Penguin Critical Anthologies. Harmondsworth, Eng.: Penguin, 1970.

Williams, Raymond. *The English Novel: From Dickens to Lawrence.* New York and London: Oxford UP, 1970.

Wilson, Angus. *The World of Charles Dickens.* London: Secker & Warburg, 1970.

Collins, Philip A. W., ed. *Dickens: The Critical Heritage.* London: Routledge & Kegan Paul, 1971.

Gold, Joseph. *The Stature of Dickens: A Centenary Bibliography.* Toronto: U of Toronto P, 1971.

Gomme, A. H. *Dickens.* Literature in Perspective. London: Evans, 1971.

Kincaid, James R. *Dickens and the Rhetoric of Laughter.* Oxford: Oxford UP, 1971.

Manning, Sylvia Bank. *Dickens as Satirist.* London: Yale UP, 1971.

Miller, J. Hillis, and David Borowitz. *Charles Dickens and George Cruikshank.* Los Angeles: William Clark Memorial Library, 1971.

Nisbet, Ada, and Blake Nevius, eds. *Dickens Centennial Essays.* Berkeley: U of California P, 1971.

Watt, Ian, ed. *The Victorian Novel: Modern Essays in Criticism.* Oxford: Oxford UP, 1971.

Welsh, Alexander. *The City of Dickens.* Oxford: Oxford UP, 1971.

Gold, Joseph. *Charles Dickens: Radical Moralist.* London: Oxford UP, 1972.

Goldberg, Michael. *Carlyle and Dickens.* Athens: U of Georgia P, 1972.

Hewitt, Douglas. *The Approach to Fiction: Good and Bad Novels.* London: Longmans, 1972.

Hobsbaum, Philip. *A Reader's Guide to Charles Dickens.* New York: Farrar, Straus, & Giroux, 1972.

Hornback, Bert G. *"Noah's Arkitecture": A Study of Dickens' Mythology.* Athens: Ohio UP, 1972.

Kotzin, Michael C. *Dickens and the Fairy Tale.* Bowling Green, OH: Bowling Green UP, 1972.

Oddie, William. *Dickens and Carlyle.* London: Centenary, 1972.

Amalric, Jean-Claude, ed. *Studies in the Later Dickens*. Montpellier, France: Université Paul Valery, 1973.

Carey, John. *The Violent Effigy*. London: Faber and Faber, 1973. Rev. ed. London: Faber, 1991.

Lary, N. M. *Dostoevsky and Dickens: A Study of Literary Influence*. London: Routledge & Kegan Paul, 1973.

Lohrli, Anne. *Household Words: A Weekly Journal 1850–1859*. Toronto: U of Toronto P, 1973.

Williams, Raymond. *The Country and the City*. New York and London: Oxford UP, 1973.

Basch, Françoise. *Relative Creatures: Victorian Women in Society and the Novel, 1837–67*. Translated by Anthony Rudolf. London: Lane, 1974.

Buckley, Jerome. "Dickens, David and Pip." *Season of Youth: The Bildungsroman from Dickens to Golding*, 28–62. Cambridge, MA: Harvard UP, 1974.

Stewart, Garrett. *Dickens and the Trials of Imagination*. Cambridge, MA: Harvard UP, 1974.

Buckley, Jerome H. *The Worlds of Victorian Fiction*. Cambridge, MA: Harvard UP, 1975.

Churchill, R. C., ed. *A Bibliography of Dickensian Criticism, 1836–1975*. New York: Garland, 1975.

Collins, Philip A. W., ed. *Charles Dickens: The Public Readings*. Oxford: Clarendon, 1975.

Cunningham, Valentine. *Everywhere Spoken Against: Dissent in the Victorian Novel*. Oxford: Oxford UP, 1975.

Friedman, Norman. *Form and Meaning in Fiction*. Athens: U of Georgia P, 1975.

Harbage, Alfred B. *A Kind of Power: The Shakespeare-Dickens Analogy*. Philadelphia: American Philosophical Society, 1975.

Kaplan, Fred. *Dickens and Mesmerism: "The Hidden Springs of Fiction."* Princeton, NJ: Princeton UP, 1975.

DeVries, Duane. *Dickens's Apprentice Years: The Making of a Novelist*. Totowa, NJ: Barnes & Noble, 1976.

Eagleton, Terry. "Charles Dickens." *Criticism and Ideology: A Study in Marxist Literary Theory*, 125–30. London: NLB Press. New edition London: Verso, 2006.

Gilmour, Robin. Review of Garrett Stewart, *Dickens and the Trials of Imagination*. *Dickensian* 72.1 (January 1976): 39–40.

Guerard, Albert J. *The Triumph of the Novel: Dickens, Dostoevsky, Faulkner*. New York: Oxford UP, 1976.

Sutherland, John L. *Victorian Novelists and Publishers.* Chicago: U of Chicago P; London: Athlone, 1976.

Thurley, Geoffrey. *The Dickens Myth: Its Genesis and Structure.* New York: St. Martin's, 1976.

Newsom, Robert. *Dickens on the Romantic Side of Familiar Things:* Bleak House *and the Novel Tradition.* New York: Columbia UP, 1977.

Patten, Robert. "A Surprising Transformation: Dickens and the Hearth." In *Nature and the Victorian Imagination,* edited by U. C. Knoepflmacher and G. B. Tennyson, 153–70. Berkeley: U of California P, 1977.

Spence, Gordon. *Charles Dickens as a Familiar Essayist.* Salzburg: Institut for Englische Sprache und Literatur, 1977.

Westburg, Barry. *The Confessional Fictions of Charles Dickens.* Dekalb: Northern Illinois UP, 1977.

Collins, Philip A. W. "Charles Dickens." In *Victorian Fiction: A Second Guide to Research,* edited by George Ford, 34–113. New York: Modern Language Association, 1978.

Patten, Robert. *Charles Dickens and His Publishers.* Oxford: Clarendon P, 1978.

Pope, Norris. *Dickens and Charity.* New York: Columbia UP, 1978.

Romano, John. *Dickens and Reality.* New York: Columbia UP, 1978.

Slater, Michael, ed. *Dickens on America and the Americans.* Austin and London: U of Texas P, 1978.

Steig, Michael. *Dickens and Phiz.* Bloomington: Indiana UP, 1978.

Worth, George J. *Dickensian Melodrama: A Reading of the Novels.* Lawrence: U of Kansas P, 1978.

Arac, Jonathan. *Commissioned Spirits: The Shaping of Social Motion in Dickens, Carlyle, Melville, and Hawthorne.* New Brunswick, NJ: Rutgers UP, 1979.

Caserio, Robert. *Plot, Story, and the Novel.* Princeton, NJ: Princeton UP, 1979.

Fenstermaker, John J. *Charles Dickens, 1940–1975: An Analytical Subject Index to Periodical Criticism of the Novels and Christmas Books.* Boston: G. K. Hall, 1979.

Horton, Susan. *Interpreting Interpreting: Interpreting Dickens' Dombey.* Baltimore, MD: Johns Hopkins UP, 1979.

Kurrik, Maire Jaanus. *Literature and Negation.* New York: Columbia UP, 1979.

Mackenzie, Norman and Jeanne MacKenzie. *Dickens: A Life.* Oxford: Oxford UP, 1979.

Schwarzbach, F. S. *Dickens and the City.* London: Athlone, 1979.

Stone, Harry. *Dickens and the Invisible World: Fairy Tales, Fantasy, and Novel Making*. Bloomington: Indiana UP, 1979.

Wheeler, Michael. *The Art of Allusion in Victorian Fiction*. London: Macmillan, 1979.

1980s

Cohen, Jane. *Charles Dickens and His Original Illustrators*. Columbus: Ohio State UP, 1980.

Gallagher, Catherine. "*Hard Times* and *North and South*: The Family and Society in Two Industrial Novels." *Arizona Quarterly* 36.1 (1980): 70–95.

Garrett, Peter. *The Victorian Multiplot Novel: Studies in Dialogical Form*, 23–51. New Haven, CT and London: Yale UP, 1980.

Nabokov, Vladimir. *Lectures on Literature*. Edited by Fredson Bowers, 62–124. New York: Harcourt, Brace, Jovanovich, 1980.

Polhemus, Robert M. *Comic Faith: The Great Tradition from Austen to Joyce*. Chicago and London: U of Chicago P, 1980.

Sadoff, Diane. "Storytelling and the Figure of the Father." *PMLA* 95 (March 1980): 234–45.

Sanders, Andrew. Review of Norman and Jeanne MacKenzie, *Dickens: A Life*. *Dickensian* 76.1 (Spring 1980): 44–45.

Stone, Donald D. *The Romantic Impulse in Victorian Fiction*. Cambridge, MA and London: Harvard UP, 1980.

Bernard, Catherine A. "Dickens and Victorian Dream Theory." In *Victorian Science and Victorian Values: Literary Perspectives*, edited by James Paradis and Thomas Postlewait, 197–216. New York: New York Academy of Sciences, Vol. 360, 1981. Reprint, New Brunswick, NJ: Rutgers UP, 1985.

Carlisle, Janice. *The Sense of an Audience: Dickens, Thackeray, and George Eliot at Mid-Century*. Athens: U of Georgia P, 1981.

Collins, Philip A. W., ed. *Dickens: Interviews and Recollections*. 2 vols. Totowa, NJ: Barnes & Noble, 1981.

Dahl, Christopher C. "Fitzjames Stephen, Charles Dickens, and Double Reviewing." *Victorian Periodicals Review* 14.2 (Summer 1981): 51–58.

David, Deirdre. *Fictions of Resolution in Three Victorian Novels*. London: Macmillan, 1981.

Gilmour, Robin. *The Idea of the Gentleman in the Victorian Novel*. London: Allen & Unwin, 1981.

Hanzo, Thomas A. "Paternity and the Subject in *Bleak House*." In *The Fictional Father: Lacanian Readings of the Text*, edited by Robert Con Davis, 27–47. Amherst: U of Massachusetts P, 1981.

Hill, Nancy K. *A Reformer's Art: Dickens's Picturesque and Grotesque Imagery*. Athens: Ohio UP, 1981.

Hornback, Bert G. *"The Hero of My Life": Essays on Dickens*. Athens: Ohio UP, 1981.

Horton, Susan. *The Reader in the Dickens World*. Pittsburgh, PA: U of Pittsburgh P, 1981.

Kaplan, Fred, ed. *Charles Dickens' Book of Memoranda*. New York: New York Public Library, 1981.

Kauffman, Linda. "The Letter and the Spirit in *Hard Times* and *The Sound and the Fury*." *Mississippi Quarterly: The Journal of Southern Culture* 34.3 (Summer 1981): 299–313.

Klein, Michael, and Gillian Parker, eds. *The English Novel and the Movies*. New York: Ungar; 1981.

Klieneberger, H. R. *The Novel in England and Germany: A Comparative Study*. London: Wolff, 1981.

Kucich, John. *Excess and Restraint in the Novels of Charles Dickens*. Athens: U of Georgia P, 1981.

Lambert, Mark. *Dickens and the Suspended Quotation*. New Haven, CT and London: Yale UP, 1981.

McMaster, Rowland, and Juliet McMaster. "Dickens and the Horrific." *The Novel from Sterne to James: Essays on the Relation of Literature to Life*, 37–53. Totowa, NJ: Barnes & Noble, 1981.

Miller, D. A. "The Novel and the Police." *Glyph: Johns Hopkins Textual Studies*. Vol. 8., 127–47. Baltimore, MD: Johns Hopkins UP, 1981.

Moseley, Merritt. "Faulkner's Dickensian Humor in *The Sound and the Fury*." *Notes on Mississippi Writers* 13.1 (1981): 7–13.

Nelson, Harland S. *Charles Dickens*. Boston: Twayne, 1981.

Newman, S. J. *Dickens at Play*. New York: St. Martin's, 1981.

Newsom, Robert. "Recent Dickens Studies." *Dickens Studies Annual* 9 (1981): 265–86.

Walder, Dennis. *Dickens and Religion*. London: Allen and Unwin, 1981.

Webb, Igor. *From Custom to Capital: The English Novel and the Industrial Revolution*. Ithaca NY: Cornell UP, 1981.

Amalric, Jean-Claude. "Shaw as a Critic of Dickens." *The Independent Shavian* 19.3 (1982): 63–68.

Armstrong, Nancy. "Dickens Between Two Disciplines: A Problem for Theories of Reading." *Semiotica* 38 (1982): 243–75.

Barickman, Richard. *Corrupt Relations: Dickens, Thackeray, Trollope, Collins, and the Victorian Sexual System.* New York: Columbia UP, 1982.

Brown, James M. *Dickens: Novelist in the Market Place.* London: Macmillan, 1982.

Cohn, Alan M. and K. K. Collins. *The Cumulated Dickens Checklist 1970–79.* Troy, NY: Whitson, 1982.

Johnson, Wendell Stacy, ed. *Charles Dickens: New Perspectives.* Englewood Cliffs, NJ: Prentice-Hall, 1982.

LaRocque, Geraldine E. "*A Tale of Two Cities* and *Absalom! Absalom.*" *Mississippi Quarterly: The Journal of Southern Culture* 35.3 (Summer 1982): 301–4.

Lerner, Laurence. *The Literary Imagination: Essays on Literature and Society.* Totowa, NJ: Barnes & Noble, 1982.

Qualls, Barry V. *The Secular Pilgrims of Victorian Fiction: The Novel as Book of Life.* Cambridge: Cambridge UP, 1982.

Sadoff, Dianne F. *Monsters of Affection: Dickens, Eliot, and Brontë on Fatherhood.* Baltimore, MD: Johns Hopkins UP, 1982.

Sanders, Andrew. *Charles Dickens: Resurrectionist.* London: Macmillan, 1982.

Simpson, David. *Fetishism and Imagination: Dickens, Melville, Conrad.* Baltimore, MD: Johns Hopkins UP, 1982.

Thomas, Deborah. *Dickens and the Short Story.* Philadelphia: U of Pennsylvania P, 1982.

Docherty, Thomas. *Reading (Absent) Character: Towards a Theory of Characterization in Fiction.* Oxford: Clarendon P, 1983.

Giddings, Robert, ed. *The Changing World of Charles Dickens.* Totowa, NJ: Barnes & Noble, 1983.

Hardy, Barbara. *Charles Dickens, The Writer and His Work.* Windsor, England: Profile Books, 1983.

Miller, D. A. "Discipline in Different Voices: Bureaucracy, Police, Family, and *Bleak House.*" *Representations* 1 (February 1983): 58–79.

Senf, Carol A. "*Bleak House:* Dickens, Esther, and the Androgynous Mind." *Victorian Newsletter* 64 (Fall 1983): 21–27.

Slater, Michael. *Dickens and Women.* London: Dent, 1983.

Brooks, Chris. *Signs for the Times: Symbolic Realism in the Mid-Victorian World.* London: Allen & Unwin, 1984.

Chase, Karen. *Eros and Psyche: The Representation of Personality in Charlotte Brontë, Charles Dickens, and George Eliot.* New York: Methuen, 1984.

Cox, Don Richard, ed. *Sexuality and Victorian Literature.* Knoxville: U of Tennessee P, 1984.

Feltes, N. N. "The Moment of *Pickwick,* or the Production of a Commodity Text." *Literature and History* 10 (Autumn 1984): 203–17.

Frank, Lawrence. *Charles Dickens and the Romantic Self.* Lincoln: U of Nebraska P, 1984.

Grant, Allan. *A Preface to Dickens.* London and New York: Longman, 1984.

Higbie, Robert. *Character and Structure in the English Novel.* Gainesville: UP of Florida, 1984.

Hollington, Michael. *Dickens and the Grotesque.* London: Helm, 1984.

Langland, Elizabeth. *Society in the Novel.* Chapel Hill: U of North Carolina P, 1984.

Moss, Sidney P. *Charles Dickens's Quarrel With America.* Troy, NY: Whitson, 1984.

Page, Norman. *A Dickens Companion.* New York: Schocken, 1984.

Paroissien, David. "Editorial: Occasion, Chance, and Change." *Dickens Quarterly* 1.1 (March 1984): 1.

Stewart, Garrett. *Death Sentences: Styles of Dying in British Fiction.* Cambridge, MA: Harvard UP, 1984.

———. "Signing Off: Dickens and Thackeray, Woolf and Beckett." In *Philosophical Approaches to Literature: New Essays on Nineteenth and Twentieth-Century Texts,* edited by William E. Cain, 117–39. Lewisburg: Bucknell UP, 1984.

Blain, Virginia. "Double Vision and the Double Standard in *Bleak House*: A Feminist Perspective." *Literature and History* 11 (Spring 1985): 31–46.

Chesterton Review: The Journal of the G. K. Chesterton Institute 11.4 (November 1985). Special Issue on Dickens and Chesterton.

Connor, Steven. *Charles Dickens.* Oxford: Blackwell, 1985.

Gallagher, Catherine. *The Industrial Reformation of English Fiction: Social Discourse and Narrative Form, 1832–1867.* Chicago: U of Chicago P, 1985.

Goldberg, Michael. "Gigantic Philistines." *Lectures on Carlyle and His Era.* Santa Cruz: University Library, U of California P, 1985.

Hardy, Barbara. *Forms of Feeling in Victorian Fiction.* London: Owen, 1985.

Kucich, John. "Dickens's Fantastic Rhetoric: Semantics of Reality and Unreality in *Our Mutual Friend.*" *Dickens Studies Annual* 14 (1985): 167–90.

Larson, Janet L. *Dickens and the Broken Scripture.* Athens: U of Georgia P, 1985.

Laurence, Dan H. and Martin Quinn, eds. *Shaw on Dickens*. New York: Frederick Ungar, 1985.

Magnet, Myron. *Dickens and the Social Order*. Philadelphia: U of Pennsylvania P, 1985.

Paroissien, David. *Selected Letters of Charles Dickens*. Boston: Twayne, 1985.

Schlicke, Paul. *Dickens and Popular Entertainment*. London: Allen & Unwin, 1985.

Sedgwick, Eve Kosofsky. "Up the Postern Stair: *Edwin Drood* and the Homophobia of Empire." *Between Men: English Literature and Male Homosocial Desire*, 180–200. New York: Columbia UP, 1985.

Vargish, Thomas. *The Providential Aesthetic in Victorian Fiction*. Charlottesville: UP of Virginia, 1985.

Zwinger, Lynda. "The Fear of the Father: Dombey and Daughter." *Nineteenth-Century Fiction* 39.4 (March 1985): 420–40.

Cohan, Steve. *Violation and Repair in the English Novel: The Paradigm of Experience from Richardson to Woolf*. Detroit, MI: Wayne State UP, 1986.

Daldry, Graham. *Charles Dickens and the Form of the Novel: Fiction and Narrative in Dickens's Work*. Totowa, NJ: Barnes & Noble, 1986.

Derus, David L. "Gissing and Chesterton as Critics of Dickens." *The Chesterton Review: The Journal of the G. K. Chesterton Institute* 12.1 (February 1986): 71–81.

Eldredge, Patricia R. "The Lost Self of Esther Summerson: A Horneyean Interpretation of *Bleak House*." *Literary Review* 24.2 (Winter 1981): 252–78. Reprinted in *Third Force Psychology and the Study of Literature*, edited by Bernard J. Paris, 136–55. Rutherford, NJ: Fairleigh Dickinson UP, 1986.

Flint, Kate. *Dickens*. London: Harvester, 1986.

Hara, Eiichi. "Stories Present and Absent in *Great Expectations*." *ELH* 53.3 (Fall 1986): 593–614.

Hawthorn, Jeremy, ed. *The Nineteenth-Century British Novel*. London: Edward Arnold, 1986.

Hough, Graham. "Language and Reality in *Bleak House*." In *Realism in European Literature*, edited by Nicholas Boyle and Martin Swales, 50–67. Cambridge: Cambridge UP, 1986.

Lukacher, Ned. "Dialectical Images: Benjamin/Dickens/Freud." *Primal Scene: Literature, Philosophy, Psychoanalysis*, 275–336. Ithaca, NY and London: Cornell UP, 1986.

McGowan, John P. *Representation and Revelation: Victorian Realism from Carlyle to Yeats*. Columbia: U of Missouri P, 1986.

Myers, Margaret. "The Lost Self: Gender in *David Copperfield.*" In *Gender Studies: New Directions in Feminist Criticism,* edited by Judith Spector, 120–32. Bowling Green, OH: Popular P, 1986.

Raina, Badri. *Dickens and the Dialectic of Growth.* Madison: U of Wisconsin P, 1986.

Sell, Roger D. "Dickens and the New Historicism." In *The Nineteenth-Century British Novel,* edited by Jeremy Hawthorn, 63–80. London: Edward Arnold, 1986.

Tambling, Jeremy. "Prison-bound: Dickens and Foucault." *Essays in Criticism* 36 (January 1986): 11–31.

Baldick, Chris. "The Galvanic World: Carlyle and the Dickens Monster." In *Frankenstein's Shadow: Myth, Monstrosity and Nineteenth-Century Writing,* 103–20. Oxford and New York: Oxford UP, 1987.

Boheemen, Christine van. *The Novel as Family Romance: Language, Gender, and Authority from Fielding to Joyce.* Ithaca, NY: Cornell UP, 1987.

Bolton, H. Philip. *Dickens Dramatized.* New York: G. K. Hall, 1987.

Brown, Carolyn. "'Great Expectations': Masculinity and Modernity." *Essays and Studies* 40 (1987): 60–74.

Collins, Philip A. W. "Dickens and the City." In *Visions of the Modern City: Essays in History, Art, and Literature,* edited by William Sharpe and Leonard Wallock, 101–21. Baltimore, MD and London: Johns Hopkins UP, 1987.

Craig, David M. "The Interplay of City and Self in *Oliver Twist, David Copperfield* and *Great Expectations.*" *Dickens Studies Annual* 16 (1987): 17–38.

Feltes, N. N. "Realism, Consensus, and 'Exclusion Itself': Interpellating the Victorian Bourgeois." *Textual Practice* 1.3 (Winter 1987): 297–308.

Hawthorn, Jeremy. *Bleak House: An Introduction to the Variety of Criticism.* London: Macmillan, 1987.

Kaplan, Fred. *Sacred Tears: Sentimentality in Victorian Literature.* Princeton, NJ: Princeton UP, 1987.

Kucich, John. *Repression in Victorian Fiction: Charlotte Brontë, George Eliot, and Charles Dickens.* Berkeley: U of California P, 1987.

McMaster, Juliet. *Dickens the Designer.* Totowa, NJ: Barnes & Noble, 1987.

Meckier, Jerome. *Hidden Rivalries in Victorian Fiction.* Lexington: UP of Kentucky, 1987.

Morris, Christopher D. "The Bad Faith of Pip's Bad Faith: Deconstructing *Great Expectations.*" *ELH* 54.4 (Winter 1987): 941–55.

Stone, Harry. *Dickens's Working Notes for his Novels.* Chicago: U of Chicago P, 1987.

Watkins, Gwen. *Dickens in Search of Himself: Recurrent Themes and Characters in the Work of Charles Dickens.* London: Macmillan, 1987.

Welsh, Alexander. *From Copyright to Copperfield.* Cambridge, MA and London: Harvard UP, 1987.

Allen, Michael. *Charles Dickens's Childhood.* London: Macmillan, 1988.

Bentley, Nicholas, Michael Slater, and Nina Burgis. *The Dickens Index.* Oxford: Oxford UP, 1988.

Bodenheimer, Rosemarie. *The Politics of Story in Victorian Social Fiction.* Ithaca, NY and London: Cornell UP, 1988.

Kaplan, Fred. *Dickens: A Biography.* London: Hodder & Stoughton, 1988. Reprint, Baltimore, MD: Johns Hopkins UP, 1998.

Levine, George. "*Little Dorrit* and Three Kinds of Science." *Darwin and the Novelists: Patterns of Science in Victorian Fiction,* 153–76. Cambridge, MA and London: Harvard UP, 1988.

Miller, D. A. *The Novel and the Police.* Berkeley: U of California P, 1988.

Page, Norman. *A Dickens Chronology.* Boston: G. K. Hall, 1988.

Poovey, Mary. "The Man-of-Letters Hero: *David Copperfield* and the Professional Writer." *Uneven Developments: The Ideological Work of Gender in Mid-Victorian England,* 89–125. Chicago: U of Chicago P, 1988.

Shattock, Joanne, ed. *Dickens and Other Victorians: Essays in Honour of Philip Collins.* London: Macmillan, 1988.

Trotter, David. *Circulation: Defoe, Dickens, and the Economies of the Novel.* New York: St. Martin's, 1988.

Childers, Joseph W. "History, Totality, Opposition: The New Historicism and *Little Dorrit.*" *Dickens Quarterly* 6 (September 1989): 150–57.

Chittick, Kathryn. *The Critical Reception of Charles Dickens 1833–1841.* New York: Garland, 1989.

Eigner, Edwin. *The Dickens Pantomime.* Berkeley: U of California P, 1989.

Lettis, Richard. *The Dickens Aesthetic.* New York: AMS Press, 1989.

MacKay, Carol Hanberry, ed. *Dramatic Dickens.* London: Macmillan, 1989.

Michie, Helena. "'Who is this in Pain?': Scarring, Disfigurement, and Female Identity in *Bleak House* and *Our Mutual Friend.*" *Novel* 22 (1989): 199–212.

Newcomb, Mildred. *The Imagined World of Charles Dickens.* Columbus: Ohio State UP, 1989.

1990s

Ackroyd, Peter. *Dickens,* London: Minerva, 1990.

Armstrong, Frances. *Dickens and the Concept of Home.* Ann Arbor, MI: UMI Research P, 1990.

Chittick, Kathryn. *Dickens and the 1830s.* Cambridge: Cambridge UP, 1990.

Davis, Paul. *The Lives and Times of Ebenezer Scrooge.* New Haven, CT: Yale UP, 1990.

Hardy, Barbara. "The Talkative Woman in Shakespeare, Dickens, and George Eliot." In *Problems for Feminist Criticism,* edited by Sally Minogue, 15–45. London: Routledge, 1990.

Hopkins, Sandra. "'Wooman, Lovely Wooman': Four Dickens Heroines and the Critics." In *Problems for Feminist Criticism,* edited by Sally Minogue, 109–44. London: Routledge, 1990.

Lettis, Richard. *Dickens on Literature: A Continuing Study of His Aesthetic.* New York: AMS Press, 1990.

Levit, Fred. *A Dickens Glossary.* New York: Garland, 1990.

Meckier, Jerome. *Innocent Abroad: Charles Dickens's American Engagements.* Lexington: UP of Kentucky, 1990.

Minogue, Sally, ed. *Problems for Feminist Criticism.* London: Routledge, 1990.

Ryals, Clyde de L. *A World of Possibilities: Romantic Irony in Victorian Literature.* Columbus: Ohio State UP, 1990.

Alexander, Doris. *Creating Characters with Charles Dickens.* University Park: Penn State UP, 1991.

Cummings, Katherine. *Telling Tales: The Hysteric's Seduction in Fiction and Theory.* Stanford, CA: Stanford UP, 1991.

Jaffe, Audrey. *Vanishing Points: Dickens, Narrative, and the Subject of Omniscience.* Berkeley: U of California P, 1991.

Morris, Pam. *Dickens's Class Consciousness: A Marginal View.* London: Macmillan, 1991.

Perera, Suvendrini. *Reaches of Empire: The English Novel from Edgewater to Dickens.* New York: Columbia UP, 1991.

Zwinger, Lynda. *Daughters, Fathers and the Novel: The Sentimental Romance of Heterosexuality.* Madison and London: U of Wisconsin P, 1991.

David, Deirdre. "Children of Empire: Victorian Imperialism and Sexual Politics in Dickens and Kipling." In *Gender and Discourse in Victorian Literature and Art,* edited by Antony H. Harrison and Beverly Taylor, 124–42. DeKalb: Northern Illinois UP, 1992.

Duncan, Ian. *Modern Romance and Transformations of the Novel: The Gothic, Scott, and Dickens*. Cambridge; New York: Cambridge UP, 1992.

Golden, Morris. *Dickens Imagining Himself: Six Encounters with a Changing World*. Lanham, MD: UP of America, 1992.

Ingham, Patricia. *Dickens, Women & Language*. London: Harvester, 1992.

Lucas, John. *Charles Dickens: The Major Novels*. New York: Penguin, 1992.

Maxwell, Richard. *The Mysteries of Paris and London*. Charlottesville: UP of Virginia, 1992.

Milbank, Alison. *Daughters of the House: Modes of the Gothic in Victorian Fiction*. New York: St. Martin's, 1992.

Moglen, Helene. "Theorizing Fiction/Fictionalizing Theory: The Case of *Dombey and Son*." *Victorian Studies* 35 (1992): 159–84.

Morgan, Nicholas H. *Secret Journeys: Theory and Practice in Reading Dickens*. Cranbury, NJ: Associated UP, 1992.

Sadrin, Anny. "Charlotte Dickens: The Female Narrator of *Bleak House*." *Dickens Quarterly* 9 (June 1992): 47–57.

Fulweiler, Howard W. *"Here a Captive Heart Busted": Studies in the Sentimental Journey of Modern Literature*. New York: Fordham UP, 1993.

Holbrook, David. *Charles Dickens and the Image of Woman*. London: New York UP, 1993.

McKnight, Natalie. *Idiots, Madmen, and Other Prisoners in Dickens*. New York: St. Martin's, 1993.

Poovey, Mary. "Reading History in Literature: Speculation and Virtue in *Our Mutual Friend*." In *Historical Criticism and the Challenge of Theory*, edited by Janet Levarie Smarr, 42–80. Urbanna-Champlain: U of Illinois P, 1993.

Andrews, Malcolm. *Dickens and the Grown-Up Child*. London: Macmillan, 1994.

Houston, Gail Turley. *Consuming Fictions: Gender, Class, and Hunger in Dickens's Novels*. Carbondale: Southern Illinois UP, 1994.

Jaffe, Audrey. "Spectacular Sympathy: Visuality and Ideology in Dickens's *A Christmas Carol*." *PMLA* 109 (1994): 254–65.

Kucich, John. "Charles Dickens." In *The Columbia History of the British Novel*, edited by John Richetti et al., 381–406. New York: Columbia UP, 1994.

Murray, Brian. *Charles Dickens*. New York: Continuum, 1994.

Nunokawa, Jeff. *The Afterlife of Property: Domestic Security and the Victorian Novel*. Princeton, NJ: Princeton UP, 1994.

Sadrin, Anny. *Parentage and Inheritance in the Novels of Charles Dickens*. Cambridge: Cambridge UP, 1994.

Slater, Michael, ed. *Sketches by Boz and Other Early Papers 1833–1839*. Dent Uniform Edition of Dickens's Journalism. Vol. 1. London: J. M. Dent, 1994.

Suchoff, David. *Critical Theory and the Novel: Mass Society and Cultural Criticism in Dickens, Melville, and Kafka*. Madison: U of Wisconsin P, 1994.

Stone, Harry. *The Night Side of Dickens*. Columbus: Ohio State UP, 1994.

Futrell, Michael H. "Dostoevskii and Dickens." In *Dostoevskii and Britain*, edited by W. J. Leatherbarrow, 83–122. Oxford: Berg, 1995.

Hollington, Michael, ed. *Charles Dickens: Critical Assessments*. 4 vols. London: Helm, 1995.

Jordan, John O. and Robert L. Patten, eds. *Literature in the Marketplace: Nineteenth-Century British Publishing and Reading Practices*. Cambridge: Cambridge UP, 1995.

Miller, Andrew H. "Rearranging the Furniture of *Our Mutual Friend*." *Novels Behind Glass: Commodity, Culture, and Victorian Narrative*. Cambridge: Cambridge UP, 1995.

Newlin, George. *Everyone in Dickens*. 3 vols. Westport, CT: Greenwood, 1995.

Reed, John R. *Dickens and Thackeray: Punishment and Forgiveness*. Athens: Ohio UP, 1995.

Tambling, Jeremy. *Dickens, Violence and the Modern State*. London: Macmillan, 1995.

Connor, Steven, ed. *Charles Dickens*. Longman Critical Readers. London: Longman, 1996.

Gager, Valerie L. *Shakespeare and Dickens: The Dynamics of Influence*. Cambridge: Cambridge UP, 1996.

Ginsburg, Michael Peled. *Economies of Change: Form and Transformation in the Nineteenth-Century Novel*. Stanford, CA: Stanford UP, 1996.

Guy, Josephine M. *The Victorian Social-Problem Novel*. London: Macmillan, 1996.

Lubitz, Rita. *Marital Power in Dickens's Fiction*. New York: Peter Lang, 1996.

Newlin, George, ed. *Every Thing in Dickens*. Westport, CT: Greenwood Press, 1996.

Pointer, Michael. *Charles Dickens on the Screen: The Film, Television, and Video Adaptations*. Metuchen, NJ: Scarecrow Press, 1996.

Rosenberg, Brian. *Little Dorrit's Shadows: Character and Contradiction in Dickens*. Columbia: U of Missouri P, 1996.

Schad, John, ed. *Dickens Refigured: Bodies, Desires and Other Histories*. Manchester, UK: Manchester UP, 1996.

Slater, Michael, ed. *'The Amusements of the People' and Other Papers: Reports, Essays and Reviews 1834–1851*. Dent Uniform Edition of Dickens's Journalism. Vol. 2. London: J. M. Dent, 1996.

Small, Helen. "A Pulse of 124: Charles Dickens and a Pathology of the Mid-Victorian Reading Public." In *The Practice and Representation of Reading in England*, edited by James Raven, Helen Small, and Naomi Tadmor, 263–90. Cambridge: Cambridge UP, 1996.

Smith, Grahame. *Charles Dickens: A Literary Life*. New York: St. Martin's, 1996.

Bynum, George B., and Wolfgang Mieder. *The Proverbial Charles Dickens: An Index to Proverbs in the Works of Charles Dickens*. New York: Peter Lang, 1997.

Hawes, Donald. *Who's Who in Dickens*. New York and London: Routledge, 1997.

Palmer, William J. *Dickens and New Historicism*. New York: St. Martin's, 1997.

Paris, Bernard J. *Imagined Human Beings: A Psychological Approach to Character and Conflict in Literature*. New York: New York UP, 1997.

Peters, Laura. Review of Jeremy Tambling, *Dickens, Violence and the Modern State*. *Dickensian* 93.2 (Summer 1997): 145–46.

Rainsford, Dominic. *Authorship, Ethics and the Reader: Blake, Dickens, Joyce*. London: Macmillan; New York: St. Martin's, 1997.

Waters, Catherine. *Dickens and the Politics of the Family*. Cambridge: Cambridge UP, 1997.

Ayres, Brenda. *Dissenting Women in Dickens's Novels: The Subversion of Domestic Ideology*. Westport, CT: Greenwood, 1998.

Baumgarten, Murray, and H. M. Daleski, eds. *Homes and Homelessness in the Victorian Imagination*. New York: AMS Press, 1998.

Cohen, Monica. *Professional Domesticity in the Victorian Novel*. Cambridge: Cambridge UP, 1998.

Cordery, Gareth. "Foucault, Dickens, and *David Copperfield*." *Victorian Literature and Culture* 26.1 (1998): 71–85.

Dever, Carolyn. *Death and the Mother from Dickens to Freud*. Cambridge: Cambridge UP, 1998.

Epstein, Norrie. *The Friendly Dickens*. New York: Viking, 1998.

Higbie, Robert. *Dickens and Imagination*. Gainesville: UP of Florida, 1998.

Peters, Catherine. *Charles Dickens*. Gloucestershire, Eng.: Sutton, 1998.

Slater, Michael, ed. *'Gone Astray' and Other Papers from Household Words 1851–1859*. Dent Uniform Edition of Dickens's Journalism. Vol. 3. London: J. M. Dent, 1998.

Vlock, Deborah M. *Dickens, Novel Reading, and the Victorian Popular Theatre.* Cambridge: Cambridge UP, 1998.

Wolfreys, Julian. *Writing London: The Trace of the Urban Text from Blake to Dickens.* London: Macmillan; New York: St Martin's, 1998.

Glavin, John. *After Dickens: Reading, Adaptation, and Performance.* Cambridge: Cambridge UP, 1999.

Hochman, Baruch, and Ilja Wachs. *Dickens: The Orphan Condition.* Rutherford, NJ: Fairleigh Dickinson UP, 1999.

Lenard, Mary. *Preaching Pity: Dickens, Gaskell, and Sentimentalism in Victorian Culture.* New York: Peter Lang, 1999.

Sadrin, Anny, ed. *Dickens, Europe and the New Worlds.* London: Macmillan, 1999.

Sanders, Andrew. *Dickens and the Spirit of the Age.* Oxford: Clarendon P, 1999.

Schlicke, Paul, comp. "Charles Dickens." In *Cambridge Bibliography of English Literature.* 3rd ed. Vol. 4: 1800–1900, edited by Joanne Shattock, 1181–1273. Cambridge: Cambridge UP, 1999.

———, ed. *Oxford Reader's Companion to Dickens.* Oxford: Oxford UP, 1999.

Schor, Hilary. *Dickens and the Daughter of the House.* Cambridge UP, 1999.

Slater, Michael. *An Intelligent Person's Guide to Dickens.* London: Duckworth, 1999.

Steward, Douglas. "Anti-Oedipalizing *Great Expectations*: Masochism, Subjectivity, Capitalism." *Literature and Psychology* 45.3 (1999): 29–50.

2000s

Allen, Richard. "Literature, Nation and Revolution: *A Tale of Two Cities.*" In *Literature and Nation: Britain and India, 1800–1990,* edited by Richard Allen and Harish Trivedi, 55–66. London: Open University, 2000.

Bowen, John. *Other Dickens: Pickwick to Chuzzlewit.* Oxford: Oxford UP, 2000.

Chase, Karen, and Michael Levenson. *The Spectacle of Intimacy: A Public Life for the Victorian Family.* Princeton, NJ: Princeton UP, 2000.

Cockshut, A. O. J. "Children's Death in Dickens: A Chapter in the History of Taste." In *Representations of Childhood Death,* edited by Gillian Avery et al., 133–53. Basingstoke, Eng.: Macmillan; New York: St. Martin's, 2000.

Jacobson, Wendy S., ed. *Dickens and the Children of Empire.* New York: Palgrave, 2000.

Morgentaler, Goldie. *Dickens and Heredity: Like Begets Like.* London: Macmillan, 2000.

Newsom, Robert. *Charles Dickens Revisited*. New York: Twayne, 2000.

Slater, Michael, and John Drew, eds. *'The Uncommercial Traveller' and Other Papers 1859–1870*. Dent Uniform Edition of Dickens's Journalism. Vol. 4. London: J. M. Dent, 2000.

Wolfreys, Julian. "'I Wants to Make Your Flesh Creep': Notes toward a Reading of the Comic-Gothic in Dickens." In *Victorian Gothic: Literary and Cultural Manifestations in the Nineteenth Century*, edited by Ruth Robbins and Julian Wolfreys, 31–59. New York: Palgrave, 2000.

Anger, Suzy, ed. *Knowing the Past: Victorian Literature and Culture*. Ithaca, NY: Cornell UP, 2001.

Bevis, Matthew. "Temporizing Dickens." *Review of English Studies: A Quarterly Journal of English Literature and the English Language* 52 (May 2001): 171–91.

Bodenheimer, Rosemarie. "Knowing and Telling in Dickens's Retrospects." In *Knowing the Past: Victorian Literature and Culture*, edited by Suzy Anger, 215–33. Ithaca, NY: Cornell UP, 2001.

Cronin, Michael. "Gissing's Criticism of Dickens." In *A Garland for Gissing*, edited by Bouwe Postmus, 23–31. Amsterdam: Rodopi, 2001.

Dowling, Andrew. *Manliness and the Male Novelist in Victorian Literature*. Aldershot, Eng.: Ashgate, 2001.

John, Juliet. *Dickens's Villains: Melodrama, Character, Popular Culture*. Oxford: Oxford UP, 2001.

Jordan, John O., ed. *The Cambridge Companion to Charles Dickens*. Cambridge: Cambridge UP, 2001.

Mengham, Rod. *Charles Dickens*. Plymouth, England: Northcote House, 2001.

Poovey, Mary. "The Structure of Anxiety in Political Economy and *Hard Times*." In *Knowing the Past: Victorian Literature and Culture*, edited by Suzy Anger, 151–71. Ithaca, NY: Cornell UP, 2001.

Robbins, Bruce. "How to be a Benefactor without any Money: The Chill of *Great Expectations*." In *Knowing the Past: Victorian Literature and Culture*, edited by Suzy Anger, 172–91. Ithaca, NY: Cornell UP, 2001.

Robson, Catherine. *Men in Wonderland: The Lost Girlhood of the Victorian Gentleman*. Princeton, NJ: Princeton UP, 2001.

Schilling, Bernard N. *The Rain of Years: Great Expectations and the World of Dickens*. Rochester, NY: U of Rochester P, 2001.

Tambling, Jeremy. *Lost in the American City: Dickens, James and Kafka*. Basingstoke, Eng.: Palgrave, 2001.

Ackroyd, Peter. *Dickens: Public Life and Private Passion.* London: Hydra, 2002.

Gardiner, John. *The Victorians: An Age in Retrospect,* 161–79. London: Hambledon & London, 2002.

Gaylin, Ann. *Eavesdropping in the Novel from Austen to Proust.* Cambridge: Cambridge UP, 2002.

Parker, David. *The Doughty Street Novels.* New York: AMS Press, 2002.

Pykett, Lyn. *Charles Dickens.* Critical Issues Series. London: Palgrave, 2002.

Rem, Tore. *Dickens, Melodrama, and the Parodic Imagination.* New York: AMS Press, 2002.

Sirabian, Robert H. *Charles Dickens: Life, Work, and Criticism.* Toronto: York UP, 2002.

Smiley, Jane. *Charles Dickens.* New York: Viking, 2002.

Bigelow, Gordon. *Fiction, Famine, and the Rise of Economics in Victorian Britain and Ireland.* Cambridge: Cambridge UP, 2003.

Campbell, Elizabeth A. *Fortune's Wheel: Dickens and the Iconography of Women's Time.* Athens: Ohio UP, 2003.

Clayton, Jay. *Dickens in Cyberspace: The Afterlife of the Nineteenth Century in Postmodern Culture.* New York: Oxford UP, 2003.

Drew, John M. L. *Dickens the Journalist.* London: Palgrave Macmillan, 2003.

Friedman, Stanley. *Dickens's Fiction: Tapestries of Conscience.* New York: AMS Press, 2003.

Garrett, Peter K. "Dickens." *Gothic Reflections: Narrative Force in Nineteenth-Century Fiction,* 141–67. Ithaca, NY: Cornell UP, 2003.

Glavin, John. *Dickens on Screen.* Cambridge: Cambridge UP, 2003.

Karl, Frederick R. "Recent Dickens Studies." *Victorian Literature and Culture* 31.2 (2003): 593–611.

Markels, Julian. *The Marxian Imagination: Representing Class in Literature.* New York: Monthly Review P, 2003.

Rodensky, Lisa. *The Crime in Mind: Criminal Responsibility and the Victorian Novel.* Oxford: Oxford UP, 2003.

Russell, Corinna, ed. *Lives of Victorian Figures I: Eliot, Dickens and Tennyson By Their Contemporaries.* London: Pickering & Chatto, 2003.

Sawyer, Robert. *Victorian Appropriations of Shakespeare: George Eliot, A. C. Swinburne, Robert Browning, and Charles Dickens.* Madison, NJ: Fairleigh Dickinson UP, 2003.

Sicher, Efraim. *Rereading the City, Rereading Dickens: Representation, the Novel, and Urban Realism.* New York: AMS Press, 2003.

Simmons, James R., Jr. "No Expectations at All: Women in Charles Dickens's *Great Expectations* (1861)." In *Women in Literature: Reading through the Lens of Gender,* edited by Jerilyn Fisher and Ellen Silber, 124–26. Westport, CT: Greenwood, 2003.

Smith, Grahame. *Dickens and the Dream of Cinema.* Manchester, England: Manchester UP, 2003.

Woloch, Alex. *The One vs. the Many: Minor Characters and the Space of the Protagonist in the Novel.* Princeton, NJ: Princeton UP, 2003.

Armstrong, Mary A. "Multiplicities of Longing: The Queer Desires of *Bleak House* and *Little Dorrit*." *Nineteenth Century Studies* 18 (2004): 59–79.

Cole, Natalie Bell. "'Amen in a Wrong Place': Charles Dickens Imagines the Victorian Church." In *Victorian Religious Discourse: New Directions in Criticism,* edited by Jude V. Nixon, 205–34. Basingstoke, Eng.: Palgrave Macmillan, 2004.

DeVries, Duane. *General Studies of Charles Dickens and His Writings and Collected Editions of his Works: An Annotated Bibliography.* New York: AMS Press, 2004.

James, Elizabeth. *Charles Dickens.* British Library Writers Lives Series. New York and Oxford: Oxford UP, 2004.

Monod, Sylvère. "Dickens Biography: Past, Present, and Future: An Outline of History." *Biography and Source Studies* 8 (2004): 139–61.

Moore, Grace. *Dickens and Empire: Discourses of Class, Race and Colonialism in the Works of Charles Dickens.* Aldershot, Eng.: Ashgate, 2004.

Morris, Pam. *Imagining Inclusive Society in Nineteenth-Century Novels: The Code of Sincerity in the Public Sphere.* Baltimore, MD: Johns Hopkins UP, 2004.

Newey, Vincent. *The Scriptures of Charles Dickens: Novels of Ideology, Novels of the Self.* Aldershot, Eng. and Burlington, VT: Ashgate, 2004.

Robinson, Alan. *Imagining London 1770–1900.* London: Palgrave Macmillan, 2004.

Zangen, Britta. *Our Daughters Must Be Wives: Marriageable Young Women in the Novels of Dickens, Eliot, and Hardy.* Frankfurt, Germany: Peter Lang, 2004.

Dailey, Donna. *Charles Dickens.* New York: Chelsea House, 2005.

Eagleton, Terry. *The English Novel: An Introduction.* Malden, MA: Blackwell, 2005.

Andrews, Malcolm. *Charles Dickens and his Performing Selves: Dickens and the Public Readings.* Oxford: Oxford UP, 2006.

Hasseler, Terri. "Recent Dickens Studies: 2004." *Dickens Studies Annual* 37 (2006): 137–215.

Loutitt, Chriss. Review of Andrew Dowling, *Manliness and the Male Novelist in Victorian Literature* and Martin A. Danahy, *Gender at Work: Victorian Culture, Literature, and Masculinity*. *Dickens Quarterly* 23.3 (September 2006): 199–202.

McKnight, Natalie. Review of Britta Zangen, *Our Daughters Must Be Wives*. *Dickens Quarterly* 23.2 (June 2006): 127–29.

Hawes, Donald. *Charles Dickens*. London and New York: Continuum, 2007.

Paroissien, David, ed. *A Companion to Charles Dickens*. Malden, MA: Blackwell, 2008.

Index

Ackroyd, Peter, 46, 56, 214–15, 235, 295, 301
Adorno, Theodor, 202
aesthetic criticism, 23, 32, 65, 148, 161, 196, 199, 212, 220, 223–24, 229, 243
Aldington, Richard, 98, 114, 276
Alexander, Doris, 224, 235, 295
Allen, Michael, 212, 235, 294
Allen, Richard, 244, 257, 299
Allen, Walter, 98, 99, 114, 278
Althusser, Louis, 195, 198, 245, 249
Altick, Richard, 256
Amalric, Jean-Claude, 56, 151, 165, 286
Andrews, Malcolm, 226, 235, 255, 257, 296, 302
Anger, Suzy, 244, 257, 300
Arac, Jonathan, 163, 165, 287
Armstrong, Frances, 225, 235, 295
Armstrong, Isobel, 187
Armstrong, Mary, 248, 257, 302
Armstrong, Nancy, 171, 205, 289
Arnold, Matthew, 50, 96, 98, 164, 199, 204, 214
Arnold Newsletter, (journal) 164
Arnoldian, The, (journal) 164
Auden, W. H., 120
Austen, Jane, 41, 96, 98, 106, 109, 228
Axton, William F., 129, 137, 150, 282
Ayres, Brenda, 187, 205, 298

Bagehot, Walter, 22, 27, 265
Baker, Ernest A., 82–84, 87, 274
Baker, Joseph E., 92, 114, 276

Bakhtin, Mikhail, 171, 172, 173, 198, 204
Baldick, Chris, 231, 235, 293
Balzac, Honoré, 80, 98
Barickman, Richard, 181–82, 205, 290
Barrett (Browning), Elizabeth, 15
Barrie, J. M., 186
Barthes, Roland, 170, 174, 178, 250
Basch, Françoise, 157, 159, 165, 286
Bataille, Georges, 178
Baumgarten, Maury, 212, 233, 235, 246, 298
Bayley, John, 120
Bayne, Peter, 22, 27, 265
Beach, Joseph Warren, 70, 87, 273
Beadnell, Maria, 77, 101, 104, 250
Belloc, Hillaire, 71–72, 87, 272
Benham, William, 75, 77
Benjamin, Walter, 177, 178, 190, 202, 242, 253
Benson, Arthur C., 54, 56, 270
Bentham, Jeremy, 93
Bentley, Nicholas, 4, 8, 294
Bernard, Catherine A., 189, 205, 288
Bevington, Merle Mowbray, 2, 8, 275
Bevis, Matthew, 252, 253, 257, 300
Bigelow, Gordon, 245, 257, 301
Biron, H. C., 54, 56, 70
Blain, Virginia, 182, 205, 291
Blake, William, 50, 75, 102, 173
Blanchard, E. L., 16, 27, 263
Bloomsbury Group, 67, 71
Boas, Guy, 84, 87, 275
Bodenheimer, Rosemarie, 198, 205, 244, 257, 294, 300
Boege, Fred C., 5, 8, 107, 114, 277
Bolton, H. Philip, 3, 8, 293

306 ♦ INDEX

Booth, Bradford, 92, 115, 277
Borowitz, David, 142, 167, 285
Boswell, James, 34
Bowen, John, 241, 257, 299
Boz Club, 47
Bradford, Gamaliel, 69
Brimley, George, 18, 27, 264
Brooks, Chris, 172, 205, 290
Brown, Carolyn, 185, 205, 293
Brown, Ivor, 123, 137, 141, 281
Brown, James M., 195–96, 205, 290
Browne, Hablot K., 38, 161
Buckley, Jerome H., 154, 165, 286
Buller, Charles, 13, 27, 263
Bunyan, John, 54, 151, 230
Burdett-Coutts, Angela, 3, 105
Burgis, Nina, 4, 8, 294
Burton, Richard, 52, 56, 64–65, 87, 269, 271
Bush, Douglas, 110–11, 115, 279
Butt, John, 105–6, 109, 115, 119–20, 133, 135, 137, 142, 277, 278
Bynum, George B., 3, 8, 298
Byron, Lord (George Gordon), 13
Byronic hero, 101

Cain, William, 173, 211, 291
Cambridge University, 65, 66, 72, 96, 109, 122, 144, 255
Campbell, Elizabeth, 247–48, 257, 301
Canning, Albert, 52, 56, 270
Carey, John, 155–56, 165, 174, 184, 196, 205, 286
caricature, 12, 15, 19, 20, 22, 23, 25, 37–38, 43, 68, 81, 98, 157, 173, 245, 251
Carlisle, Janice, 229, 235, 288
Carlyle, Thomas, 19, 34, 39, 55, 63, 153–54, 230, 231
Carpenter, Edward, 55
Caserio, Robert, 164, 165, 287
Cason, Clarence E., 67, 87, 272
Cecil, David, 72, 73, 87, 163, 274
Cervantes, Miguel de, 54, 77

Chapman, Raymond, 132, 137, 283
Chase, Karen, 189, 205, 247, 257, 290, 299
Chaucer, Geoffrey, 109, 228
Chesterton, G. K., 2, 38, 44, 47–50, 52, 53, 54, 56–57, 63, 73, 74, 77, 79, 93, 94, 111, 113, 119, 121, 135, 144, 146, 147, 159, 176, 222, 256, 269, 270, 271, 273, 277
Childers, Joseph W., 199, 205, 294
Chittick, Kathryn, 6, 8, 12, 26, 28, 294, 295
Christie, O. F., 82, 87, 275
Church, Richard, 99, 115, 277
Churchill, R. C., 5, 8, 97, 115, 276, 286
Cixous, Hélène, 178
Clayton, Jay, 253, 257, 301
Cleghorn, Thomas, 16, 28, 264
Cockshut, A. O. J., 120–21, 137, 250, 257, 278, 280, 294
Cohan, Steve, 231, 235, 292
Cohen, Jane, 212, 235, 288
Cohen, Monica, 187, 205, 298
Cohn, Alan, 4, 8, 150, 290
Cold War, 153
Cole, Natalie Bell, 249, 257, 302
Collins, K. K., 4, 8, 290
Collins, Norman, 70, 87, 274
Collins, Philip A. W., 2, 5, 6, 8, 12, 17, 18, 20, 26, 28, 122–23, 129, 137, 142, 155, 165, 223, 249, 280, 281, 282, 284, 285, 286, 287, 288, 293
Collins, Wilkie, 38, 123
colonialism, 201, 204, 246, 247
Compton-Rickett, Arthur, 45, 57, 64, 269
Connor, Steven, 196–97, 204, 205, 291, 297
Conrad, Joseph, 97, 201
Coolidge, Archibald, 135, 138, 282
Cordery, Gareth, 204, 205, 298
Coveney, Peter, 110, 115, 279
Cowper, William, 74

Cox, C. B., 113, 114, 115, 279
Cox, Don R., 232, 235, 291
Craig, David, 220
Croker, John Wilson, 15, 28, 263
Cronin, Michael, 43–44, 57, 300
Cross, Wilbur, 42, 54, 57, 268, 270
Crotch, William Walter, 40, 57, 64, 87, 271
Crotchet Castle (Peacock), 154
Cruikshank, George, 161
Cruse, Amy, 5, 9, 274
cultural studies (cultural criticism), 96, 102, 148, 161, 163–64, 170, 176, 179, 180–83, 188, 192–93, 197–98, 202–4, 216, 220–21, 223, 229, 233, 239–40, 242–44, 245, 247, 253, 256
Cummings, Katherine, 183, 206, 295
Cunningham, Valerie, 157, 165, 286
Curtis, Gerald, 203, 206

Dabney, Ross, 136, 138, 145, 282
Dahl, Christopher C., 244, 257, 288
Dailey, Donna, 240, 257, 302
Daldry, Graham, 223, 235, 292
Daleski, H. M., 147, 165, 233, 235, 284, 298
Dallas, E. S., 22–23, 28, 265
Danahay, Martin, 256
Dark, Sidney, 63, 87, 271
Darwin, Bernard, 74, 87, 91, 115, 274, 275
Darwin, Charles, 191–92, 231
Davey, Samuel, 39, 57, 153, 165, 266
David, Deirdre, 184, 206, 288, 295
Davis, Earle R., 123–24, 138, 281
Davis, Paul, 233, 235, 295
Davis, Robert G., 107, 115, 277
Dawson, William J., 51, 57, 269
deconstruction (critical methodology), 111, 131, 170, 173–74, 190, 197, 200, 204, 231–32, 253
Defoe, Daniel, 75
De Man, Paul, 163, 177

Derrida, Jacques, 163, 170, 173, 175, 176, 180, 190, 192
Derus, David L., 50, 57, 292
Dever, Carolyn, 193, 206, 298
DeVries, Duane, 5, 9, 159, 165, 286, 302
Dexter, Walter, 3, 9, 45–46, 275
Dickens, Catherine Hogarth (the novelist's wife), 35, 37, 63, 78, 100–101, 102, 214, 225
Dickens, Charles, works by:
All the Year Round, 3, 31, 161, 252–53
American Notes for General Circulation, 15, 81, 182, 221, 242
Barnaby Rudge, 35, 126, 177, 220, 221, 250–51
Bleak House, 18, 22, 32, 35, 65, 68, 83, 104–5, 111, 112, 134, 147, 151, 160, 171, 174, 175–76, 179, 182, 183, 185, 188–89, 191, 192, 194, 201, 218, 221, 224–25, 231, 233, 245, 248, 251
"Bride's Chamber, The," 225
Christmas Carol, A, 15–16, 105, 153, 176, 233–34, 249
Cricket on the Hearth, The, 16
David Copperfield, 17, 21, 22, 34, 35, 36, 41, 65, 67, 73, 76, 78, 81, 83, 134, 145, 151, 154, 160, 175–77, 183, 184, 192, 194, 204, 218, 224–25, 233, 244, 249
Dombey and Son, 16, 35, 43, 83, 108, 126–27, 130, 131, 141, 144, 145, 164, 175–76, 177, 184–85, 186, 192, 200, 201, 224–25
"George Silverman's Explanation," 225
Great Expectations, 21, 22, 36, 38, 51, 52, 55, 73, 76, 83, 99, 107, 134, 145–46, 154, 159, 160, 174–75, 176–77, 180, 185,

Dickens, Charles, works by:
  Great Expectations (continued), 187, 191, 194, 216, 224–25, 229, 231, 233, 241, 244, 248, 249, 250
  Hard Times, 19, 55, 78, 81, 83, 96, 97, 130, 131, 134, 145, 151, 153–54, 171, 195, 198, 226, 232–33, 244, 245
  Household Words, 2, 3, 31, 35, 132–33, 252
  Little Dorrit, 20, 21, 22, 35, 55, 77, 78, 83, 95, 106, 127, 131, 134, 145, 151, 154, 177, 187, 189, 194, 199, 202, 204, 223, 224–25, 231, 245, 248, 251
  Martin Chuzzlewit, 16, 22, 35, 43, 68, 182, 192, 221, 228, 242, 246
  Master Humphrey's Clock, 14
  Mystery of Edwin Drood, The, 76, 188, 201
  Nicholas Nickleby, 13, 104, 126, 177, 220, 221, 250
  Old Curiosity Shop, The, 14, 35, 40, 126, 175–76, 247, 248
  Oliver Twist, 35, 98–99, 104, 126, 131, 160, 176–77, 194, 198, 233, 244, 249, 250
  Our Mutual Friend, 21, 22–24, 35, 76, 78, 83, 127, 131, 134, 147, 151, 171, 175–76, 179, 184, 185, 188, 200, 202, 220, 224–25, 249
  Pickwick Papers, 12, 13, 22, 35, 48, 52, 54, 104, 126, 147, 195, 202, 250
  Sketches by 'Boz,' 12, 13, 159, 160–61, 223
  Tale of Two Cities, A, 20–21, 81, 83, 86, 134, 153–54, 223, 226, 244
  Uncommercial Traveler, The, 160–61, 249

Dickens, Elizabeth (the novelist's mother), 102, 182, 187, 193, 214, 225
Dickens, Henry (the novelist's son), 75, 87, 273
Dickens, John (the novelist's father), 21, 102, 213, 214
Dickens, Mary (the novelist's daughter), 75, 87, 267
Dickens Fellowship, 32, 45–47, 53, 92, 212
Dickens House, 250
Dickens Journals Online, 252–53
Dickens Quarterly (journal), 150, 164, 254
Dickens Studies (journal), 129, 149
Dickens Studies Annual (journal), 4, 149, 150, 213, 254
Dickens Studies Newsletter (journal), 149–50
Dickensian (journal), 45–47, 56, 129, 149–50, 164, 182, 219, 234, 254
Dickensians, 38, 44, 47, 48, 50, 53, 63, 64, 70, 73, 76, 77, 82, 106, 133, 144, 158, 199, 212, 250
Docherty, Thomas, 172, 206, 290
Donovan, Frank, 135, 138, 283
Donzelot, Jacques, 203, 206
Dostoevsky, Fyodor, 80, 129, 165
Dowling, Andrew, 242, 258, 300
drama, 3, 71, 79, 119, 129, 162, 251
dramatic poetry, 44, 72, 96
Drew, John M. L., 252–53, 258, 260, 300, 301
Duncan, Ian, 199–200, 206, 296
Dyson, A. E., 120, 138, 147–48, 155, 165, 283, 284

Eagles, John, 16, 28, 264
Eagleton, Terry, 158, 159, 165, 194, 196–97, 206, 245–46, 258, 286, 302
Easson, Angus, 3
Edgar, David, 220
Edgar, Pelham, 71, 87, 274

eighteenth-century novel, 102, 221, 228, 232
Eigner, Edwin, 193, 212, 222, 235, 294
Eisenstein, Sergei, 254, 258, 276
Eldredge, Patricia, 191, 206, 292
Eliot, George (Marian Evans), 19, 20, 27, 28, 32, 96, 136, 144, 145, 158, 172, 246, 264
Eliot, T. S., 68, 87, 96, 272
Ellis, Sarah Stickney, 184
Ellis, Stewart, 35–36, 58, 270
Elton, Oliver, 65–66, 88, 271
Empson, William, 122, 138, 281
Engel, Monroe, 113–14, 115, 120, 279
Engels, Frederick, 81
Epstein, Norrie, 216, 235, 298
Evans, B. Ifor, 94, 115, 275
Evans, Marian. *See* Eliot, George
evolution (scientific theory), 231

Fabianism, 54
Fanger, Donald, 165, 281
Faulkner, William, 106, 124, 133, 226
Feltes, N. N., 195, 206, 291, 293
feminism (feminist criticism), 135, 141, 142, 157, 170, 174, 176, 177, 181–88, 200, 201, 202, 204, 214, 247–48, 256
Fenstermaker, John J., 4, 5, 9, 287
Fido, Martin, 134–35, 138, 142–43, 166, 283, 284
Fielding, Henry, 13, 49, 77, 96, 109, 124
Fielding, Kenneth J., 2, 3, 9, 107, 115, 121, 129, 130, 131, 135, 138, 223, 278, 279, 280, 281, 282, 283
Figgis, Darrel, 54, 48, 270
First World War, 53, 63, 92
FitzGerald, Edward, 75
Fitzgerald, Percy, 47, 58, 269, 270
Flaubert, Gustave, 19, 98

Fleissner, Robert, 155, 166, 227, 281
Flint, Kate, 174, 181, 206, 292
Ford, Ford Madox, 69, 88, 273
Ford, George, 5, 6, 9, 12, 20, 21, 23, 28, 92, 111, 115, 119, 120, 138, 195, 278, 279, 280, 281
Ford, Richard, 13, 28, 263
formalist criticism, 13, 32, 83, 86, 94, 96, 98, 107, 110, 120, 127, 128, 130, 134, 137, 148, 159, 170, 198, 199, 200, 212, 214, 216, 229
Forster, E. M., 24, 68, 69, 85, 88, 96, 113, 159, 173, 178, 242, 274
Forster, John, 5, 9, 18, 28, 32, 33–36, 47, 53, 58, 63, 73–74, 76, 77, 78, 82, 88, 100, 101, 103–4, 130, 134, 146, 213, 255, 264, 266
Forster Collection, Victoria & Albert Museum (London), 133
Forsyth, William, 21, 28, 265
Foucault, Michel, 69, 175, 177, 180, 190, 192, 193, 198, 203, 204, 214, 230, 231, 242, 244, 248
Frank, Lawrence, 190, 206, 291
Frankfurt School (philosophical group), 193, 202
French Revolution, 51, 86, 244
Freudian psychology, 102, 107, 110, 125, 130, 163, 186, 187, 188, 189, 190, 191, 193
Friedman, Norman, 159, 166, 278, 286
Friedman, Stanley, 251–52, 258, 301
Frye, Northrop, 131, 138, 173, 199, 283
Fulweiler, Howard W., 232, 235, 296
Futrell, Michael H., 165, 297
Fyfe, Thomas, 3, 9, 271

Gadd, W. L., 3, 10, 269
Gager, Valerie L., 227, 235, 297
Gallagher, Catherine, 195, 206, 288, 291

Galsworthy, John, 67, 88, 273
Gardiner, John, 7, 9, 258, 301
Garis, Robert, 127–29, 138, 145, 158, 160, 166, 174, 281
Garrett, Peter K., 171, 174, 207, 251, 258, 288, 301
Gaylin, Ann, 251, 258, 301
Gelpi, Barbara Charlesworth, 154
gender studies, 183, 184, 185, 186, 191–92, 198, 200, 201, 204, 248, 256
Gerould, Gordon, 94–95, 115, 276
Giddings, Robert, 220, 236, 290
Gilmour, Robin, 156, 166, 229, 236, 286, 288
Ginsburg, Michael Peled, 179, 207, 297
Gissing, George, 2, 36, 42–44, 48, 52, 56, 58, 73, 111, 144, 256, 268, 272
Glavin, John, 181, 207, 253, 254, 258, 299, 301
Goethe, Johann Wolfgang von, 144
Gold, Joseph, 4, 9, 142, 152–53, 166, 284, 285
Goldberg, Michael, 153, 166, 285, 291
Golden, Morris, 196, 207, 296
Goldman, Lucien, 196
Goldsmith, Oliver, 34
Gomme, A. H., 143, 166, 285
Grant, Allan, 220–21, 236, 291
Graves, Robert, 135
Greene, Graham, 120
Gregor, Ian, 131, 140, 284
Greimas, A. J., 173
Gross, John, 121, 135, 138, 281
Grubb, Gerald G., 107, 115, 277
Guerard, Albert, 154–55, 165, 166, 286
Guiliano, Edward, 150
Guy, Josephine M., 232, 236, 297

Hamley, E. B., 21, 28, 265
Hanzo, Thomas, 188–89, 207, 288
Hara, Eiichi, 174, 207, 292
Harbage, Alfred B., 155, 166, 286
Hardy, Barbara, 120, 143, 166, 186, 187, 207, 283, 284, 290, 291, 295
Hardy, Thomas, 53–54, 172, 246
Harrison, Antony, 184
Harrison, Frederic, 40, 58, 267
Harvard University, 99, 109, 255
Harvey, W. J., 120, 172, 207, 229
Hasseler, Terri, 5, 9, 303
Hawes, Donald, 3, 9, 254, 255, 258, 298, 303
Hawthorn, Jeremy, 174, 207, 292, 293
Hawthorne, Nathaniel, 124
Hayward, Abraham, 13, 28, 263
Hegel, Georg Wilhelm Friedrich, 163
Heidegger, Martin, 190
Henley, W. E., 40, 58, 267
Heroes and Hero-Worship (Carlyle), 34, 39
Hewitt, Douglas, 154, 166, 285
Hibbert, Christopher, 130, 138, 283
Higbie, Robert, 172–73, 193–94, 207, 291, 298
high seriousness (critical principle), 50, 52, 97, 144
Hill, Nancy K., 218–19, 236, 289
Hobsbaum, Philip, 141, 166, 285
Hochman, Baruch, 194, 207, 233, 236, 299
Hogarth, Catherine. *See* Dickens, Catherine Hogarth
Hogarth, George, 12, 28, 263
Hogarth, Georgina, 36
Hogarth, Mary, 101, 126, 219, 250
Hogarth, William, 66, 219, 222, 230
Holbrook, David, 186–87, 207, 296
Hollington, Michael, 6, 9, 26, 28, 172, 207, 291, 297
Homer, 31
Hood, Thomas, 14, 29, 263
Hopkins, Sandra, 186, 207, 295
Hoppé, A. J., 36

Hornback, Bert, 152, 166, 218, 236, 285, 289
Horne, R. H., 15, 28, 263
Horney, Karen, 191
Horton, Susan, 164, 166, 171, 207, 287, 289
Hough, Graham, 221, 236, 292
House, Humphry, 3, 93–94, 107–8, 110, 111, 115, 120, 122, 136, 142, 152, 185, 196, 221, 249, 256, 275, 278
House, Madeline, 3, 9, 108, 130, 281
Houston, Gail Turley, 200, 207, 296
Howells, William Dean, 41–42, 58–59, 135, 267, 268
Hughes, Helen S., 71, 88, 274
Hume, David, 90
Hunt, Brian Desmond, 233
Hunt, Leigh, 63
Hutton, Laurence, 42, 59, 267
Hutton, R. H., 26, 29, 266
Huxley, Aldous, 69, 88, 135, 273

idealism (in literature), 25, 42, 48, 86, 186
Idylls of the King (Tennyson), 224
imperialism, 184, 202, 216, 247
Industrial Revolution, 195
Ingham, Patricia, 184, 207, 296

Jackson, Holbrook, 51–52, 59, 269
Jackson, T. A., 80–82, 86, 88, 93, 107, 108, 110, 130, 136, 203, 274
Jacobson, Wendy S., 246, 258, 299
Jaffe, Audrey, 175–76, 207, 295, 296
James, Elizabeth, 240, 258, 302
James, Henry, 23–24, 27, 29, 39, 42, 43, 63, 65, 68, 69, 83, 85, 96, 113, 119, 124, 144, 145, 163, 172, 178, 266
Jameson, Frederic, 7, 199, 245
Jarmuth, Sylvia L., 135, 138, 283
Jeffrey, Francis, 63, 119

John, Juliet, 251, 258, 300
Johnson, E. D. H., 134–35, 138, 141, 284
Johnson, Edgar, 3, 5, 6, 9, 32, 56, 59, 91, 101, 103–6, 107, 110, 111, 112–13, 116, 119, 120, 129, 130, 146, 213, 255, 277, 278, 279, 281, 282, 283
Johnson, Samuel, 34
Johnson, Wendell Stacy, 220, 236, 290
Jordan, John O., 4, 9, 202, 208, 213, 297, 300

Kant, Immanuel, 143
Kapital (Marx), 55, 203
Kaplan, Fred, 4, 150, 193, 213–14, 232, 236, 286, 289, 293, 294
Karl, Frederick R., 7, 10, 125, 138, 239, 258, 281, 301
Kauffman, Linda, 226, 236, 289
Kayser, Wolfgang, 172
Keats, John, 15, 256
Kent, Charles, 32, 59, 266
Kettle, Arnold, 98–99, 116, 277
Kidd, H. H., 67, 88, 273
Kierkegaard, Søren, 159
Kincaid, James R., 151, 156, 167, 246, 285
Kingsmill, Hugh (H. K. Lunn), 76–77, 88, 101, 274
Kitton, F. G. (Frederick George), 4, 10, 36, 38–39, 44, 45, 47, 59, 74, 82, 88, 267, 268, 269, 270
Klein, Michael, 233, 236, 289
Klieneberger, H. R., 226, 236, 289
Knoepflmacher, U. C., 161, 223
Kotzin, Michael, 162, 167, 285
Kristeva, Julia, 178, 248
Kucich, John, 181, 192–93, 208, 220, 236, 258, 289, 291, 293, 296
Kurrik, Maire Jaanus, 163, 167, 287

Lacan, Jacques, 170, 175, 178, 180, 188–89, 190, 191, 198

LaCapra, Dominic, 203
Lambert, Mark, 218, 236, 289
Landor, Walter Savage, 34
Lane, Lauriat, Jr., 26, 119, 138, 279, 280
Lang, Andrew, 2, 53
Langland, Elizabeth, 172, 208, 291
LaRocque, Geraldine E., 226, 237, 290
Larson, Janet, 173–74, 208, 291
Lary, N. M., 165, 167, 286
Laski, Harold, 81, 88, 273
Laurence, Dan H., 56, 59, 292
Lawrence, D. H., 64, 186
Leacock, Stephen, 77–78, 88, 271, 274
Leavis, F. R., 24, 72, 73, 88, 96–97, 98, 110, 116, 122, 135, 144–47, 154, 155, 159, 160, 163, 167, 198, 228, 229, 276, 281, 284
Leavis, Q. D., 24, 27, 29, 72–73, 88, 122, 144–47, 154, 155, 159, 160, 163, 167, 174, 198, 229, 274, 277, 284
Leech, John, 38
Lehmann, R. C., 3, 10, 270
Lenard, Mary, 187–88, 208, 299
Lerner, Gerda, 248
Lerner, Laurence, 229–30, 237, 290
Lettis, Richard, 223–24, 237, 294, 295
Levenson, Michael, 247, 257, 299
Levine, George, 223, 231, 237, 294
Levit, Fred, 3, 10, 295
Lewes, George Henry, 32–34, 41, 59, 119, 144, 266
Lewis, C. S., 186
Ley, J. W. T., 36, 56, 59, 62, 63, 88, 271, 272, 273
Lindsay, Jack, 101–2, 109, 110, 116, 119, 277
Lister, Thomas Henry, 13, 29, 263
Livingston, Flora, 3, 10, 274
Lodge, David, 130, 139, 282
Lohrli, Anne, 2, 10, 286

Loutitt, Chriss, 256, 258, 303
Lovett, Robert, 71, 88, 274
Lubbock, Percy, 24, 65, 68, 69, 71, 89, 96, 159, 272
Lubitz, Rita, 187, 208, 297
Lucas, John, 130, 139, 143–44, 167, 224–25, 237, 282, 284, 296
Lukacher, Ned, 190–91, 208, 292
Lukács, Georg, 86, 89, 157, 281
Lunn, Hugh Kingsmill. *See* Kingsmill, Hugh

MacDonald, George, 186
Mack, Maynard, 131
MacKenzie, Compton, 64
MacKenzie, Jeanne, 162, 167, 287
MacKenzie, Norman, 162, 167, 287
MacKenzie, Robert Shelton, 31–32, 59, 266
Magnet, Myron, 221, 237, 292
Manheim, Leonard, 124, 139, 278, 282
Manning, John, 123, 139, 279
Manning, Sylvia Bank, 151, 167, 285
Mansbridge, Albert, 91, 116
Marcus, Steven, 119, 120, 125–27, 139, 147, 241, 280, 282
Markels, Julian, 245, 258, 301
Martineau, Harriet, 19, 29, 264
Marx, Karl, 55, 80, 81, 82, 149
Marxist criticism, 80–82, 86, 107, 110, 130, 146, 148–49, 158–59, 190, 194–98, 204, 214, 244, 245, 255–56
Marzials, Frank, 36–37, 59, 267
Maslow, Abraham, 191
Masson, David, 17–18, 29, 119, 264, 265
materialism, 86, 192, 202, 216
Matz, B. W. (Bertram Waldrom), 36, 45–46, 51, 53, 60, 268
Maugham, W. Somerset, 97, 116, 276
Maurois, Andre, 29, 79, 89, 273, 274
Maxwell, Richard, 177, 180, 208, 243, 296

McCabe, Bernard, 128–29, 139, 282
McCarthy, Justin, 17, 29, 267
McCarthy, Patrick, 233
McGowan, John P., 230, 237, 292
McKnight, Natalie, 177, 208, 255, 258, 296, 303
McMaster, Juliet, 222, 229, 237, 289, 293
McMaster, Rowland, 229, 237, 289
Meckier, Jerome, 217, 221, 237, 293, 295
melodrama, 19, 49, 62, 68, 70, 120, 123, 160, 251
Melville, Herman, 124, 179
Mengham, Rod, 240, 258, 300
Meynell, Alice, 44, 54, 60, 269, 270
Michie, Helena, 185, 208, 294
Mieder, Wolfgang, 3, 8, 298
Milbank, Alison, 186, 187, 208, 296
Mill, John Stuart, 154
Miller, Andrew H., 202, 208, 297
Miller, D. A., 69, 175, 180, 204, 208, 244, 289, 290, 294
Miller, J. Hillis, 6, 80, 89, 94, 111–13, 114, 116, 119, 120, 122, 128, 129, 130–31, 139, 142, 143, 151, 152, 163, 167, 170, 174, 202, 208, 221, 244, 279, 283, 285
Millett, Kate, 141–42, 167, 183, 284
Milne, James, 50, 60, 269
Milton, John, 31, 50, 109
Minogue, Sally, 185–86, 209, 295
Miyoshi, Masao, 132, 139, 284
Modern Language Association, 4, 5, 92, 149
modernism (modernist movement), 7, 40, 47, 50, 54, 64, 67–69, 71–73, 76–78, 99, 102, 103, 109, 212, 223, 234
Moers, Ellen, 110, 116, 280
Moglen, Helen, 186, 209, 296
Monod, Sylvère, 6, 7, 10, 112, 116, 129, 133–34, 139, 201, 223, 279, 283, 302
Moore, Grace, 247, 259, 302

Mordell, Albert, 20, 29, 272
More, Paul Elmer, 50, 60, 96, 269
Morgan, Nicholas H., 176, 209, 296
Morgentaler, Goldie, 249, 259, 299
Morris, Christopher, 174–75, 209, 293
Morris, Pam, 198, 209, 245, 259, 295, 302
Morris, William, 55
Moseley, Merritt, 226, 237, 289
Moss, Sidney P., 217, 237, 291
Mottram, R. H., 91, 117
Muir, Edwin, 68–69, 89, 273, 282
Murray, Brian, 215–16, 237, 296
Murry, John Middleton, 63, 89, 272
Myers, Margaret, 184, 209, 293

Nabokoff, Vladimir, 228, 237, 270
Nabokov, Vladimir, 228, 237, 288
narrative (theory of), 44, 144, 163, 172, 174, 179, 182, 189, 193, 197, 202–3, 204, 223, 229, 241, 244, 245, 246, 251
Nelson, Harland, 217–18, 237, 239, 289
New Criticism, 65, 71, 130, 145, 170, 212, 220
new historicism, 34, 170, 176, 196–203, 220, 244–47, 256
Newcomb, Mildred, 224, 237, 294
Newey, Vincent, 249, 259, 302
Newlin, George, 3–4, 10, 297
Newman, S. J., 217, 237, 289
Newsom, Robert, 160, 162, 167, 239–40, 259, 287, 289, 300
Nineteenth-Century Fiction (journal), 164
Nineteenth-Century Prose (journal), 164
Nisbet, Ada, 5, 10, 76, 106–7, 110, 117, 142, 167, 277, 281, 285
Noyes, Alfred, 92, 117, 275
Nunokawa, Jeffrey, 202, 209, 296

O'Connor, Frank (Michael O'Donovan), 99–100, 117, 278
Oddie, William, 153–54, 167, 285
O'Donovan, Michael. *See* O'Connor, Frank
"Of Queen's Gardens" (Ruskin), 142
Oliphant, Margaret, 29, 38, 60, 265, 267
Orwell, George, 68, 84–85, 89, 91, 93, 119, 121, 135, 152, 174, 222, 275
Osborne, Charles, 3, 10, 274
Owen, Robert, 51
Oxford University, 109, 162, 255
Oxford University Press, 2, 94

Page, Norman, 3, 10, 291, 294
Palmer, William J., 203, 209, 298
Paradis, James, 189
Paris, Bernard J., 191, 209, 298
Parker, David, 250–51, 259, 301
Parker, Gillian, 233, 236, 289
Paroissien, David, 3, 10, 150, 167, 252, 254, 291, 292, 303
Partlow, Robert, 142, 149–50, 167, 284, 285
Pater, Walter, 63
Patten, Robert, 142, 150, 161, 167, 168, 195, 202, 208, 209, 285, 287, 297
Peacock, Thomas Love, 154
Pearce, Roy Harvey, 131
Pearson, Gabriel, 121–22, 135, 138, 139, 279, 281
Pearson, Hesketh, 101, 110, 117, 276
Pêcheux, Michel, 195
Perera, Suvendrini, 201, 209, 295
performance theory, 181, 213
Peters, Catherine, 216, 237, 298
Peters, Laura, 178, 209, 298
Peyrouton, Noel, 6, 129, 139, 168, 282
Phelps, William, 52–53, 60, 271
Philip, Alexander, 3, 10, 269

Phillips, Walter C., 65, 89, 271
Philpotts, Trey, 178, 209
"Phiz." *See* Browne, Hablot Knight
Pierce, Gilbert, 3, 10, 266
Pike, James S., 153, 168, 275
Pilgrim's Progress (Bunyan), 106, 151
Pointer, Michael, 234, 238, 297
Polhemus, Robert, 228, 233, 238, 288
Poovey, Mary, 183, 187, 200, 209, 244, 259, 294, 296, 300
Pope, Norris, 157, 168, 287
Pope-Hennessy, Una, 100–101, 104, 108, 110, 117, 276
post-colonial studies, 201, 246
Postlewait, Thomas, 189
postmodernism (postmodern studies), 204, 214, 215, 216, 220–21, 227, 239, 241–44, 253
poststructuralism (literary methodology), 155, 163, 164, 171, 172, 181, 189, 197, 218, 221, 224, 227, 229, 241, 244
Poulet, Georges, 112
Powys, John C., 62–63, 89, 271
Praz, Mario, 108–9, 111, 113, 117, 278
Price, Martin, 120, 139, 283
Priestley, J. B., 141
Pritchett, V. S., 95–96, 117, 276
Propp, Vladimir, 173
psychological criticism, 6, 7, 72–73, 76, 83, 85–86, 94, 96, 101–2, 103, 104, 120, 124–25, 134, 136, 146–47, 154–55, 163, 182–83, 184, 186–87, 188–94, 204, 224
Pugh, Edwin, 50–51, 60, 80, 269
Pykett, Lynn, 1, 10, 242, 259, 301

Qualls, Barry, 230, 238, 290
queer theory, 188, 248
Quiller-Couch, Arthur, 66, 89, 272
Quinn, Martin, 56, 59, 292

Rabelais, François, 54

Raina, Badri, 197–98, 209, 293
Rainey, Lillian, 67, 89, 272
Rainsford, Dominic, 179–80, 210, 298
Rantavaara, Irma, 5, 10, 276
Rathburn, Robert, 110–11
reaction against the Victorians, 5, 45, 46
reading (theories of), 65, 96, 113–14, 171, 172, 174, 180–81, 182, 188–89, 197, 243
realism (in literature), 20, 26, 32, 41, 42, 44, 47, 48, 70, 83, 85, 99, 105, 108, 124, 125, 131, 132, 157, 158, 160, 172, 185, 195, 221, 228, 230, 252
Reed, John R., 226–27, 238, 297
religion (in Dickens), 66, 82, 93, 123, 219, 227, 249
Rem, Tore, 251, 259, 301
Resnick Stephen, 245
Richards, I. A., 65
Richardson, Samuel, 66, 96, 109
Robbins, Bruce, 244, 259, 300
Robinson, Alan, 243, 244, 259, 302
Robson, Catherine, 247, 259, 300
Rodensky, Lisa, 244, 259, 301
Rogers, Samuel, 63
romance (literary genre), 25, 51, 99, 100, 192, 199–200, 228, 231
Romano, John, 160, 168, 287
Romantic poets, 102, 221
Romanticism (Romantic movement), 101, 160, 165, 190, 194, 224, 228, 231–32, 240, 243
Rosenberg, Brian, 178–79, 210, 297
Rouse, H. Blair, 27, 29, 277
Rousseau, Jean Jacques, 125
Royal Shakespeare Company, 220
Ruskin, John, 19, 29, 55, 119, 142, 154, 265
Russell, Corinna, 6, 10, 259, 301
Ryals, Clyde deL., 231–32, 238, 295

Sadoff, Diane, 189, 210, 288, 290

Sadrin, Anny, 201, 204, 210, 296, 299
Saintsbury, George, 40–41, 60, 98, 267, 268, 269, 271
Sala, George Augustus, 31, 60, 266
Sanders, Andrew, 162, 168, 219–20, 223, 234, 238, 288, 290, 299
Santayana, George, 66, 89, 98, 119, 272
satire, 22, 25, 37, 52, 66, 131, 151, 157, 251
Sawyer, Charles J., 74
Sawyer, Robert, 251, 259, 301
Schad, John, 179, 210, 297
Schiller, Friedrich, 144
Schilling, Bernard N., 250, 259, 300
Schlicke, Paul, 4, 10, 222, 238, 261, 292, 299
Schor, Hilary, 185, 210, 299
Schwarzbach, F. S., 163–64, 168, 176, 180, 243, 287
Scott, Sir Walter, 13, 40, 41, 73, 199–200
Second World War, 7, 84, 100
Sedgwick, Eve Kosofsky, 188, 210, 248, 292
Sell, Roger D., 199, 203, 210, 293
semiotics, 174
Senf, Carol A., 182, 210, 290
sensationalism (sensational novels), 33, 38, 65, 71, 109
Seymour, Robert, 77
Shakespeare, William, 1, 13, 15, 31, 32, 40, 46, 50, 63, 66, 72, 74, 77, 84, 94, 98, 102, 109, 119, 120, 141, 155, 186, 221, 227, 228, 239, 251
Sharpe, William, 123
Shattock, Joanne, 223, 238, 261, 294
Shaw, George Bernard, 53, 54–55, 56, 60–61, 80, 95, 107, 119, 203, 271
Shorter, Clement, 42, 44, 61, 268
Sicher, Efraim, 233, 243, 244, 259, 301

Simmons, James R., Jr., 248, 259, 302
Simpson, David, 179, 210, 290
Simpson, Richard, 19, 29, 264
Sirabian, Robert H., 240, 260, 301
Sitwell, Osbert, 71, 89, 274, 275
Slater, Michael, 2, 4, 8, 10–11, 142, 164, 168, 182–83, 184, 186, 210, 217, 219, 234, 238, 252, 255, 260, 285, 287, 290, 294, 297, 298, 299, 300
Small, Helen, 203, 210, 298
Smiles, Samuel, 39
Smiley, Jane, 1, 11, 215, 238, 240–41, 260, 301
Smith, Grahame, 136–37, 140, 181, 210, 216, 238, 246, 253–54, 260, 283, 298, 302
Smollett, Tobias, 13, 49, 96, 124
Spence, Gordon, 160–61, 168, 287
Spilka, Mark, 120, 124, 140, 174, 279, 280, 281
Stang, Richard, 113, 114, 117, 142, 279
Staples, Leslie, 46
Steig, Michael, 161, 168, 287
Stephen, James, 21
Stephen, James Fitzjames, 20–21, 29–30, 44, 119, 244, 264, 265
Stephen, Leslie, 21, 30, 37–38, 61, 267, 269
Sterne, Laurence, 13
Stevenson, Lionel, 95, 112, 113, 114, 117, 276, 280
Stevenson, Robert Louis, 47
Steward, Douglas, 191, 211, 299
Stewart, Garrett, 156–57, 159, 168, 173, 194, 211, 286, 291
Stoehr, Taylor, 124–25, 140, 158, 160, 282
Stone, Donald, 228, 238, 288
Stone, Harry, 2, 11, 132–33, 140, 141, 142, 162, 168, 193–94, 223, 225, 238, 280, 283, 288, 293, 297
Storey, Gladys, 110, 117, 275

Storey, Graham, 3, 9, 108, 223, 281
Stothert, James Augustine, 18, 30, 264
Stott, George, 25–26, 30, 266
Strachey, Lytton, 77, 89
Straus, Ralph, 73–74, 90, 256, 260, 273, 274
Suchoff, David, 202, 211, 299
Sucksmith, Harvey Peter, 144, 158, 168, 285
Sussman, Herbert, 131–32, 140, 283
Sutherland, John, 161, 168, 223, 287
Swinburne, A. C., 44, 61, 268
Symons, Julian, 103, 117, 277

Taine, Hippolyte, 19, 30, 264
Tambling, Jeremy, 69, 177–78, 211, 242–43, 244, 260, 293, 297, 300
Taylor, Beverly, 184
Tennyson, Alfred, 15, 46, 224, 226
Tennyson, G. B., 161
Ternan, Ellen, 35, 70, 74, 75–76, 77, 78, 79, 100, 101, 106, 108, 110, 130, 182, 183, 214, 225
Thackeray, William Makepeace, 16, 17, 52, 64, 226, 264
Third Force Psychology, 191
Thomas, Deborah, 219, 238, 290
Thurley, Geoffrey, 158–59, 168, 287
Tillotson, Geoffrey, 182
Tillotson, Kathleen, 3, 108, 109, 112, 115, 117, 120, 129, 131, 133, 135, 140, 142, 278, 280, 284
Timko, Michael, 150
Todorov, Tzvetan, 173, 178
Tolstoy, Leo, 47, 158
Tomlin, E. W. F., 141, 168, 284
Trilling, Lionel, 106, 117, 120, 128, 245, 260, 278
Trollope, Anthony, 154, 164
Trollopian (journal), 164
Trotter, David, 201, 211, 220, 294

Van Amerongen, J. B., 129, 140, 272

Van Boheemen, Christine, 191–92, 205, 293
Van Dyke, Henry, 54, 61, 270
Van Ghent, Dorothy, 99, 118, 120, 143, 277, 278
Vanity Fair (Thackeray), 17
Vann, J. Don, 4, 11, 284
Vargish, Thomas, 230, 238, 292
Victoria & Albert Museum (London), 133
Vietnam conflict, 153
Vlock, Deborah, 180, 211, 299

Wachs, Ilja, 194, 207, 236, 299
Wagenknecht, Edward, 69–70, 90, 95, 118, 129–30, 133, 140, 273, 274, 276, 282
Walder, Dennis, 219, 238, 289
Walker, Hugh, 52, 61, 271
Wall, Stephen, 6, 11, 285
Wallace, Alfred, 53
Wallock, Leonard, 123
Walters, J. Cuming, 46, 53, 61, 270, 273
Ward, Adolphus, 36, 43, 61, 266
Warner, Charles Dudley, 42
Warner, Rex, 96, 118, 276
Waters, Catherine, 203, 211, 298
Watkins, Gwen, 192, 211, 294
Watt, Ian, 142, 168, 285
Watt, James Crabbe, 39, 61, 266
Way We Live Now, The (Trollope), 154
Webb, Igor, 195, 211, 289
Wells, H. G., 68
Welsh, Alexander, 150–51, 163, 168, 174, 176, 180, 193, 211, 243, 285, 294
Westburg, Barry, 159–60, 168, 287
Weygandt, Cornelius, 66, 90, 272
Wheeler, Michael, 173, 211, 288
Whipple, Edwin P., 17, 19, 22, 24–25, 30, 264, 265, 266
White, Hayden, 203
Whitman, Walt, 21, 30, 265

Wilde, Oscar, 40
Wilkins, William Glyde, 47, 61, 270
Williams, Emlyn, 141
Williams, Mary, 3, 11, 269
Williams, Orlo, 67–68, 90, 272
Williams, Raymond, 142, 148–49, 158, 168–69, 194, 245, 279, 281, 285, 286
Wilson, Angus, 1, 11, 107, 118, 119, 120, 122, 140, 143, 169, 277, 278, 280, 285
Wilson, Arthur H., 113, 114, 118, 280
Wilson, Edmund, 4, 11, 44, 61, 84, 85–86, 90, 91, 95, 104, 106, 110, 111, 114, 119, 121, 124, 128, 130, 133, 135, 141, 146–47, 148, 153, 174, 275
Wing, George, 135, 140, 284
Wolfreys, Julian, 180–81, 211, 243, 251, 260, 299, 300
Woloch, Alex, 241–42, 260, 302
Woman in White, The (Wilkie Collins), 38
Woolcott, Alexander, 49
Woolf, Virginia, 21, 30, 67, 68, 90, 272
Wordsworth, William, 16
Worth, George, 160, 169, 287
Wright, Thomas, 74–76, 77, 79, 90, 100, 101, 106, 107, 274

Yale University, 109, 255

Zabel, Morton Dauwen, 109–10, 118, 119, 279
Zangen, Britta, 248, 255, 260, 302
Zweig, Stefan, 80, 80, 272
Zwinger, Lynda, 184–85, 211, 292, 295

Mazzeno traces critics' attitudes toward Charles Dickens, beginning with his phenomenal popularity during his lifetime and continuing after his death through a half century of debunking ... Mazzeno does a remarkable job of providing succinct summaries and evaluations of eighteen decades of critical commentary on Dickens's life and work ... An invaluable tool.

—CHOICE

The most impressive — and by far the most detailed — of attempts to analyze, categorize, and evaluate Dickens criticism in English.

—DICKENS QUARTERLY

Even veteran Dickensians will benefit from Mazzeno's clear insight into the origins and consequences of critical shifts in Dickens studies.

—STUDIES IN ENGLISH LITERATURE

CPSIA information can be obtained at www.ICGtesting.com
Printed in the USA
LVOW041917040712

288791LV00003B/89/P